American Flintknappers

american flintknappers

STONE AGE ART IN THE AGE OF COMPUTERS

John C. Whittaker

University of Texas Press
Austin

Copyright © 2004 by the University of Texas Press
All rights reserved

ISBN 978-0-292-70266-0

First edition, 2004

Requests for permission to reproduce material from this work should be sent to Permissions, University of Texas Press, Box 7819, Austin, TX 78713-7819.
utpress.utexas.edu/index.php/rp-form

♾ The paper used in this book meets the minimum requirements of ANSI/NISO Z39.48-1992 (R1997) (Permanence of Paper).

Library of Congress Cataloging-in-Publication Data

Whittaker, John C. John Charles), 1953–
    American flintknappers : Stone Age art in the age of computers / John C. Whittaker
      p.   cm.
Includes bibliographical references and index.
    ISBN 0-292-70163-2 (hardcover : alk. paper) — ISBN 0-292-70266-3 (pbk. : alk. paper)
    1. Flintknapping. 2. Stone implements. I. Title.
TT293.W45 2004
621.9′32—dc22

2003017053

Dedication

My wife Kathy Kamp has put up with my knapping habits for years, listened to my knap-in stories, discussed my analysis, saved me from malevolent computers, and been my most understanding and forthrightly critical reader and colleague. Our daughter April wears "the pretty ones" and pays a parent the supreme compliment of occasionally telling her friends he's "cool." You are both my inspiration always.

Contents

Acknowledgments	xi
1. Introduction: Coming to the Knap-in	*1*
The Knap-in Ethos	4
Sources of Information	8
The Knap-in at Fort Osage	14
2. Making Stone Tools: The World's Oldest Craft	*17*
The Processes of Flintknapping	18
Tools and the Knappers' Ethos	25
3. From Fakes and Experiments to Knap-ins: The Roots of Modern Flintknapping	*34*
Charlie Shewey	34
Early Archaeologists and Fakers	37
Native Knappers	40
Mack Tussinger and the Oklahoma Eccentrics	40
Daniel, Howe, and Others	46
McCormick the Folsom Fluter	47
Bryon Rinehart and Grey Ghosts	50
Richard Warren—Scale Work and Lap Knapping	53
Patterns in the Early Modern Knappers	57
Halvor Skavlem and the Hobby Knapper	58
Archaeology and Replication	59

Knapping Newsletters	61
The First Knap-ins	64
Waldorf and *The Art of Flintknapping*	65
Transition to the Current Scene	66
The Current Scene	70

4. The Knap-in: People and Organization — 72

Bob Hunt, Organizer at Fort Osage	72
George Eklund, Commercial Knapper	76
Jim Regan, Copper Toolsmith	77
Gene Stapleton, Dealing in Stone	79
Percy Atkinson: Gourds, Axes, and Philosophy	81
D. C. and Val Waldorf, Knap-in Professionals	83
Ingrid Jones, Knapper Spouse	84
Knapper Demography	86
A Continent of Knap-ins	92
Mid-West Flintknappers' Convention, June 1993	94
Pine City Knap-in	97
Evergreen Lake Knap-in, July 1996	99
Genesee Valley Flint Knappers Association Knap-in, August 1996	101
Flint Ridge Knap-in, August 1996	107
Knap-in Generalities	111

5. Knappers at the Knap-in — 112

Culture and Community of Practice	113
Performance	114
Learning to Knap	118
Learning the Ethos	123
Politics, Gender, and Ethnicity	125
Expressions of Identity	128
The Chipping Keeps You Going: Why Knappers Knap	136

6. Status and Stones — 147

The Knap-in as Egalitarian Event	148
Ooga-Booga, a Ritual of Inclusion	153
Status and Competition in Knapping	156
Talking with Stone: Ritual Exchanges and the Expression of Status	163

7. Art, Craft, or Reproduction: Knapper Esthetics — 169

- Stone Tools as Art and Folk Art — 172
- Two Knappers, Two Attitudes — 180
- The Ideal Point: Common Esthetic Rules — 180
- The Rules in Action: Knapping Contests — 186
- Imitation as Esthetic Goal — 193
- Point Types and Artistic Choices — 194
- Replicas and the Art of Knapping — 200

8. Can't Never Have Too Much Flint: The Lore of Stone — 203

- The Mystique of Stone — 208
- The Qualities of Stone — 210
- The Quest for Stone — 211
- Decreasing Resources — 222

9. Modern Stone Age Economics — 227

- Frank Stevens, Knap-in Entrepreneur — 228
- A Trip to Quartzite — 230
- Market Knapping — 235
- Art Knapping — 237
- Dale Cannon and Stone Knives — 241

10. Knappers, Collectors, Archaeologists: Ethics and Conflicts — 249

- Replicas, Fakes, and Art — 250
- Fakes, Replicas, and Ethics — 251
- Murmurings at the Knap-in — 251
- Woody's Dreams and Knappers' Nightmares — 253
- Fakes and Archaeology — 262
- Counting Knappers and Points — 263
- Markets, Again — 267
- The World of Collecting — 269
- Authentication — 275
- Archaeological Impacts of Modern Knapping: Collections — 279
- The Creation and Destruction of Sites — 282
- Epilogue: Sin and Society — 284

11. Silicon and Society   *289*
    Silicon Connections   290
    Forming and Breaking   297
    The Future   301

Appendix A. Knapper Mail Survey Questionnaire   309

Appendix B. Fall 1996 Fort Osage Knap-in Registration   314

Appendix C. New York Knap-in Contest Rules, 1994   316

Appendix D. New York Knap-in Contest Rules, 1996   318

Bibliography   320

Notes   345

Index   347

Acknowledgments

It's been a ten-year project, resulting in a book, some other writings, masses of paper documentation, and piles of stone tools and debitage, so obviously I had a lot of help. My first debt of gratitude is to all my knapping friends. Many of your names appear in this book, and those who do not are also remembered with thanks. No blame attaches to my friends, informants, and readers for any obstinacy, oversight, or error in my personal interpretations of the knapping world. I try not to be smug, but I remember daily that I chose the right profession—I actually get paid to teach anthropology and to research archaeological sites and knap-ins. Lucky is the anthropologist who gets to spend his research time with such interesting and friendly folk, and lucky is anyone who can find such a wide and welcoming group of friends. Some special assists come to mind:

Bob Hunt first welcomed me to Fort Osage and has been a genial host and supportive friend. Charlie Shewey, Larry Nelson, Dick Grybush, Jack Holland, Bob Patten, Errett Callahan, Gene Stapleton, and others helped me research knapping history. Woody Blackwell, Roy Motley, Glen Leesman, George Eklund, Jeff Gower, Marty Reuter, Mike Stafford, Larry Alexander, Carolyn Johnson, and many more are remembered for long discussions and sometimes unrepeatable stories about collecting, the market, and fakes, aspects of the knapping that I saw less directly than the knap-ins themselves. Jeff Oberloh, D. C. and Val Waldorf, David Klostermeier, Larry Kinsella, Bob Keiper, and others gave me videos and other knap-in documentation. Jeff Behrnes,

Bob Hunt, and Art Magruder provided knapping mailing lists. Richard Sanchez's thoughtful emails helped make this Luddite aware of the growing importance of computers in the knapping world.

Amy Henderson drew figures 2.1, 2.2, 3.10, 5.1, and 7.4. Sarah DeLong took many of the artifact photos and helped prepare illustrations. Derek McLean produced most of the color plates. Pete Bostrom, Errett Callahan, Larry Nelson, Larry Scheiber, Gene Stapleton, Gene Titmus, Val Waldorf, and James Wood provided various illustrations.

My Grinnell knapping friends and students, among them Mark Bro, Matt Graesch, Tom Harvey, Mike He Crow, Don Jay, Steve Owens, Byron Worley, Bill Eichmann, Grant McCall, Matt Hedman, Alex Woods, Byll Bryce, Ann Feltovich, Mike Wells, Lara Gaasland-Tatro, Carl Drexler, and many others over the years have been my Friday afternoon home "knap-in," a sounding board and sympathetic audience, and companions on knapping adventures.

Many archaeological and anthropological colleagues have discussed the knappers and my research with me, among them John Reynolds, Phil Geib, Stan Ahler, Miranda Warburton, Jack Holland, Doug Caulkins, Jon Andelson, Chuck Hilton, and Chris Downum. Mike Stafford and Lucy Lewis Johnson also reviewed the manuscript for the press and gave usefully critical comments. Many other friends read and commented on parts.

Theresa May, University of Texas Press editor, and others there did such a fine job on my previous book that I was eager to work with them again. Moreover, they had faith that this book would be worth publishing, too, and would eventually get completed. Research grants from Grinnell College supported various aspects of this work, and the color plates were made possible by the generosity of the Cranbrook Institute of Science, Gerry Goth, and Grinnell College.

J.C.W.

American Flintknappers

Introduction: Coming to the Knap-in

On the battered toolbox is a worn bumper sticker: "Only the Rocks Live Forever." A pile of rocks lies beside the box, angular lumps of pink and grey chert, a flat nodule with a brown crust like French bread, and a scatter of sharp flakes and fragments of several materials. The tools inside the box are not those envisioned by Craftsman or Sears. A couple of pieces of battered deer antler jut out beside a heavy, dinted copper rod and bits of copper wire set in wooden and plastic handles. This is the modern tool kit of the world's most ancient craft, flintknapping (Figure 1.1). The flintknapper shapes rocks into arrowheads, knives, and other prehistoric tools. Rocks are central to the flintknappers' world, but more interesting than how stones are shaped is the way knapping shapes the people who work them.

Stone tools are treasures to be discovered, masterpieces to be created, mysteries to be explored, keys to the understanding of ancient times. They can carry you back to a heroic past, far from the anonymous mechanized mob life of today, where the hunter pitted his skill and courage against the mammoth, and craftsmen were revered. For stone tools, some men (and most, but not all, knappers are men) will crawl through muck or walk miles in the sun, carry loads that make their knees ache, accumulate backyards piled high with rocks, risk painful injury and the ridicule of their neighbors, pay astounding sums of money, and worry more about knapping problems than their jobs or marriages. People who understand this are unusual and share a special

Figure 1.1. A knapper's tool kit. Bob Hunt has a typically large outfit, which reflects his use of copper tools and fondness for working large pieces.

sympathy that cuts through the shell of other social differences. They will use up their vacation time driving overloaded cars across the continent to spend a weekend with others like them, to talk about rocks, swap rocks, break rocks, and, above all, to be a flintknapper among flintknappers.

I am as bad as many, and stone tools have been a continuing theme in my life, if not an obsession, since I was a boy. I began flintknapping, making stone tools, in 1973 when I was a college student studying archaeology, and I have pursued the craft ever since, cunningly making it all respectable by including stone tools as part of my professional academic life. Like quite a few of my archaeological colleagues, I make stone tools for experimental purposes, duplicating prehistoric knapping to learn what the tools are good for, how much effort it takes to make them, what the waste products look like, and patterns of manufacture, damage, repair, destruction, and discard.

As an academically oriented knapper, I was vaguely aware that there were a few people who made stone tools as a hobby, or even sold them as replicas to museums, or as fakes to collectors, but I rarely met them or knew much about them. In the 1970s and 1980s, however, a number of amateurs were crossing the lines, making contacts in the academic world and contributions to the professional literature that I read, and the number of nonacademic knappers was expanding and becoming more organized and visible. I got on a couple of mailing lists, started getting some newsletters, and learned that there were regular meets, called "knap-ins," being held in several states. The closest knap-in to me was at Fort Osage, near Kansas City, Missouri, so without knowing quite what to expect, I put my tools and some rocks in the back of my car, and drove out to Fort Osage one weekend in September 1990.

As I got out of my car in the parking lot, I knew I had found a home, for the air was filled with the unmistakable sharp crack of stone being flaked. There were, in fact, more knappers than I had ever seen in one place before, fifty or sixty. Some were selling stone, or tools, or points they had made, but mostly they were knapping, working the stone, watching each other, and exchanging ideas (Figure 1.2). As I wandered through for the first time, I was staggered by the number of knappers, the diversity of techniques and tools, and the virtuosity of some of the craftsmanship. I had not realized anything like this existed, and, as it turned out, only three of the other knappers were archaeologists.

Figure 1.2. The knap-in scene. The center of the Fort Osage Knap-in, May 1998.

Introduction

As I became familiar with the Fort Osage knappers, I realized that their craft was as important to many of them as it is to me, and maybe more so, and that the knap-in was a major social event. The knappers were developing a small-scale society, with its own events, symbols, rules, and ethics. There were complicated economic transactions, competition and expression of status, exchange of information, and the development of social networks; in short, all sorts of things that anthropologists find interesting. I was also intrigued that an obsolete and difficult craft which I had assumed was of mostly academic interest could attract so many devoted followers. As a practicing knapper, who makes stone tools both for fun and as part of my professional archaeological interests, I already had a skill which gave me common ground with and an entrée to this society of craftsmen. Having watched the development of knapping in academic circles in my lifetime, I realized that knapping was experiencing a boom among nonacademic craftsmen, and I decided that I had an unusual chance to watch and participate in the formation of a small informal community, a process of considerable anthropological interest. I don't intend to burden readers with loads of anthropological theory, but as certain issues come up, it is useful to explain why anthropologists, archaeologists, folklorists, sociologists, and other scholars should find the modern knappers interesting, and why I look at them the way I do.

The Knap-in Ethos

I started seriously studying the knap-in with several general concerns (beyond a convenient academic excuse to have some weekend fun). My first interest was in why people knapped, what it meant to them. I also wanted to know how an informal group like this developed, and what determined the directions of development. All groups of people have rules which guide the behavior of members, determine who is recruited and allowed to belong, and prescribe how new members are incorporated. In anthropological terms the knappers form a sodality, a voluntary association with a specific purpose.

However, knappers can also be considered as a subculture, a smaller unit within American culture as a whole, which in some ways recognizes itself as different and adheres to a set of shared beliefs and rules (Spradley 1970). Subcultural groups like this have always interested anthropologists, and there are many recent anthropological and journalistic discussions of subcultural groups within the United States. Often subcultures are defined by ethnic, racial, or socioeconomic traits, and may find themselves in conflict with other groups, especially the dominant majority around them. Examples include tribal groups (Foley 1995), religious minorities (Bloom 2000), and street people (Spradley 1970; Fleisher 1995). Conflicts involving disadvantaged, suppressed, or militant subcultures create troubling issues in current American society, but are less relevant to the knapping world. In part this is because membership in the knapping world is voluntary and carries no stigma, and knappers have few agendas to promote.

Voluntary groups that take on subcultural status include some people united by an unusual lifestyle, like senior citizens living in RVs (Counts and Counts 1996). Occupational subcultures form among groups engaged in common pursuits, such as police (Barker 1999), firefighters (McCarl 1985) surgeons (Katz 1999), baseball professionals (Gmelch and Weiner 1998), and criminals (Fleisher 1998; Sikes 1997). Later I will discuss such groups as "communities of practice." Artisans and hobbyists are similar—for example, falconers (Bodio 1984), Civil War reenactors (Horwitz 1998), or wood-carvers (Cooper 1980). Such groups are so common that any reader will surely be a member of one or several and will recognize that they are held together not only by common interests, but by developing social bonds, rules for behavior, and ways of looking at the world. Membership becomes an important part of the identity of members that they announce and manipulate in various ways.

How individuals and groups create an identity for themselves and express it to others has also been of interest to anthropologists for many years (Goffman 1959, 1971; Rubinstein 1995; Brown and Mussell 1984). Our individual identities are partly defined by our memberships in different groups, and our obedience to the rules of these groups. When we interact with others, their understanding of the possible memberships affects how they see us, and we attempt to manage the opinions of others by showing or concealing information about our affiliations. In a nation of almost 300 million people, where many feel ignored, anonymous, and suffocated, open expression of membership in small, comprehensible groups becomes increasingly important.

The knappers I was seeing at Fort Osage form a community in themselves, but are connected to knappers holding similar events elsewhere in the country, and part of a larger national and even somewhat international network of knappers. Knap-ins are a fairly new phenomenon and are still in the process of growing, changing, and defining themselves. I wanted to see how new members were incorporated, how novices learned not just to knap, but to be knappers, and how ethics, rules, and beliefs about knapping were developed and transmitted. Anthropologists talk about the body of shared ideas, values, beliefs, perceptions, symbols, and rules for behavior as "culture," and a shared culture is what unites the people of a society. At the knap-ins, I could watch the development of a society of knappers, with a subculture that was part of mainstream America, but also distinct from other groups within our country.

As I became a knap-in regular, I learned the peculiar ethos of the knap-in, the culturally defined and shared beliefs about how things ought to be, that lies behind many of the rules of proper behavior. As I eventually discovered, modern knap-ins across the country share a common ethos, and the knappers who go to them, and even most knappers who do not, are bound together by shared ideas. Although there are disagreements, conflicts, and violations, an overall knapping ethos can be stated as a series of fundamental beliefs:

(1) Knapping is an art, meaning both a special skill and an esthetic product.
(2) Knapping is fun and interesting, part of the heritage of all people.
(3) Knappers should teach others in order to perpetuate the tradition and share the art and pleasure of knapping.
(4) There are many ways of knapping and many different kinds of knowledge; diversity is good.
(5) Knapping should be enjoyed as a source of fellowship and social interaction; thus competition, hierarchy, and even too much organization are to be avoided.
(6) Knapped art should be promoted honestly; selling modern work as antiquities is bad.

Because much of what follows reflects on the knap-in ethos, it is worth expanding a bit here. Any art or craft involves the application of skill and knowledge. Chapter 2 explains briefly the mechanics of the art of knapping, how it is done today, and what different techniques mean to those who use them.

Part of any culture is its history and traditions. The historical development of the modern knapping world is discussed in Chapter 3, with an emphasis on knappers outside of archaeology.

Knappers perform their art for the sake of its beauty and for the fun of a challenging craft. Chapters 4 and 5 are about the people of the knap-ins, why the craft of knapping attracts them, and who becomes a knapper. Because knapping is primarily done for pleasure, although as we will see there can be economic motives too, it should be shared with the public and with other knappers. Knappers mostly agree that it is the duty of all knappers, and part of the purpose of knap-ins, to promote knapping as an art and hobby, to teach anyone who is interested, and to share techniques with other knappers.

The knap-in is a public arena where knappers perform their craft and interact with other knappers. One of the pleasures of knapping is the fellowship of like-minded friends. Knap-ins are very explicitly expected to be fun, even if you conduct some business there, too. As a result, overt competition, hierarchical leadership, and even anything that smacks of formal organization are discouraged in a number of ways. Of course, some organization is necessary, and some knappers are more central to the knap-in than others. The organization of knap-ins will be a focus of Chapter 4. Similarly, knap-ins attempt to be inclusive, valuing the contributions of individuals at all levels of skill and knowledge. In a craft where learning new tricks is important, and there are many different ways of knapping, diversity is valued, and the fellowship of knap-ins also forbids that knappers of lesser skill be discouraged or discriminated against. Naturally, there are differences in the status of individual knappers, often based on their skill. Knappers do engage in competition for reputation, markets, and status within the group. Chapter 6 considers the importance of status and the ways knappers express it, and also how the knap-in society curbs competition and divisive elements and encourages inclusion.

Modern knappers know full well that their craft has little practical application in today's world; it is a craft performed for its own sake. Knappers find beauty and inspiration in stone, in prehistoric artifacts, and in the knapped art they make. Knappers refer constantly to knapping as art, and non-knappers also recognize the esthetic qualities of stonework. The esthetics of knapping will be discussed at length in Chapter 7.

Knapping and archaeology relate in ways that are partly friendly and beneficial, and partly hostile and inimical. The public perception of prehistoric and modern artifacts as art objects has created a sizable market for both. Many knappers fund their hobby by selling their work, and a few earn their living through knapping and related activities. Because knappers perceive themselves as artists, the consensus is that points should be sold as art. Selling modern work as ancient is dishonest and cheats the knapper of his credit as an artist. There are, of course, some knappers who do not feel this way, and many of the points made by knappers are eventually bought and sold as fake antiquities, even when the knapper who made them disapproves. The history behind this situation, the market for flaked stone artifacts, and the arguments about ethics in the knapping world are discussed in Chapter 9. The impact of modern knapping on archaeology is also considered in Chapter 10.

The knap-in ethos has created a subculture of modern craftsmen pursuing an ancient craft. It ties them together with bonds of shared ideals and with beliefs about the meaning of knapping. However, the knapping world is constantly changing. The patterns of variation and disagreement among knappers, wider social trends, and the way societies form and dissolve mean that knapping twenty years hence may be as different as the knapping world was twenty years ago. Chapter 11 discusses some recent trends, the forces that hold knappers together and pull them apart, and what the knap-in means in the wider American society.

Sources of Information

This particular fieldwork posed some unusual challenges for me as an anthropologist. First, the group I was studying only assembled for short times at weekend knap-ins, so I could only witness knap-in interactions a few times, separated by long intervals. As it turned out, I have attended the Fort Osage Knap-in twice yearly from September 1990 to the present, with only a couple missed sessions. I tried to get some idea of how the Fort Osage Knap-in compared to other knap-ins, at least in the Midwest, by attending a few others: the Mid-West Flintknappers' Convention in Illinois (June 1993), the Minnesota Knappers Guild Knap-in (June 1996, 1999, and 2001), the Evergreen Lake Knap-in (July 1996), the Genesee Valley Knap-in in New York (August 1996), and the Flint Ridge Knap-in in Ohio (August 1996).

Many knappers I knew from Fort Osage turned up at these other knap-ins as well, strengthening my opinion that the knap-in culture is shared across the country. I also talked to knappers in other contexts: atlatl competitions, rock shops, artifact shows, via phone and email, and in visits to friends. For many knappers, the knapping world continues as a major social force and personal focus much beyond the knap-in itself, and in the last few years, the Internet has provided an important new medium for maintaining ties within the knap-in community. However, for me, the knapping ethnography was only one project in the midst of teaching and all the other things I was doing, so my ideas grew by fits and starts, and I often came back to thinking about the knap-ins wishing that I had paid more attention to something the time before.

All anthropologists must be concerned with their relationships with the people they study. In my case, I felt that there were several diplomatic and ethical considerations. The knappers as a group are interested in thinking about knapping, and about themselves as knappers. They produce their own literature and read some archaeological publications, and obviously would read anything I wrote about them. The first rule of anthropological ethics is to avoid harming your informants, even unintentionally. In a literate and self-aware group like the knappers, the usual anthropological problem of ensuring that the informant is protected and necessary confidentiality maintained became complicated. On the one hand, I was recording individuals, and their individuality and human personalities are important. Most of my friends are proud of their status as knappers and craftsmen, and some publicize themselves for commercial purposes. I felt it would be silly and even offensive to attempt to conceal the names of my informants or disconnect most of the information from the individuals, as anthropological convention often expects. Furthermore, I regard this study as documentation of a historic phenomenon that I hope will be of interest some years into the future. The identities of some of the individuals involved are a crucial part of the record.

Those knappers whom I formally interviewed and taped gave their permission for the material to be quoted and used. As in most ethnographies, the bulk of my information comes from public conversations, never intended to be secret, in which I was one participant. On the other hand, as in all groups, there are tensions and hostilities, and people say things about others that they do not want passed around, or reveal to the interviewer information that they would probably not shout out in public. Some knappers were sensitive about economic information, others about personal relationships or ethical stances. For this reason, while this study is about individuals and their work as well as the group, in some sections I have felt it was better to keep the information vague or anonymous, while in others I explicitly use the knappers' names, with deep appreciation for the help and friendship that make this possible. This results in a slight imbalance; my view of the knap-in may be a bit rose-tinted at times, or at least less specific about some of the incidents of conflict and disagreement, and I had to restrain my natural temptation to tell certain juicy and revealing stories. This sometimes means that I must report one knapper's story as I heard it and slight the knowledge that someone else disagreed vehemently. I was unable to independently verify some contradictory stories.

My view is also biased in that it represents a collection of both systematic and unsystematic data—stories, conversations, observations, guesses, and rumors, as well as formal interviews and questionnaires. There are certain blind spots. Some people are reluctant to talk to me, a professional archaeologist, about activities they know I consider unethical. Some knappers, especially those most heavily involved in faking artifacts, tend to be rather paranoid, and my information about the shadier side of knapping is thus more often secondhand and imprecise.

Even after several years there are knappers whom I have seen many times, and may even know by name, but with whom I have never had much interaction. Usually there is no particular reason. No ethnographer can talk to everyone about everything, and some people simply fail to catch your eye for one reason or another, or no reason at all, or they may be too busy to talk when you are available. As far as I can tell, this is how we all experience life, so my view of the knap-in is no more biased than anyone else's, but it is one individual's view, and surely differs from that of any other knapper.

I relied on several major sources of information. First and foremost was participating in the knap-ins. The hallmark of anthropology as a discipline, what makes us different from related fields like sociology, is that we consider "participant observation" a primary method of doing research. Being there, participating in events, becoming as much as possible a member of the group you are studying, is a technique that anthropologists have always used and view with pride. When successful, participant observation gives you unique "feel" and insight into a culture. If you are accepted as a member of the group, you may have access to people, events, and meanings that are denied to the outsider. However, participant observation creates its own peculiar biases. First, you may have to let go of some of your own ways of doing and seeing, and blend in, accepting the rules and following the behavior patterns of the host culture. This process of internalization can bias you, too; most anthropologists develop a strong emotional attachment to the culture they work with. I truly love the knap-ins, and I cannot count the number of friends I have made through my knapping activities. I consider myself, and am accepted by others, as a true member of the knap-in community. On the other hand, no matter how well you blend in, it is impossible in most situations for the anthropologist to completely lose his or her outsider identity. The anthropological enterprise inherently involves doing things that no one else is doing: observing, recording, analyzing, questioning.

As a participant observer at knap-ins, I had far fewer difficulties than anthropologists working with the Yanomamo, the Trobrianders, or even French villagers. I did not have to learn difficult languages, eat strange and repulsive foods, live in the jungle, risk exotic diseases, or entrust my life to Third World airlines. I considered this good research design. More seriously, the knappers were part of a culture I already understood. We spoke the same language, obeyed the same laws, followed similar customs, shared some beliefs, and considered ourselves members of the political unit and culture of America. On a superficial level, I was acceptable from the beginning and shared some of my general identity with all the other knappers. However, small groups form their own subcultures, and individuals define part of their identity as membership in these smaller units. We all have multiple overlapping identities, including, in my case, American, Iowan, archaeologist, father and husband in my nuclear family, member of the larger Whittaker family, alumnus of various educational institutions, professor at another, sports team member, and so on. Some of these identities only manifest themselves at certain times; I am only an Iowan in important ways for events like voting, state fairs, and taxation, and when someone in Arizona asks me where I live.

As I will show, "knapper" is another identity that is extremely important to the subculture of the knap-in and the individuals who form it. That identity usually includes a particular set of skills, and if I had not already known them, or wanted to learn, it would have been difficult for me to understand what was going on at knap-ins or to be accepted as a member. This was especially so because one of my other identities, "archaeologist," clashed with my identity as knap-in participant, at least in the eyes of some others. Not only was I an academic, and therefore expected to be a bit snooty, I was an archaeologist, and expected to disapprove of nonprofessional excavation of sites, the commercial market in artifacts, and faking antiquities. I do, in fact, disapprove of all these things, and it took a while for some people to realize that while I might not approve of some of the things they did, I was willing to treat them as humans, refraining from attacking them while sharing our common interests. I also did not try to hide the fact that I was recording things and intending to write about the knappers and knap-ins. Quite a few other knappers take photos and videos, and even write about knapping, so I did not appear too strange in this. As a known academic, I was regarded with suspicion by a few knappers and had to endure occasional semi-joking comments about spying for the IRS. A few of the more paranoid knappers never did talk freely to me, but the fact that I spent much of my time at the knap-ins sitting with other knappers, making an acceptable standard of arrowhead, discussing the same issues, and offering and accepting advice on technique, went a long way to establishing that I was a genuine knapper, a decent sort, and relatively harmless. Everyone goes through a process of establishing an identity as an acceptable member that is much like mine; each has more, or fewer, individual complications.

Being a knapper, and eventually a Fort Osage regular, thus gave me access to the bulk of my information. I took photos and notes as I strolled through the knap-in, and sat up late at night typing a detailed journal of observations. I snooped shamelessly, eavesdropped when I politely could, and asked pointed questions as I knapped. As I became a recognized regular, made friends, and got to be known as a reasonably friendly archaeologist who wanted to write about the knap-in, many people actively helped me, calling events to my attention, introducing me to friends, bringing artifacts to show me, or telling me the latest gossip. Between 1992 and 1994, I did a series of formal taped interviews with about fifteen knappers. I had a set series of questions about how they started knapping, what they made, and what knapping meant to them, that I later expanded into a broader mail survey. I interviewed Fort Osage regulars at several levels of skill; inevitably, I interviewed those I felt comfortable with at the time, so not nearly all of the knappers I consider important were interviewed. Another source of documentation that I used for the knap-ins themselves has been videotapes made by other knappers. Some of these the makers advertised for sale to the knapping community, others were given to me by friends.

A second major data set was the mail questionnaire I designed with the help of my wife Kathy and the computer expertise of my student Matt Hedman (Whittaker and Hedman 1996, 1997). In four pages, it asked for a lot of detail about such things as how knappers got started, what interested them, who taught them and who did they teach, what they made, whether they sold things, what they did at knap-ins, what other crafts they participated in, and why they liked knapping (Appendix A). I sent this questionnaire to all of the 364 knappers who had signed in at Fort Osage up to Spring 1994 or were on Bob Hunt's list to get Fort Osage mailings, and to 183 (a randomly selected 13.8 percent) of the 1,327 names collected up to early 1992 by Jeff Behrnes when he was editing *The Flint Knapper's Exchange* newsletter. The response rate was about 34 percent for the Fort Osage list, which is adequate, although as it turned out, not all of those who responded actually went to Fort Osage Knap-ins. Only about 19 percent of the names from Behrnes's list responded, which is a rather poor return rate, although not unusual for mail surveys. The low response rate is partly explained by the list's being less up-to-date and including fewer people who knew me. In the end I had a sample of 90 Fort Osage knappers and 70 others. The idea was to give me a wider and more systematic cross-section of knappers than I was able to get just talking to people at knap-ins, and to see if there were any geographical patterns. Was the Fort Osage Knap-in typical of knappers everywhere? There are some useful patterns, although surveys of this sort are not really random samples. I randomly selected the people to get mailings, but only some of them were interested enough to respond, so there is an inherent bias in the results. Nevertheless, I feel that the most interesting patterns are borne out by my less systematic observations, and I will refer to the survey data from time to time. Respondents were promised confidentiality, and although most of them signed their names, I do not attribute any information from the survey to individual knappers.

A final source of information on the knapping world is the writings of the knappers themselves. These include several newsletters and, in the last few years, computer communications over the Internet. The Web page and mail servers such as "The Tarp" carry much the same kind of conversations and exchanges as one can hear at knap-ins.

Instructional videos have also become quite common and often contain not just information on techniques, but a look at how the video maker feels about knapping in general. I will discuss all of these in their place.

I reference a lot of these sources because they are publicly available documents that others interested in the modern knapping scene can perhaps find and use. The newsletter *Chips,* published by Val and D. C. Waldorf, is particularly relevant to the Fort Osage Knap-in because the Waldorfs and a number of others who regularly write articles for them are knappers I met at Fort Osage.

The Knap-in at Fort Osage

My visits to Fort Osage, like those of many other knappers, have developed a familiar pattern. I know what to expect, who I want to see, what I intend to do. How a person becomes a knapper, and how a knapper becomes a part of a knap-in, are topics I will discuss at length. First, however, it helps to have a mental picture of the knap-in itself.

The first time I headed for Fort Osage, I had a hard time finding it. Struggling through the traffic of the Missouri side of Kansas City, you eventually reach surrounding suburbs and countryside, and the small town of Buckner on State Highway 24. From there, assuming you find all the oddly angled and not always well-marked intersections, you can get to Sibley. Over the years, the old houses, apparently permanent garage sales, and rattling bridge over the rail line supplying coal to a power plant have become familiar, in a hamlet small enough to see a fox run across the road at night. Crossing the bridge you pass a cemetery and find yourself at the museum and entrance to the state park. Fort Osage is the site of the first fort built in the new Louisiana Purchase. The fort was constructed by William Clark in 1808 and in use as a military strongpoint and trading post until 1827 (Roberts 1988). Today there is a partial reconstruction of the fort on the original foundations, looking out over the Missouri River. A few hundred yards away from the fort, at the entrance to the park, is a small visitor center and museum, with a parking lot and a large garage in back. Between 1991 and 1995 the knap-in was held behind the museum, on the parking lot and under the shelter of the garage and awnings. Since then it has been returned to its original site, which is the large parking lot used for overflow visitors, in the area between the museum and the fort, and off to one side. The park and fort offer a picturesque setting and provide basic facilities such as toilets, picnic tables, parking, and large areas of lawn where the knap-in can set up and knappers can camp overnight.

On arriving, I generally park close to the knap-in, but not as close as many of the knappers, who have trailers full of rock to sell, or cars stuffed with knapping equipment, or points, tools, and other items to display or market. Bob Hunt and other organizers, with the help of knappers who arrive early, set up a large, open tent, with tarps on the ground to keep chips out of the grass. Knappers bring tables and folding chairs to supplement picnic benches from the park. As knappers arrive, the knap-in develops into clusters of people under the main tent, and under private shelters or on tables set up around it. Others park their vehicles and open the back to spread their wares or set up their chairs on tarps to catch the debris.

The first few times I came, I put up a tent out in the field and camped on site, as many knappers do. As taking notes became more important and I began to rely on my laptop computer, an electrical outlet became necessary. For a while I tried typing my notes in the evening, sitting on a log that I dragged into the men's restroom, with my computer plugged into the shaving outlet. Moths found the glow of my computer screen attractive, and slapping at Missouri's aggressive mosquitoes disrupted my thoughts and produced incomprehensible typographic errors in my notes. After a couple of knap-ins I began to imitate many of the other knappers, especially those who bring wives, driving twenty minutes into town to stay in a motel. The Scottish Inn in Grain Valley was closest and cheapest, and I picked up a lot of good stories around the pool in the evenings and over dinner. In the morning the room doors would open one by one, each disclosing a sleepy knapper headed for his vehicle, and I even found a broken arrowhead on the asphalt of the parking lot one day. Having a shower instead of a cold wash under the park faucets probably improved my presence as an interviewer, too.

Once I find a parking place at the knap-in, I usually wander through, greeting friends, seeing who is there, doing an initial scout before unloading my knapping gear. I travel light compared to many knappers. I don't bring large amounts of stone, and my kit fills just one small toolbox, but I also have my recording equipment to manage. The tape recorder can be left in the car until I am actually interviewing someone, but I usually have a camera at hand and carry my clipboard everywhere. Set-up is much more elaborate for some knappers, especially those who have commercial interests. Others just like to have the proper amenities, like a tipi instead of a tent, or a long table with cases for display, or an awning so they can set up shade away from the main crowd.

I generally park my tool kit under the main tent and knap with knap-in organizer Bob Hunt and several others who usually join that group. Most knappers have habitual positions, and little groups of friends will assemble in their own areas at each knap-in, but there is a lot of flow as well. A few knappers sit and knap most of the time, but the majority wander around, visiting friends, watching others, purchasing supplies, and gossiping between bouts of knapping. There is a continual buzz of conversation mingling with the din of knapping: the crack, crack, crack, clatter of fracturing stone and falling flakes. Among the seated knappers, visitors wend their way, cautiously handling a finished point on one table, peering over another knapper's shoulder to ask questions, or hastily dragging a small child off a pile of sharp flakes.

A knap-in is an occasion to knap, but more importantly, an occasion to be a knapper among other knappers. Stone tools are made, but so too are contacts, lessons, status, and meaning. Over the years, the knap-in at Fort Osage has grown from a small group of friends to a major event, with all the trappings of a small temporary culture, a short tribal gathering. As such, it has its own rules and organization. Although there is little obvious formal structure to the knap-in, there are, in fact, regular patterns of behavior and expectations, and certain key individuals shape the flow of events and the experiences of other knappers like myself.

Before I discuss the social life of knap-ins and the meanings of the craft, it will be useful to explain a little bit of the history and techniques of flintknapping.

Making Stone Tools:
The World's Oldest Craft

*A*t most shows displaying arts, crafts, or hobbies, the emphasis is on the objects. Tomatoes, wood carvings, dogs, guns, model trains, paintings, and quilts are "shown." Although artists or owners may be working on them or actively showing them off, the object, not the action, is the focus of the event. Knap-ins are very different: they are all about the act of knapping. Artifact shows, which are also common, make a good contrast. They are much more typical shows, displaying the same kind of objects made by knappers. They even involve some of the same people, but although there may be knappers knapping and displaying their work at some artifact shows, the event itself is structured around displaying objects, mostly prehistoric stone tools.

At knap-ins, people knap. The activity defines the event, and that focus makes knap-ins different from most other gatherings of artisans. Knappers come to a knap-in to knap companionably in the company of other knappers, to watch others and learn from them and compare techniques, and to display their own abilities. Spectators also come to watch, but knap-ins are not demonstrations. The stone tools that the knappers make are evidence of their skill, and are bought and sold, admired and exchanged within the knap-in and among outsiders, but the focus of the event remains on the knapping, and the knapping performance is intended for the insider, not the spectator. Not everyone knaps at a knap-in, and no one spends all his or her time knapping, but the event remains a knap-in, not a primitive craft show. In order to understand the knappers and the meanings of their craft, it is necessary to understand a little of the techniques of flintknapping and the technical language of the flintknapper.

Stone tools are part of everyone's heritage. No matter who you are, at some point in the past, your ancestors made stone tools. They are the oldest artifacts we can document. The first recognizable cutting and pounding tools are found in African deposits dating between 2 and 3 million years ago, where they are associated with the hominid forms that are the ancestors of all of us. Tools of more perishable materials such as wood were surely important, too, but stone tools preserve well and thus are disproportionately important to archaeologists. They also changed through time, and distinctive forms are associated with particular times and places, so they can be readily used as chronological markers, as well as shedding light on human activities and technological skills.

Modern American knappers are not much interested in Old World stone tools, which are often quite simple, especially the older forms. They imitate almost exclusively American forms, and here, too, they are not interested in the simple tools. Most stone tools everywhere were just scraps of stone with a little bit of work to shape a useful edge. Such simple tools are well known to archaeologists and collectors, but knappers rarely make them, unless they intend to use them, as some do. Modern knappers prefer the more complex forms, "arrowheads" and other types lumped by archaeologists under the terms "biface" and "projectile point." A biface is any tool that is worked on both sides of a piece of stone, but normally the term refers to a relatively large, flat cutting tool. Projectile point is the archaeologists' term for small symmetrical bifaces that could have been used to tip arrows, spears, or sometimes knives.

A few basic techniques were used to make all the different kinds of stone tools. Much more detailed descriptions and instructional information can be found in a number of sources, including my *Flintknapping: Making and Understanding Stone Tools* (Whittaker 1994) and other books and videos listed in the bibliography.

The Processes of Flintknapping

Flaked stone tools are made by fracturing brittle, homogeneous stones. The process is now mostly called knapping or flintknapping in the English-speaking world. The word is from Germanic roots meaning "to break with a sharp blow" and was first applied to gunflint makers in England, and then to other stone workers. Only some stone can be worked by knapping. It must be homogeneous, without large flaws, crystals, bedding planes, or other irregularities. Most knapping stone is composed of various forms of silica, and among the most common types are flint or chert, which are sedimentary, and obsidian, which is a volcanic glass.

Knappable stone breaks with a conchoidal fracture. The most familiar example to most people is the cone that a BB punches out of a plate glass window. By varying the forces, angles, and positions of the blow, the knapper manipulates the fracture and controls the shape of the flake (the piece removed) and the core (the piece from which the flake is struck). Flakes and cores have distinctive features resulting from conchoidal fracture (Figure 2.1). These include the platform where the blow falls, the bulb of percussion, which is a distorted form of the cone of conchoidal fracture, and other traits shown in Figure 2.2.

In order to flake, a stone must have that glassy conchoidal fracture, and the glassier it is, the more easily it fractures and the sharper the edges. Stone with irregularities, bedding planes, crystal structure, or distinct grains does not flake well. The texture and flaking properties of some of the sedimentary stones like chert can be improved by heat treating. As stone is central to the world of the knapper, Chapter 8 will discuss it in detail.

Knapping is an intellectual as well as physical activity. The knapper must watch and control a number of variables, and each blow must respond to existing conditions, correcting errors left by previous blows or overcoming flaws in the material. Each blow either prepares the way for further work or creates difficulties, and a good knapper is constantly aware of both long-term strategy (what is this piece going to become, and what is required to get it there?) and the immediate problems of each flake removal.

Several basic principles must be observed each time the knapper strikes a blow. The platform angle (the angle between the surface where the blow falls and the adjacent surface from which the flake is removed) must be less than 90 degrees. The blow must also strike the platform at an angle less than 90 degrees (see Figure 2.1). The fracture tends to run under the greatest mass of material; thus the flake will tend to follow ridges on the face of the core. If there is no ridge to fol-

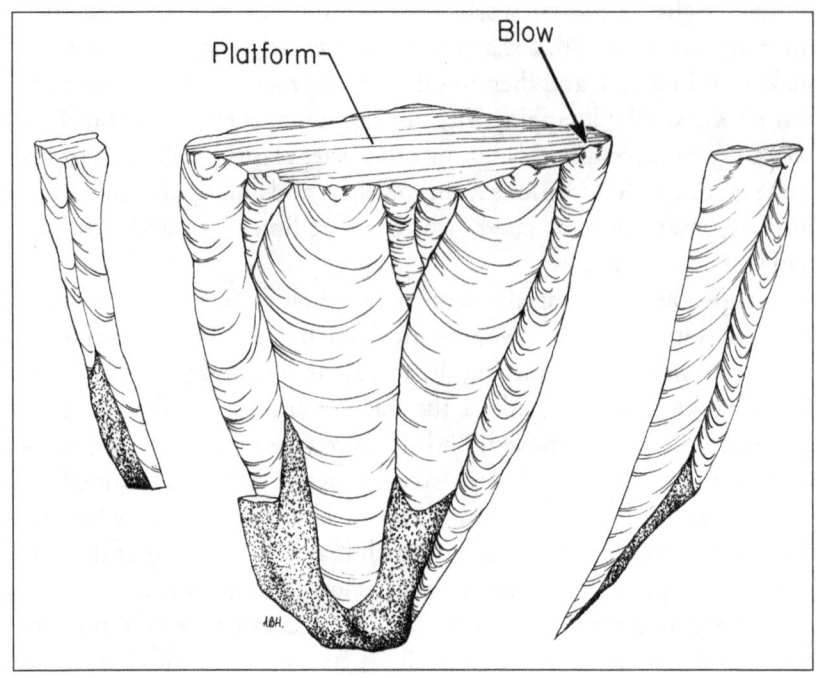

Figure 2.1. Typical core and flakes. The flake on the left has terminated in a step fracture, while that on the right ends in a more desirable feathered termination. Drawing by Amy Henderson.

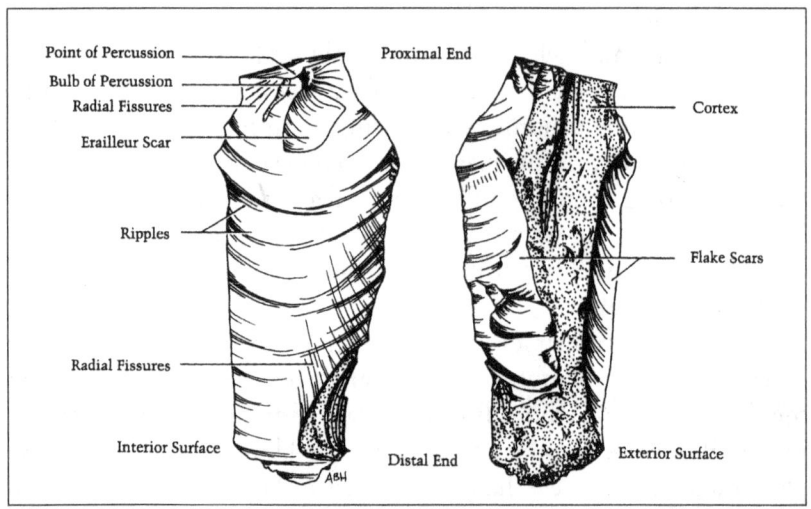

Figure 2.2. Features of a typical flake (Whittaker 1994 Figure 2.3, drawing by Amy Henderson).

low, the flake will spread out and be short and rounded. Knappers also try to control the way the flake terminates. A feather termination is sharp and leaves a smooth surface on the core. A step or hinge termination means the flake does not have a good cutting edge, and leaves a step on the core that will interfere with further flake removals. Brittle stone can also be fragile, and a misdirected or too forceful blow can easily snap a point instead of removing the desired flake.

There are several ways of applying force to the stone to remove flakes: direct percussion, indirect percussion, and pressure flaking. Each method has distinctive consequences.

Percussion Techniques

The simplest and most obvious way to remove a flake is by directly striking the stone with another object. The earliest crude stone tools were made by direct percussion, but later work can show great refinement. There are two major forms, referred to somewhat misleadingly by knappers as "hard hammer" and "soft hammer" percussion.

Hard hammer percussion usually refers to the use of a stone ham-

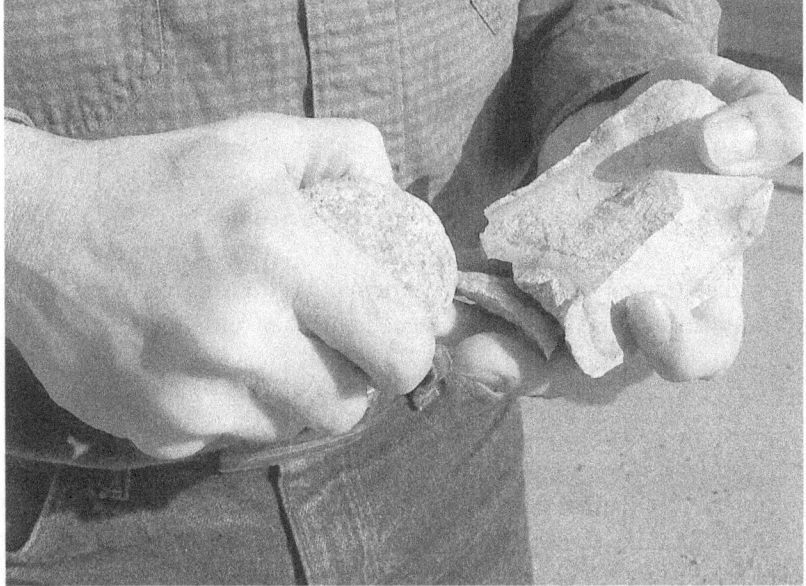

Figure 2.3. Hard hammer percussion with a stone hammer. The knapper uses a precision grip on the pebble hammerstone because not much force is needed. The blow strikes the top of the core, and the flake comes off the underlying surface. Photo by Sarah DeLong.

mer to strike the core (Figure 2.3). In addition, hard hammer percussion most often implies working a simple core and removing relatively large flakes by striking a flat platform, as in Figure 2.1.

Soft hammer percussion, on the other hand, often means the use of a hammer of antler, wood, bone, or other material softer and more resilient than stone. Many modern knappers now use copper (Figure 2.4). Such tools are often called batons or billets. Soft hammers are less effective than hard for removing large flakes from normal cores, so the use of a soft hammer often implies that bifaces are being worked. In working a biface, the blows fall on the edges, rather than on the flat platform surfaces of normal cores. The edges of bifaces in production are generally strengthened by intentionally dulling them, because a thin, sharp edge will crush under the blow rather than transmitting the force to a clean flake fracture. The flakes produced in making bifaces have somewhat different traits from the normal hard hammer core flake and are often referred to as biface thinning flakes. Some confusion arises because it is possible for a skilled knapper to thin bifaces and make the typical flakes using a stone hammer, especially if the hammerstone is relatively soft. Hammers of all degrees of hardness can be used somewhat interchangeably, and the difference in the kinds of flakes produced depends in part on how the hammer is used and what form of artifact is being worked. Nevertheless, it is easier and more usual to use relatively hard hammers on cores, and relatively soft hammers on bifaces. Quite often, a large flake struck with a hard hammer is thinned and shaped with a soft hammer to make a finished bifacial tool, or a preform that can be finished by pressure flaking as described below.

Indirect percussion means that the blow is transmitted to the stone through an intermediate punch, usually made of antler or copper. This is a relatively uncommon technique, though there are several knappers who use different styles of indirect percussion to thin bifaces. However, because the punch can be small, and can be placed very precisely, indirect percussion has some advantages over direct percussion techniques and is also sometimes used for making blades (long, straight flakes) or for notching projectile points. The disadvantage is that tools must be held with both hands, making it more difficult to stabilize the piece that is being worked, and many knappers find it slow and clumsy. Those who are adept at indirect percussion, however, consider it every bit as good as more common techniques (Figures 2.5, 2.6).

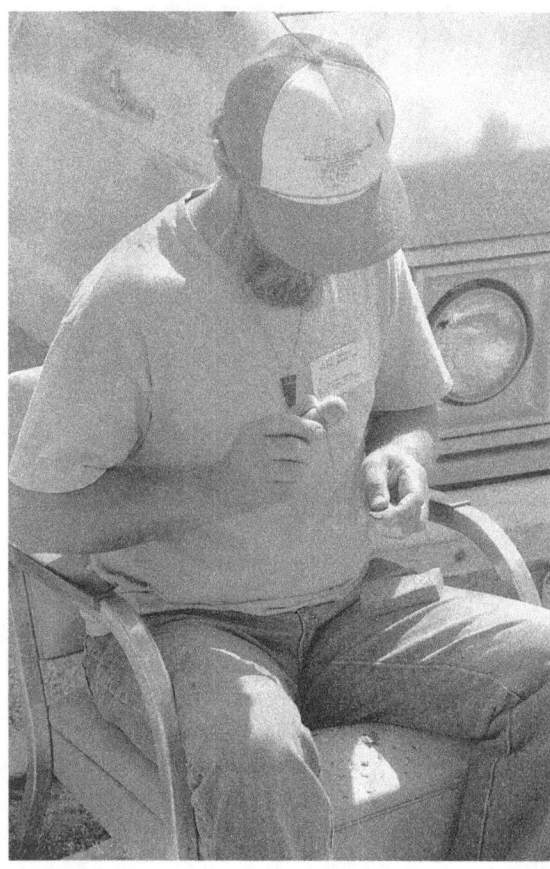

Figure 2.4. Soft hammer percussion with a small copper billet. Ron Fuller holds the piece he is working "freehand." Many knappers rest larger pieces on their thighs.

Pressure Flaking

The final category of knapping techniques is pressure flaking. In pressure flaking, the force is applied by pressing instead of striking (Figures 2.7, 2.8, 2.9). This allows great precision, but generally limits the amount of force. Pressure flaking is most often used for the final work on refined tools like arrow points and for notching and other details that cannot be done by percussion. It is quite common to begin pieces by percussion to remove large amounts of material, and use pressure flaking to straighten the edges, add notches, barbs, or other details, and leave a regular pattern of flake scars across the face of the point.

In pressure flaking, the point is held on a pad of some sort in the hand or occasionally on a bench or table (Figure 2.7), while the other hand presses the tool against the edge of the stone, directing the force

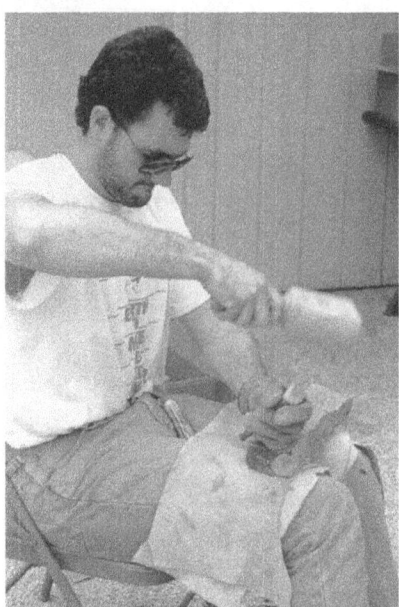 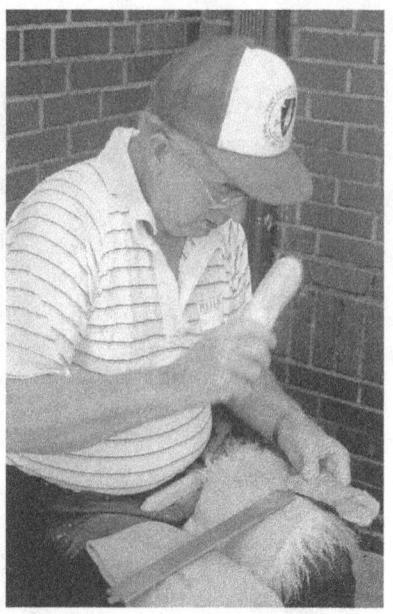

Figure 2.5. Indirect percussion with a large antler punch. Mike Stafford is making a square axe out of Danish flint. Fort Osage, 1991.

Figure 2.6. Ted Frank has an unusual indirect percussion technique. He lays a copper bar across his lap, with the end resting against the platform edge of a biface, and strikes it with an antler billet to drive a flake off the underside of the biface. Fort Osage, 1994.

both inward, to make the flake run across the face being worked, and downward, which begins the fracture. Pressure flaking can be made more powerful by adding the pressure of the legs, or the leverage of a longer tool, called an Ishi stick by many knappers (Harwood 1988b), which is held under the arm (Figure 2.8). The name honors Ishi, last survivor of a group of California Indians. His flintknapping skills and tools were recorded by a number of early anthropologists (Nelson 1916; Shackley 2001) and are admired by modern knappers. It is also possible to remove very long flakes (called blades by archaeologists) from a core by pressing with a chest crutch or other tool that allows the body weight to be brought to bear (Figure 2.9).

Mechanical lever devices have also been used by modern knappers to remove large flakes by pressure. The most common lever device to be seen today is the "fluting jig," which is used by some knappers to flute Clovis and Folsom points (Blackwell 1994a,b). These points have a single large flake scar, or flute, that runs from the base up toward the tip, thinning the base of the point for hafting (Ahler and Geib 2000). There is no good evidence that lever devices for flaking were used anywhere in prehistory.

Tools and the Knapper's Ethos

The discussion above has been necessary to summarize some of the specialized technology and language of the knapper and to illustrate a little of the variation in techniques. Like all technologies, the details are infinite and complex, and the language used to discuss them is esoteric, but this is part of the world of any craftsman. Knappers, like all craftworkers and artists, from gunsmiths and wood-carvers to quilters and weavers, find the details of their work fascinating and argue and discuss them constantly. The debates and exchange of information are not just to learn and teach, but also to state positions that reflect one's identity and beliefs, membership, knowledge, and skill.

Figure 2.7. D. C. Waldorf pressure flaking on a bench. Fort Osage, 1998.

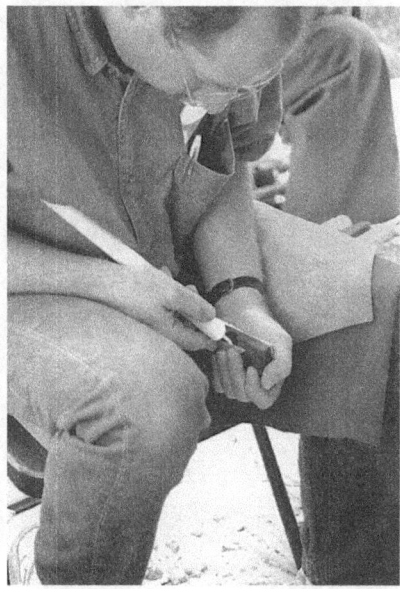

Figure 2.8. Quentin Wells pressure flaking into hand pad with an Ishi stick. The long handle and the pressure of the legs add force. Fort Osage, 1998.

Figure 2.9. Alan Cantrell making obsidian pressure blades with a chest crutch. The boards form a vise holding the core, and the antler tip of the crutch rests on the platform. A previous long blade of black obsidian lies on the edge of the leather pad. Fort Osage, 1997.

Copper tools are a good example of how the details of technology reflect deeper themes in the knappers' world. Traditional knapping tools almost everywhere were stone, bone, antler, and wood. There were a few exceptions. Copper was sometimes used for the working tip of pressure flakers in regions where there were large sources of pure native copper, as in the upper Midwestern United States (Whittaker and Romano 1996), and also where early metal use overlapped with late Stone Age technology, as in ancient Egypt and Scandinavia (Stafford 1998). Gunflints and other Industrial Age stone survivals were made with steel hammers. However, archaeologically oriented knappers trying to re-create prehistoric stone tools usually attempt to use equipment that ancient knappers would have used. For some kinds of experiments, the tools used do not matter. If you want to know how well a stone knife works, it makes little difference whether you flaked it with copper or antler. However, if you want to estimate how long it took a prehistoric knapper to make a Folsom point, you need to use the tools that would have been available then and reach a sufficient level of skill to use them efficiently.

Some early experimenters were limited by their ignorance or the availability of correct materials. Cushing (1895) tells of using a bone toothbrush handle, and many knappers started with nails or other metal as pressure flaking points. Even many serious experimental knappers prefer copper pressure flakers over antler because the copper, being a bit harder, makes it easier to remove consistent flakes and the copper tip requires less frequent resharpening.

In the early days of knap-ins in the late 1970s and early '80s, knappers were already arguing about copper versus antler in pressure flaking. Most agreed that copper was easier to use, and many felt that there was little difference in the results (e.g., Callahan and Titmus 1980). Others felt that not only did copper produce subtle differences in the flakes and edges of points, but that because it was significantly easier to use and not available to most prehistoric people, replications made with copper were not as good and taught us little about prehistoric knapping (Callahan and Crabtree 1979: 24; Del Bene 1979). J. B. Sollberger, a much-admired Texas knapper, went so far as to say, "I had lots of fun with copper but regret the wasted years of its use" (Sollberger 1979b), because he felt it prevented him from really understanding how Folsom points were made. Currently, the vast majority of knappers use copper pressure flakers, and there is little discussion of them (Figure 2.10).

Arguments about copper in recent years focus almost entirely on copper billets for "soft hammer" percussion. Not all knappers find it easy to obtain good antler. Large antlers for percussion billets are difficult to get and often expensive. Ordinary deer antler is mostly too small for heavy percussion work, and moose antler is the preferred material. Antler billets also wear out and have to be replaced. Knappers have tried a number of substitutes. The archaeologically oriented knapper literature in the 1970s had a number of discussions of tool materials. People were trying hard wood billets, and phenolic resin as a synthetic antlerlike material that was actually cheaper than antler (Callahan 1978b).

Copper is easily made into tools with shapes and handles familiar to the modern hand. More importantly, it is somewhat harder and heavier than antler, although softer than many hammerstones. This means that the hammer can contact a smaller surface, and the fracture of the flake begins more rapidly, with less shock to the piece. Great force can be applied and large flakes removed, and less careful preparation of platforms is necessary. Copper is the right density and hardness to be used both as a hard hammer for striking flakes off a core and as a soft hammer for making bifaces. Copper is relatively cheap and readily available. These are considerable advantages to the commercial and hobby knappers, who care less about experimenting with past technologies than turning out a nice arrowhead quickly and without breaking it. The choice of tools thus says something about a knapper's goals and orientation (Figure 2.11).

Even in recent history, it is often difficult to pin down events and timing with any precision, so the origins of copper billets are vague. George Eklund is one of the founders of the Fort Osage Knap-in and is often credited with introducing copper billets for biface work. As a teenager learning to knap he used both antler and copper pressure flakers, and when Charlie Shewey, an older knapper, convinced him that he could make points much more efficiently by doing the early work with percussion, he hit on the idea of copper instead of antler billets. He doesn't remember exactly when this happened, but he was using copper billets by 1979, when my colleague Chris Downum witnessed a demonstration for the Wichita State University field school. Chris, being an archaeologist, thought copper billets were somewhat out-

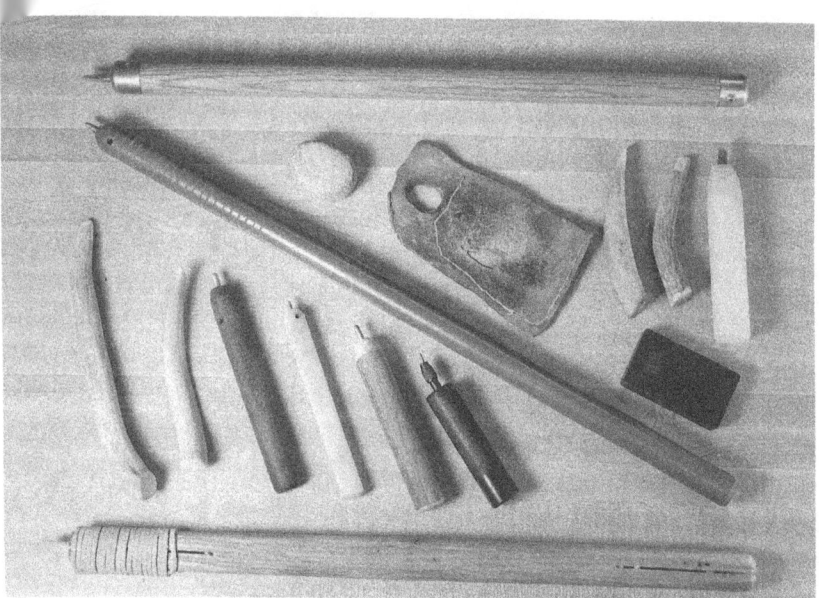

Figure 2.10. Array of pressure flaking tools: Three long "Ishi sticks" include a wooden model by Earnie Jones with a copper cap on the butt holding extra tips (top), a typical black nylon handle design (diagonal), and one I made to use antler tips (bottom). Bottom left flakers are two antler tines, then copper-tipped forms made by Frank Stevens and Jim Regan, one of my minimalist broom handle flakers, and a more complex flaker from Gene Stapleton. Upper right are a pebble to abrade platforms, my leather hand pad, a rubber pad from Dale Cannon, and three notchers—bone and antler, and a nylon-handled one by Jim Regan. Photo by Sarah DeLong.

landish and remembered them well. George was probably important in popularizing copper billets among the Midwestern knappers, but others were also using them and probably came up with the idea independently. Videotapes of the Fort Osage and Texas knap-ins for 1988 show that copper billets had already taken a strong hold in Texas and the Midwest. However, a 1988 California knap-in video shows no copper. This may be because the Californians used mostly obsidian, which requires more delicacy, but there are also significant differences in knappers' attitudes toward copper.

Today, a large majority of the Fort Osage knappers use copper billets, as do probably most American nonacademic knappers. However, the choice of tools is a symbolic decision that knappers can use to align themselves with differing philosophies. Several of the most admired

Figure 2.11. Group of knapping hammers: On the left, four antler billets, including a fancy eagle head by Terry Karrow, with an oak billet and a hammerstone upper right. On the right, seven copper tools: a Gene Stapleton copper ball, a "copper bopper" from "Nine Fingers" Jerry Calvert, two milled forms from Gene Stapleton, Jim Regan's paddle design, a larger version by Tom Richter, and a hammer from Ted Frank. In the center are a modern abrading stone and a flattened copper tube punch for indirect percussion. Photo by Sarah DeLong.

Fort Osage knappers, including Bob Patten and Jim Spears, use only antler and other "primitive" materials. Sometimes this is an expression of virtuosity: antler is seen as more difficult to use than copper, especially in making thin and fragile bifaces. Many also believe that there are subtle differences in the flake scars, and points knapped with traditional tools thus look more authentic. Knappers concerned with archaeological experimentation, including most academic knappers, point out that using tools that were not available in the past is a poor way to understand prehistoric knapping. There is also a personal esthetic involved, and similar choices are seen in other crafts. For instance, woodworking friends tell me that there are cabinetmakers who refuse to use power tools.

Probably the most vocal "traditionalist" is Errett Callahan (1994, 1999, 2000). He particularly dislikes copper billets, and feels that a true "master" knapper can only work with traditional gear. "If it wasn't done in the past, it's not traditional. Traditionalism is not just a fad; it's something we believe in, a way of life. It is not a search for the easy way out, a search for more efficient tools and clever tricks. Traditionalism is a commitment to preserving traditions of value; for it is by means of traditions that value systems are passed on. *Traditions perpetuate values. Innovations undermine values*" (Callahan 2000: 11).

The Fort Osage knappers, most of whom use copper, find Callahan's views extreme, to put it politely. They point out that the line drawn for traditionalism is highly arbitrary—Callahan himself is a leader in promoting art knapping that goes beyond anything produced in prehistory, even if he claims that traditional techniques are the only legitimate way to make it. The dominant view among Fort Osage knappers seems to be "live and let live" (Blackwell 1997a). Different tools are seen as requiring slightly different, but equally respectable, skills, and "copper bopper" knappers are annoyed by the moralizing tone of some of the traditionalists. Many knappers who use copper express admiration for those who don't, or feel a bit apologetic about using copper, since it is "not authentic" for most of prehistory, but they reject the implication that traditional knapping is necessarily superior. When Tony Romano and I published an article on prehistoric copper pressure flakers (Whittaker and Romano 1996), it was immediately used by some knappers to bolster the traditional nature of all copper tools, even though the article applied only to a limited time and part of North America, and did not deal with the issue of copper billets at all.

A number of possible prehistoric copper billets have been found. Woody Blackwell lent me one he had acquired from a collector who hunts copper artifacts in Minnesota with a metal detector. It was a small, flat lump of copper with the slight mushrooming and pitting that might be expected from knapping use, although it is better described as a soft hammerstone than a billet. Unfortunately, an artifact with no context like this is worthless as archaeological evidence. We don't know where it came from, what it was with, how old it is, or even if it is really prehistoric at all. Until some copper billets are documented by proper and well-recorded excavation, the best we can say is that they seem to be out there. Again, however, some knappers are eager to see this as vindication of the "traditional" nature of their knapping.

A similarly fraught topic is lapidary knapping, more often called lap knapping, flake over grinding, or f.o.g. In lap knapping, the preform is

Figure 2.12. Lap knapping: a demonstration piece by Dale Cannon showing ground surface partly pressure-flaked, with the upper left edge given final treatment. Photo by Sarah DeLong.

prepared not by flaking, but by grinding, to produce a perfectly smooth surface which is then covered with regular patterned flake scars in a single series of pressure flakes (Figure 2.12). There were actually a few prehistoric cultures where this technique was used, although, of course, the surfaces were ground by hand rather than with power lapidary wheels. As we shall see, the art- and knife-collector-oriented knappers are most likely to use lap knapping, and again, some other knappers are dismissive of such nontraditional techniques.

The variations in technique discussed above reflect two facets of the thinking of modern knappers. The range of possible techniques, choices among them, and individual variations reflect the individuality of the craftsman and the possibility of expressing a point of view in the way you perform a craft. Knappers tend to develop their own little tricks, and tools to suit themselves, and are generally proud of their own way of working and possessive of their personal tool kit. However, knappers who use fluting jigs, copper billets, or flake over grinding techniques often sound slightly defensive in the face of criticism that they are not really "traditional." Tradition and authenticity are very strong values among knappers. Without the sense of tradition and continuity, you lose some of the connection to the past that attracts most knappers. Whether they make nothing but copies of prehistoric points using copper tools, or do careful replicative experiments with antler tools, or produce fantasy knives with a combination of ancient and modern techniques, all knappers refer to "tradition" as part of their emotional attachment to knapping. These issues will be raised again later.

From Fakes and Experiments to Knap-ins: The Roots of Modern Flintknapping

Modern *flintknapping* can be fancifully pictured as a tree with two roots. The first of these is the interest of academic archaeologists in understanding stone tools, and the second, the craft tradition of knappers who make stone tools for curiosity, fun, and profit. The soil which nourishes both these modern knapping traditions is the ancient heritage of stone tool craftsmanship common to all our ancestors.

Part of the culture of the knap-in concerns the traditions of modern flintknapping and the various historical reasons for making stone tools in a modern world. The archaeological and the nonacademic roots of modern knapping intertwine, but both were essential in shaping the modern knap-in, and each played a somewhat different role. It should be no surprise that the academic knappers wrote about what they learned. The nonacademic knappers, for a variety of reasons, are poorly documented, and the purpose of this chapter is thus to explore the roots of modern knapping, with an emphasis on the neglected parts.

Charlie Shewey

Charlie Shewey died in November 2002, and the Fort Osage knap-in lost one of its most respected figures. For years he was a regular, walking carefully with his cane among the tents and tables at the Fort Osage Knap-in, stopping frequently to greet friends with a firm handshake or a lengthy story. The other knappers regarded Charlie with the

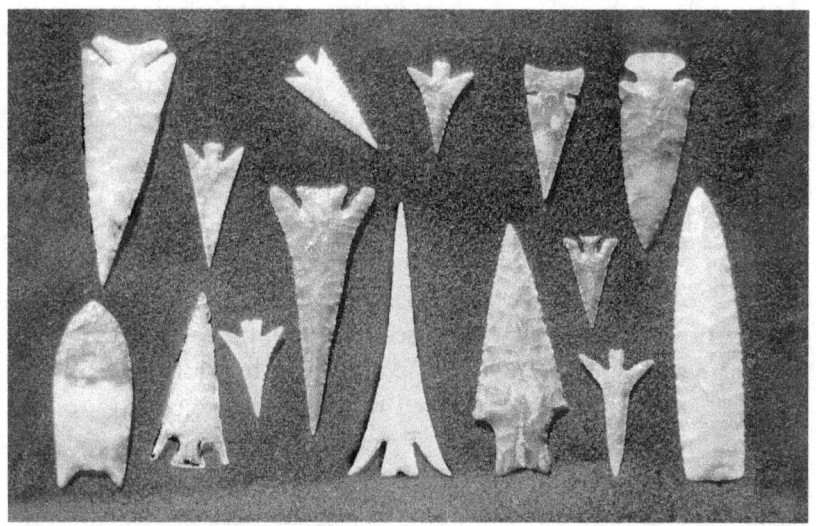

Figure 3.1. Small points by Charlie Shewey.

respect due to a senior statesman, for Charlie was a knapper before most of us were born, and an expert knapper when almost no one else approached the levels of skill common today. Although when I knew him, he was no longer an active knapper, Charlie had a huge influence on the Fort Osage Knap-ins, more than is immediately apparent.

Charlie Shewey helped teach Bob Hunt and several other key knappers and was a charter member of the group of knappers who started the Fort Osage Knap-in. Charlie was born in Oklahoma in 1911 and started collecting arrowheads as a boy, at a time when points had little commercial value. As he remembers it, the usual response when he asked neighboring farmers if he could look for points on their land was "Sure, but why ain't you doing something useful?" When he was twelve, his scoutmaster taught him how to make small "bird points" by pressure, and Charlie worked out percussion for himself (Shewey and Waldorf 1998). By the 1930s he was making points as good as those of most modern knappers, and better than most of his contemporaries (Figure 3.1). Arthritis ended Charlie's knapping, although I have seen him show beginners how to do something.

On one occasion, Charlie Shewey was passing out a "business card" at the knap-in. Under his name it read, "A poor, pitable, old and infirm critter. Would-be collector of stone artifacts. Seeking to upgrade an abominable accumulation of rejected relics. Lowest possible prices paid. Interested in Flint Knapping and related skills. WorldWide." Most of this was outrageous hyperbole. The small labeled drawing of a point by Ishi, also on his card, is more accurate. If you knew Charlie at all, or even just eavesdropped for a few minutes at a knap-in, you soon learned that he had an immense and unique collection. The Ishi point was one of three he owned, the point type he considered rarest of all and most difficult to collect. Ishi, the last survivor of the Yana of California, lived for about five years at the University of California's Museum of Anthropology in San Francisco. He did flintknapping and other demonstrations for the public, but points made by Ishi are rare. Moreover, as a skillful knapper attached to a tragic personal story of the destruction of Indian cultures, he is regarded as a sort of deity by knappers. At one knap-in where Charlie showed us his Ishi points, one knapper confided to me, only partly in jest, that after handling a point by Ishi he would now feel unable to wash his hands for a few days.

Bringing the Ishi points to show other knappers was typical of Charlie. Talkative and generous with information, Charlie had a vast fund of stories and knowledge of artifacts, collectors, archaeologists, and flintknapping. As a senior knapper and respected expert, he influenced other knappers in their understanding of archaeology and the details of different point types, and specimens in his collections served as models and inspiration.

As a collector, Charlie also represented one of the reasons why knap-ins, and the whole hobby of knapping, exist. Most knappers start from an interest in collecting artifacts, and collectors also provide the major market impetus for knapping, a topic I will discuss in detail later.

Charlie Shewey was something of a patron of the arts among flintknappers. His vast range of experience with all sorts of artifacts gave him a very knowledgeable eye, and his judgment on points, modern or ancient, was respected by all the Fort Osage knappers. If he liked a knapper's work, he would buy from him regularly, and he said he had hundreds of points by each of several modern knappers, at a time when very few collectors were interested in modern knapping. He not only encouraged some of these knappers by praising their work publicly, but by paying them a lot of money for their points. Their knapping was surely influenced by what Charlie liked.

In the course of collecting artifacts and learning how to knap, Charlie Shewey met many of the old commercial knappers and collectors, and quite a few archaeologists. The relationships between archaeologists and artifact collectors are complex and will be discussed later. As a collector, Charlie had mixed experiences with archaeologists. Some respected his knowledge, others wanted nothing to do with any non-archaeological artifact collector. It took us a while to get friendly, and for a while I found it slightly embarrassing to be introduced to his friends at the knap-in as "This here's John Whittaker, he's an archaeologist, but he's OK." This chapter owes a great deal to Charlie. He probably knew as much about the early days of knapping, which are largely undocumented, as anyone, and much of my information about early knappers comes from Charlie, as does a lot of the historical lore among other knappers. Charlie was the Fort Osage knappers' main link to knapping history, but we have to start the history of knapping well beyond even Charlie's memory.

Early Archaeologists and Fakers

Experiments with prehistoric technology were only a small part of archaeology as it developed in the late nineteenth century (see L. Johnson 1978 for a thorough history of flintknapping in archaeology). Stone tool making survived long enough to be recorded in a few native cultures, mostly in the New World. As a result, some of the basic techniques and features of stone tools were apparent to early American anthropologists, making experiments with stone flaking somewhat less urgent than in Europe, where arguments about how to recognize the earliest stone tools were the impetus for much of the experimentation. A number of early American anthropologists, inspired by observing Indian knappers, or by archaeological finds of stone tools, did learn some flintknapping. A few described their own experiments and their observations of native knappers and applied some of this information to interpreting archaeological finds. Some of the first knapping archaeologists were influential figures. Frank Hamilton Cushing (1895) was one of the founders of Southwestern archaeology and ethnology, and William Henry Holmes (1891, 1919), who pioneered a number of modern lithic ideas, was the head of the Bureau of American Ethnology. Nevertheless, flintknapping experiments remained a very minor byway in the path of early archaeology. This remained true until the 1960s, although there were a number of important and quite good studies from time to time in the preceding eighty years.

While early academic archaeology showed little interest in knapping, and most people considered the making of stone tools a lost art, a surprising number of laymen were figuring out the basic techniques of flintknapping, and making stone tools to satisfy their curiosity or to fill their pockets. Although records of early nonacademic knappers are scarce, it seems that fakers picked up the craft even faster than archaeologists, perhaps having more immediate incentive. In Europe, there were traditions of gunflint making and masonry that maintained some knowledge of knapping (Whittaker 2001a, 2001b), and it is not surprising that as scholars became interested in "antiquities," a number of individuals turned knapping skills to profit by producing fakes. It is more surprising, to a modern archaeologist anyway, that the archaeologists showed so little interest in learning the techniques from those who knew them, or at least observing them with an eye toward applying the information to understanding prehistoric stone tools. There were a few exceptions, such as Sydney Skertchly (1879), who worked with gunflint makers, and Sir John Evans (1866, 1872) and Augustus Henry Lane Fox Pitt-Rivers (1906), two of the founders of British prehistoric studies, but they had little impact.

Jacques Boucher de Perthes, a French customs official, conducted excavations in the Pleistocene gravels around Abbeville between 1840 and 1860. Here he found handaxes and other early stone tools in the same strata as the bones of mammoths and other extinct "antediluvian" creatures. It took quite a while for him to overcome the established opinion that humans had only been in the world for a few thousand years since Adam and Eve, but eventually his finds were recognized as one of the convincing pieces of evidence for much greater human antiquity. One might expect a customs official to have a suspicious turn of mind, but to Boucher de Perthes goes the dubious honor of being probably the first archaeologist to be fooled by fake stone tools. Spurred by offers of rewards, his workers produced numerous spurious "finds," and, blinded by his enthusiasm for an eccentric (but largely correct) view of prehistory, Boucher de Perthes accepted and published a variety of fakes and absurdly interpreted natural rocks (Rieth 1970). When I was a young anthropology student at Cornell University, poking around in the old books in the library, I came across his *Antiquités*

Celtiques et Antédiluviennes (Celtic and Pre-Flood Antiquities, 1847). I opened this pioneering work with awe, and was horrified to see that alongside handaxes and fossils he had published things that even I could see at a glance were rubbish. It was probably a good lesson.

In the 1860s the English scholar Sir John Lubbock, writing his bestseller *Pre-Historic Times* (1890, 352), felt it necessary to explain the differences between weathered ancient flints and fresh forgeries. This was not only to demonstrate the great age and man-made origin of handaxes and other finds, but because Edward Simpson, alias "Flint Jack," and other fakers were producing flint handaxes and other antiquities for sale. The story of Flint Jack is a sad one: antiquarians were willing enough to buy his stone tools, but when he was found to be a counterfeiter, they reviled him and showed no interest in learning from his skills (Blacking 1953; Marsden 1983; Frank 1991). He died a pauper, and the best we can say of this story is that neither the scholars nor the knapper inspire much admiration.

In America, Thomas Wilson of the Smithsonian was complaining about fakes by 1888. Someone had given the museum eight points that had apparently been reworked from old specimens and given unusual notches, a feature that Wilson noted might increase their sale value from a couple of cents each to fifty or seventy-five. Wilson seems to have been more annoyed by the economic fraud than the destruction of real artifacts and production of fakes, and like a true bureaucrat he concluded: "A law is sorely needed in the United States by which these fine gentlemen can be prosecuted for such deceitful practices, as they now can be for passing base money" (1888, 555).

Albert Jenks (1900) recorded another counterfeiter, Lewis Ericson. Ericson was born of Norwegian parents in Wisconsin in 1873 and, during an illness as a youth, discovered that he could remove chips from old arrowheads by biting on them. Perhaps he was feverish. In any case, he wisely substituted a set of steel pincers for his teeth and began crunching out fishhooks, eccentrics, and barbed "fish spears," using old points as raw material. After smearing his points with dirt to disguise the new scars, he could sell them to collectors for up to six dollars, "while at two or three dollars the demand was greater than the supply" (295). Jenks estimated that Ericson and a neighbor had made over a thousand points, and remarked that one reason he was able to deceive so many archaeologists and collectors was that they "refuse to disclose to one another the source of their alleged treasures" (293). Jenks noted that others in the area were also selling fakes, but were not as skilled at making them.

Native Knappers

Another poorly documented aspect of the early history of modern flintknapping concerns the few native people who made stone tools into modern times. Ethnographic records of surviving knappers in the nineteenth century contributed to archaeological understanding and early experiments (Ellis 1965; Holmes 1919). Although most Native American groups seem to have quickly abandoned stone tools when metals became available, some knowledge certainly survived, and it is likely that a number of unrecorded Indian knappers made arrowheads for home use and perhaps tourist sale. Two individual knappers are accorded legendary status by modern knappers (Harwood 1988a, 1999, 2001a, 2001b). Ishi, the last survivor of the Yana in California, spent his last years (1911–1916) at the University of California's Museum of Anthropology in San Francisco (Kroeber 1961). His flintknapping skills were recorded by several anthropologists (Nelson 1916) and continue to be of interest to archaeologists (Shackley 2001) and impressive to modern knappers (Figure 3.2). Another California Indian, Ted Orcutt (1862–1946), knapped huge obsidian blades for ceremonial use and sale, and also apparently made thousands of points commercially (Harwood 1988a, 1999), but seems never to have attracted the attention of anthropologists, despite wide public interest in Ishi during Orcutt's lifetime.

Mack Tussinger and the Oklahoma Eccentrics

In the late 1930s Mack Tussinger came to the attention of archaeologists when large numbers of peculiar chipped stone artifacts (Figure 3.3) began to circulate among collectors and dealers in Oklahoma and Missouri (Clements and Reed 1939; Ellis 1940). Tussinger claimed to have found a huge cache of 3,500 eccentric flints in 1926 (Clements and Reed 1939) or 1921 (Ellis 1940; Heeringa and Elsing 1960; Iler 1996) in a low mound on the Elk River in Oklahoma, interred with a group of human burials. He dug the flints up, took them home, and reburied them. Charlie Shewey knew Tussinger and says he claimed the reburial was because the flints came from the property of his cousin, who would have wanted a share if he had known where they were found.

Figure 3.2. Ishi's points. Photo of Lithic Casting Lab casts of points from Charlie Shewey's collection. Center point is cast to look like obsidian but was actually glass. Photo by Sarah DeLong.

Tussinger began selling his "finds" to local dealers and collectors. According to Ellis, "The first specimens sold were small, relatively simple, and all made from local material from the Peoria, Oklahoma, quarries. . . . Later points were larger, more complex, and of a wide variety of flint" (1940, 122). Tussinger's prices also climbed from as little as twenty-five cents to as much as fifty dollars, a considerable sum in those days.

Forrest Clements, from the Department of Anthropology at the University of Oklahoma, and Alfred Reed, who was apparently a collector and amateur archaeologist associated with the Oklahoma State Archaeological Society, analyzed some 900 of Tussinger's specimens, which Reed had acquired, and interviewed Tussinger. Clements and Reed also visited the site, where nothing was left but "a barely perceptible rise on the field level and a difference in color of the earth" (1939, 28). Reed arranged a lease on the site, and a field crew from the University excavated it in 1937. They found large disturbed areas that indicated previous digging, and scattered human bone, plus six eccentric

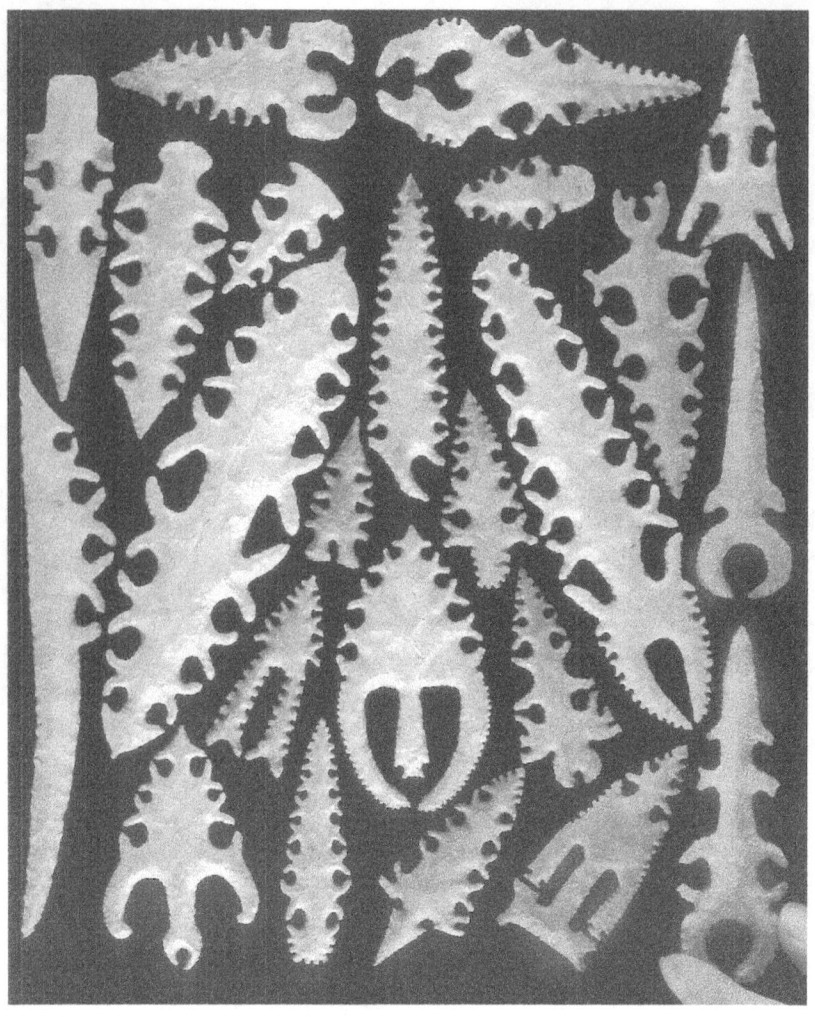

Figure 3.3. A group of Mack Tussinger's eccentrics, with finger for scale. Photo by Pete Bostrom, Lithic Casting Lab.

flints. However, only one of these was possibly in undisturbed position, and the other artifacts were normal Plains sherds and points. Back in the laboratory, they examined all the eccentrics, looking for evidence of metal flaking tools or acid weathering, but found neither. They considered the artifacts reminiscent of Maya eccentrics. Actually, most were simply long bifaces or points with the edges almost obsessively serrated and barbed. The notching style is distinctive, as is the fondness for small attached arrowhead forms on bases and barbs (Bostrom 2003). Tussinger's notching skills are still impressive today, but his points look nothing like real Maya eccentrics. (See Figure 9.1 for a modern replica, and Stuart 1989, Willey 1972, Willey et al. 1965, Woods and Titmus 1996 for ancient examples.) Clements and Reed concluded that there was no evidence of forgery, but the circumstances of the find were "unsatisfactory," and they recommended that Tussinger's artifacts should not be dismissed, or accepted, just yet.

Clements asked H. Holmes Ellis, who ran the Lithic Laboratory at the Museum of the Ohio State Archaeological and Historical Society, to have another look. Ellis is in some ways the forefather of modern scientific knapping. His laboratory collected ethnographic accounts of knapping techniques and experimented with them, and Ellis had published a major report in 1939 (Ellis 1965).

Ellis analyzed two hundred specimens from the Reed collection and was much more definite in his conclusions than Clements and Reed. He noted that the eccentrics "did not conform to any known pattern within the area of their occurrence" (1965, 123), and only superficially resembled Maya eccentrics. They still had some small, loosely attached flake remnants, typical of freshly chipped pieces. The edges, where recent chipping would be most obvious, had been treated with some dark organic substance, unlike prehistoric patinas. The overall flaking patterns, and the form of most of the objects, suggested that they had been reworked from prehistoric bifaces and intentionally aged.

The feelings among collectors also seem to have been mixed (Reeder 1936, 1937a, 1937b). In March of 1936, *Hobbies: The Magazine for Collectors* ran a photograph of Tussinger specimens captioned "These delicate implements, says Charles W. Grimes, owner, came from a mound in southwest Missouri. What is the opinion of collectors as to their use?" A followup in the January 1937 issue explained that now there was more information available, and gave Tussinger as the finder, and Oklahoma as the location. Clements and Reed were cited as believing them genuine, and the Maya connection was mentioned. A final note the next month appears to refer to the same material, and warns that according to a Mr. Benedict, who "has first-hand information[,] . . . fancy spears may be fakes" made by a Southwestern Indian from old points.

Tussinger apparently started small in the late 1920s, and it was only around 1936 or so that he began selling large numbers of larger pieces and asking higher prices. I think he was trying to take advantage of recent news of the destruction of one of the most important sites in America. Between 1933 and 1935, a large Caddoan burial mound, part of a mound and village complex in Spiro, Oklahoma, was butchered by commercial diggers (Brown 1996; Clements 1945; Hamilton 1952; Phillips and Brown 1984). Spiro Mound, more properly the Craig mound at Spiro, and often called the Temple Mound by contemporary writers, was an incredibly rich site. Elite burials on wooden litters were accompanied by outstanding objects such as shells engraved with "Southern Cult" designs, wooden masks, hafted copper axes, and the like. The looters called themselves "The Pocola Mining Company," which pretty much indicates their approach to archaeology. In 1935 the outrageous destruction of the site finally aroused archaeologists and responsible citizens. Oklahoma passed a site preservation law and the looters were evicted, but they not only snuck back and continued the rape of the main mound with a series of tunnels, but attempted to dynamite it when they were finished. Of course, the looters kept no records and destroyed untold amounts of evidence, as they were only interested in salable artifacts. They were not even very careful in recovering those, especially as they grew increasingly hasty and began to suspect that others in the group were selling things behind their backs. Charlie Shewey remembered seeing backdirt piles full of bits of engraved shell and rotted cloth. As the thieves hauled out their loot, it was quickly sold on the spot to dealers and collectors and dispersed all over the country.

Fortunately, an amateur archaeologist, Henry Hamilton, interviewed some of the looters after the destruction of the mound and collected as much information as possible on the finds, tracing them through chains of buyers (Hamilton 1952). Subsequent excavations of the remains of the site (Orr 1946; Brown 1966a, 1966b, 1996) and various analyses of artifacts from it (Bell 1947; Brown 1971, 1976, 1996; Phillips and Brown 1984) have recovered a lot of information, but also show how much was lost. While the site was being looted, amazing finds flooded the market and made quite a splash in the news and among collectors. The news stimulated further plundering of nearby sites, and when the supply of real artifacts ran out, fakes rapidly filled the gap.

Among the Spiro finds were a number of massive flaked and ground stone maces, large bifaces, and projectile points (see Brown 1996,

431–503). Nothing like Tussinger's eccentrics was clearly traceable to Spiro, but one similar piece was found by University of Oklahoma crews in the looters' backdirt, and an Arkansas collector claimed to have found eleven more in a burial in the mound (Ellis 1940). My guess is that Tussinger responded to the great find at Spiro by increasing his production and sales of fakes from a supposedly similar site. He may even have passed some pieces to an Arkansas friend to help bolster the authenticity of his "find" with a false Spiro provenience for a few similar specimens. This is admittedly speculation, but Charlie Shewey's memories of Tussinger make it seem plausible.

Charlie knew Tussinger, as they were both active in the world of artifact collecting. He told pretty much the same story about Tussinger's eccentrics as I found in the articles cited above, including the details of the supposed find and the real origin of the artifacts. When I interviewed Charlie, he added that a man named Willard Elsing ended up with many of Tussinger's eccentrics and even wrote a crazy book about them. Pete Bostrom, whose Lithic Casting Lab produces fine casts of artifacts, was able to show me a copy. *Treasure from a Pre-Historic Age* (Heeringa and Elsing 1960) is a fifteen-page pamphlet written by Irene Heeringa and illustrated by Elsing for his private Oak Crest Museum near Joplin, Missouri. It is an absurd attempt to connect the Oklahoma fakes to Maya eccentrics, the Easter Island symbol system, and the fictional ancient continent of Mu. I spoke to Mr. Elsing in 2001, and he assured me that he would still "stake his life" on the authenticity of Tussinger's eccentrics, but was not forthcoming on details. A few others still believe in them, too (Iler 1996), but the evidence is strongly against an ancient origin, let alone any Mayan connection.

Mack Tussinger's "find" was dismissed and dropped out of the archaeological literature, and Tussinger died twenty or thirty years ago, but according to Charlie, he continued his career as a faker for some time. Charlie dealt with him on behalf of other collectors. He remembers Tussinger having lots of marvelous maces and spuds. Such things were found at Spiro and may have been his inspiration; Charlie remembered that he copied some Spiro artifacts, making them out of novaculite rather than the proper cherts. When Charlie asked him how every month he came up with things no one else could find, he claimed that because he was part Indian he could talk to the Indians up in the hills and get them to sell him heirlooms. "One time he had a statue, almost four feet tall, made of some kind of volcanic stone, that he claimed he'd dug in Spiro Mound, recently, you see. And I said, 'How could you get that out of Spiro Mound when it's been leveled since 1935?'" Tussinger claimed there was a corner of the mound on another landowner's property that had not been dug until he got there. Charlie remembered an area which had been left alone by the University of Oklahoma archaeologists because they knew the mound did not extend there. The statue "was *obviously* as modern as hell," but Charlie's client wanted it so badly he paid $2,500 for it. "I was down [to Spiro] sometime after that, and looked, and there was a place over on that side of the fence you could have put a car in. Somebody had gone there and dug a helluva hole. There was nothing there . . . so he dug that hole I guess to show a place where he'd dug that thing out of."

Charlie's verdict on Tussinger was "He was a master crook," and I have told his story at length to give some idea of the convoluted world of fakery. I suppose if there is a moral to the stories of Tussinger and other fakers at the dawn of modern knapping, it is that although some of them developed considerable skill and knowledge, neither the scientific community nor the collectors could trust them. As a result, they cast suspicion on all knappers for many years and are remembered as cheats rather than craftsmen.

Daniel, Howe, and Others

On the same pages of *Hobbies* cited above are advertisements for H. T. Daniel, Dardanelle, Arkansas, "Largest Dealer in the South." The long list of ethnographic and archaeological artifacts includes points priced from twenty-five cents to a dollar, and a few small items from the "Great Temple Mound." When I asked Charlie Shewey about other early knappers, he mentioned Daniel and Lear Howe, although

> they weren't really knappers, they were just crooks. They were primarily making stuff out of broken projectile points. H. T. Daniel made all these nose rings and fish gigs, and turtles and rabbits and different things out of them, always out of broken projectile points, and later on Lear Howe started doing the same thing. Each one of them served five years with Uncle Sam up at Joliet. . . . They would advertise 20,000 genuine Indian relics. Then they would say "Fulsom" instead of Folsom, not spelling it correct, they would spell everything wrong, "Cluvis-

es," instead of Clovis—they thought that was protecting them. But they found out it didn't—misspelling things and selling them as real genuine ancient pieces. Somebody turned them in to the postal service.

I was unable to confirm any of this from independent sources, but it would certainly be easy and profitable for dealers with large inventories of real artifacts to enlarge their business by cranking out fakes or buying them from others, and such dealings are still common today. Whether or not the opinion of the time, as remembered by Charlie Shewey, is right about Howe and Daniel, they were two of many who helped develop the market for both real stone tools and fakes.

McCormick the Folsom Fluter

In the 1920s and 1930s, finds of stone points with the bones of extinct animals proved that humans had been in North America during the Pleistocene. These points are now described as "fluted," typically with a single large thinning flake running up the point from the base. The two major types recognized by early archaeologists are the larger, earlier Clovis point and the smaller, more finely worked, and later Folsom point.

Another early knapper of Charlie Shewey's acquaintance was Marvin McCormick, who was one of the first knappers to produce an acceptable fluted point (Figure 3.4; see also Figure 7.12). This became his specialty, and he turned out vast numbers of them; "hundreds of thousands," or "boxcar loads," were two of the expressions I heard. According to Charlie, McCormick was still working into the 1970s.

Like most of the early knapper/fakers, and for that matter, like most knappers now, McCormick began by collecting prehistoric points. He was three years older than Charlie Shewey, and Charlie knew him before World War II.

> He used to be a cowboy out there in southeast Colorado, he knew where all the sites were, blowouts and everything. [Blowouts are areas of wind erosion.] He told me, during the Honest to God Depression, he and his wife would go out constantly looking for arrowheads, to sell. You could sell those nice little three-inch side-notched points for ten cents apiece. If he

Figure 3.4. Fluted points (left) and others bought as antiquities in the 1950s, but probably made by Marvin McCormick. They show characteristic traits: made of Alibates chert, they are a bit too thick for real Folsom points.

found a Clovis, or an Agate Basin, or something, he could get as much as fifty cents for it. He said everybody out there was doing it, so that whole country out there was looked over with a fine-toothed comb in the twenties and thirties. Everybody was going out every day trying to find Indian relics. There was a guy down in Liberal, Kansas, about fifty miles away, that was coming about once a month up there to Pritchet, to buy points people had found.

This general situation, and the price structure, are visible in advertising like the H. T. Daniel ads mentioned above.

McCormick's knapping techniques were crude by modern standards, but effective. He used an iron plow bolt to knap a rough shape. One of his favorite materials was colorful Alibates chert from Texas. Charlie said he would strike with the center of the bolt, eventually wearing the bolt down to an hourglass shape. "That was the only percussion he knew, he didn't know real percussion. He'd pound on the edges of the thing, and he'd take his bolt and hit, and say, 'I wish to hell I knew how to do this like the Indians did.' I'd try to explain to him about normal percussion, I'd say, 'Well it's so dang *easy*,' but it didn't suit him. A lot of people don't like any kind of a change, change of environment, change of job, change of anything." Despite this handicap, McCormick was able to make nice, thin Folsom blanks by pressure flaking with an iron nail wrapped in rawhide. "He was so damn good at pressure, and had the strength of a buffalo bull, so he didn't need the percussion." He removed pressure flakes with an upward motion that sometimes brought his hand against the edge of the point, and so he always wore heavy leather gloves, and Larry Nelson told me that he had eye damage from flicking flakes into his face. The final fluting was done by indirect percussion, using an iron spike as a punch.

McCormick was not only one of the first to successfully flute points, but also one of the first to use heat treatment. He preferred to use Alibates chert, and sometimes Edwards Plateau cherts, both of which heat treat well. He claimed to have learned arrowhead making and heat treating from his great-uncle, who had been a teamster with ox-drawn freight wagons on the Santa Fe Trail and may have learned in his turn from Indians. Charlie Shewey believed that McCormick worked as an aide-de-camp for Frank H. H. Roberts, who conducted some of the first excavations of Folsom sites (Waldorf 1997). I was unable to confirm this; McCormick is not listed among the expedition members of the several seasons (1934–1940) at Lindenmeier (Wilmsen and Roberts 1978) or mentioned among the helpers and visitors Roberts acknowledged in his reports (Roberts 1936, 1937). Nevertheless, Roberts's work in Colorado may have been McCormick's inspiration for making Folsom and other fluted points. After the Folsom finds in 1926 and the subsequent development of archaeological and collector interest in Paleoindian points (Wormington 1949, 49), McCormick's ability to make them, at a time when few could, would have been a definite economic advantage. Although the estimates of "boxcar loads" and the like may be exaggerations, he was productive. Charlie Shewey claimed McCormick told him he made about fourteen points a day, five days a week, for many years. As we will see later, this seems a remarkably high number, even in comparison to some very productive modern knappers. McCormick sold mostly to dealers, in large job lots. His primary customer was one Monroe Nowatny of San Antonio, Texas, who also bought from Rinehart and Warren, and reputedly once ordered five thousand points at one time from McCormick (Waldorf 1997).

Bryon Rinehart and Grey Ghosts

The so-called Grey Ghosts are a class of flaked stone artifact spanning the period beginning just after World War II and continuing up to the present, and made by several people (Figure 3.5). Grey Ghost–type points are very large bifaces, sort of exaggerated arrowheads, often with notching or serrations or other decoration untypical of prehistoric work (Figure 3.6). The most characteristic trait is their manufacture. They are flaked from slabs, using some sort of lever device, which removes huge, flat pressure flakes. Because the slabbed surfaces are flat, the flakes expand and sometimes terminate in small step fractures at or past the centerline of the piece. The edges are then finished with relatively steep pressure retouch, producing a flat, beveled cross-section. Typical examples are rather ugly and not considered

Figure 3.5. Three early modern knappers at Gustine, Texas, Summer 1977. Left to right, Richard Warren was famous for his lap knapping, as well as making Grey Ghosts; Bryon Rinehart is considered the classic Grey Ghost maker; and Larry Nelson is another early amateur knapper and Warren's friend. Photo courtesy of Larry Nelson.

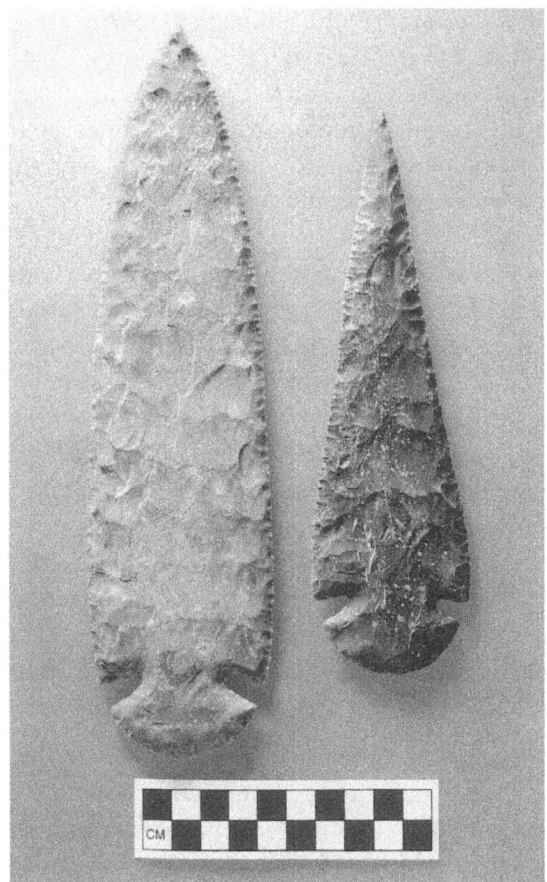

Figure 3.6. Grey Ghosts. Specimen on right was made by Dave Tussinger in 1999; the other may be his work but is also typical of Rinehart. Photo by Sarah DeLong.

good work by most knappers, but the better ones are not too bad. All are impressively large and sometimes elaborately notched. The name most often associated with Grey Ghosts is Bryon Rinehart, or Brian Reinhardt.[1]

Rinehart began his knapping career making ordinary points by normal means sometime before World War II. After a stint in the war, he came up with the idea of sawing blanks from the tabular Edwards Plateau chert that occurred in his part of Texas, near Gustine. This is a medium-quality grey or brownish chert with white spots or speckles, and when the slabs are sawed, one can obtain pieces the right width for a large point 12 to 18 inches long. His other idea was a lever device for rapidly removing large flakes. He kept this device secret, and Errett Callahan and J. B. Sollberger were reputedly met at shotgun point when they tried to visit him (Waldorf 1997), although they were eventually on friendly terms (J. A. Harwood 2001; Callahan 2001b). Charlie Shewey told me the lever device was a metal-tipped pressure flaker on a long handle fixed to a fulcrum of some sort, perhaps an eyebolt. The slab being flaked would be held partly upright, at the correct angle, in a support, so the pressure tool could be applied to the edges, and when the handle was pulled up, enough pressure could be generated to remove huge flakes. D. C. Waldorf (1995a) has experimented with such a device. According to Matt Trout, a current Texas knapper (Trout 1997), Rinehart shared his secret with at least one other knapper, a hobby knapper named McGee. The jig used by McGee held the point on a flat wooden base, with the flaking lever hinged vertically to the base (Trout 1997). Despite the secrecy of Rinehart and others, the idea of a mechanical flaking jig is fairly simple, and a number of people, including other makers of Grey Ghost–type material, as well as some other commercial knappers, must have developed or used them.

According to Charlie, Rinehart "never was a real knapper, I mean, he used a fulcrum for his stuff." Although many of his artifacts sold as antiquities, and Callahan (2001b) thinks he was inspired by the Spiro finds, Rinehart's points were not replicas of genuine prehistoric types.

> Rinehart wasn't even trying to make his stuff look old. Why, even his better work, it still wasn't like anything the Indians did. Some of his better stuff don't look too bad. But some of the others—awful, rough horrible-looking stuff, and he'd make *shapes*, like he'd have an eighteen-inch corner-tang knife with a big curve in it somewhere. In fact, we used to make fun in a way, by saying, "I can tell it's his a hundred yards away, all you got to do is hold it up to the skyline so you can see the shape of it." Cause he didn't give a damn about the shapes, he made them absolutely atrocious. He didn't try to make them look like the Indians'.

Rinehart was also prolific. According to Waldorf (1997), who got most of his information from Charlie Shewey, as I did, Rinehart only sold points by the gross, with no points under 9 inches long. Many were sold in shops along the western parts of Route 66, and Rinehart got twenty-five cents an inch for his work. Matt Trout told me in 1997 that the lore among Texas knappers is that Rinehart only sold in orders of 10,000 inches, at a dollar per inch, and demanded payment in gold coins. Everyone agrees that he was immensely prolific, and according to Trout "every junk antique store" in central Texas has one of his pieces. I saw one in a Colorado Indian arts store that had been given an elaborate turquoise and gold handle in the form of a kachina. It was the ugliest and most expensive thing in the store.

Bryon Rinehart died around 1982 (J. A. Harwood 2001) of lung cancer or emphysema, but Charlie thought his son had continued making Grey Ghosts for a while. Two other knappers are named as doing Grey Ghost–type work recently, Richard Warren, better known as one of the early lap knapping artists, and Dave Tussinger, son of the early faker. Others may well have been in the business, too.

Richard Warren—Scale Work and Lap Knapping

Larry Nelson is another of the older knappers at Fort Osage, a stocky man who appears quietly on the edges of the knap-in from time to time. In 1997, when I was trying to work out some of this history, Bob Hunt told me Larry would be a good source. We sat under the trees at the edge of the parking lot on a hot day, and he showed me a tray of points by various old knappers, especially Richard Warren.

Richard Warren has had considerable influence on some of the Fort Osage knappers. Although knap-in lore remembers him mostly as an eccentric and eventually paranoid faker, he also receives credit as one of the first art knappers. Both Larry Nelson, who says he was Warren's best friend, and Charlie Shewey argue that although much of Warren's work was sold by dealers as ancient, Warren himself did not attempt to deceive and should not be called a faker. He made two different styles of knapped pieces. One was the big lever-flaked "Grey Ghost"–type points that some knappers call "scale" work. Warren's were better made and used nicer material than Rinehart's. Larry Nelson says that Warren's lever device was more sophisticated and versatile than most, and he could work points with a lenticular cross-section, so his Grey Ghosts were not as flat as Rinehart's. Warren's other points were made by conventional pressure flaking on smaller pieces, at least some of which were ground first. This is now called lap knapping. He imitated fine parallel oblique-flaked late Paleoindian points, especially a form called Yuma or Angostura points, which are long, narrow lanceolate or triangular points (Figure 3.7). Jim Hopper (see Chapter 6), who was largely responsible for spreading lap knapping among the Fort Osage knappers, was inspired by Warren, as were some other knappers, although Warren was very secretive about his techniques.

Larry Nelson himself had learned to knap well before he met Richard Warren. An uncle who was a trapper in Wyoming but also made and sold arrowheads during the Depression started Larry knapping around 1948. Larry figured out heat treating in 1950, when his mother burned a pair of blue jeans that had one of his points in the pocket and he tried to reflake it. Larry eventually trained as an engineer and wrote a master's thesis on the effects of heat treating flint (Nelson 1968) that is one of the earliest scientific discussions of this topic. Meanwhile, he was able to earn "spending money" by selling points, trying to avoid the dealers who wanted to resell them as antiquities.

Larry Nelson met Richard Warren around 1958 while exploring a Missouri cave (Nelson 2002). Caves, it seems, fascinated Warren throughout his life.

> We heard grunting and groaning and clunking and here came Rich and his brother out of the back cave. We didn't know they were in there. They were way in the back looking at the drip stone. We became friends. We were looking for arrowheads, but we hadn't had much luck that day. I said, "Well, I can make these things." And he said, "You can?" And so I started giving him tips on flintknapping and then when I finished up engineering school at Rolla, Missouri, we went our separate ways.

They met again later in Denver, and after Warren became a skillful knapper, they occasionally worked together, with Warren turning out blanks that Nelson finished.

Charlie Shewey also knew Richard Warren, and claims that when they first met, Warren was making mostly the larger "scale" pieces, but Charlie convinced him that he could do as well selling fewer of his finer pieces for higher prices. Charlie bought several hundred of Warren's pieces in the years he knew him, but stopped when Warren "killed the goose that laid the golden egg" by continually raising his prices.

Larry Nelson told me

> the Grey Ghosts were Warren's bread and butter, but he found it very boring to crank them out. He called them "big ugly spears." And they were straight as a string and ugly grey Texas

[chert]. He made a few eccentrics. One time some guy selling this kitsch-type Indian art wanted a bunch of flint thunderbirds, so Rich made the lenticular blades and had me put the shapes in them because he didn't want to do it, it was so boring. And there was one piece of real dark Texas that was almost black, so I made a flint bat out of it, which really cracked him up. I have no idea where that artifact wound up.

Warren sold mostly to dealers, including Munroe Nowatny, and Nelson thought that a lot of his work was exported to Germany and Japan. Like Rinehart, he was prolific. He, too, sold by the inch, and Nelson guessed he must have made at least 100,000 inches of Grey Ghosts in his career.

Grey Ghosts and finer point replicas allowed Richard Warren to support himself as a professional knapper living a "middle middle-class" lifestyle, but late in his career he became interested in more ambitious knapping art, beyond even the perfect pressure flaking on some of his finer points. He wrote a letter to *Flintknappers' Exchange* (Warren 1978) saying that as an isolated commercial knapper, he was surprised to learn how many other knappers there were. He did not describe his commercial work, but stated that his interests were now focused on "teleolithics," which he described by saying: "I'm curious as to what can be done with flint if one picks up where the best Stone Age knappers abandoned the craft, and pursues it for art's sake."

Larry Nelson showed me a photograph of an art piece (Figure 3.8) in which Warren had knapped six large eccentric bifaces, finely flaked and elaborately notched, and mounted them on a marble stand with three as uprights and the others intertwined among them. It was not

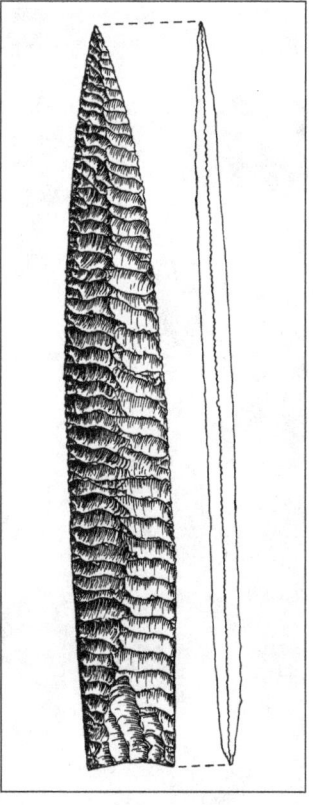

Figure 3.7. A finely flaked point by Richard Warren. Drawing by Val Waldorf.

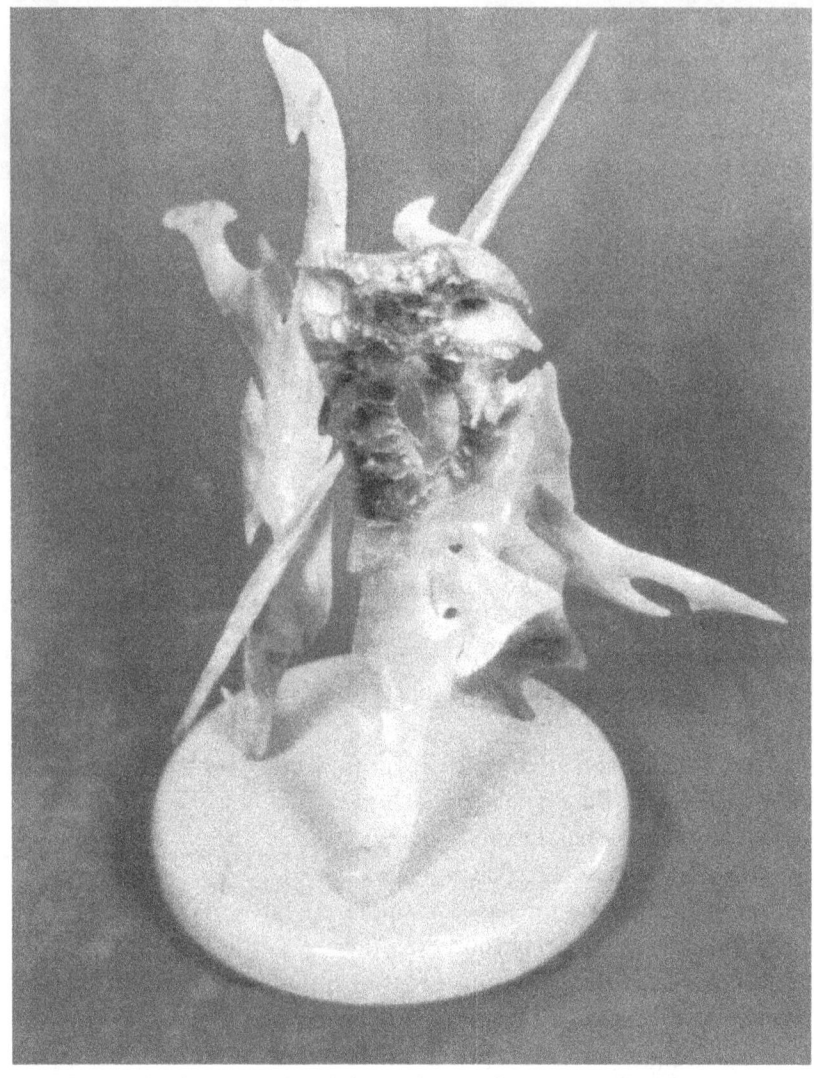

Figure 3.8. Richard Warren's "Teleolithic" sculpture. Photo courtesy of Larry Nelson.

only very impressive to a knapper, but an attractive piece of abstract sculpture.

Dave Waldorf (1997) met Warren when he lived in Missouri, but Warren moved a lot, always trying to live near a source of good stone. Larry Nelson first knew him in Missouri, then ran into him again in Denver, after which they both moved back to Missouri. Later Warren moved to Llano, Texas, to be closer to his raw materials, then on to Oregon when he started chipping Oregon agate, then to Montana as he became more paranoid and antisocial, and eventually back to Oregon. Like Rinehart, Warren was very secretive and refused to show anyone his shop or techniques. Larry Nelson was sworn to secrecy and is still somewhat reticent. After some personal tragedies, Warren apparently became increasingly unstable, committing suicide around 1992 or 1993. A more exotic rumor among knappers is that he faked his death to escape from either the IRS or contract killers hired by defrauded artifact collectors.

Patterns in the Early Modern Knappers

Warren represents a trend among the commercial knappers, even more apparent today, to straddle the fence between faking and "art knapping." The Grey Ghost–type artifacts represent a borderline category. They are not replicas of genuine artifacts and, if sold honestly, could simply be knapped art. Unfortunately, most such things have usually been palmed off on less knowledgeable collectors and tourists as spectacular antiquities. The superfinely flaked points and eccentric forms made by Warren and other modern knappers are similarly ambiguous artifacts. They are not really replicas, and knowledgeable modern collectors buy them for what they are, but they can also be dishonestly sold at high prices as ancient art to less experienced customers.

In the past, when the archaeology and prehistoric artifact types were less well known, eccentric and unusual fake stone tools could and did fool many experts. The collectors in particular were easier to fool in Tussinger's day because collectors tend to be secretive about the real sources of their artifacts and unreliable in recording and reporting provenience information. Both collectors and archaeologists occasionally become easy victims because they desire to believe in a spectacular or interesting find, to the point of disregarding suspicious evidence.

Faking also responds to market patterns and to archaeological trends. New and spectacular finds have inspired many imitators. Today, the high price of some scarce forms, such as Paleoindian fluted points, and the demand for truly superior pieces affect what modern knappers make. Both the honest art knapper and the faker are affected. In Chapters 9 and 10 I will discuss the current market for flaked stone.

Halvor Skavlem and the Hobby Knapper

While most of the known early nonacademic knappers were out-and-out fakers, or made pieces that were usually sold as fakes, there must also have been many unknown hobby knappers, just as these form the majority today. Since archaeology as a profession was not very interested in experimental stone tool making until the 1960s, no one paid much attention to them. A California amateur named Joseph Barbieri applied his knapping skills to interpreting stone implements from Lake Mohave (Barbieri 1937), producing an unusually insightful analysis. He even discussed some of the important variables in knapping, such as platform angles, platform preparation, and the angle of the blow. Although pictures of Barbieri's work (Harris 1926) suggest a pretty competent knapper, no one seems to have been much impressed; archaeology was not yet ready to listen to knappers.

One exception to the anonymity of most amateur knappers was Halvor Skavlem. Skavlem was a Norwegian immigrant living in Wisconsin who began experimenting with flintknapping around 1912. He became proficient enough to attract local attention, and even some national notice when an article in the *Atlantic Monthly* (Stewart 1923) described him. Apparently the article resulted in numerous letters to the author from others who also wanted credit for rediscovering a "lost art," which supports my suspicion that there were many more amateur knappers than we know about, even in the 1920s.

Skavlem is known to archaeologists today because Alonzo Pond, who knew him as a boy and went on to become an archaeologist, published *Primitive Methods of Working Stone Based on Experiments of Halvor L. Skavlem* (Pond 1930). For many years this monograph was one of the few sources an aspiring knapper could turn to for instruction. It was actually quite a good piece of work, considering ethnographic accounts, techniques of knapping based on Skavlem's ideas, pecked and ground implements, and experiments in felling trees with stone axes. Along the way it dismissed the old tale that arrowheads can be made by dripping water on hot rocks, described British gunflint makers, considered the difference between natural and human flaking, and provided an early consideration of the mechanics of flaking.

Stewart (1923) portrays Skavlem himself as quite a character. He was a retired farmer who took up knapping, archaeology, and natural history as hobbies and worked with the early archaeologists in Wisconsin.

He knapped with bone pressure flakers and hammerstones, rather than the metal tools of most fakers of his day, because he was interested in figuring out "how the Indians did it." The pictures of his work in Pond show competent small points, rather crude by the standards of today's knap-in, but perfectly adequate replicas. It appears from the pictures that he had not fully worked out methods of thinning by pressure or percussion. Skavlem does not seem to have attempted to sell his work or otherwise profit from it. Although Stewart says his work was in demand in museums as far away as Canada and France, he says Skavlem knapped purely out of love of the craft and curiosity, with no ulterior motive. Amateurs like Skavlem continue to make up a large portion of the knap-in knappers, and there must be many more hobby knappers who have never made contact with the rest of the knapping world. Charlie Shewey, Larry Nelson, and several others among the modern knappers I know or have heard of were similarly precocious self-taught knappers who received little or no public recognition.

Archaeology and Replication

In the 1960s the field of archaeology increasingly shifted away from description and chronology and toward attempts to understand how cultures were organized and to explain processes of change and adaptation. These new emphases required studying how specific tools were made and used in order to understand what people were doing and how they made a living in their environment. As a result, experiments in making and using all sorts of artifacts, which had always been a small part of archaeology, became much more important. Not only did more archaeologists begin to experiment with stone tools, but the field was now willing to look to some of the nonacademic experts.

The two names most associated with the florescence of scientific flintknapping are Don Crabtree and François Bordes (Figure 3.9). Don Crabtree (1912–1980) was an American who began knapping as a youth (Callahan and Crabtree 1979; Johnson 1978; Knudson 1982). He never finished a college education, but was employed by several institutions as a paleontologist and lithic technologist. Between 1941 and World War II he worked at the Lithic Laboratory of the Ohio Historical Society under H. Holmes Ellis (Callahan and Crabtree 1979, 27). This was after Ellis's major experimental study of flintworking techniques (Ellis 1965) was originally published in 1939, and it is not clear how much

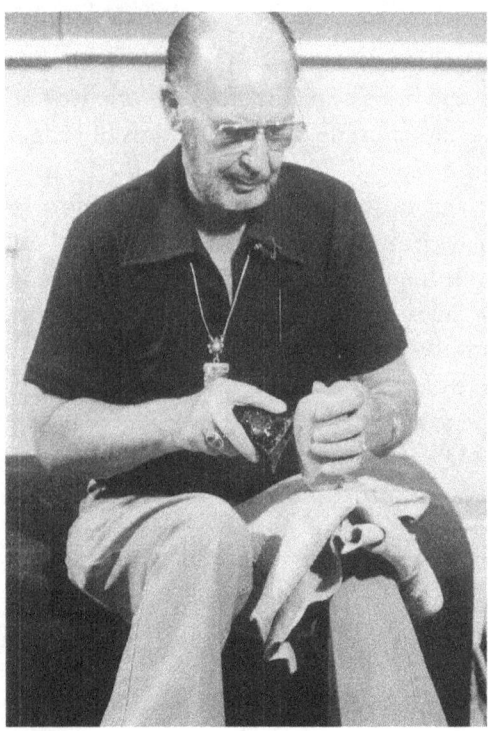

Figure 3.9. Don Crabtree making percussion blades during a visit to the University of Lethbridge, 1979. Photo courtesy of James Woods.

influence Ellis had on Crabtree's interests and skill. After World War II Crabtree was diverted into business pursuits, but continued his lithic experiments as a hobby. After he gave some demonstrations to archaeological groups in Idaho, Earl Swanson of Idaho State University convinced him to become involved in academic archaeology. Crabtree eventually published a number of important articles that helped to define lithic experimentation as a legitimate field (e.g., Crabtree 1966, 1968, 1972).

With Swanson's help, Crabtree obtained National Science Foundation support in 1964 to attend a lithic conference in Les Eyzies, France, where he met François Bordes and Jacques Tixier, two important French prehistorians who were promoting experimental knapping on their side of the Atlantic (Jelinek 1965, 1982). The conference began a long and fruitful interchange between Bordes and Crabtree (1969) and, more importantly, impressed a number of influential archaeologists with the value of lithic experiments.

Crabtree and Bordes were only the best known of those who stimulated the growth of academic knapping, and others would have done so without them, simply because the intellectual climate in archaeology was right. Nevertheless, the influence of both men went beyond their published works. They helped to establish knapping as a useful part of archaeology and inspired and trained other knappers. Crabtree had an especially strong influence on the American scene. Starting in 1968, Crabtree taught a summer field school in flintknapping at Washington State University, and many currently active academic knappers were trained there, or in its successor, run by Jeff Flenniken, a professional archaeologist who was a student of Crabtree. As the learning genealogy in Chapter 5 shows, Crabtree influenced Errett Callahan and J. B. Sollberger (as well as others whose connections are not shown), and they in turn affected many other knappers, including some of the Fort Osage group. Errett Callahan, for instance, calculates that between 1971 and 1996 he taught 781 students, mostly in weeklong workshops. This does not count innumerable public demonstrations.

From the late 1960s to the early 1980s there was a brief period when a number of nonacademic knappers with interests in serious archaeology were able to contribute both to archaeological thinking about stone tools and to the development of the knapping community as it stands today. Don Crabtree was only the most prominent; others include J. B. Sollberger, Gene Titmus, L. W. Patterson, Errett Callahan, and Bob Patten (Callahan 1979a; Patten 1978a, 1978b, 1978d, 1979, 1980; Patterson 1975, 1978b, 1979a, 1980, 1981, 1982, 1988, 1990; Patterson and Sollberger 1978; Sollberger 1968, 1978b, 1979a, 1985, 1986; Sollberger and Callahan 1978; Sollberger and Patterson 1976; Titmus 1980, 1985; Titmus and Callahan 1980; Titmus and Woods 1986). Some of these knappers were extremely prolific writers; the references above are only a selection intended to show characteristic interests and outlets. Although they tended to write for smaller regional journals and knapping newsletters, their work influenced both knapping technique and archaeological analysis. Serious knappers such as these helped bring together the archaeologists and the nonacademic knappers, and from these two roots grew the modern knap-in.

Knapping Newsletters

One of the factors which crystallized the knapping world, and continues to play an important role, was the newsletter. The first of these was *The Newsletter of Lithic Technology*, which eventually became large and established enough to drop the "newsletter" and consider itself a journal, becoming *Lithic Technology*. It was begun in 1972 with Ruthann Knudson and Guy Muto as editors and continued under various editors until expiring in 1988. George Odell revived *Lithic Technology* in a larger and more formal format in 1993. From the first, articles in *Lithic Technology* consistently dealt with the analysis and interpretation of stone tools, rather than with knapping per se. Although many of the people involved with *Lithic Technology* as writers or editors were knappers, and some were involved with the development of knap-ins as well, *Lithic Technology* always remained at a distance from the knap-in world. Even as knap-ins began to be organized, and despite the archaeological bent of early knap-ins, they were never advertised in *The Newsletter of Lithic Technology* and rarely reported on. *Lithic Technology* reflected the growing interest in stone tools among archaeologists, and provided an outlet for the work of some of the archaeologically oriented nonacademic knappers, but did not reach much beyond.

In 1978, Errett Callahan and Jacqueline Nichols established an alternative newsletter, *Flintknappers' Exchange*. Their first editorial statement described their goal as providing an "informal, non-academic, and non-statistical medium of exchange . . . to reach not only academic knappers but the non-academic craftsmen—amateur or expert—commercial knappers, and others" (Callahan 1978a, 2). The material in *Flintknappers' Exchange* emphasized practical knapping, rather than archaeological analysis, although archaeological implications of knapping were often considered and the tone was fairly serious. There was a great deal of input from archaeologically involved nonacademic knappers, and even some from commercial knappers like Warren and Waldorf, as well as from a few archaeologists. In the first two issues, which set the tone and included themes that are still being discussed today, there were articles about archaeological analysis, from the knapper's perspective, of points (Patten 1978b, 1978c; Stanford 1978; Sollberger 1978a) and debitage (Dubuc and Nichols 1978); editorials about bringing knappers and archaeologists together, sponsoring a series of regional knap-ins, and documenting modern sites (Callahan 1978a, 1978b, 1978d; Nichols 1978a); discussion of knapping theory (Cresson 1978; Bradley 1978; Nichols 1978b); experiments in using stone tools (Callahan 1978c); and numerous knapping tips concerned with helping the beginner (Patterson 1978a; Johnson 1978; Cohen

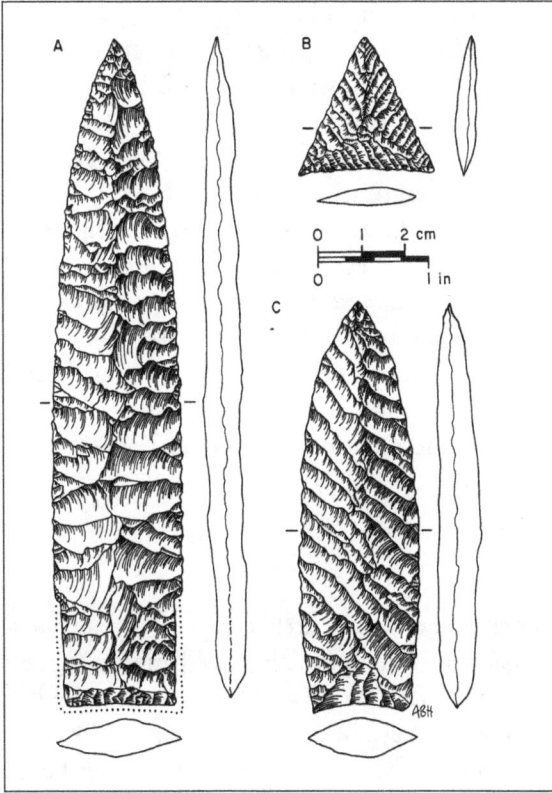

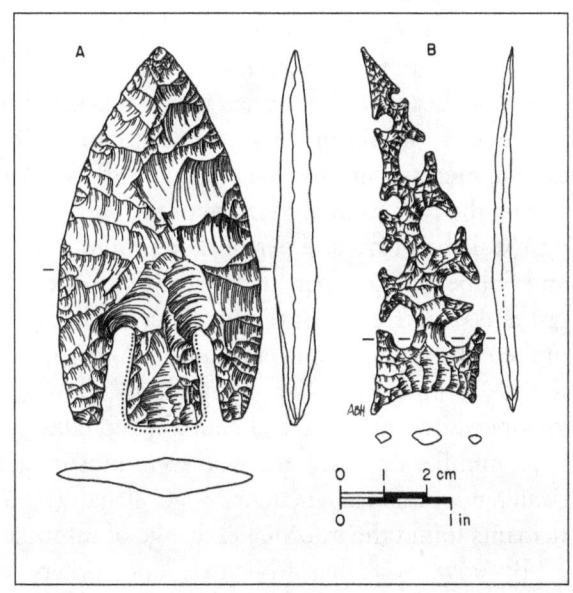

Figure 3.10. Selected points by knappers of the 1970s knapping renaissance. After drawings by Errett Callahan published in Flintknappers' Exchange. 3.10A: (A) Jeff Flenniken, (B) Don Crabtree, (C) Rob Bonnichsen. 3.10B: (A) J. B. Sollberger, (B) Gene Titmus.

1978) or trying new tools (Patten 1978a; Sollberger 1978c, 1978d; Callahan 1978e). *Flintknappers' Exchange* initiated a series of interviews with well-known knappers of the day and illustrated their work (Sollberger and Callahan 1978; Bonnichsen and Callahan 1978; Figure 3.10).

Flintknappers' Exchange lasted only four years (1978–1981), but had some important effects. For the first time, there was a source for tips on a variety of knapping techniques. Lines of communication among all sorts of different knappers were opened; by the end, there were over seven hundred subscribers. *Flintknappers' Exchange* also began to promote and publicize knapping events, including the first knap-ins. Rereading my old issues of *Flintknappers' Exchange* twenty years later, I was struck again by how much they influenced me and other knappers, and how well they reflected the ferment of ideas and growth of knapping in those years.

The First Knap-ins

Knap-ins began as small gatherings of archaeologists and archaeologically oriented knappers. Errett Callahan told me that credit for the first knap-in should go to Ruthann Knudson, who organized an informal knapping session with Errett, herself, Carl Fagan, and Bennie Keel one afternoon when Callahan was giving a presentation for her at Wright State in 1971. By this standard, perhaps the lithic technology conference at Les Eyzies in 1964 should be awarded the title of first knap-in. There were, of course, many other small gatherings of knappers, both academic and other, which remain unrecorded.

An early gathering that probably had more influence on future developments than most was held at J. B. Sollberger's home in Dallas during the 1975 Annual Meeting of the Society for American Archaeology (Callahan 1976 and personal communication). As well as Callahan and Sollberger, knappers included Robson Bonnichsen (an archaeologist and Crabtree student) and a couple of dozen friends and students of these three. Although Callahan (1976) dignified the occasion by calling it "a lithic workshop symposium," it was quite informal, with knappers sitting in a circle, knapping and talking, and mingling with a large number of observers, who were mostly archaeologists from the conference and local amateurs. As Callahan (1976) recalled it, the participants found the informal exchange of information very useful.

By 1978, Callahan, Nichols, and others were organizing the

newsletter *Flintknappers' Exchange* and promoting other knapping workshops (Nichols 1978a). They were also trying to come up with a name for them. In a letter to me in 1997 Callahan explained, "It was Crabtree who coined the term 'knap-in.' We put out feelers in FE and over the phones and mails for a good name for these get-togethers. Crabtree sent in a whole page full of suggestions. We (Jackie and I) picked 'knap-in' and it's stuck." They were using the word in the third issue of *Flintknappers' Exchange* in 1978 as if it were already accepted, although Nichols (1978b, 3) asked if anyone could think of a better term. A list of humorous options from Crabtree was published in the next issue (Nichols 1979), but apparently no one offered serious alternatives. Bob Patten, who was involved in some of these early gatherings, told me in 1997 that he remembers his wife Laurie independently suggesting "knap-in." Whatever the source or sources, the choice is not surprising; American society had just come through the age of the sit-in, love-in, be-in, and others, so "knap-in" would have seemed a natural addition to the vocabulary. In 1979 the first two events to be announced as "knap-ins" (in *Flintknappers' Exchange)* took place in April at the Casper, Wyoming, meeting of the Wyoming Archaeological Society (Callahan and Nichols 1979), and in May at Lake Belton, Texas (Patterson 1979b). Participating knappers were primarily professional and amateur archaeologists.[2] Both knap-ins focused on demonstrations and experiments.

Waldorf and *The Art of Flintknapping*

One of the frustrations of learning to knap in the early 1970s and before was that there was essentially no instructional literature. There were a few archaeological accounts in relatively obscure publications (Ellis 1965; Pond 1930), Crabtree's classic *An Introduction to Flintworking* (1972), which was largely a set of illustrated definitions, one amusing but not very detailed small book (Mewhinney 1957), and a few ephemeral popular pamphlets produced for Boy Scouts and others, which were as likely to be misleading as helpful (e.g., Reese 1957). It was also very difficult to find other knappers, even in the archaeological circles of my undergraduate days. For amateurs with no archaeological connections it was even worse. The beginnings of knap-ins and newsletters in the late 1970s began to improve this situation, and a few other important and helpful works came out (e.g., Callahan 1979a), but there was still no basic manual for learning to knap. Finally, in 1979, D. C. Waldorf published his second edition of *The Art of Flintknapping*.

Waldorf, at that time a commercial knapper making and selling ordinary point replicas, had written a first edition in 1975. He and his wife Val sold a few out of their shop and eventually by mail order. The second edition was much expanded and improved, with illustrations by Val, who is a trained artist. It also received wider publicity, as Callahan reviewed it favorably in *Flintknappers' Exchange* (1979b, 1979c), praising it as "an excellent textbook" with "professional attitudes in the commercial field." I was among many who immediately ordered a copy. In the next few years, as communication of all sorts grew among knappers, *The Art of Flint Knapping* soon reached a wide audience. Archaeologists like myself might grumble at the use of some terms, but here at last was a fairly detailed, accurate, well-illustrated guide to the basics of flintknapping, by someone who really knew how to do it on an expert level. The Waldorfs have continued to revise and improve *The Art of Flint Knapping*, now in its fourth edition, and estimate that they have sold over forty thousand copies. *The Art of Flint Knapping* was immensely influential in starting many knappers, popularizing some techniques and artifact types, improving communication among knappers, especially in the nonacademic circles, and making the Waldorfs well-known figures. As a result of this success, the Waldorfs were among those who influenced the beginnings of a number of knappers and knap-ins, including Fort Osage, and were the logical people to start a newsletter. The resulting *Chips*, and more recently the Waldorfs' Web page with essentially the same content, became the dominant communication line in the knap-in world (Figure 3.11).

Transition to the Current Scene

Flintknappers' Exchange had folded in 1981, but knapping had developed a momentum of its own. Knap-ins continued to grow and spread, and knappers, both archaeological and nonacademic, became more numerous, skillful, and connected. Experiments and lithic analyses based on knapping became common in the archaeological literature, but changes were already in the wind. Archaeological interest soon began to turn away from experiments with primitive technology. In lithic replication studies, several influential archaeologists reacted to

Figure 3.11. Chips *newsletter team in action: Val Waldorf (camera), D. C. Waldorf, and Dane Martin interview Charlie Shewey (center). Fort Osage, May 1998.*

the overoptimistic statements of some knappers (e.g., Flenniken 1984) with equally excessive criticisms that knapping experiments were not living up to their promise and had little potential for advancing archaeological theory (Binford and Nichols 1979; Thomas 1986). Sadly, the critics were more widely heard.

Some knap-ins continued to have an archaeological emphasis, but increasingly most knap-ins were dominated by the nonacademic knappers and used for fun and exchange rather than to work out archaeological problems. Academic knappers began increasingly to ignore or distance themselves from knap-ins. As this is a source of hard feelings among some knappers, it is worth explaining. Archaeologists are not as completely opposed to amateurs and artifact collectors as some seem to believe; many amateur archaeologists do good archaeological work and are accepted as colleagues by the professionals. The Society for American Archaeology, the major professional organization, for instance, presents a yearly Crabtree Award to an outstanding avocational archaeologist.

Even collectors are not always entirely disliked. Those who keep records, collect only surface material, and communicate with the archaeologists often have good relationships with the professional community. However, all collecting does diminish the artifacts on sites, and thus the potential to interpret both the sites and the artifacts from them. Collectors point out that if they did not pick up the artifacts, they might never be seen or might be destroyed by farming and erosion. This is often true, but unless the information about where the artifact was found stays with the artifact, the artifact, however pretty, is of limited use for understanding prehistory. The worst offenders are those who dig up sites looking for artifacts to collect or sell. Without proper documentation, this is just destruction, and theft of the heritage of all people.

Charlie Shewey was a good example of why archaeologists like myself have mixed feelings about artifact collecting. On the one hand, Charlie was sincerely interested in archaeology and the interpretive value of artifacts and had some good contacts among professional archaeologists. He was extremely knowledgeable and eager to share what he knew. His collecting preserved some artifacts and the information associated with them, which might otherwise be lost. On the other hand, the collection itself was the goal, not the use of the artifacts to interpret the past, and much of the documentation existed only in Charlie's memory. Now that he has died, a lot of the information about his specimens has perished with him, and these specimens have ceased to be of much archaeological value. Charlie and other collectors pour a lot of money into buying artifacts, and this, of course, is part of the impetus for unscrupulous diggers to loot sites. Charlie, for instance, bought things from the looters of Spiro. Charlie often said he hated the guys who dig up sites as much as anyone, and many of his artifacts were surface finds or came from old collections made long ago; nevertheless, collectors continue to create a lucrative market for artifacts, which promotes the destruction of sites by looters.

Like Charlie, many collectors are obsessive about their hobby. One specimen of a type, or of an artist's work, is not enough. I finally asked Charlie how many points he thought he had. "Well, I imagine I've got at least half a million points all together, old and new, because one time over fifty years ago my brother and I even counted the old points we had, and we had over a quarter of a million old points that he and I had found, and I have them all now since he's passed away. I've got an awful lot of them since I've been collecting so damn long." Charlie started collecting before World War II, when prices for artifacts were often relatively low. Following a stint as a fighter pilot on the carrier *Lexington* in that war, Charlie flew for TWA. He sought out and bought fine artifacts before the market inflated. "I live in a little-bitty damn house. It's too bad to have as good a collection as I've got and no proper place to show it. I really spent my money on artifacts instead of buying houses." Consequently, his collection was huge and included some rare items.

The avidity with which some people collect artifacts fuels a growing market, and the monetary value of artifacts encourages people to destroy sites for them and to create fakes that muddle the archaeological record. In the minds of many archaeologists, this tars all collectors with the same brush. I shall say more about fakes later; for the moment it is enough to note that the ambivalent feelings archaeologists have toward collectors, and the resentment collectors feel about it, help explain why archaeologists felt increasingly alienated from knap-ins as they became more nonacademic and commercial.

The nonacademic knapping world had continued to grow, with a number of knap-ins established in the early 1980s. In 1984, Ray Harwood, based in California, started a newsletter, the *Flintknapping Digest*, which provided inspiration and its mailing list to the Waldorfs when they took over with *Chips* in 1989 (Harwood 1991). A decade of changes were plain to see. Like *Flintknappers' Exchange, Chips* aimed to improve communication among all knappers and originally hoped to be the voice of a "Flint Knappers' Guild International." The idea of a guild was soon abandoned, as most knappers were not eager to be organized in such a formal way. Archaeologists and nonacademic but archaeologically oriented knappers had been the main contributors to *Flintknappers' Exchange*. A few of these contributed to *Chips*, but most of the contributions were from the growing ranks of commercial or hobby knappers. The themes in the first year, which set the tone, can be compared to those described above in *Flintknappers' Exchange*. Several articles reported on regional knapper gossip or knap-ins, with an emphasis on who was there and what they could do rather than on experimental problems (Frederick 1989a, 1989b; Moore 1989c; V. Waldorf 1989b, 1989c; Harwood 1989). There were numerous practical knapping tips dealing with copper billets (Moore 1989b), notching (Scheiber 1989c; D. Waldorf 1989a), Danish daggers (Sheward 1989), Folsom and other Paleoindian points (Imel 1989a, 1989b), pressure flakers (Merlie 1989b), and the like. Holland (1989) provided a short report on an archaeological conference dealing with Paleoindian problems. Knapping humor was a prominent part of *Chips* from the first, with humorous essays, poems, and cartoons by Val Waldorf, H. R. Moore, M. Dothager, and Larry Scheiber. Ethical issues, especially fakes and marking of points, were discussed in several letters and editorials (Callahan 1989; Blake 1989; D. Waldorf 1989d; Merlie 1989a). An interview with Jim Spears in the first issue (D. Waldorf 1989c) was probably an idea borrowed from the series in *Flintknappers' Exchange*. The most noticeable difference between *Chips* and *Flintknappers' Exchange* was the increased commercial emphasis. *Chips* provided a medium for advertising stone, tools, points, and lessons, as well as for noncommercial announcements of knap-ins.

Several other newsletters in the 1980s and 1990s *(The Flint Knapper's Exchange, The Flint Knappers Digest)* were similar to *Chips,* while the Minnesota Knappers Guild's *The Platform* was more local and archaeological in tone. With the dominance of *Chips* and the rise of the Internet, the other newsletters died out. Currently, *Chips* and the Waldorfs' similar Web page, The Knappers Corner, as well as the other Web pages devoted to knapping, continue a mix of commercials, knap-in announcements and accounts, knapping tips, and stories.

The Current Scene

The knap-in now is different from the first knap-ins of the late 1970s and early 1980s. The increase in communication among knappers fostered by the newsletters, the knap-ins themselves, and now the Internet has created many new knappers and brought older ones out of obscurity. Knap-ins like Fort Osage, which usually started with half a dozen friends in a backyard, now attract fifty to three hundred knappers, plus a large crowd of related craftsmen, hangers-on, and public. Although there are knappers at most knap-ins who have strong archaeological interests, and a few knap-ins where archaeological concerns are prominent, most current knap-ins are dominated by knappers who knap for fun. The commercial possibilities of knapping are also well represented. Knapping supports several small businesses selling tools, raw material, and other primitive goods, a surprising number of knappers who make most or all of their living through knapping or related activities, and numerous dealers who buy and sell modern points and antiquities. Many knappers see participation in the market for stonework as a way of supporting their hobby; others continue the old tradition of faking; and others are trying to bring knapping to a new level as a legitimate craft art, issues to be discussed later. As knapping has grown more popular and more commercial, the archaeological profession has largely withdrawn from the knap-in scene, troubled by some ethical issues and distracted by shifts within the discipline, which has become more fragmented, more esoteric, and less interested in straightforward problems of technology and experimentation. At the same time, the archaeological profession is increasingly aware that it must become more relevant and responsive to the rest of the world. After all, public money provides most archaeological funding, and the interest of voters is the ultimate force creating public and governmental interest in protecting prehistoric sites from development and looting. I don't expect knap-ins to become more archaeological, but I do try to drag friends and colleagues to them, not just for fun, but because here is a large audience interested in archaeology, some of whom can perhaps be swayed toward a more archaeological view of artifacts. Knappers are also a group of people with all sorts of knowledge useful to archaeologists. As a man with a foot on each shore, I would like to see some reunification.

The Knap-in: People and Organization

Although they are relatively informal events, each knap-in relies on a core of individuals who make the necessary arrangements, spread the word, and attract other knappers. Like any society, a knap-in is more than the sum of its parts, but certain individuals affect the flavor of each knap-in. Describing a few of the key individuals at Fort Osage will help provide a framework for understanding how the knap-in works. Although my choice of individuals to describe is biased by my own particular experience, they are all people who most of the other knappers would recognize as important regulars, in the sense that "it wouldn't be the same without him." For instance, when I began interviewing, and asked Bob Hunt who I should talk to, the names he came up with were pretty much the same ones I had already observed were important regulars at Fort Osage.

Bob Hunt, Organizer at Fort Osage

Bob Hunt sits on his five-gallon bucket at the heart of the knap-in. He wears a baseball cap that says "Fort Osage Knap-in 1991," and a dusty T-shirt. Behind him are a couple of cases of pieces he is proud of, beside him sits his tool chest with bumper sticker "Only the Rocks Live Forever," and at his feet are piles of flakes and nodules of stone. He works steadily, bent over a slab of flint with a copper billet in his hand, but looking up to talk to the other knappers around him. Bob is the quintessential knap-in knapper, proud of his skill and his identity as a knapper, dedicated to a hobby that interests him more than his job as an equipment engineer for Southwestern Bell. Because he is sociable and a good organizer, as well as a good knapper who enjoys spending a lot of time knapping, Bob was the main founder of the Fort Osage Knap-in and has remained its primary mover (Figure 4.1).

Bob likes outdoor activities, fishing, hunting, and camping. He shoots and collects guns, and used to walk the fields, surface collecting artifacts, until knapping took over as a hobby. Bob's wife bought a stone cross that sparked Bob's curiosity, and he eventually met the man who made it and learned basic pressure flaking from him. Around 1977 he started knapping with friends in Illinois, including Dave Klostermeier and Larry Kinsella, who were soon to start the Fairview Heights Knap-in. Bob learned a bit from them, and Fred Bollinger, an Illinois knapper, taught him percussion flaking. After a few years, Bob moved to the Kansas City area, where he met Charlie Shewey and some other knappers. A number of friends started getting together weekly to knap and talk stone tools. No formal organization was created, but these knappers became the core of the Fort Osage Knap-in and helped organize it. They included Charlie Shewey, Don Dreisoerner, Roy Motley, Bill Morton, Al Meister, Jim Dixon, Don McCardie, George Eklund, and Carl Dowell. Don Dreisoerner in particular often served as another contact and organizer in the early days of the knap-in. In 1984, Bob and his friends decided they should hold a knap-in like the Illinois knappers. Bob remembers only six or seven people came to the first Fort Osage Knap-in, all locals or Illinois friends. They were all crowded together in one of the fort's

Figure 4.1. Bob Hunt—Sunday at Fort Osage, 1995.

dark blockhouses. However, as word spread in the next couple of years, the local knappers became more numerous, knappers came from farther away, and the knap-in began to grow. Other knap-ins were also forming around this time. For a while the Fort Osage Knap-ins were held alongside a "rendezvous" of black powder enthusiasts and frontier reenactors.

Bob also had the advantage of a large supply of raw material, mostly from the St. Louis area. He says his fondness for making very large pieces is a result of having lots of material when he was learning. Bob generally brings buckets of Burlington chert to the knap-in to sell. The geological happenstance of plentiful chert is also why there are so many artifact collectors and flintknappers in the Midwest.

Bob was lucky in having a convenient, picturesque, and welcoming state park as a knap-in site. The Fort Osage State Park provides features that knap-in organizers consider essential to the success of a knap-in (see also Spears 1994). There is a good space for setting up shelters and spreading out the knappers, with access to plenty of parking. The knap-in has been held in two areas of the park over the years. It started in the grassy area between the visitor center and the fort, joining the rendezvous for a while. When I first attended, the knap-in was still there, although the rendezvous had found another site. The next year, however, the knap-in moved to the parking lot and garage behind the visitor center, which provided more shelter and closer bathrooms. By 1996 it had outgrown that area and returned to the original location.[1] The visitor center and the reconstructed fort provide bathrooms, recently supplemented with porta-potties. While the knap-in was behind the center, there were convenient electrical outlets, and knapping and other activities were more likely to continue into the night. Now a few people knap and socialize by lantern light, but the evenings seem less eventful.

The fort, or rather the Jackson County Parks Association, also provides some of the necessary communications network and organization of the knap-in. The park sets various rules (where the knap-in can set up, restrictions on alcohol and camping, etc.) and collects an entry fee. Knappers sign in at the museum, and Bob Hunt maintains the mailing list, but the park actually mails out the twice-yearly knap-in announcements. From the fort's point of view, the knap-in is another attraction that brings in the public, increasing visitation and fees. The actual participants in the knap-in number only one to three hundred and pay reduced entry fees, but several hundred visitors come to the fort over the course of a knap-in weekend.

Food and lodging are essential for knap-ins, too. Almost all knap-ins are in locations where participants can camp. This is one option at Fort Osage, but many knappers drive a few miles to one of the hotels in the suburbs of Kansas City. The availability of food has varied. Knap-in organizers frequently try to attract some sort of food vendor. For a while, the fort personnel, dressed in their nineteenth-century costumes, served a dinner of stew or other camp cookery one or two evenings. They charged five dollars and you could eat on a fort porch overlooking the river, a view better than most fancy restaurants can offer. This also kept the knappers together and promoted continuing into the evening. Some knappers always preferred to go into town and find a restaurant. Eventually the fort, for a variety of reasons, stopped cooking. Currently, a local Boy Scout troop sets up a field kitchen and serves three meals a day, including hamburgers and the like for lunch and steak or roast turkey dinners.

The role of the organizer is largely behind the scenes. Bob, Don, and others find food vendors, negotiate with the fort, and solve problems as they arise, but spend most of their time just being knappers like the rest. The organizers set up the tent and facilities with the help of early arrivals. As the knap-in winds down on Sunday, they gather the knappers who are left, and everyone helps take down the tent, pick up trash, move debitage to a dump area, and generally police the grounds.

Most knap-ins abhor the idea of formal bosses, organizations, rules, and hierarchy. They remind me of the hunter-gatherer societies of anthropological literature. Leadership in such groups tends to be ad hoc, with those who are respected for a particular skill organizing certain activities, but otherwise described by one anthropologist as "One word from the chief, and each man does as he pleases" (Chagnon 1997, 27). Similarly, knap-in organizers have to lead by personal character, insofar as they lead at all. They tend to be charismatic or at least sociable, and to have assembled a local group of knapping friends who can help put together a knap-in. The local knapping group in turn helps to attract other knappers as it begins to publicize the knap-in. Knap-in leaders tend to be respected for their knapping skills, although they are not necessarily "top" knappers. However, if they are, or if they can attract some of the more renowned knappers, others will come to their knap-in just because they know that so-and-so will be there. This is especially true of less-skilled knappers who are attempting to improve their skills. One of the reasons Fort Osage is a large and popular knap-in is because a number of well-known knappers frequently attend.

George Eklund, Commercial Knapper

George Eklund is one of the commercial knappers and was also an early member of the Fort Osage group. He started knapping as a teenager, after hunting arrowheads in Missouri. He used a hammer to make flakes and pressure-flaked with an upward motion he had found pictured in a cheap tourist book. After a nasty accident when his hand slipped and he slashed himself on a piece of obsidian, he realized a downward motion was better, and also began using copper grounding rod instead of deer antler for his pressure tools. Charlie Shewey taught him percussion flaking, which made him much more efficient.

George is a big, burly man with huge arms and hands that he wraps with medical tape for protection before a day of knapping. He is renowned as the "fastest" knapper at Fort Osage, doing massive percussion on large pieces, but he is also capable of fine pressure work. He makes his living through knapping and related pursuits, so he has to be efficient. He turns out literally tons of blanks, which other knappers buy and finish, and also makes the typical large Midwestern Archaic points and a range of large things like Mississippian hoes. Although he says he does not sell things as fakes, much of his work is clearly purchased by the dealers who do buy for the fake antiquities market. George also deals in artifacts, antique cash registers and jukeboxes, and other primitive crafts, and gives flintknapping lessons.

George influenced a number of the Fort Osage knappers in their knapping styles. He is credited by many with introducing copper billets, or at least being one of those who invented them. Copper billets are especially characteristic of the Fort Osage group, although widely used by other American knappers. The copper billet is an important invention in knapping because it allows faster reduction of stone and thinning with less risk of breakage, concerns which are especially important to commercial knappers. George also claims to have invented two of the art forms in which points are sold by knappers. For a while he made points only partly knapped from a large flake, still attached as if growing out of the stone. A number of other knappers also made these. At one knap-in he was selling rustic frames in which a

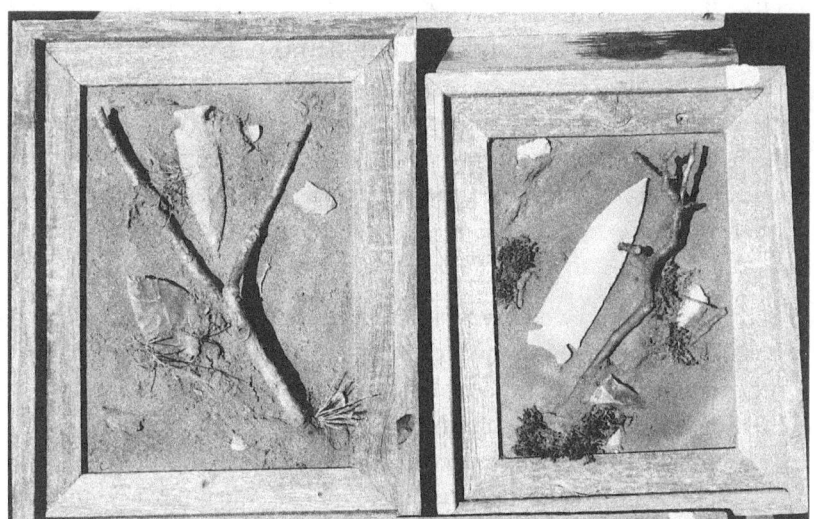

Figure 4.2. Two of George Eklund's frames with the modern points as "found." These, perhaps, aim at the same market as the plastic gun and dyed feather headdress pseudo-antiques found in many gift shops and decorator catalogs. It also appeals to the knapper, expressing the connection to the past and to finding artifacts. Fort Osage, 1997.

point was mounted on dirt and weeds, as if just found on the surface of a field (Figure 4.2). Another knapper, impressed, described the frames in detail on the Internet. Others have tried it, but it does not seem to have become as popular as I expected.

Jim Regan, Copper Toolsmith

As copper tools became popular, a number of knappers began to fill the demand by finding copper sources and selling tools. Jim Regan, a tall ash-blond Minnesotan, was one of the founders of the Minnesota Knappers Guild and the Pine City Knap-in, and one of my first friends at Fort Osage. He usually set up under the central tent on a picnic table, where he displayed an ever-expanding line of copper tools. His most typical product was a flat bar billet with a wooden or plastic handle (see Figure 2.10), in several sizes. He also sold round billets, punches, and both long and short nylon-handled pressure flakers where an adjustable length of copper wire is held in place by an Allen screw. Jim designed and produced the most popular model of fluting jig seen at the knap-ins, and also dealt in stone and antler.

Jim's interest in knapping, Indians, and primitive crafts was spurred as a boy by a cigar box of prehistoric points a neighbor gave him. Around 1985 Alan Jiranek, a scrimshaw artist who works with knappers, showed him a bit of knapping, and he began to try to learn, eventually coming to the Fort Osage Knap-in, where Bob Hunt and others taught him the basics. At the time, the Fort Osage knappers were using copper rod billets, and Jim, a mechanical designer educated in drafting and engineering, started to evolve tools that suited him better.

> For instance, my wooden handled billet. A nice comfortable wooden handle but all the weight to the billet is up forward to the hand so you can get a real nice whip which works well for removing stacks and so on on points. That tool has become extremely popular with lots of knappers. . . .
>
> I like coming up with a tool that will help me flintknap, and I started making them to sell because they worked so well, and out of necessity. I come from the land of No Flint, Minnesota, so I would sell tools to get money to buy flint.

Jim sold at knap-ins and also had a Xeroxed price list and advertisements in various newsletters, which brought in a steady stream of mail orders. Most of the profits went into his knapping, which can be an expensive hobby. Jim traveled to several knap-ins a year, usually with his wife Pat. Pat does not knap, but was one of the circle of wives who socialize among themselves and incidentally help keep the knap-ins, and the knappers, running smoothly. Jim was also the point man for the Pine City event near his home. He liked using different stones, and at knap-ins he could buy from other knappers most of the material he used for several hours of knapping a week. As an entrepreneur, Jim was typical of many knappers who have developed a product, a tool, a raw material, or a stone source in order to fund their interest in knapping.

Jim died unexpectedly at fifty-three of a heart attack in August 2000, while sorting stone for another knapper at his home in Minnesota. As always when one of the circle dies, a number of tributes appeared on the Internet email listserve The Tarp. Jim was important to the knap-ins beyond his toolmaking because, as his friend Dave Plankers wrote, "He was a wonderful ambassador for flintknapping, always willing to share his tarp with anyone who wanted to learn to knap." The Minnesota knappers in particular considered him their main mentor.

Figure 4.3. "You can't afford not to buy it!" Gene Stapleton (kneeling, left) explains the virtues of his wares to Glenn Leesman.

Gene Stapleton, Dealing in Stone

Gene Stapleton (Figure 4.3) leans against his red pickup, pipe jutting from his square jaw, and argues vigorously with another knapper. "You know what this stone is here, right? No? Well, it's the same as that stuff, but you have to heat it just right or it ain't worth shit." He tosses the nodule brusquely back into the pile of stone, while the other knapper winces.

Stone is one of the basic resources of the knap-in and, as we will see, is both symbolically and economically important. There are a few individuals, not always knappers, who specialize in selling stone. A few of them are trying to make a living at this and other knapping-related pursuits. More typical is Gene Stapleton, one of many knappers who make a point of collecting and selling large amounts of stone. Typically, this satisfies an interest in geology and a knapper's love of stone, helps fund his knapping interests, and keeps him deeply involved in the knap-in world.

Although at any knap-in Gene is likely to have a ton or two of Oregon obsidian, Texas cherts, Missouri Burlington chert, and Arkansas novaculite, Gene's specialty is fine exotic stone. He obviously relishes the extensive and Byzantine networks he uses to obtain stone from Australia, England, and Mexico, as well as the States. He also travels to a series of knap-ins and rock shows all over the country, where he buys and sells stone, as well as collecting some himself. Gene likes to heat treat stone and sell it as large flakes or partly bifaced blanks. This allows him to select the especially choice pieces he needs for his style of knapping. Gene is unusual in experimenting with chemical treatments of his stone. He dyes some of his novaculite and has studied chemical aging and coloring in some detail.

Gene does good business in stone, and also sells copper tools and Carborundum stones for abraders, but says he does not usually sell his points. His interest in choice stone sources reflects in part the way he knaps. He favors large Scottsbluff forms and fluted points, using fine and often exotic materials prepared by grinding to get very regular flake scar patterns. Gene knew J. D. Sollberger, and he flutes with the same kind of lever device that Sollberger popularized. His points are often spectacular, oversized and finely flaked with huge flutes, although he also makes points that are closer to prehistoric prototypes.

Fluting suits Gene's character. One of his other interests is motorcycle racing, and taking the longest flute possible off a large point may not get your heart pumping as fast, but it also involves an element of risk. Gene gets a lot of attention when he flutes, because other knappers also like the drama. Gene adds to this atmosphere by proclaiming "I just don't give a damn!" and tossing away failures with a theatrical air of carelessness. Whether his point flutes successfully, as it usually does, or snaps in half, the audience can count on a good show. Gene doesn't mind being known as a "hard-ass." He is an encyclopedia of knowledge about stone, knapping, and archaeological geology, but also opinionated and often loud and profane in expressing his views, which is somewhat contrary to knap-in norms. He can alternate between patiently teaching a knapper who asks a question and driving the next one away with brutal criticism. He can be either annoyingly hard-headed in his stone sales or unexpectedly generous. His unpredictability and willingness to be outrageous make for some uneven relationships with other knappers, but the varied interactions among all sorts of colorful people with unusual skills and esoteric knowledge are one reason knap-ins are endlessly fascinating.

Percy Atkinson: Gourds, Axes, and Philosophy

Percy is another knapper everyone knows as a character (Figure 4.4). He defines the word "spry." If you ask him how old he is, he runs off a few paces, jumps up in the air and clicks his heels, does a jig step or two, falls into a boxer's stance and spars toward you, then thumps his chest and says, "Seventy-two years old!" Percy has had a lot of lives. A farm boy from Illinois, he served in World War II as a seaman on the same carrier as Charlie Shewey, although they did not know each other, and lost a couple of fingers in a kamikaze attack. As a young man, he was a bantamweight boxer, but he claims his good health comes from walking a dozen miles a day as a postman for thirty-five years, not smoking or drinking, and downing a glass of vinegar every morning. After retiring from the post office, he worked in construction for a while, and owned a contract cleaning company. When he finally retired again from all this, he needed something to do, and an interest in Cherokee ancestors in his mother's family expanded into reading history and working in native crafts. He joined an earth science club, and at a rock and mineral show saw a demonstration of knapping by John Mondino, one of the Fort Osage knappers. "I pulled up a chair and ceased to watch anything else there." He eventually badgered John into giving him some lessons and was on his way.

Percy deprecates himself, because he never had more than a grade-school education, but he is visibly intelligent and well read. He speaks with a nineteenth-century rhetorical flourish and vivid relish about anything from politics to history to the great photographic artists. He is so articulate and talkative that by the end of a knap-in he is usually hoarse, and the other knappers regard him as something of a camp philosopher. I was one of a group watching Jim Spears at the May 1995 knap-in, when Jim, who is extraordinarily good at thinning bifaces, made a rare mistake and snapped his piece. One of the newer knappers blurted out, "Gosh, I'm glad you did that!" and everyone looked shocked. Blushing, the newcomer hastily explained that it was only because he felt better knowing that the experts made mistakes, too, and Percy laid a fatherly hand on his shoulder. "When that happens, you

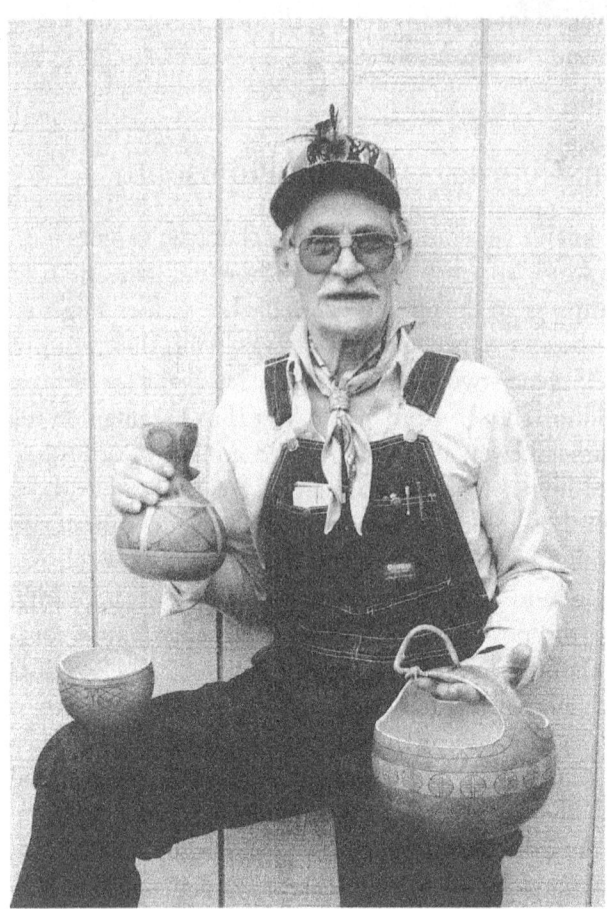

Figure 4.4. Percy Atkinson with some of his gourds. Fort Osage, 1995.

may be pretty sad, thinking about what a fine and beautiful point you just broke, and now it will never be anything more than worthless junk, but experiences like that are what make you a better knapper, and a better person."

Percy talks often about patience; how he was a fighter as a boy, and too often angry as a man, and how important it is to be patient and not let the world upset you. He is, in fact, almost the only Fort Osage knapper I have seen make ground stone axes and other objects by correct old techniques, pecking and grinding them for hours. In recent years he has done less knapping and stonework and has been growing bottle gourds and making a variety of artfully decorated gourd containers. Like many of the knappers, Percy has a wide interest in primitive crafts; as many others also do, he has made a niche for himself by developing skill in a craft that no one else is doing. His gourds are admired, and he usually has a long order list. Typically, too, the money is not the real incentive.

D. C. and Val Waldorf, Knap-in Professionals

All the knappers I know started knapping because of an interest in primitive crafts or prehistory, not because it seemed like a profitable profession. This is true even of those who eventually became professional, or heavily commercial, because they saw advantages in knapping over other possible careers. Dave and Val Waldorf are among the few knappers who really make their living by knapping and related activities. They have some influence on a large part of the American knapping world both because of their skills and because they run the *Chips* newsletter, which is one of the most important strands of the knapping information network. For many years, *The Art of Flint Knapping*, which D. C. wrote and Val illustrated, was the only really usable manual for beginning knappers and sparked the interest of many.

D. C. started his career by finding that his boyhood hobby of making points had potential as a commercial craft (Waldorf 1980). Eventually he became a commercial knapper in the 1970s, making points that mostly moved into the fake antiquities market in Ohio. Today he says, "I just wanted to make good quality reproductions and I was not happy about seeing my work misrepresented down the line, but I couldn't stop them unless I quit knapping, and if I did that I would have had to go back to work for my dad, which was even worse!" He married Val, and they moved to Branson, Missouri, in 1974. Living in Missouri, D. C. met Bob Hunt, Charlie Shewey, and others, and was eventually one of the knappers who helped start Bob Hunt and encouraged him to set up a knap-in. Val is an artist, and once she hitched up with Dave, she turned her talents to illustrating lithics. She is, incidentally, one of the few female knappers at Fort Osage, although she only knaps occasionally. Dave and Val operated The Flint Shop in Branson, selling stone and points to tourists and by mail order. They changed the name to Mound Builder Arts and Trading Company after publishing the first edition of *The Art of Flint Knapping* in 1975 and adding it to their mail business. Dave and Val started *Chips* in 1989 as a commercial venture, and to encourage knapping in general by helping knappers find and communicate with one another. Subscriptions and advertising turn some profit for the Waldorfs, knap-in announcements run for free, and many of the knappers at Fort Osage and other knap-ins contribute articles and commentary concerning knapping news and events, knapping techniques, and stone artifacts. *Chips* has been a major forum for discussion of current issues such as ethical concerns and is one of the most useful documents of recent knapping history. The Knapper's Corner Web page, which they added in 1996, is essentially the electronic version of *Chips* with some additional links and information.

Making a living as a flintknapper requires some versatility. Many other commercial knappers make much of their income dealing in stone, but the Waldorfs have tried other avenues. Writing and publishing are one aspect of this. Dave also continues to make and sell points, increasingly marketing them as signed work by a known artist rather than replicas. He makes the usual range of large Midwestern Archaic points, but also is one of the few knappers who make Danish Neolithic daggers, which are perhaps the most complex and spectacular of all prehistoric stone tools. Val, meanwhile, has done lithic illustrations for a number of archaeologists, as well as much of the artwork for *Chips, The Art of Flint Knapping,* and a book of point types, *Story in Stone.* She sells her original drawings, once published, and in 1996 the Waldorfs began marketing what they intend to be a series of collectable ceramic mugs. The first shows several styles of fluted points and a mammoth hunting scene; the second a number of points by top modern knappers. Dane and Mary Martin now collaborate with the Waldorfs to edit *Chips* and the Knapper's Corner Web page. The Waldorfs and Martins have expanded into making a series of instructional videos featuring Dave and other knappers, marketed through The Knapper's Corner.

Ingrid Jones, Knapper Spouse

Various readers commented that I write about the knappers using "he," "him," and "his." I am not trying to buck the modern preference for nonsexist writing, but the Fort Osage Knap-in is very much a male event. I have seen fewer than a dozen female knappers in all the years I have been attending. This is true of the knapping world in general; female knappers are rare, although perhaps a bit less so among academic knappers than at knap-ins. My 160 survey respondents included only 2 female knappers. Nevertheless, a fair number of women are regulars at Fort Osage. They usually come because their husband or boyfriend is a knapper, and they find a variety of things to do.

I met Ingrid Jones one of the first times I went to Fort Osage. She was teasing Bob Hunt with a plush toy moose, which she said should be the knap-in mascot, even if its antlers were too soft to make billets. It turned out she had bought it on a tour of the local flea markets and antique stores with a group of the knap-in wives. Ingrid came to the knap-in with her husband Earnie, who was one of the first of the hospitable regulars I met. Earnie learned to knap after taking a class from Larry Kinsella at Cahokia Mounds State Park in Illinois and going to some of the early Fort Osage Knap-ins. Ingrid was involved with the Society for Creative Anachronism, a medieval reenactment group, and Earnie had been a member of various archery societies in the 1960s. Ingrid says the knap-ins remind them both of these other hobbies, where the bonds of an unusual shared interest hold a diverse group together and create friendships.

Over the years, a group of a dozen or so wives got quite friendly, developing a regular routine of dropping off their knapping menfolk and going out to shop and tour for the day before rejoining the men for dinner. They also spent some time at the knap-in, with varying degrees of interest in it. Ingrid and a couple of others eventually learned how to make "dream catchers" from one of the other craftsmen at the knap-in. Ingrid became quite proficient and began making dream catchers in all sizes, from wall hangings to earrings for sale at the knap-in and other events. Earnie made and sold copper pressure flakers and other tools, so they could set up together and cooperate on watching the stand. Ingrid's dream catchers and other jewelry eventually eclipsed the copper tools, and by 1996 they had to set up a small open tent to accommodate her wares.

A number of other wives work with some craft compatible with knapping or help their husbands sell things. Don Kylberg's wife Annette, for instance, mounted points with wire wrappings for pendants and earrings. Don, who organized one of the Texas knap-ins, told me that his preference for knapping small, fine points was in part because that provided the raw material for his wife's jewelry and made a hobby they both enjoyed. A couple of other wives appeared at one knap-in without their husbands, having joined forces to form a small company selling knapping stone.

Many husbands joke about how their wives tolerate their knapping habits, or interfere with them. Some of the joking has the bite of truth, and the wives who do come to knap-ins are considered a power to reckon with. Sharon Mondino and Pat Regan have more than once made everyone stop knapping and assemble for a group photo. Everyone rather liked this, and Sharon made and sold copies. It was a considerable help to me in learning to identify various knappers by name. More to the point, I do not think any of the knappers could have successfully organized a group photo; in a group that tries hard to remain unorganized and without hierarchy, only the wives had such overarching authority.

Knapper Demography

The assorted individuals described above give a personalized sample of the range of activities and characters, and the varying emphases that knappers put on their knap-in participation. While each is a unique individual, each also represents common themes among the knappers. Knappers come to Fort Osage to knap, to meet other knappers and exchange information, to buy, sell, and trade raw materials, tools, and points. The mail survey I conducted in 1994 (Appendix A) gives a somewhat more quantified idea of who knappers are and what knappers say they like to do at knap-ins.

One hundred sixty knappers responded to the survey, 90 who said they went to Fort Osage at least once, and 70 who did not. As the differences in these two groups reflect some idiosyncrasies of the Fort Osage event, it will be useful to separate them for some purposes.

Knappers from thirty-seven states plus Guam and Ontario responded; 18 states were represented among responses from Fort Osage knappers, with twenty-eight knappers from Missouri, thirteen from Kansas, and eight each from Illinois and Texas (Table 4.1). The Midwest and Texas were also strongly represented in the non–Fort Osage group. If we look at the mailing lists as a whole, we can see the geographical patterns of modern knapping a bit better (Figure 4.5). Although these lists had some biases to begin with and are now several years out of date, if we were to add all the new knappers who have surfaced or learned in the last few years, the patterns would probably be pretty much the same. Texas, Missouri, Illinois, and California are the four states with the most knappers. California and the West Coast in general are under-

Table 4.1
Locations of Knappers Responding to the Mail Survey

State	Fort Osage	Non–Fort Osage
MO	28	6
KS	13	0
IL	8	10
TX	8	11
MN	7	0
CO	5	2
IA	4	1
AR	3	3
GA	2	0
IN	2	0
OK	2	2
WI	2	0
LA	1	1
MS	1	2
NY	1	3
OR	1	0
TN	1	1
VA	1	2
CA	0	3
NJ	0	2
OH	0	2
WV	0	2

(Single non–Fort Osage knappers responded from AL, AK, AZ, CT, FL, GU, ID, KY, MI, MT, NC, ND, NM, ON, SD, UT, and WY.)

represented at Fort Osage and in my information generally, and Oregon is probably especially underrepresented. The high numbers in California probably reflect large overall population.[2] Concentrations of knappers in the Midwest and Texas reflect in part the availability of raw material. The East Coast, where material is relatively scarce, has fewer knappers. The presence of an enthusiastic group in New York is an

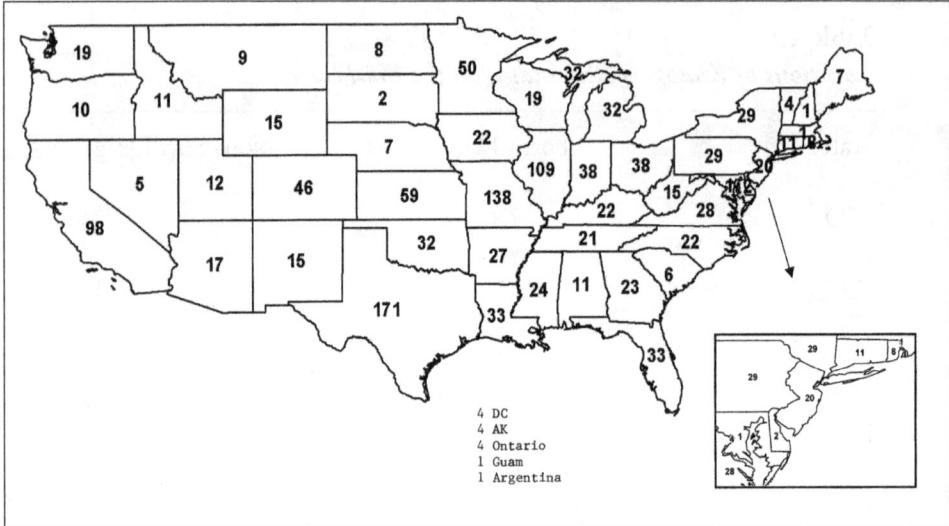

Figure 4.5. Map of knapper locations from 1994 mail lists.

exception and probably explains the relatively high number of New York knappers. There is a feedback loop involved in knapper populations. Knappers tend to cluster where there is raw material. Where there are already some knappers, and raw material, knap-ins get started. Knap-ins, and enthusiastic knappers, create more knappers.

Most knappers are men; only two female knappers responded to the survey. I will discuss why this is so later. It is hard to guess how many female knappers are out there.

The average age of the knappers in both groups of responses was similar, 49.3 years for all the responses, with a range from 18 to 85 (Figure 4.6). Most knappers tend to be settled adults, often retired. There are a lot of new knappers, but these are not necessarily young folk. Ten knappers with forty or more years of knapping experience responded. The Fort Osage responses included more younger knappers, probably because that list was more up-to-date at the time of the survey and thus included more beginners. This is also reflected in the years people have been knapping (Figure 4.7). Fort Osage knappers claimed an average of 11.2 years of experience, while for non–Fort Osage knappers the average was 15 years. Knappers were also asked to rank their skill level as "beginner," "competent" (making normal point replicas), "skilled" (capable of large, thin bifaces, fluted points, etc.), or "expert." Of the

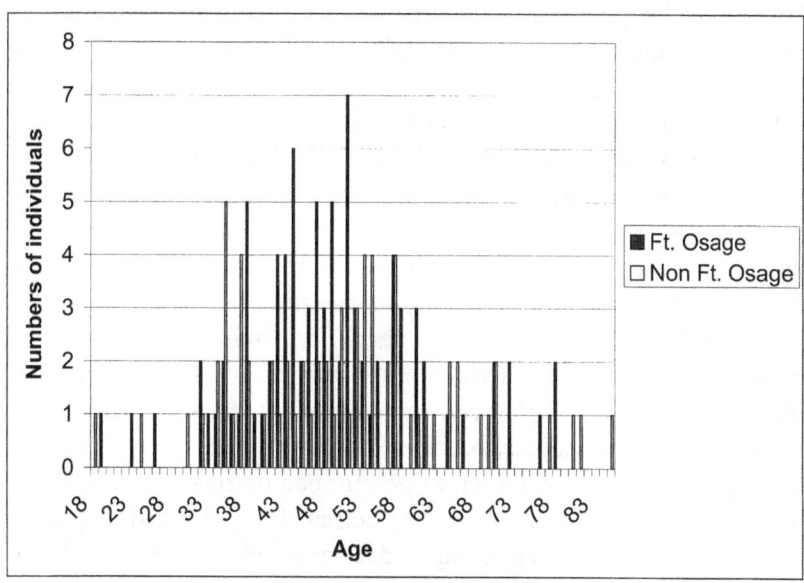

Figure 4.6. Ages of knappers responding to mail survey.

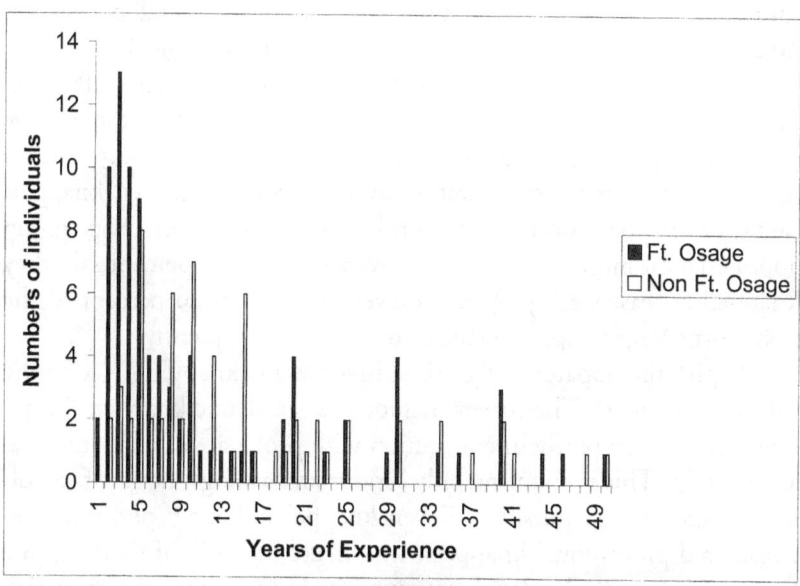

Figure 4.7. Number of years of experience claimed by knappers responding to mail survey.

Fort Osage knappers, 26 percent considered themselves beginners, 44 percent competent, 20 percent skilled, and 8 percent expert. The non–Fort Osage responses were, respectively, 20 percent, 43 percent, 23 percent, and 13 percent. This means that one-fifth to one-quarter of knappers saw themselves as beginners, reflecting a growing craft.

Knappers come from diverse backgrounds. I know knapping dentists (four of them!), engineers, artists, mechanics, electricians, software designers, factory workers and supervisors, bulldozer operators, farmers, and, of course, archaeologists, to mention only a few. Knappers whose background includes art or design, or making things with their hands, often mention this when asked why they began knapping or like to do it. Some feel that craftsmen of various sorts are predisposed to become good knappers, but I can't confirm that. Of 153 knappers ranking their educational level, 27 percent had finished high school, 50 percent had gone to college, and 23 percent had advanced degrees of some sort. The Fort Osage group had fewer college graduates and relatively more high-school-educated knappers than the non–Fort Osage group, but advanced degrees were equal. The knappers thus tend to be well educated as a group; comparable statistics for U.S. white males in 1994 are that 82 percent finished high school and 26 percent completed four years of college, but only about 9 percent of the overall population holds advanced degrees (United States Census Bureau 1995).

Some knappers are almost fanatically devoted to their craft. Even including all the less-dedicated knappers who responded, the average time the responding knappers estimated they knap was 24.5 hours a month. That is more than half an average work week! Ten knappers said they knapped 100 hours a month or more. The Fort Osage group appeared a bit more dedicated than average. Sixty-six percent said they knapped at least weekly by themselves, while only 49 percent of the non–Fort Osage knappers claimed to knap this frequently.

Despite the apparent huge time investment, knapping is a hobby for most knappers. The survey included 12 "academic knappers," who, like myself, knap partly in connection with professional or avocational archaeology. This is counting only serious archaeology, not artifact collecting and related pursuits. Eleven knappers, about 7 percent, were considered professional knappers, who make the bulk of their income from knapping and related activities such as selling raw material. Another 23 (14 percent) were considered "heavy commercial knappers," estimated to sell over a hundred points or $1,000 worth of knapping-

Table 4.2
Percentages of Responding Knappers Who Said They Do a Particular Activity at Knap-ins

	Always	Sometimes	Never
Knap	45	28	26
Watch	68	22	3
Talk	61	23	10
Film	6	33	59
Buy material	22	51	23
Sell material	9	18	72
Buy Points	7	28	62
Sell Points	9	17	72
Buy Other	18	40	40
Sell Other	6	11	83

Total of 141 responses, but the percent totals do not add up to 100% because some knappers did not answer all questions.

related material a year. The rest of the knappers in the survey (114, 71 percent) are essentially hobby knappers who flake primarily for fun, although 47 of these said they sometimes sell points, often seeing this as a way to defray the costs of their hobby. Almost half of all knappers (not counting academic knappers) in the survey (67, 42 percent) said they "never" sell points, and 5 of the hundred-hours-per-month knappers were hobbyists.

The survey also asked knappers what they like to do at knap-ins (Table 4.2; Whittaker and Hedman 1996). Not all of the non–Fort Osage knappers actually go to knap-ins, so only 57 of them answered this, and only 84 of the Fort Osage group. As one might expect, almost everyone watches and talks to other knappers. In conversation, knappers constantly refer to the companionship and social pleasures of knap-ins and the potential for learning from others as reasons why they like knap-ins. I was surprised to find that around 10 percent of the respondents appear to be either wallflowers or strong, silent types who claim they "never" talk to others at knap-ins. Since knapping with others in public is one of the main activities, distinctive features, and purposes of knap-ins, it was even more surprising that a quarter of the knappers said they "never" knap at knap-ins and less than half of them "always" do. When I reviewed the responses, I found that in fact several of the knappers who claim not to knap at knap-ins are guys I have watched knapping at Fort Osage. Apparently, knapping at the knap-in is less important in the minds of some regulars than it seems to me.

Another reason for getting together is to exchange points, tools, and especially raw material. The opinion of many knappers is that Fort Osage has a slightly more commercial flavor than some other knap-ins, but the survey did not support this very strongly. Only 9–10 percent of all knappers "always" sell points at knap-ins, and 70–73 percent "never" do, with both the higher percentages coming from the Fort Osage responses. Sales of stone seem to be a little higher at Fort Osage than elsewhere. Most knappers (70–74 percent) "never" sell material at knap-ins. Both the Fort Osage and other knappers have about the same percentage (25 percent and 30 percent) who do sell stone at knap-ins. However, about half (51 percent) of Fort Osage knappers "always" or "usually" buy stone at the knap-in, while only 34 percent of the non–Fort Osage group do the same. I am not sure why this should be the case, since so many of the Fort Osage knappers come from stone-rich states, and 53 percent of them said they collect most of their stone at the source, only slightly fewer than the 59 percent of non–Fort Osage knappers who do the same. Nevertheless, knap-ins were the most important source of stone for 23 percent of Fort Osage knappers, compared to 7 percent of knappers who do not go to Fort Osage. An additional implication of these figures is that a relatively small number of knappers are moving the bulk of the stone. This commerce will be discussed later.

A Continent of Knap-ins

Not only stone moves among knap-ins. Although there are regional groups, some of the same knappers show up at events all over the country, and some knappers wear out more rubber on asphalt than they do copper on flint. Leroy Jines sets up his tarp under a canopy next to the parking lot and his truck at Fort Osage, a white-bearded man with an open face and dusty tan overalls, surrounded by piles of bifaces roughed out of stone from all over the country. Leroy rarely makes a finished point. He prefers collecting material and knapping it into bifaces that he sells to other knappers, who will finish them. "Once you've done the biface work, you've solved all the puzzles," he says. Besides, collecting the material is one excuse to travel around the country. Home is the Panhandle of Texas, but as a semi-retired auctioneer and businessman, Leroy spends much of his time going from knap-in to quarry to knap-in in his camper, accompanied by his wife Ann and a friendly little dog named Shadow. He habitually chronicles his knap-in and quarry adventures in messages to The Tarp email group. The bifaces around him document his travels equally well, and he emailed me a summary of 2001.

> Last year we traveled a bit more than 33,000 miles. We collected Edwards and Georgetown flint in Central Texas. Then South to the Fredericksberg area for Pedernales; at Uvalde we gathered Pedernales from the Nueces River gravel bars. Also farther south to San Antonio for Edwards chert. We collected Kay County chert from south Central Kansas on the way to Fort Osage. I got a bit of Florida chert from around Gainesville, Florida, picked up some Coastal plains chert from around Dothan, Alabama. Last June we went to knap-ins at Davis Creek, California for obsidian and dacite and the weekend following Davis Creek we went to a knap-in at Glass Buttes, Oregon for more obsidian and dacite. Picked up some Burlington on the way home from Ft Osage. We attended knap-ins at Water Creek Arkansas and went to a novaculite quarry near Malvern, Ark. after the event and got 800 lbs, then Moundville, Alabama where a bunch of us went on an atlatl feral pig hunt after the knap-in, but didn't even see a pig, Steve Behrnes knap-in in Louisiana where I picked up some small pieces of Citronel chert. Mark Bracken's knap-in in NW Georgia, Paynes Prairie knap-in near Gainesville, Florida, Ft Osage in Missouri twice, Flint Ridge Ohio, Pigg Farm knap-in in Indiana where we went on a canoe float trip with Jeff Pigg after the knap-in, Bob Patten's near Denver, Colorado where I saw the most abo style knapping, Letchworth, New York had the grandest sight seeing views of the Gennessee River Valley, Ron Fuller's knap-in in NE Oklahoma where we set out trotlines across Spavinaw Creek and caught enough fish to feed 60 peo-

ple a fish supper, Quartzsite, Arizona where I got some Imperial Jasper (out of Mexico) from one of the venders, 5 knap-ins in the Central Texas area and events at several other places. I believe the most memorable event was Flint Ridge. There was such a diversity of primitive and modern crafts. It was also the biggest event with Spring Ft Osage coming a close second. The best camping area was Davis Creek, California with tall pines and a creek beside the camping area. We attended 23 events total which worked out pretty close to every other weekend. We started in mid January and finished around the first of November. In the Winter I cook and work the rock gathered during my travels throughout the year.

All knap-ins have strong similarities, with knapping, socializing, and exchange as the main activities. However, there is a lot of variation, and a different "feel" to each knap-in. This is usually attributable to the core group of knappers at each, and what they attempt to organize, encourage, or avoid. In 1996, twenty-four different knap-ins were advertised in *Chips;* in 2001, there were thirty-seven (Table 4.3). The geographical pattern visible in the knapper demography can be seen in the knap-ins, although there has been some change through time. It has not been possible for me to visit all, or even very many, of the possible knap-ins, but a few capsule descriptions will help to show the range of variation and how Fort Osage fits the patterns.

Mid-West Flintknappers' Convention, June 1993

One of the smaller knap-ins, and the first knap-in other than Fort Osage that I attended, is the Mid-West Flintknappers' Convention, often referred to as the Fairview Heights Knap-in, and now officially the Devil's Hole Knap-in, although in the same location. When I parked in front of the picnic shelter that housed the knappers, the first knappers I saw, including the organizers, were people I knew from Fort Osage, and I felt right at home. The Fairview Heights Knap-in bills itself as "the oldest in the midwest." It was started in 1980 by David Klostermeier and Larry Kinsella. Dave Klostermeier is Site Administrator at the Missouri First State Capitol State Historic Site. Larry Kinsella grew up on a farm that is now part of the park where the knap-in is

Table 4.3
Knap-in Calendar for 2001

Jan 1–Feb 1	5th Annual Quartzite Knap-in	AZ
Jan 25–28	Joe Miller's Knap-in	TX
Feb 23–25	4th Annual Paynes Prairie Primitive Arts Festival	FL
Mar 16–18	Maxdale Texas Knap-in	TX
Mar 30–Apr 1	Moundville Alabama Knap-in	AL
Mar 30–Apr 1	Southwest Louisiana Knap-in	LA
Apr 3–7	5th Annual North Georgia Knap-in	GA
Apr 7–8	Winter Break Knap-in	WA
May 4–6	Water Creek Knap-in	AR
May 5–6	Old Stone Fort Knap-in	TN
May 18–20	Fort Osage Knap-in	MO
June 1–3	1st Annual Ooga-Booga Convention and Knap-in	TX
June 1–3	Devil's Hole (Fairview Heights) Knap-in	IL
June 2–3	Wrightwood California Knap-in	CA
June 2–3	Knap-in at the Trailside Museum	NE
June 9–10	Colorado Front Range Knap-in	CO
June 15–17	Southern Indiana Knap-in	IN
June 16–17	Davis Creek California Knap-in	CA
June 23–24	Gathering at Glass Buttes	OR
June 29–30	Minnesota Knappers Guild Knap-in	MN
June 30–Jul 1	Elk Park Knap-in	PA
July 7–8	1st Annual Chickasaw Trace Knap-in	TN
July 7–8	Upper Missouri River Knap-in	MT
July 12–15	Evergreen Lake Knap-in	IL
July 27–29	Crab Orchard Knap-in	VA
July 28–29	Stu and Rose Murdoc's Knap-in	WA
Aug 10–12	Puget Sound Knappers' Pig Roast and Knap-in	WA
Aug 17–19	Pigg Farm Knap-in	IN
Aug 18–19	Old Stone Fort Knap-in	TN
Aug 24–26	Stone Tool Craftsman's Show	NY
Aug 31–Sept 2	Flint Ridge Knap-in	OH
Sept 1–3	Medicine Creek Knap-in	WA

Sept 14–16	Fort Osage Knap-in	MO
Sept 21–22	1st Annual Ozark Mt Primitive Skills Gathering	MO
Oct 5–7	7th Annual Kansas Knap-in	KS
Oct 19–21	Clinch River 2nd Annual Primitive Skills Knap-in	TN
Oct 19–21	1st Guadalupe River Knap-in	TX

held. He hunted points all over the hills of the park, which were fields then, and eventually became involved with professional archaeologists working in the area. Although he is a carpenter by profession, he has worked on numerous professional excavation projects. Because both Dave and Larry have archaeological backgrounds, the Fairview Heights Knap-in emphasized archaeology more than most and originally had a somewhat different core group. Although it has become more like Fort Osage in recent years, some of the archaeological origins are still visible. When I was there in 1993, Larry invited a number of interested knappers over to his house in the evening to watch a video he and Dave had just made, documenting the atlatl weights and other spear thrower parts from the famous Archaic site of Indian Knoll in Kentucky. Several other knappers had brought atlatls and threw spears throughout the day. Others besides myself noted the atlatl theme, but when Gene Stapleton commented that he enjoyed having a focus for the knap-in that way, Larry assured him that it was largely coincidence. This anti-organizational attitude is typical of the Midwestern knappers.

Nevertheless, the Fairview Heights Knap-in seemed to me more formally organized than the Fort Osage Knap-in. There was no registration fee, but a can on a table collected a suggested dollar from each knapper to cover the costs of mailing announcements of the next knap-in. At 1:00 on Saturday, the height of the knap-in, there was a drawing for registration prizes donated by the knappers.

About eighty people signed the register. Not all of these were knappers, but probably there were sixty to seventy knappers present at one time or another during the event. The knapping was relatively serious, too, as it usually is at Fort Osage. Most of the knappers seemed to spend much of their time actually knapping. This may have been, in part, because, with the knap-in more concentrated under the one shelter, there was less need to move around to see what others were doing and exchange gossip.

Pine City Knap-in

In 1989, Tony Romano, Gene Altiere, and Jim Regan organized what became the Minnesota Knappers Guild (Figure 4.8) and began holding a public knap-in. Gene edited a newsletter called *The Platform* for several years (1989–1995). *The Platform* carried few advertisements and was concerned mostly with local knapping news and announcements, knapping tips (mostly by Jim Regan, the group's most accomplished

Figure 4.8. Tony Romano watches Jim Regan flute a Clovis point with the lever device Jim designed and sold. Fort Osage, 1994.

The Knap-in: People and Organization

knapper), and an unusual archaeological presence. Professional archaeologists contributed descriptions of projects with a relevance to knappers (Peters 1994), and there was a series describing Minnesota stone resources aimed at both archaeological and knapping interests (Bakken 1993; Gonsior 1992; Romano 1993, 1994). The newsletter lapsed, but the Guild remains as a loose group of knappers whose members do demonstrations for educational organizations, as well as hosting an annual knap-in. By 1996, the Pine City Knap-in was a good example of the well-established smaller knap-ins. Jim Regan was the official contact and organizer, the knap-in is in Tony Romano's hometown, and the two of them took care of setting up, with the help of some of the other local knappers and early arrivals. In June 1996, fifty-seven people signed the registration list, but several of these were visitors rather than knappers, or wives or children, so perhaps thirty-five to forty knappers were present. I came because Tony, Jim, and Gene were friends from Fort Osage. Tony and Jim were regulars there, and many of the other Minnesota knappers also go to the Fort Osage Knap-in at least once in a while.

The Pine City Knap-in is held on the grounds of the Minnesota Historical Society's Northwest Trading Post Historic Site. A log fort, actually a trading post rather than a military establishment, has been reconstructed on the site of the original structure, built in 1803–1804 on the banks of the Snake River. The post serves as a backdrop; the knap-in is supposed to set up far enough away that it does not mar the view for visitors or block the parking areas. One large open tent sufficed to cover the knap-in, and only a couple of knappers set up outside it (Figure 4.9). The knap-in felt very relaxed, partly because, with fewer than half as many knappers, there was less of a crowd than at Fort Osage. There was less to see, less milling around, and less of a tendency for the knappers to knap in separate groups. The atmosphere also seemed somewhat less commercial. Tony Romano in particular works with local amateur and professional archaeologists, and several come to the knap-in. The knap-in publicity includes an invitation to the public to bring artifacts for the archaeologists and others to identify. There were fewer of the more commercial knappers, only a few knappers had much stone to sell, and only a couple of people with other crafts were set up. Nevertheless, there was the usual exchange and selling among the knappers, and to visitors to the fort who stopped to see the knap-in.

The only special event associated with this knap-in was a drawing

Figure 4.9. The knap-in at Pine City in 1996 was small and intimate, occupying only one tent.

for "door prizes." Most of the knappers donated something, and anyone who had signed the registration sheet and was present got to go up and pick a prize as his or her name was called.

The Pine City Knap-in has grown a bit since my first visit, but remains one of the smaller knap-ins, reflecting the efforts of a small group of active and enthusiastic knappers. Holding a knap-in is a good way to get to meet other knappers, especially if you are a bit out of the way up in Minnesota. Visiting knappers also bring stone to sell and trade, highly desirable in such a stone-poor area.

Evergreen Lake Knap-in, July 1996

The Evergreen Lake Knap-in, in Comlara Park near Normal, Illinois, is one of the new knap-ins, started in 1995. The organizing core is Glenn Leesman, Paul Schilkofski, and Tim Lindenbaum. They and several other knappers were meeting regularly at Glenn's house and going to other knap-ins. They decided they could do just as well with a knap-in of their own, and there was no other major knap-in scheduled in July.

Part of the motivation for holding a knap-in, at least potentially, is commercial. Knap-in organizers do not usually stand to profit directly, but the opportunity to sell points to the public and material to other knappers is important to some knappers. Glenn is very much into buying and selling modern points and building a collection of ancient specimens. The knapping style of the group that knaps at Glenn's house reflects his insistence that points should be good replicas, although the three organizers have different preferences. Paul Schilkofski likes to make fluted points; his fluting jig is inscribed "Flutin' Fool." Tim prefers Dalton-related forms, and Glenn makes the range of Midwestern Archaic points, but also some of the smaller, less spectacular forms that are often found, but less often made, by modern knappers.

The Evergreen Lake Knap-in thus had a somewhat more commercial feel to me than some other knap-ins. There were several dealers there, including one with a large display of ground-stone gorgets, axes, and bannerstones. Several circulated through the knap-in, buying points. There was a lot of stone for sale; in fact, Bob Hunt complained that he was not selling much of his Burlington chert, because there was so much exotic stone.

As the knap-in was so new, the organizers were feeling some strain, and told me that it was more work than they expected. The site in Comlara Park they got for free, because on other occasions they did demonstrations for the park. They felt that the nearby motel accommodations were better than at some other knap-ins, an advantage, but that their food vendor was not good enough and they would have to try to arrange something like the Boy Scouts, as at Fort Osage. Meanwhile, there were continual small problems that had to be solved. For instance, on the first morning the park had left the showers locked, and a park employee with a key had to be hunted down so the camping knappers could get cleaned up.

Despite being new, the knap-in was well attended. There are a lot of Midwestern knappers, and with no competing knap-ins, sixty-eight people registered, almost all knappers or vendors of knapping-related goods. Almost all were from the Midwest: forty-four from Illinois, eleven from Missouri, six from Indiana, two from Iowa, and one each from Ohio and Wisconsin. The four others were from Georgia, Louisiana, Texas, and Colorado. Many of the knappers were Fort Osage regulars as well. This knap-in, too, has grown and become a bit more diverse in subsequent years.

While maintaining the usual loose atmosphere of knap-ins, the organizers had set up a couple of special things. Their announcements in *Chips* noted that there would be atlatl and sling demonstrations. I got to try a staff sling, a medieval weapon new to me, and several people had atlatls and primitive bows to show off, let others try, or sell. Early in the knap-in there was an impromptu trip to Glenn Leesman's house to look at his collection of artifacts and his knapping workshop.

There was also a prize drawing. Such drawings seem to be getting common at knap-ins. They can be used to raise money to cover expenses of organizing an event and using a public site, and they serve as a focal moment, briefly bringing most of the knappers together in one place where announcements can be made. There was no registration fee for the knap-in, but knappers were asked to contribute items for the drawing, and tickets were sold at two dollars a shot. There were around thirty prizes, mostly points, but also slabs or nodules of stone, a couple of blanks, a pack of artifact collector cards, some bead necklaces, a knap-in cap, a knapper T-shirt, a copy of Waldorf's book, and a raccoon skin. The drawing was an occasion for friendly jokes; Steve Behrnes and Brad Arles, who had just had birthdays, were presented with cupcakes and eggs of silly putty for them to knap. The drawing was run by Paul Schilkofski, who held the pot with tickets while someone's young son drew them. George Pelfrey held up each piece as it was drawn for, and the crowd commented on it. George would say, "this here's Glenn's idea of a Snyder point," and someone would shout, "it looks like a Clovis to me." The joking and public display of each prize with the donor's name provided some low-key recognition of skill and generosity, without violating the knap-in taboo on overt competition, which I will discuss later.

Genesee Valley Flint Knappers Association Knap-in, August 1996

I wanted to see this New York Knap-in because it had several unusual features. It reflects an enthusiastic local group in a part of the country where there are relatively few knappers and little usable stone. It had a reputation as being fun, but more organized than most knap-ins; my Midwestern friends were strongly divided over whether they liked this or not. The announcements gave the full title as "Seventh Annual Stone Tool Technology Show and Genesee Valley Flint Knappers Association Knap-in." Both the formality of the title and the presence of an "Association" reflect the unusually formal organization, and the use of the word "Show" reflects a concern with knapping as an art and with public education. The Genesee Valley Flint Knappers Association has even gone so far as to register as a nonprofit organization and, in January 1997, started a newsletter. The formal name of the knap-in is, however, too much of a mouthful; most knappers refer to it as the Castile Knap-in after the nearby town where it used to be held, or simply as the New York Knap-in or the Genesee Knap-in.

I had to fly in to visit the New York Knap-in, and I was met by Kenny Wallace and Dana Klein, the organizers. Dana and his wife Kay even lent me a battered old Blazer for the weekend. This allowed me to explore the spectacular gorges at Letchworth State Park, although when I rose early to catch the vultures roosting on the ledges, the Blazer backfired like a cannon as I pulled over beside the gorge, and by the time I could look over the cliff edge, the vultures had flung themselves off and were soaring at top speed away from me, leaving only white guano on the rocks and a black feather drifting down the breeze.

Thursday before the knap-in I was given a tour of Kenny's workshop, decorated with antlers on the outside and knapper clutter on the inside. Besides knapping, Kenny enjoys bartering, for instance, exchanging a flint knife for the spectacular full-color mammoth tattoo on his right shoulder. ("Hurt, but it's worth it.") He is the lead knapper among the group of locals who knap together from time to time. Around 1990 they formally organized as the Genesee Valley Flint Knappers Association and began holding a small knap-in in the city park in Castile. As the knap-in grew, they planned to move it to Letchworth State Park. This entailed some increased restrictions, such as not selling prehistoric artifacts, but offered a large facility with bathrooms, parking lots, and shelters in a scenic park. The knap-in moved to Letchworth in 1994, combining with the Moses Vancampen Long Rifle Mountain People Primitive Encampment, a fur-trade-era reenactors "rendezvous." New Yorkers seem to have a fondness for long titles. Having two different but compatible events and groups of people brings in a larger audience and more potential customers (Figure 4.10).

The Genesee knappers emphasize knapping as an art form, and this emphasis extends to many aspects of the knap-in. For one thing, there were more non-knapping artists and a greater diversity of crafts on display than I have seen at any other knap-in (see V. Waldorf 1993 for a similar account). Antler carvers were especially common. Antler carvers and scrimshaw artists are natural associates of knappers, and a number

Figure 4.10. Kenny Wallace spends time in both the rendezvous and the knap-in, so he dresses up in period clothes, which knappers usually avoid. Dana Klein is in the background. His clothes pass for either rendezvous costume or knapper shabby. Genesee Knap-in, 1996.

of them collaborate in making stone knives with fancy handles and other multimedia artifacts. I have an impression they are becoming more common at knap-ins generally, and more knappers are trying their hands at carving and scrimshaw, too. At Letchworth a number of the wood and antler carvers as well as a couple of knappers were from the New York Iroquoian tribes, giving a much stronger Native American presence at this knap-in than I have seen anywhere else.

The disadvantage of having all the other crafts and combining with the rendezvous is that there was less actual knapping at this knap-in than at others. The organizers had set up a ring of chairs under the main shelter. Dana explained that the "knapping circle" was an intentional arrangement that they hoped would promote fellowship, but there were times when it was almost deserted, and it never seemed to me to be the center that was intended. I, for instance, hardly knapped at all, as there were so many things I wanted to see and so many new people to talk to. Most of the action for most people was at the tables under the two large shelters, where knappers and other craftsmen had their displays. The event was well advertised, and there were a lot of visitors passing through. In fact, Dana told me that the Friday was mostly for the knappers and the weekend was partly "the price we have to pay" for the knap-in. The opportunity to sell brings knappers and other artists, but the mass of park visitors who come through also bring some headaches. As Dana put it, "How many times can you stand answering the same dumb questions about making arrowheads with hot rocks and water?" The many visitors also meant knappers and other artists seemed less willing to leave their displays untended than at smaller events like Fort Osage. The necessity of tending displays also kept some knappers out of the central knapping area, and a few knapped at their tables or wherever they had set up.

On Friday, we set up the knap-in, and knappers began to arrive, hanging out in the camping areas, knapping a bit, and gossiping over home-brewed beer distributed by Joe Hewitt. His "Knapper Beer" label features a Clovis point as "the Mark of Excellence" and the slogan "After two or three Knappers anything you make will look a whole lot better."

On Saturday, as the event really got under way, some of the differences from most knap-ins appeared. This one had a schedule of events running throughout the day. There were several formal demonstrations. Three of the local knappers, Tom Pedlow, Joe Hewitt, and Dan Long, demonstrated local clay pottery, cordage, and pine pitch hafting, respectively. Dick Parker, one of the rare individuals who makes and sells ground-stone axes and similar tools, demonstrated some of his techniques. Craig Ratzat, an Oregon professional knapper, brought a huge load of obsidian for sale and demonstrated how he spalls it. Meanwhile, Bob Berg, who makes and sells atlatls, had set up a target course, after a lengthy safety discussion with park officials, and there were to be atlatl contests (Figure 4.11). Atlatls, also called spear throwers, were used on most continents before the bow and arrow. Basically a stick with a hook on one end, an atlatl gives a mechanical advantage that allows a light spear to be thrown much farther than is possible by just throwing it like a javelin. Over in the rendezvous encampment,

Figure 4.11. Bob Berg and his atlatl shop at the Genesee Knap-in, 1996.

there were tents to wander through and reenactors selling nineteenth-century crafts. Now and then they would fire off a cannon or black powder rifle, to the irritation of knappers trying to concentrate on a persnickety stroke.

The Genesee Valley Knappers knap-in also featured a knapping competition, which was another reason I wanted to be there. In Chapter 7 I will discuss how this event expresses esthetic ideals and reflects both competition for status and the rejection of a competitive atmosphere. There was also a "Howdy" award, named after a deceased member. Ballots were handed out at registration, and knappers voted the award to whoever they felt contributed most to their knap-in experience. In addition, the Genesee Valley Knappers Association has started the tradition of a yearly vote among themselves for knappers who have contributed most to the advancement and appreciation of the art. The names of these people are inscribed on stones to be used for a "Wall of Fame" in a knapping museum that remains a long-term dream of the group.

The Midwestern knappers that I have seen are, for the most part, firmly set against the idea of awards, hierarchy, and competition among knappers, a topic I will discuss at length later. The New York knappers formed an unusually organized group and have also felt the need for formal recognition of certain knappers and their achievements. They phrase this carefully in terms of recognition and promotion of the art of knapping and explicitly eschew the idea of competition. This fence-straddling seems to have been successful so far; I saw no indications of active competition for the awards or jealousy and conceit among the "competitors." Perhaps the emphasis on recognition developed in part because they are somewhat isolated from the rest of the knapping world; few of the New York group get down to the Midwestern knap-ins, and the Midwestern knappers, like the really mobile knappers from elsewhere whom I meet at Fort Osage, rarely get up to New York. I hear that this, too, is changing, as the New York Knap-in developed a reputation as an enjoyable and different knap-in.

When I visited the New York knappers, I was hospitably greeted with samples of black Onondaga chert and other New York materials. My first attempts to work it were pretty ugly, and the other knappers viewed them with both sympathy and friendly derision. The New York knappers are perversely proud of the difficulty of working New York cherts, and of the scarcity of high-quality material that reduces them to such straits. Still, good material is much desired, and the Genesee Valley knappers have even mounted expeditions, sending some members to Texas with a van to bring back flint (Klein 1994). One reason for holding a knap-in is to bring in material. As the New York Knap-in becomes better known and knappers come from farther away, the Genesee Valley group gains access to a greater diversity of material. I heard a number of comments from Fort Osage knappers between 1994 and 1996 that the New York knappers were better than they thought they were once they got their hands on good material, and that it was worthwhile going up there because good stone was easy to sell.

I will discuss the economics of stone later, but as I said, stone resources are a strong influence on the location and popularity of some knap-ins. The Texas knap-ins have always had the advantage that virtually unlimited supplies of good chert were readily collected, although the distance Midwestern knappers have to transport it offsets this somewhat. The knappers in Oregon and parts of California likewise are close to obsidian sources, but for some reason, there have not been large and long-standing knap-ins along the West Coast. Richardson's Rock Ranch in Oregon, which began hosting a knap-in in 1993, is a commercial rock shop that plainly hopes to profit by attracting knappers to relatively cheap stone. The only knap-in I have attended where local stone sources were a defining feature was the knap-in at Flint Ridge, Ohio.

Flint Ridge Knap-in, August 1996

The Flint Ridge Knap-in was started around 1990, and the organizers in 1996 were listed as Carl Fry, Roy Miller, and Dan Minard. The site was Mason's Campground, a trailer park on the edge of the Flint Ridge State Memorial, a park protecting prehistoric quarry areas. The campground also sold some stone, and offered the opportunity to dig for flint (by hand) and buy what you collect. From what I heard, this was more of a draw in previous years; many knappers who go to Flint Ridge either have their own sources, like Roy Miller, who is a commercial knapper, or have discovered that digging flint without machinery is a backbreaking job.

Only a couple of knappers were seriously digging at Mason's in 1996. One of them was Gerry Goth, a Michigan knapper I knew from Fort Osage (Figure 4.12). As he puts it, he "has the flint bug, bad" and

Figure 4.12. Gerry Goth in his flint quarry hole at Flint Ridge, 1996. Except for the modern tools, this gives a pretty good idea of what the prehistoric mining operations there were like.

is as much interested in collecting stone as knapping. He sells a little, swaps a lot, and collects other knappers' work, but he does it strictly for fun. When I arrived, he had already been there a couple of days and had opened a hole more than 2 meters in diameter and a meter deep, digging down through 60 centimeters or so of topsoil, shattered flint, and the debris of other diggers to flint bedrock. I worked with Gerry off and on for the next two days, to see what it was like, as did Craig Ferrell, a West Virginia knapper.

The flint bedrock is seams, blocks, and plates of chert, with clay-filled fissures running here and there. Gerry had several sledgehammers and chisels to pound into the cracks, and the flint could be broken out in chunks. This was not the most productive pit Gerry had worked; the flint was coming out in pieces usually not more than 10 to 15 cm long. The color was largely a creamy white, not the more desirable clear chalcedony or colorful tan, yellow, purplish, or grey with dendritic mottling that is sometimes found. It was warm, but shady, in the woods and far enough from the road and knap-in that we heard little except the ringing pound of sledges on Gerry's homemade chisels, the grating sound of flint being pried loose (which Gerry claims is his favorite music, the Goth Symphony in Flint Miner), and the melodic clatter of lumps of flint tossed out of the pit onto the "keeper" pile. Many of the plates of flint were roughly vertical, and if you could dig in steps, starting a face at one level and working back, you could pry the flint out relatively efficiently. Some was badly broken up, weather-cracked, and worthless. The good pieces were correspondingly hard to get out. A few worms and beetle grubs turned up in the clay, and once a small salamander, opening its mouth in a silent bark.

It was hard work digging with steel tools and must have been vastly harder in prehistoric times with only stone mauls and antler wedges. The weight of flint we obtained seemed only slightly more than the sweat we perspired. By the time I left, Gerry had removed 200–300 pounds of good material, for which he would pay "Mason's House of Flint" twenty cents a pound. It could be sold for one to two dollars a pound or more, depending on whether it was heat-treated and slabbed and whether it was nice and colorful. Considering that this was the result of three men working much of two days, it should be obvious that Gerry is not digging flint as a profit-making enterprise.

Besides the flint digging, which was minor this time, the Flint Ridge Knap-in seemed quite different to me from other knap-ins. The physical arrangement had much to do with this. About half the knappers set up along a lane at the edge of the campground, with some scattered in among the campers, and the other half of the event was across the road under tents and other individual shelters in an open field. There was no central knapping area, and I felt there was less sense of community than at most knap-ins. I never did find any registration for knappers like myself; if you were camping you paid a camping fee, and if you were set up as a vendor, an additional ten dollars, but most knap-ins try to register all knappers for a mailing list and hand out name tags. As an ethnographer who has never been good at remembering names, I found it a serious disadvantage not to have name tags, and many of the people at this knap-in were new to me. There was a good deal of non-local stone for sale, including Craig Ratzat's trailer of 6,500 pounds of Oregon obsidian, which he had brought to Ohio after the New York Knap-in. There were a number of other crafts for sale, including several different atlatl styles, because an atlatl contest was planned.

As the knap-in went on, more organization became apparent. There was a primitive archery competition on Saturday, organized by Gary

Hardy, a local knapper. The atlatl contest was on Sunday, organized by Ray Strischek, who is not a knapper but had a whole tent hung with atlatls and darts. So, too, did Bob Berg from New York, who teaches primitive skills and makes and sells atlatls under the name of Thunderbird Atlatl. Atlatl enthusiasts form a group that has been growing in parallel to the knappers. There is some overlap, with knappers like myself who are interested in atlatls, and atlatlists who knap, and a growing trend to link atlatl events to knap-ins. However, atlatl contestants seem to be a bit more diverse than knap-in participants. Men dominate both, but there are more women and children active in the atlatl groups. At Flint Ridge, forty-four people participated in the atlatl event, mostly men, but there were several women and children.

I participated in the atlatl contests and placed second in one event, which reflected more the relatively low scores than my skill, since I had only had an atlatl for a couple of weeks at that point. Even the "experts" did not live up to the potential of the weapon at this point in the history of sport atlatling. I was struck by how compatible the atlatl competition was to the knap-ins in some ways. It was a notably noncompetitive competition. There was a lot of mutual comparing of gear and technique, and coaching of beginners. The small audience was nonpartisan, and entrants encouraged each other without much bias. Winning brought no great fame (a certificate and mention in *The Atlatl*, newsletter of the World Atlatl Association), and losing no public notoriety, although no doubt some were disappointed in their performance. Ray and several volunteers organized participants, recorded scores, and enforced safety rules without much fuss, so although the nature of the event demanded some structure, it was still quite informal.

The local knapping group and organizers have united as the Flint Ridge Lithic Society. There was a formal meeting on Sunday to discuss what to do about the knap-in next year. The campground owners, the Masons, were elderly, and it looked like a new site was needed. After some discussion, several people volunteered to look into possibilities. On Sunday evening, an auction was held to help defray costs of the knap-in.

The auction was held in the campground's central shelter, which had not been used for knapping. An audience of about seventy sat in rows of chairs and came and went. I figured that to be a good estimate of the number of knappers at the knap-in; many were not present at the auction, but campers filled the gaps. A man I did not know served as auctioneer, and Bob Berg was the assistant, holding up the items, identifying the donors, and making humorous comments. As at the drawings at other knap-ins, the display of donations was important. There were about sixty items, quite diverse. There were a few points, of course, but the rest of the stuff ranged from atlatls, billets, claw pendants, dream catchers, earrings, and flint, to prybars, pipestone, safety glasses, and a Zuni belt buckle. At the end the auctioneers announced that they had raised $1,082.

Knap-in Generalities

All knap-ins have some features in common. Sites tend to be similar, because certain facilities are needed. At all knap-ins, knapping with other knappers is the most common and defining activity. Exchange and sale of materials and points are almost equally important, and the various educational and entertainment activities set up by individuals or the organizers are common, but definitely secondary. Each knap-in relies on a small group of local knappers to organize it, often spearheaded by a particularly enthusiastic individual or two.

The knappers' world is relatively small, and many knappers attend several knap-ins every year. The knap-ins are scheduled with this in mind, to prevent too much overlap and conflict.

Each knap-in develops traditions and a consistent flavor, which depend in large part on the organizers and the knappers who become regulars. However, each individual knap-in at a location is slightly different from year to year. Nevertheless, any knapper who has been to a couple of knap-ins should feel comfortable at any other and find people he has met before. This is part of the charm for many knappers, and one reason that knappers feel some unity as a group and some fellowship with all other knappers, even strangers. The similarity of different knap-ins, and their uniqueness, provide both a common ground of experience and the adventure of new experiences.

With a general picture of the Fort Osage Knap-in and some idea of the range of variation in other knap-ins, we can begin to look in detail at some of the interesting features of the modern knapping world and how the knapping subculture operates as a society.

Knappers at the Knap-in

A couple of years ago I received an email message:

My name is Matt Graesch and I am a student majoring in geology at Iowa State University. I have been an avid knapper for a good portion of my life. I was pleased to notice by chance this afternoon that you are at Grinnell. I have admired your work for some time and would like to ask a few questions.

Is there an Iowa organization of knappers? If so, how can I get in touch? I have had a hard time finding others who are interested and at present know no one else who knaps. Do any knap-ins occur in Iowa?

Is there an area in south east Iowa or north east Missouri where I can collect (legally) Burlington chert? I am at my wits end trying to keep myself supplied with lithics. I am tired of obsidian (I have exhausted the local rock shop's supply anyway) and the assorted cherts I come up with in the glacial till are too small and fractured to allow points larger than an inch. Does a decent source of available material occur in the near area? In short, where do you get your rock? I know I can buy some kinds over the net, but my financial situation as a student limits this.

I am sorry if I seem to be asking so many questions but I feel that I have knapped in anonymity for too long. I wish to be in contact with others who don't think it's weird that my front yard is covered in chips of rock or look at me funny when I am outside at ten at night hitting two rocks together!

The inquisitive student turned out to live in Des Moines, so I invited him to come join the small group of my students and friends who knap together many Friday afternoons, and he soon became a regular. As we became friends, he expressed an interest in going to Fort Osage, and we traveled to the knap-in together several times.

The first time we went together to Fort Osage, I introduced Matt to my friends, and as he is not at all shy, he was soon sitting with Bob Hunt and others, making points and talking. Matt had several interests besides knapping that he shared with many knappers. He made bows and hunted with them, he collected artifacts and knew Midwestern point types well, and he had a lot of detailed knowledge about rocks, their formation, and their geographic distribution. Expertise in these things gained him immediate respect. Over the next few knap-ins, it also became obvious that he was an enthusiastic knapper who was developing considerable skill and should be encouraged.

As I watched Matt interact with the other knappers and remembered my own early experiences, I realized that the knapping world has consistent ways of training and incorporating new members. All cultures do, and the processes of recruiting and including new members reflect things that the group as a whole considers important.

Culture and Community of Practice

When anthropologists talk about culture, they often mean several different but interconnected things. They might mean a group of people, from a small band to a huge nation, that share a basic way of life. More properly, the people form a society, and their culture refers to less tangible aspects, their shared rules and beliefs and common patterns of behavior. We might also refer to material culture, the objects humans create and use, which, of course, result from behavior governed by the rules of a culture.

For our purposes here, I emphasize culture as a system of shared ideas that provide "standards for deciding what is . . . for deciding what can be . . . for deciding how one feels about it, . . . for deciding what to do about it, and . . . for deciding how to go about doing it" (Goodenough 1961, 522). Anthropologists often say that a good ethnography, a description of a culture, should specify what a stranger to that society would have to know in order to act appropriately in any social event (Goodenough 1957; Frake 1964). Anthropologists differ on whether you can or should focus a study on the abstract cultural rules that govern behavior, or whether it is necessary to also consider the behavior itself, since what people do frequently differs from some of the rules they claim to obey, or at least expresses contradictions and variations. Most anthropologists find that behavior and rules are most usefully considered together.

Related fields use similar concepts. For instance, Etienne Wenger, who writes about theories of knowledge and learning, and Jean Lave, an anthropologist interested in learning, use the term "community of practice" to emphasize the social nature of learning (Lave and Wenger 1991; Wenger 1998). Not only do most people learn best as part of ongoing social interactions, but social groups form around particular activities and bodies of knowledge or "practice." Familiar examples are military units, the workers in an office, sports teams, or construction crews. Such groups form small communities with their own sets of rules, or cultures. Members learn not just how to do the job, but how to fit in socially. Individuals in communities of practice also define some of their personal identities through membership and participation in the community, and thus the body of knowledge carried by members of a community or culture must include not just rules, but beliefs, feelings, and emotions. These concepts fit perfectly the world of the knap-in, where to belong you learn not just to knap, but to be a knapper.

Performance

As we have seen, knappers do many things at a knap-in. The underlying meaning of many of the activities is to demonstrate that the people doing them are knappers. Actually, as I mentioned before, not all who are thought of as knappers, or who are at least considered knap-in regulars, actually knap very much or are very good at it. There are even some, like some of the vendors and wives, who do not knap at all, but who are definitely considered members of the knap-in community. Each member of the knap-in establishes some sort of identity, a reason for others to accept him or her as part of the group. The group as a whole also maintains an identity by establishing rules for membership, usually unspoken, activities that unify members, and symbols that can be used by individuals to show that they belong.

For most regulars at Fort Osage, knapping, actually making stone tools, is important because it does three things: First, knapping is one of the most important ways of establishing an identity and showing membership. Knapping in public demonstrates to others that you are a knapper, you belong, and you adhere to the ideals of the knap-in. Second, knapping at a knap-in also reflects the important belief that by practicing and teaching an ancient craft, knappers are preserving a heritage common to all people. Knapping knowledge should be freely taught, and anyone can watch you at the knap-in and learn. Finally, public knapping gives others the opportunity to evaluate your skills and rank you among the knappers.

Knapping not only produces stone tools, but a flow of information. This is why the opportunity to knap with others is one of the main reasons for the existence of knap-ins, and why the emphasis on public performance of a craft is one of the things that distinguish knap-ins from other events.

Knapping performance is an important part of incorporating new knappers. "Newbies" are often given a piece of stone by more experienced friends. This is seen as a way of encouraging them, but the off-hand comment that often goes with the stone is "see what you can do with that." It is considered polite to show appreciation of the gift by actually making something of it and then showing the result to the giver, so this also serves as a test of competence.

On one occasion, a visitor asked Bob Hunt to make a fluted Clovis point so he could see how fluting was done. Bob made the point and fluted one side with his lever device, a modern tool that probably had no parallel in Clovis times. Over the course of the preceding year and a couple of knap-ins, Matt had bought a fluting jig from Jim Regan, fluted everything in sight with it until he had mastered that technique, and then begun to experiment with fluting by direct percussion. Bob handed Matt the almost finished Clovis and asked him to demonstrate for the visitor the final flute by direct percussion "the way they would have done it." Matt set up the platform by pressure flaking, ground it smooth with his abrader, braced the point against a pad on his leg, and struck a decisive blow with his copper billet. There was the sharp crack of a successful flake, and the point was passed around to show that both methods of fluting were equally good. Matt was very pleased: not only had he passed the test and publicly displayed his skill, but Bob had openly acknowledged that Matt was an equal member of the community whose individual skills were valued.

There is a lot of variation in the way knappers treat knapping performance at knap-ins. A few, including some very respected knappers, provide an exception to the rule that knap-ins are for knapping, by not knapping at all, or by doing only basic work rather than showing off their skill. The knappers who don't knap tend to be at both ends of the spectrum of skill. Most are beginners who do not knap at knap-ins either because they are embarrassed to show their lack of skill or because they are more interested in watching other knappers and learning from them, or both. A few skillful knappers have established their reputations elsewhere and may display their skill by bringing products rather than by knapping. A couple of these say that the attention they get by knapping is too distracting. There are a few, even today, who have secret tricks they do not want to reveal.

There is, however, a certain amount of pressure to knap at knap-ins. Beginners who want to learn are told repeatedly (and correctly) that the only way to do so is to practice what you are taught. Knap-ins offer an unusually good opportunity to practice and be coached by a variety of people more skillful than yourself. If you are becoming a knap-in regular and want to establish yourself as a member of the community, it is not absolutely necessary to knap, but it helps. I know several people who started coming to knap-ins as dealers or experts in some other primitive craft, without any intention of learning to knap. Often they find that they have to at least try it. The motivations are complex, and I do not know anyone who claims to have started knapping purely to fit in, but that is surely part of it.

Even some expert knappers can feel some pressure to knap publicly. If you have a skill that is not common, others will ask you to show it to them. Some top knappers intentionally collect an audience and teach them, or demonstrate a particular skill. This spreads knowledge and gives the knapper status in the group. A demonstration of lap knapping by Jim Hopper will be described in detail later. Jim had an unusual and admired technique, and knappers who saw his work wanted to see how he did it. Eventually he did a couple of formal demonstrations at Fort Osage, but lap knapping requires grinding and cutting machines, so it is not easy to do the whole process at a knap-in. Moreover, some other knappers felt that lap knapping with modern tools was in some ways "cheating." I felt it was significant that at the knap-ins following his demonstration of lap knapping, Jim was increasingly to be seen making percussion bifaces. At first they were only adequate, but it did not take him long to apply the same precision to percussion that is evident in his pressure flaking. He was soon known for making some of the thinnest large bifaces at the knap-ins, and he began spending most of his time at the knap-in making bifaces. Undoubtedly there were more reasons than just proving he could really knap, but that he surely did, too.

A performance depends on having an audience. Many knappers simply knap and do not think of themselves as performing, yet when someone stops to watch them or begins to ask questions, they respond by explaining what they are doing, pointing out tricks and problems, or even changing what they are doing to answer a question or make it more interesting for the watcher. Moreover, sociologist Erving Goffman (1959) would point out that all public action is at least potentially a performance, in the sense that it is managed in such a way as to present a particular public "face." At the knap-in, you can reduce risk and present the face of a skilled knapper by focusing on materials, forms, and techniques that are most familiar to you. It is also common to casually scatter around a few successful pieces in progress, or maybe display a case filled with your better work, to show that you know what you are doing, even if the point in your hand is a disaster.

Some knappers are more explicitly performing all the time, knapping consciously as if they had an audience, and sometimes making an effort to attract one. For instance, a knapper who wants attention can easily get it by working large pieces. Striking a large piece of flint makes a distinctive noise; if it is good quality, it may ring like a bell, and a heavy blow produces grunts of effort and the ringing crash of a large flake being detached. If you want to be flamboyant about this, you can. George Eklund, for instance, is one of the most exciting knappers to watch. He often handles large pieces and works very fast, flipping his bifaces up in the air as he turns them over to work on the other face and striking them almost before they are at rest again. He jokes and explains as he works. He knaps so fast and heatedly that it is sometimes hard to follow what he is doing, so he is not the most useful for beginners to watch, but everyone enjoys the show. George is also quite willing to slow down and explain carefully if beginners ask questions. Bob Hunt is less flamboyant, but it is well known that he likes to work gigantic pieces of flint, and it is fun to watch him solve the problems and listen as friends tease him about flaws and mistakes. The crowd remains in suspense, admiring successful flakes and laughing and groaning in sympathy when an hour's work shatters with a single blow.

Learning to Knap

Learning at a knap-in involves not just learning to knap, but learning to be a knapper. To become a member of the knap-in community, most learn to knap at least some, and all must learn how to behave at knap-ins and absorb to some degree the knap-in ethos.

Learning to knap used to be almost entirely a matter of teaching yourself. Until the 1970s, there were few knappers around, no knap-ins, and relatively little academic or public interest. There were no instructional books or videos, the network of knappers was completely undeveloped, and most of those who did knap were either academics or artifact fakers, or were regarded as fakers by both the academic and collecting communities. Nevertheless, a surprising number of people figured out how to knap, and many of the older knappers are proud that they did it all themselves, and feel that modern learners have it too easy.

Now there are several good instructional books, but the wave of the future seems to be videos. For teaching some aspects of knapping, a good video is much more effective than written words or pictures. Videos available now include some academic ones intended to demonstrate the basics of knapping to a class, and those meant for use by people trying to learn to knap, which are mostly produced by nonacademic knappers (Whittaker 1995). Classroom knapping films include a video reissue of films made of Don Crabtree in the 1970s (Crabtree 1992) and a newer video by Bruce Bradley (1989). Instructional videos made by nonacademic knappers and explicitly intended to teach knapping techniques have become both more numerous and more specialized in the last few years, and, among the better examples, include videos featuring Waldorf, Ratzat, Blackwell, Cannon, Warmuskerken, Metcalfe, and Redfearn (see the list in Bibliography). Not only do knapping videos teach (and document) various techniques, they also reflect some of the basic knapping ethos. Waldorf and Metcalfe, for instance, talk on their videos about being a knapper, how they started, and ethical concerns. All the videos offer tips and demonstrations; teaching is a value of the knapping community. The videos are, of course, recorded performances as well. They tend to be made by knappers who are articulate teachers and performers in the knap-in context as well, although there are exceptions as too many rush to cash in on the market. Several videos even incorporate knapping humor and insider jokes. Waldorf's *Caught Knapping* (1992) features a tame blue jay. Partly in response, Blackwell's fluting video (1995) includes a Rube Goldberg device controlled by a chicken. Craig Ratzat included a Band-Aid in the packaging of *Lap Knapping* (1996), and Dale Cannon (Cannon et al. 2000) sings a song.

There are vastly more aids available to would-be knappers today than in the past, and it is probably possible to buy these, work in isolation, and still learn much faster than many of us did when I was learning. However, the best way to learn to knap is still face to face. The growth of knap-ins has probably been a major influence in the explosion of knapping. Knappers learn by watching others at knap-ins, and some find mentors or begin long-term friendships. In the last five years, the Internet has created a new and influential means of communication that makes personal connections among knappers and the growth of the community even more rapid.

My mail survey asked 160 knappers how they learned. One question asked respondents who taught them what and when, in an attempt to see if any particular individuals were especially influential. A second question asked knappers to rank (1 = most important, 2 = next most important, etc.) several items under the question "How did you learn?" The choices were "taught by friends," "paid for lessons," "watched others," "read books," "looked at artifacts," "figured it out by self," "went to knap-ins," and "other" (Table 5.1). Note that when the survey was conducted in 1994, videos were still rare enough that I did not think to put them on the list, and no one cited them in the "other" category, so they had not yet had much impact. I suspect they would now receive an increasingly high score. The Internet also did not figure in the knap-in world at that point.

The help of friends was considered the most important part of learning by 27 percent of the respondents, and 23 percent ranked self-teaching as the most important. Only a few knappers said that paid lessons were most important. Reading, watching other knappers, going to knap-ins, and looking at artifacts were not first in the minds of as many knappers, but were often ranked fairly high. The importance of reading was a bit surprising, given how few books on knapping there have been

Table 5.1
Percentages of Knappers Who Learned in Particular Ways

Rank of Importance	Friends	Lessons	Watch	Read	Artifacts	Self	Knap-in	Other
1	27	4	14	14	9	23	9	4
2	6	3	18	19	13	14	13	4
3	4	3	15	15	11	6	11	1
4	5	1	13	8	8	5	13	1
5	3	1	3	7	8	5	9	0
6	1	1	1	1	5	7	4	0
7	1	1	1	0	1	1	1	1
8	0	2	0	1	1	1	0	1

Total 160 knappers, but percentage totals do not add up to 100% because some knappers did not answer all questions.

until recently. Books mentioned by name as important in another question (Who taught or influenced you?) included eleven mentions of Waldorf *(The Art of Flintknapping)*, three "books" in general, one mention of Callahan's "Basics of Biface Knapping," and one of my *Flintknapping: Making and Understanding Stone Tools.* Other comments suggest that reading was ranked high partly because reading about stone tools and prehistory inspired some knappers to begin, even if it did not teach them specific techniques. The influence of articles in *Chips, Flint Knappers Exchange,* and other newsletters was probably also reflected in this question, although the choice specified "books."

The change from individuals teaching themselves, to a network of knappers, was visible when the responses were divided into knappers with less than ten years' experience (84 of them) and those with ten years' or more experience (71). Learning from friends was important to both groups, but less important to the older knappers than the less-experienced group. However, self-teaching was far more important to the older knappers ("most important" for 35 percent) than to the less-experienced ("most important" for 12 percent). Knap-ins were most important for only 4 percent of the older group, while knap-ins were most important to 15 percent of the newer knappers. Watching and reading were also less important to the senior knappers. Paid lessons, although a minor factor for all, made more of a difference to more recent knappers.

These patterns also affected comparisons of the Fort Osage knappers with other knappers. The Fort Osage knappers by definition go to at least one knap-in and usually found them an important learning source. The non–Fort Osage knappers were a bit older on the average, and not all of them go to knap-ins.

If I had to produce a sort of average "How I first learned to knap" story, it would go like this: "I found an arrowhead, wondered how it was made, and started experimenting. I figured out a little bit, but then got stuck. Then I met X, and he taught me enough to go on from there." This is a repeated pattern in interviews, conversations, and on the survey. It is, in fact, my own knapping story as well (Whittaker 1994, 2–5). The relative importance of learning from others and figuring out things on your own has shifted over time, but the basic story is the same. As I got to know other knappers and saw that some were unusually interested in teaching, or were admired and sought out, I wondered if I could see that in my survey.

The survey asked both who taught or influenced you and whom you taught. Combining the names in these answers produced the following chart of knapper learning networks (Figure 5.1). Most of the knappers who were mentioned as teachers by more than three other knappers are Fort Osage knappers, but this is hard to evaluate. More than half of the survey responses were from Fort Osage knappers, whom we should expect to be teaching each other. On the other hand, Fort Osage is one of the most popular knap-ins, and most of the teachers cited are respected knappers, who not only make an effort to teach people, in some cases offering classes or paid lessons, but also attend a lot of knap-ins.

The learning network chart also shows how interconnected knappers are now, learning from each other and exchanging ideas. In places, several generations of learning are visible. Don Crabtree, considered by many to be the founder of modern American knapping, taught both Errett Callahan and J. B. Sollberger among the survey respondents. They, in turn, influenced many others; Callahan through his classes and Sollberger through a large group of Texas knappers who are poorly represented here. Sollberger's influence, at least in the common use of a lever device for fluting, is much greater than the chart shows. Not all

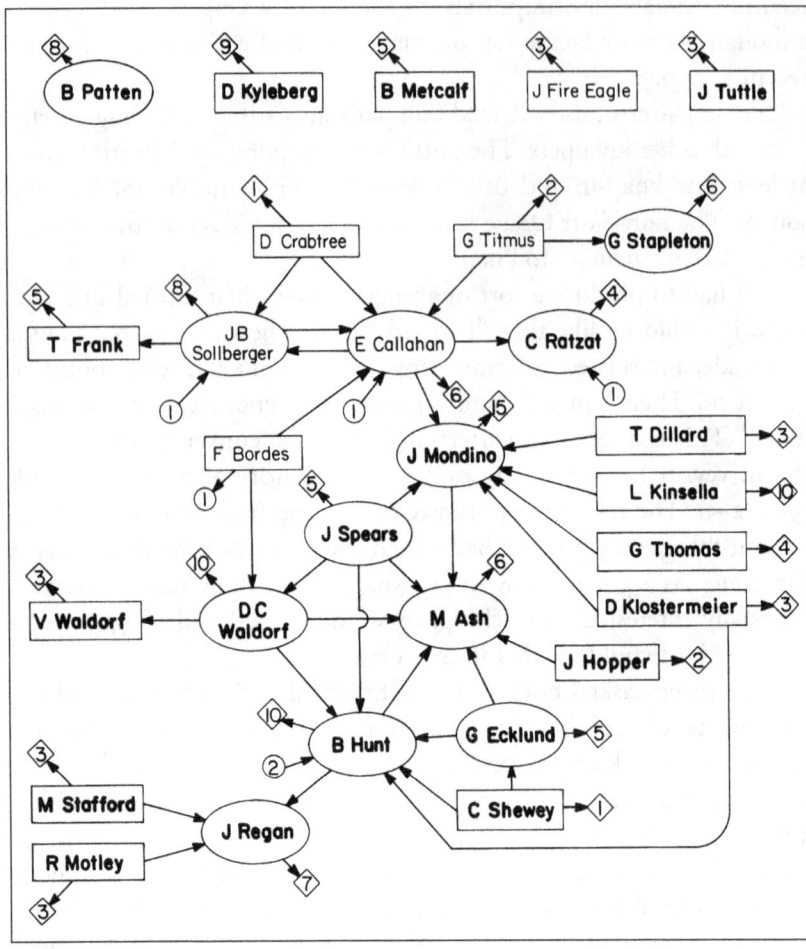

Figure 5.1. Simplified knapper learning network. Many relationships that I know to exist were not mentioned by respondents and are not included on this chart, and only some of the named knappers were survey respondents. Arrows indicate direction of information flow. Bolded names are Fort Osage knappers. Around names, the rectangles indicate people mentioned only as teachers, ovals those mentioned as both teachers and students. Numbers indicate additional individuals. Drawn by Matt Hedman, Amy Henderson.

the connections that I know about were mentioned by respondents, and as some of the people on this chart were not surveyed, or are dead, the tangle should realistically be much greater. Crabtree, Sollberger, Callahan, and Titmus all had close relations at one time or another and represent a major Western "school." All were involved in the early development of knap-ins and had strong interests in the scientific uses of knapping. Callahan taught Stafford, and Sollberger influenced Don Kylberg, Gene Stapleton, and Woody Blackwell, to mention just a few of the connections not documented by the survey. In the Midwest, D. C. Waldorf and Bob Hunt form the center of a node of knappers with Fort Osage and Midwestern connections.

Learning the Ethos

Anthropologists would say that culture is a shared body of knowledge, including rules for correct behavior. In Lave and Wenger's terms, communities of practice include knowledge about how to be a member as well as how to do the job or perform the activity. Membership in any social group requires learning a vast amount of complex and nebulous knowledge. All members of a culture learn its ways partly by being taught, and partly by observing others, and by the trial and error of participation. Making stone tools is a major part of knapping culture, but it is not the only thing necessary. Much of stone tool making is technique, which can be explicitly taught, and often is. Other parts of knap-in culture are more often absorbed than taught, as new knappers observe the behavior of those around them, listen to their comments, read the newsletters, and, most importantly, try to act as knappers at the knap-in.

I have characterized the knap-in ethos as appreciation of the art, enjoyment of the craft, sharing and teaching, and fellowship, with rejection of competition and hierarchy. It is fair to say that appreciation of knapping is foremost among these elements. It is what brings knappers together in the first place and unites even those who disagree on many other matters. It connects knappers to the non-knappers who interact with the knap-in, including collectors hostile to "fakers" and members of the public curious about arrowheads. The interest in stone tools is more often a necessary precondition for entering the knapping world than a part of the ethos that is picked up once one is a member.

Public knapping expresses and communicates the ethic of teaching and sharing knapping knowledge. The whole knap-in is set up so that knappers can circulate and exchange knowledge, ask for help, and teach the public. The loose organization avoids raising barriers to the individual quest for knowledge, but at the same time puts the burden upon the individual learner, rather than an institution or formalized teacher. This is coherent with the knap-in rejection of authority and hierarchy, and also conforms with the belief that a true knapper, who appreciates the art of knapping, should actively seek to advance in skill and understanding.

The rules that ensure good fellowship are somewhat more complex. Rejection of hierarchy and competition is important and is expressed in the very organization of the knap-in, as well as in comments and gossip among the knappers. Individuals who attempt to impose themselves on others, as bosses, authorities, or experts, are not well received. I will discuss the nature of competition and hierarchy later. For now, it is enough to say that knappers are constantly ranking themselves and others by knapping skill, but avoid admitting this and keep competition for status as much out of sight as possible. It is permissible, and common, to describe other knappers' skills with admiration, and even to flatter those knappers to their face, but it is not acceptable to boast about one's own work.

One result of the negative attitude toward hierarchy is a deep ambivalence toward authorities on knapping knowledge. It is recognized that there are many different ways of doing the same thing in knapping, and this diversity is generally valued, even as knappers argue constantly and sometimes heatedly over, for instance, the "best" way to flute a point or thin a biface. The instructions given in "how-to" texts, like Waldorf's and my own, are bound to spark disagreement from many knappers. The reception depends on how things are phrased. For instance, in my *Flintknapping* book, I tried to explain alternative techniques and point out disagreements with my theories. Knappers who were more skillful than I were generally complimentary and unoffended, although they did not hesitate to point out why their preferred technique was better. When Errett Callahan (1996a) wrote a generally favorable but quite critical review of my book, some of the Fort Osage knappers were quick to take sides against him because he was much more dogmatic in his statements than I was.

Similarly, as an academic archaeologist, I was regarded with reservations by some knappers. Although knappers, and especially collectors, are generally interested in archaeological information and respect some academic authorities, they feel slighted by the academic world. They are fond of citing instances where a knapper's practical knowledge was more accurate than an academic's theories. Gregory Perino, for example, is best described as a nonacademic archaeologist with a foot in both the scholarly world and the collecting world. His point-type book (Perino 1985) is widely cited by both archaeologists and collectors. I hear again and again knappers who in one conversation will cite Perino's book, or his judgment on a point, as conclusive evidence, and in the next conversation will provide a gleeful anecdote about how he was fooled by a fake or mistaken about a prehistoric point.

My response as an archaeologist who is trying to be an ethnographer in the knap-in culture is to keep a low profile. I have information to share, and many of my friends at Fort Osage are eager to ask me what archaeologists think about a new find in Africa or get my opinion on a point type. When not asked, I prefer to listen, since I learn more that way. On some subjects, like Midwestern point types, I am happy to defer to others who know more anyway. By trying not to exploit my academic credentials too much or set myself up as an authority, I maintain a friendly and egalitarian flow of information, learn more than I would otherwise, and adhere to the cultural rules of proper knap-in behavior.

Politics, Gender, and Ethnicity

The rules of knap-in etiquette are the more important, as knappers include a wide range of people of diverse and sometimes conflicting backgrounds and viewpoints. As I said earlier, knappers come from all walks of life. However, politically conservative viewpoints seem to dominate the discussions I hear around me at Fort Osage. As an academic and political liberal, I get teased a lot. For my part, I am amazed that some otherwise intelligent people get their news and views from people like Rush Limbaugh and Art Bell.

The survey reflects another important demographic fact: the knap-in is dominated by men. The survey mailing lists include a few extraneous people who came to knap-ins or got the newsletters but were not really knappers, but still, the lists provide the best estimate. There are seventy names (5 percent) on the two lists that are apparently female, but I am not inclined to trust this information too far. Initials and ambiguous names may conceal a few additional female knappers, but many of the female names seem to be artisans, spouses, or others rather than really being knappers. For instance, of nine females on the Fort Osage list that I know personally, only five of them are knappers. The dearth of female knappers is significant, too, when one notices in the artifact collector literature that this related hobby attracts many women, although here again men are the majority.

Knapping is a male craft, in the minds of both most knappers and most archaeologists, and perhaps the archaeological literature best explains why. Alice Kehoe (1991) suggests that the nineteenth-century picture of the warlike savage led anthropologists to describe most bifacial tools, the most interesting pieces made by knappers, as weapons, projectile points which would have been used for hunting and for war. As she points out, we might expect that many of the "projectile points" were actually used as knives. In fact, the archaeological record supports this, but knappers and archaeologists who recognize that the resharpened edges of such tools as Thebes and Dalton points indicate knife use still assign these knives to men. Men made them, men used them for male activities like butchery; such is the almost automatic assumption.

There is some reason to argue that in many cultures, stone tools were associated with activities like hunting that were most often performed by men, and thus the tools might be expected to be made by men as well. However, there are a surprising number of ethnographic accounts of women making stone tools, and even hunting (e.g., Jarvenpa and Brumbach 1995). The ethnographic record is almost certainly biased. It was largely assembled by male ethnographers who often considered male activities more interesting and important, and perhaps found it easier to participate in and observe what men were doing, so we can be fairly sure that women knapped, hunted, made tools, and performed "male" crafts much more often than existing records show. Nevertheless, even archaeologists who are overtly aware of this find it hard to shake off their biases. Joan Gero (1991) and Kenneth Sassaman (1992), for instance, argue strongly that women should not be neglected when considering stone tool manufacture and use. They correctly point out that many stone tools are simple to make; anyone can be taught to make a sharp flake in a few minutes. It makes no sense for women or even children to rely on men for such easily made necessities. However, Gero and Sassaman both end by suggesting that women at least produced simple flake tools, but cannot bring themselves to assign more complex bifaces to female knappers. One can find ethnographic support for such a situation in some societies (Bird 1993; Gorman 1995), and I bring it up here not so much to argue one way or the other as to point out how deeply the bias against female knappers has penetrated the scientific and supposedly self-aware work of anthropologists as well as popular stereotypes.

The bias against female participation in "male" activities remains strong in American society. The knap-in is overwhelmingly a male event. Knapping makes weapons and hunting gear. The knap-in community overlaps with the atlatl enthusiasts, the primitive bowyers and archers, and the black powder and rendezvous groups, also dominated by men. That said, it is important to note that there are female knappers, and there is no hostility toward them. In fact, many knappers express a desire for more female participation, and I do not recall hearing any slighting comments about the ability of women to learn knapping.

There are, in fact, some accomplished female knappers. At Fort Osage, Val Waldorf is perhaps the best known. Typically, however, she is more recognized for her skill as an artist and editor of *Chips,* and she rarely knaps at knap-ins. Several other women occasionally knap, but they are a very small presence. Most were drawn in because of the interests of a husband or boyfriend, or came with another primitive craft and took up some knapping. No female knapper is at the highest levels of knapping prestige. The better ones are readily accepted as knappers, but considered unusual enough to attract comment. When D. C. Waldorf (2000) ran an article in *Chips* on Clovis points that featured modern points by a number of knappers, one was "an obsidian Clovis made by Angela Hopkins of Pella, Iowa. She is one of our few lady knappers and a 'beginner.' Way to go Angela!"

Ethnic affiliation is another aspect of identity that looms large in contemporary America. Again, this is not reflected in my survey, but the knappers are overwhelmingly "white" as well as male. I have not attempted to collect information about knappers' race or ethnicity, either in the survey or in conversations, so my comments are largely impressionistic, but very few knappers are visibly "people of color," to use today's phrase. A number of knappers claim some Native American ancestry, and I know a few who are enrolled members of various tribes. As we shall see, there is a considerable market for stonework, and I find it surprising that Indian artists have not picked up knapping along with the other traditional and modern crafts for which there is a good market. It is not uncommon to see Indian art stores selling bow and arrow sets that look well made until you see that the artist used the hideous flake points that are mass produced in Mexico. Mike He Crow, who grew up in the Dakota community of Pine Ridge, makes bows and arrows, flutes, beadwork, and other crafts. He tells me he knows a few Native American knappers, but he is one of very few who attend knap-ins and use their knapping in craft sales.

The political conservatism and rural orientation of many knappers means that there are sometimes jokes and commentary that would be considered offensive by some oversensitive souls, and occasionally even some speech that is overtly racist. Comments about the supposed inability of some groups to achieve high civilization are especially irritating to me, as that is a racist fallacy that archaeologists often find themselves arguing against. However, on one occasion I witnessed an event that expressed for me how the knapping ethos and the normal good hearts of most people usually overcome ideological biases. A young black man from Kansas City was among the tourists at Fort Osage one day, wandering among the knappers, asking questions. He happened to hit upon two knappers I have heard expressing negative opinions about African Americans in general, and admired a point one was shaping. When he asked for more details about how it was made and expressed an interest in learning to knap, he was invited to sit down, and the two knappers spent an hour coaching him and gave him a handful of material and a basic pressure flaking kit. To be a knapper at the knap-in, you must be able to knap and willing to teach, and the values of the knap-in should take precedence over abstractions like political disagreements or racial biases.

Expressions of Identity

The knap-in ethos is conveyed by the actions and words of the knappers and also by the symbols that they use to show that they are members of the group.

One way of showing membership in a group is by demonstrating understanding of jargon or insider jokes, both requiring knowledge that only members are likely to have, and allowing both public and private signaling of membership. Knapper jargon includes the technical terms of knapping, some of the names of stones, and ways of describing stones and knapped art. All of these are covered elsewhere; here I want to consider some of the humor of knappers.

I have already discussed the performance aspect of knap-ins. Knappers also perform for the non-knapping public. There is a great deal of public interest in arrowheads and archaeology, and in crafts and hobbies, so knapping demonstrations are easy crowd pleasers for state archaeology weeks, museum open houses, local lapidary society meetings, and so on. To the knapper, the ability to show off his craft is another way of expressing identity, possessing an uncommon skill and being the focus of attention because of it. Being asked to do public demonstrations through the various networks of knappers, collectors, and archaeologists is another mark of knapping prestige. But knappers are not above playing with this concept. As Goffman (1959) points out, the performance of any social identity usually has a "front stage" of information that is presented to the audience and a "back stage" of things that are obscure or even intentionally concealed. When one performs as an "authority," it is common to demonstrate skill by making a task visibly spectacular. If you can perform it so well that it seems easy or natural to you, your authority is augmented. It is usually best if the details of technical difficulty remain mystical.

On one occasion, Tony Romano was asked to do a demonstration for Minnesota's Archaeology Week in a large chain bookstore. His friend and knapping mentor Jim Regan was not available; it was his wife Pat's birthday. However, Jim said he might manage to swing by if it was okay with Pat. Tony told me,

> I did my usual demonstration, explaining the principles of knapping, talking geology and raw materials, showed them the major techniques, answered questions. Finally a woman asks, "How long does it take to learn that?" I look up, and Jim had come in and was hanging back among the books. "You, sir," I said, "would you come up here a moment?" Jim does the "who, me?" thing and comes over. "Now, sit down here. You hold the rock like this, and the billet like this, and see if you can knock off a flake." So Jim took the tool and the piece of flint, and wham wham wham he made a beautiful biface in a couple of minutes. I just looked over at the lady and said, "See, any damn fool can do this!"

It had, of course, become obvious that this was not true.

Much knap-in humor springs from two major roots, the perceived absurdity of knapping, and stereotypes of prehistory. Knappers know full well that their craft is unusual, even eccentric. It has little practical application, and much of the public does not understand either how it is done or why it would appeal to anyone. On the other hand, a great many people have at least a passing interest in stone tools and prehistory, and perhaps a majority of adult Americans have some sort of hobby. Knappers, like many hobbyists, are devoted to their craft to the point of obsession, and this is what the humor focuses on. In this respect, it is much like the humor of other hobbies, which also pokes fun at obsession.

Knapping has not hit the mainstream of American culture, so you can not yet buy tacky mass-market T-shirts. Nevertheless, T-shirts and bumper stickers are cheap and easy to produce on a small scale, and they are a favored medium of self-expression these days. Goffman (1971) coined the term "tie-sign" to describe the "evidence about relationships, that is, about ties between persons, whether involving objects, acts, or expressions," that we all present in daily interaction. Tie-signs are a necessary part of social interaction because they are culturally coded to tell others who we are, what subgroups we are affiliated with, and thus what kinds of relationships and behavior are expected of both parties. Hodder (1982) and others have suggested that where accurate information is socially critical, the symbols will be increasingly visible and easy to read. For instance, gender is a critical social distinction in American society, and it is usually easy to tell immediately, even at a distance, whether a person is a man or a woman. Clothes, hair, and posture are strongly coded with this information, and when they have been intentionally made ambiguous; that, too, is important knowledge for social interaction.

Nevertheless, tie-signs are often ambiguous, not just because others must know enough of the meaning of your symbols to understand their message, but because the intensity of affiliation is likely to be unclear. For instance, Rubinstein (1995), discussing clothing, distinguishes between "tie-signs" that signal membership and "tie-symbols" that merely reflect support for a group or an idea. As her own examples show, this is a shaky distinction. I remember passing through "the City," the banking district of London, one fall. At closing time, the streets filled with an army of clones, a crow-flock of young men and women dressed unimaginatively in black, each with a cell phone clamped to his or her ear. For some, these outfits were doubtless a mandatory corporate uniform, with color and pattern specified by the boss. For others, the funeral attendant look-alike clothes were probably more the expression of membership in an occupational subculture, or even just registered agreement with the commercial and political ideals of the office drudge.

Naturally enough, as knap-ins became popular, some knappers began to supply personal identity advertisements, tie-signs in the form of humorous T-shirts and bumper stickers. Explaining jokes dilutes the humor, but fortunately, most knap-in examples are fairly transparent.

Several T-shirts have wide circulation. Larry Kinsella sells a T-shirt designed by his son, with a cartoon imitating the style of Garry Larson. A caveman is seen throwing back his cloak to reveal a clandestine display of atlatls and darts, with the slogan playing on a well-known NRA bumper sticker: "When atlatls are outlawed, only outlaws will have atlatls." Another shirt has a drawing of a Clovis point and the words "Grind it, Bind it, and Shove it in a Mammoth." Like the atlatl one, this reflects the stereotyped importance of hunting and weapons in the past and the somewhat macho attitude that some knappers take to the largely male world of knapping. Like much male humor, both shirts have sexual echoes. Both are also insider jokes; not many people know what an atlatl is, or that the basal edges of Clovis points were usually ground to prevent them from cutting the bindings that fastened them to the shaft. Both are also self-deprecating: knappers are really neither the rebels they sometimes like to think, nor members of a large and powerful lobby, nor eager to take on prehistoric elephants with stone tools.

When J. B. Sollberger died, Woody Blackwell, who considered him a mentor, arrived at Fort Osage with a large box of T-shirts, which he passed around as a tribute. The shirt, which I had seen previously, had a portrait of J. B. and some Clovis points and the title "J. B. Sollberger Clovis Factory." Sollberger is largely responsible for the popularity of lever devices for fluting. The T-shirt commemorated an admired knapper and poked respectful fun at his most typical product and his productivity. In addition, it draws humor from anachronism, the contrast between the idealized, individualized craftsman of Clovis times and modern mass production.

Other T-shirts have been produced as mementos of particular knap-ins, and the Fort Osage and Evergreen Lake Knap-ins have each had hats at one knap-in (Figure 5.2). Knappers also sometimes wear shirts that are not specifically knap-in-oriented, but are appropriate to a knap-in. One sees Indian art and Southwestern designs, arrowheads, archery motifs, and the shirts of various archaeological organizations.

Figure 5.2. Glenn Leesman, who organizes the Evergreen Lake Knap-in, wears T-shirt and hat from past years. Fort Osage, 1998.

George Weymouth, a wildlife artist, sells a whole line of shirts with different groups of projectile points on them.

Americans are also fond of using their cars to display their personalities and affiliations. License plates with "Knapper," "Flint," or some variant are common, and a few bumper stickers are available. Dale Cannon sells several, including a play on milk ads, "Got Flint?" and the suggestive "Wanna Grind?" These serve not just to display a knapper's affiliation, but also help advertise for Dale's Future Artifact knife sales.

The ambiguity of tie-signs is apparent in the reading of knapper T-shirts and bumper stickers. They are most important as a means of signaling your identity to other knappers. If someone approaches me, looks at my shirt, and asks, "What the heck is a Clovis?" I know he is not a knapper, but he probably has also just told me that he does not recognize this significant part of my identity. I now have the choice of explaining, thus further expressing my knapping identity, or not. At a knap-in, with visitors, newcomers, tourists, craft vendors, point purchasers, and others all milling around, it is sometimes useful to be recognized as one of the adepts. Of course, since tie-signs may be used deceptively, the burly fellow wearing the "Mammoth Meat Cutters Union—You Stab 'Em, We Slab 'Em" T-shirt may not know as much as he wants you to think. He may even be a spying anthropologist, an accusation I have faced a couple of times!

Joking serves another purpose at the knap-in besides displaying membership. It keeps your image in line with the expected egalitarian ideals of the knap-in. Even the best knappers make jokes about their work. When asked what he is making, a knapper is never making "a big Clovis point." If he is speaking to another knapper, it is usually "gravel," or "little rocks out of big ones," or something equally facetious (Figure 5.3). If the observer is another knapper, he ought to be able to figure out what is really going on anyway.

The self-deprecation and humility, false or real, that is the norm in

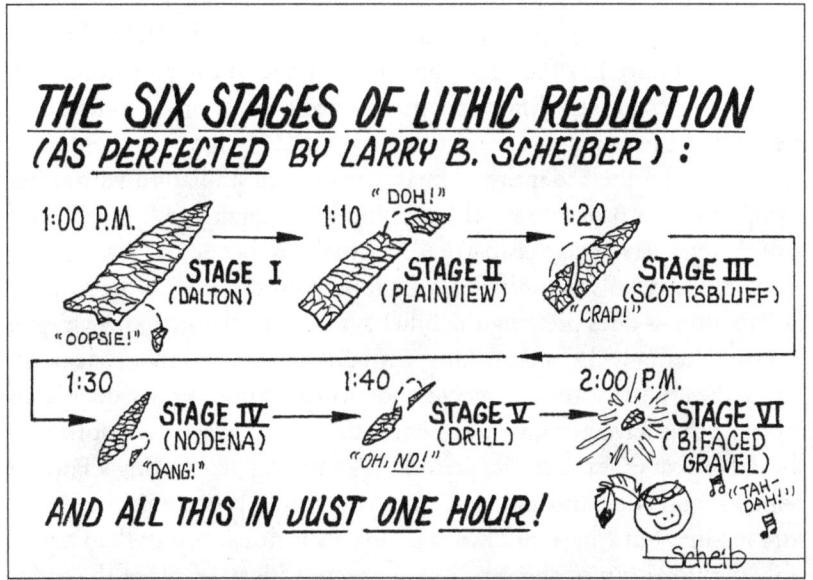

Figure 5.3. Cartoon by Scheiber—knapping production stages reinterpreted as errors. Chips 14 (2): 24, 2002. Courtesy Val Waldorf, Larry Scheiber.

knapping jokes may work as protective magic. Most people, even the least superstitious, consider it bad luck to speak too confidently about something that is desired but might not happen. George Gmelch (1971) has studied magical beliefs of American baseball players. It is well known that you must never speak about a no-hitter while a game is in progress, for fear of jinxing the pitcher, and other sports have similar taboos. Gmelch also found that baseball magic conformed to the expectations of Bronislaw Malinowski (1925), who, long ago, while working with the Trobriand Islanders, proposed that while all people count primarily on physical action to deal with predictable events, life is full of uncontrollable factors that most folk attempt to control by magic. Moreover, the riskier the proceeding, the more likely magical beliefs will be brought to bear. In the modern example of baseball, for instance, Gmelch found that fielding, in which errors are relatively rare, has few magical practices attached. In contrast, hitting and pitching are very chancy. A pitcher's best pitch may be hit for a home run, or a feeble ball may tempt a batter to swing and miss. Accordingly, players attempt to control the uncontrollable with rituals like touching their numbers, taboos on certain "unlucky" actions, and "magical" fetishes carried in their pockets.

Knapping appears to have little of the overt magic of baseball. Knappers avoid attracting bad luck by speaking confidently of the outcome, but I have not found anyone who admits to carrying good luck charms for knapping. Many knappers have clothes or personal ornaments that they wear at knap-ins, or even in daily life, but these seem more to signal their identity as knappers or their affiliation with other groups than to promote good knapping luck (Figure 5.4). Nor have I found knappers who see particular rituals as necessary for success. Some of the details of individuals' knapping procedure may be ritualistic in nature—does pressing the billet against the platform or swinging it experimentally before striking actually improve aim, or do such actions really serve to increase confidence by repeating a sequence of motions that have become meaningful because they seem to work? We should expect that the riskier actions in knapping, like fluting a Folsom point, should demand more magic than simple procedures like pressure flaking, but I have not heard of any such rituals, other than a possibly fictitious rumor that one knapper sends his wife out of the room when fluting, which could be interpreted in a number of ways.

There may be an element of magic in a knapper's preference for his

Figure 5.4. Knapper chic: Jim Grybush with arrowhead earring at Fort Osage, 1997.

or her own tools. Artisans in many crafts tend to be possessive about their tool kits, and a knapper's tool kit is a very personal possession. Most of the tools are fairly durable and not expensive, but some tools a knapper will be reluctant to lend. Many knappers make their own tools and sometimes elaborate them with carved handles, unusual machining, exotic wood, or the like (see Figure 2.10). They shape tools to fit hands, and over long use, the grips develop a high polish and comfortable personality. Again, while there may be an element of superstition in a knapper's reluctance to use an unfamiliar tool for a tricky shot, mostly it is an eminently practical recognition that familiarity and practice produce success. Knappers also like to experiment with new tools and are suckers for gadgetry. I have seen no sign that tools, even such things as fluting jigs, which are the focus of inventive attention and used in high-risk procedures, are ever decorated to attract good luck. Decorative tools and personalized equipment seem instead to be another expression of identity as a knapper and an individual.

The expression of individual identity as a knapper and of membership in the knapping community is a strong force among knappers. It pervades interactions at knap-ins and with the public; it is expressed in humor and in tools, displayed on clothing and cars. The knap-in world brings in new members, training them to make stone tools and to be part of the community. Successful new members must be willing recruits, and the importance of knapping in the lives of knap-in regulars is a bond among us. Next we must consider what it is that some people find so compelling about an ancient craft.

The Chipping Keeps You Going: Why Knappers Knap

At my second knap-in at Fort Osage, I had just met D. C. Waldorf when our chat was dramatically interrupted. A burly, bearded man wearing black leather motorcycle togs pushed through the crowd and practically fell on his knees in front of D. C. to thank him profusely for writing *The Art of Flint Knapping*. He said he had been in the hospital, almost lost his leg, and couldn't ride his motorcycle, but he found Waldorf's book and took up flintknapping instead, and it saved his life! They had a long conversation, and when the guy left, D. C. said to those of us who had been listening, "Sometimes when you can't do nothing else, the chipping keeps you going." Not everyone is as emotional about knapping as the motorcyclist, whom I never saw again, and not everyone is as committed to it in as many ways as D. C., who is a professional and gets a good deal of prestige from his skills. Nevertheless, this set me thinking about why people knap and why some find knapping sufficiently meaningful that it shapes large parts of their lives.

I knap both as part of my professional interest in archaeology and as a hobby because I think knapping is fun, but I was still surprised when I discovered how many other knappers there are. Knapping requires considerable work to learn, and until recently there have been very few sources to learn from. Knapping has almost no practical use in the modern world. Although a few outdoor survival schools teach the rudiments, I have never heard of anyone whose life was saved by knapping in a survival situation. Lots of people have at least a faint interest in prehistoric stone tools, but many of them sneer at reproductions as "fakes." The raw material is scarce, heavy, and often dirty, the waste products are sharp and messy, and the process can be dangerous. Why do so many people learn to knap and enthusiastically pursue an obsolete, impractical, and difficult art?

First some statistics. In my questionnaire I asked, "Why do you knap? What do you like about knapping?" An open-ended question like this, actually two related questions, gets a wide variety of answers (Table 5.2). Responses on the 160 questionnaires ranged from blanks and question marks to vague comments like "I enjoy it" to minute specifics such as "I love the tinkle of the thin ones that hit the pile of chips." Many responses included several things, so the answers do not add up to the number of respondents. The general patterns are close to what I hear at knap-ins.

Most knappers knap for fun, and vague comments about knapping being enjoyable or fun or satisfying were very common, but not very satisfying to my curiosity. Why is knapping fun? The most common single response category was that knapping is relaxing or therapeutic, not a surprising response given that most knappers are doing it for fun. Almost as many responses mentioned that knapping is "challenging" or used similar concepts like pride in doing something difficult, "pleasure in completing a high-risk work of art," or doing something that not many people can. I noticed that "relaxing" and "challenging" occurred together in many responses, and many of my friends at knap-ins say them in the same breath. I suspect that for many people, to be relaxing, a craft has to absorb them, require attention, and distract them from their normal life. Some of the responses confirm this. One knapper wrote, "It is the only legal activity I have discovered to get relief from job stress." (I had to wonder what else he does in his spare time!) Two others explicitly mentioned that they used knapping "to escape."

Quite a few knappers mentioned how knapping helps them understand prehistory or ancient stone tools. Almost as many claimed it gave them a feeling of connection or kinship to the past. I consider these somewhat connected, but they rarely occurred together. The few archaeologists in the sample usually mentioned knapping as a key to understanding the past and sometimes gave that as their only reason for knapping. I realized as I analyzed the responses that a few years ago I would have been similar, but now, if I am asked to explain why I knap, I always talk about what an enjoyable craft it is, as well as giving my scholarly reasons. The "understanding the past" answers were usually more vague when they were not from archaeologists, but also

Table 5.2
Survey Responses to "Why do you knap?"

45	"Relaxation, therapy," or similar
38	Challenging:
	25 used the word "challenge"
	13 used similar concepts: "pride," "accomplishment," etc.
31	Vague answers like "satisfying," "fun," "hobby," "enjoy it"
26	To understand the past—"study," "interest," "curiosity," "learn"
21	"Kinship" or "connection" with the past, similar concepts
22	"Beauty" or "art"
18	"Sell," "money," or "profit" and similar concepts
17	Vague answers like "making," "creating," "using hands"
15	Making a point:
	10 making a nice point
	3 making a point or something nice out of a rock
	2 making an authentic-looking point
14	Need products for a variety of purposes:
	4 Add types I can't find to my collection
	4 Points for bow and arrow hunting
	1 Gunflints for black powder guns
	1 Gunflints and arrowheads for hunting
	2 Experiments and museum displays
	1 Points to make arrow reproductions
	1 Flakes to study fracture mechanics
9	Social interaction, "people," "camaraderie," etc.
6	Keeping an ancient skill alive
4	Teaching others
3	Personal identity, self-expression
3	Survival skill
2	Escape the present
2	Inexpensive hobby
2	Like the sounds made by flaking

Total: 278 answers on 160 questionnaires. Numbers are the number of responses that include a particular element.

included three who noted that knapping knowledge helps them, in their artifact collecting, to identify or authenticate ancient points. Actually, I think a general curiosity about past life is more important than this question showed. The related question "What got you started knapping?" received many responses (41/183) that cited an interest in Indians, prehistoric technology, or how points were made, and even more (51/183) that mentioned collecting points. Perhaps once the initial question "how did they do this?" was answered by having learned some knapping skill, other aspects of knapping continued to hold the interest of the knappers and seemed more important to them when I asked why they knap.

More materialistic reasons occurred in a number of answers. Thirteen knappers mentioned that they can "turn a buck" or sell their artifacts. However, this was fewer than mentioned the beauty of flaked stone or called knapping "art." I was also intrigued to notice that several of the knappers in the sample who make their living by knapping, or at least sell lots of points, did not mention the economic side at all when asked why they knap.

Even in the relatively impersonal context of a mail questionnaire, the emotional attachment of some knappers to their craft was obvious. Only three explicitly said that knapping was a necessary part of their identity or self-expression, but some sent me drawings, cartoons, or knapping autobiographies, or wrote long and emotional responses to my questions. One knapper wrote that he knaps because "I deeply respectfully love it. I feel more connected to powers greater than myself. It keeps a person pretty humble [because it is difficult]."

One response that summed up many of the reasons above came not on my questionnaire, but in an email message from Barent Parslow:

> I would think that we pursue ancient crafts, not limited to flintknapping, because we have a need to connect to the lives of our ancestors and thereby renew hope for our own futures, to connect ourselves with our ancestors and understand their values. Aside from being plain simple and degenerative fun, educational, and esteem building, it is very nearly religious. There is meditation, a connection with ancestors, and personal peace and tranquility. Words fail me in the explanation. I began with hunting and have been progressing backwards, albeit slowly, ever since. These "hobbies" help me escape from the all too disappointing present.

As an archaeologist, I want to pursue for a moment the interest in the past and the related "escape from the present." Almost all knappers have at least a casual interest in prehistory. Many take this no further than liking to collect points, or enjoying primitive crafts, and have no real interest in learning anything about the archaeological meaning of artifacts or the nature of prehistoric Indian cultures. However, some are just as dedicated scholars in their way as any academic archaeologist. Many of these read all sorts of popular literature about Indians and archaeology, not always getting a very accurate picture, but others read the professional literature as well and are very well informed. Academic or amateur, scholarly professional, serious layperson, or dabbler, we all share a curiosity about the past, and more. Our interest, whether we recognize it or not, is likely to rise from deeper emotional needs.

Archaeologists often joke that they work with dead folk because they are easier to get along with than live people. Some anthropologists similarly claim that they study strange and outlandish peoples because they feel alienated from their own culture. Many a true word is spoken in jest. Not many anthropologists are really misfits or misanthropes (although I know a few), but for many of us, past or foreign cultures offer something we fail to find in our own.

Many of the Fort Osage knappers work at jobs that do not especially interest them, and several have told me that they are good knappers because they practice a lot: at the end of a day they come home from work as fast as possible, take off their work clothes, and knap for a couple of hours. Every day. The relaxation value of an absorbing craft is high, and knapping is more of a challenge than most routine jobs. In a mostly uncontrollable universe, a knapper is matched against the stone and triumphs through skill, knowledge, and wit. Practiced actions produce predictable results, and the unexpected can usually be overcome. In a world swimming in mass-produced low-quality consumer goods, a knapper strives to make something fine and unique. In a society of millions, where individuals feel lost and unimportant, knapping is an expression of individualism; knappers are proud of being among the few people who really know how to make stone tools. The craft also provides a "community of practice," a circle of friends, other craftsmen who understand and who are united by a common interest.

Then there are the esthetic and even sensuous pleasures of knapping. Good stone is beautiful material, and to the knapper who sees its potential, it often takes on a mystical spirit. Flaked stone is beautiful, too. The very act of knapping is filled with excitement. It is dynamic, forceful, precise, cunning. The dramatic crack of a good flake detaching from a core is one of the most distinctive and seductive sounds I know, and the jingle of perfect flakes among others on a tarp is music to my ears. My desk is littered with hard, sharp, shapely points, flakes too perfect to throw away, smooth fossils found in fractured nodules. I often find myself fidgeting with them, caressing surfaces, admiring colors, testing serrated edges against my finger. Many knappers admit to carrying favorite points in their pockets until they are worn smooth by handling and friction. In our archaeological work in Arizona we have occasionally found prehistoric examples of points that were already ancient when someone dropped them on our later sites, and points with intentionally dulled edges and blurred surfaces, doubtless ancient fetishes, charms, worry beads (Kamp and Whittaker 1999).

The connection to prehistory, the past, ancestors, is very important to many knappers, although they do not always say so when asked why they knap. I know only a handful of knappers who consider themselves Native Americans, although quite a few others claim some Indians in their family history. Since many Americans consider it romantic to have Indian ancestry, one might expect knappers, who are involved in all sorts of primitive crafts that are mostly derived from American Indian lifeways, to go out of their way to claim a blood connection. In fact, relatively few do so. I am aware of a couple of less skillful knappers who sell to tourists at rock shows and similar events who say that they are part Indian, or tell involved stories about how they learned from an old Indian, but I suspect some of these stories stretch the facts.

I am not sure why knappers do not rush to claim Native American connections, but can think of several possible reasons. I have already explained that the knap-in community is largely white and male. As a group, knappers tend to be firmly grounded in their own ethnic, social, and political identities and perhaps less likely than some other Americans to want to claim other ethnic affiliations. A few knappers point out that "everybody's ancestors made stone tools," but this is not a major theme. A number of the knappers participate in "reenactments" where they dress up and perform the part of fur trade or Civil War–era Americans, or even, in a couple of cases, medieval Europeans. I have never seen anyone at any of the knap-ins I have attended dress up as an Indian and play a role while knapping, although I know a few knappers who dress in some sort of primitive garb, especially when giving public demonstrations. The nature of the knap-in as an event focused on the craft does not promote play-acting, and for most knappers, role-playing "Indians" would not feel right. It is recognizably a role that does not "belong" to most knappers and is foreign to them in a way that the role of Civil War soldier is not. This is quite apart from the likelihood that the watching public would find it silly, or inappropriate, or even offensive for non-Indians to dress up in Native American garb. People are particular about how others perceive their identities, and even more so about how they perceive themselves. I talked to one knapper who claimed Mexican Indian and Spanish ancestry. He said he had been asked to join a fur-trade-era "rendezvous" group dressed in buckskins and carrying flintlocks. He declined: "Well, look at me! Which side do you think I would have been on then?"

The knap-in is tightly focused on the performance of a craft, rather than the performance of another culture or historic events, as in Civil War reenactments. The majority of the artifacts made by knappers imitate prehistoric American prototypes, but the craft itself is the thing, and it is so universal a heritage that it can be divorced from specific historic contexts.

Nevertheless, the connection that knapping forges with the past is very important to many knappers. At one of my first knap-ins, I sat on the Fort Osage balcony eating stew and looking out over the flowing river. I gradually became aware of two old knappers whom I did not know. They were discussing prehistory with a passion that became hard to ignore. Part of the argument focused on the observation, often made by modern knappers, that the finest knapping was done by the earliest Native Americans. Although this is an overgeneralization, Paleoindian points tend to be large and spectacular, and the following Archaic period is also characterized by good knapping and large points, but generally less finely made. The Woodland and later points are often undistinguished, or even crude. At this point one of the knappers expounded with considerable force a summary of American prehistory, which I have now heard a couple of times from different knappers.

Pounding on the handle of his rustic chair, he lectured us:

> The early Indian people just hunted and gathered, there weren't very many of them, and they wandered around a lot. Then they settled down and began to grow things, but it was when they learned to make the goddamned pottery that the downfall

began. Then they could store grain, and when they stored it, then the big ones began to tax the little ones. And they spread out their government by bloodlines, and used the grain they took, the taxes, to build big useless things like Monks Mound at Cahokia. And finally the government got so bad people couldn't stand it anymore, and bust it up, and they went back to the tribal level.

Then the other speaker burst out: "What the hell! It's like what we're doing right now in the United States. Why in the hell is all this stuff got to go to the federal government? The same thing is happening to our government that happened to the Indians back then, and we are falling apart."

To the archaeologist, this is a vastly oversimplified view of prehistory, but to the teller it was a compelling model, not so much for describing the past, but for explaining the universal trends of human history and the hardships that people suffer when technology and governments become too complicated.

More often, knappers just express admiration for the people of the past according to well-established stereotypes in American culture. For many Americans, the "old days" in many respects were "the *good* old days." Grandmothers on cookie packages, Southern plantations on whiskey bottles, and pyramids or Indians on herbal medicines are all common advertising devices that try to convince us that a product was made in what we believe was "the old way," that is, by hand, with careful craftsmanship. They also imply the preservation or rediscovery of forgotten wisdom. Craftsmanship is, of course, a concept common in knapper conversation and as an answer to why knappers like knapping, and carrying on the ancient tradition of stone tool making is another important value for some knappers.

Quite a few knappers are craftsmen in other crafts or work in a field that requires a similar artistic turn of mind. In professional life, Jim Regan was a machinist and inventor, Tony Romano and Gene Altiere are dentists, Mike Ash an artist, and so on. On my survey, I asked two related questions attempting to assess knappers' other interests and aptitudes. An open question, "What other hobbies or crafts are you interested in?" produced an enormous and diverse list, but 83 out of the 160 respondents said they had other craft hobbies, ranging from painting and sculpture to model airplane building, wood-carving, blacksmithing, and a variety of other primitive crafts. The second question, a list of interests that I considered related to knapping (Table 5.3), may have reduced the explicit answers in the first question, as knappers felt it redundant to explain interests that answered both questions.

Debbie Olausson (1998) also surveyed knappers, looking for connections between knapping skills and other craft interests. Her sample of 197 knappers included some of the same American knappers as mine, but had a much higher percentage of archaeologists. She compared them to 58 archaeology students at the University of Lund, Sweden, and found that compared to her archaeology students, knappers ranked themselves higher on patience, interest in shooting sports, abilities in drawing three-dimensional objects, and overall artistic talent. Perception and reality may not be the same, but the habit of making things, and enjoying the making, is strong among knappers.

Table 5.3
Percentages of Fort Osage (N = 86) and non–Fort Osage (N = 69) Knappers Pursuing "Other Related Interests"

F.O.	Non-F.O.	Related Interests
74	90	read about archaeology
85	88	visit museums
73	60	collect prehistoric artifacts
53	43	collect other knappers' work
37	53	belong to archaeological society
14	24	take courses related to archaeology
86	85	watch TV specials on archaeology
30	57	have participated in arch. project or excavation
33	37	antiques
79	69	hunt/fish
42	31	black powder/rendezvous/reenactments
63	50	archery/bow hunting
27	25	collect knives
37	47	rock hound/lapidary work/jewelry
22	21	other

I have discussed how knapping becomes an important part of the identity of many of us in the knapping world. Part of the value of art is in the unique nature of each piece, and part of the value of the artist is that he or she is an unusual individual in a world of 6 billion faceless humans. Individuality is considered a typical American value; our cultural myths embodied in popular media like novels and movies, both fictional and historic, celebrate the individual who swims against the stream, who stands out. Our historical mythology suggests that being an individual was easier in the past; modern society subjects us all to more and more restrictions, most visibly in the proliferation of legislation protecting us from ourselves, forbidding small offenses, restricting customary rights, setting up complicated mechanisms to solve small problems that become more pressing as too many people live too close together. Proficiency in an ancient craft sets you apart as an artist, and as an unusual and different person, and connects you to the legendary past of American Freedom.

It is no coincidence that many knappers hunt, fish, shoot, ride, canoe, hike, or otherwise enjoy the outdoors. This, too, is a connection with the past, when we feel humans lived more closely with nature, and with traditional freedoms to bear arms and to exploit the bounty of the earth. Quite a few knappers entered the craft because of some interest in hunting, black powder guns, archery, or outdoor survival. Stone tools, as I have said, are generally thought of as weapons and hunting gear.

Most importantly, as I have said before, the knap-in creates a society of people with common interests, a community of practice, a subculture of people embedded in the mainstream of America, but somewhat resistant to parts of American culture. As Larry Langford said to me at one knap-in, "We are all Ghost Dancers." The Ghost Dance was a revitalistic native religious movement that originated with Paiute prophets in Nevada but found its most famous and militant expression among the Plains tribes between 1889 and 1891 (Mooney 1896; Brown 1970). Participants believed that by performing the proper ceremonies of the Ghost Dance, and by living according to the old ways, they could prevent the destruction of their way of life by the encroaching federal government and European culture. The whites would be defeated and vanish, the buffalo would return, and the world would become again as it should be. The response of the United States government to this movement was military action, culminating in the slaughter at Wounded Knee in 1891.

The knappers of Fort Osage have no such sweeping millenarian hopes. Their Ghost Dance is a small, temporary resistance to the unsatisfactory world around them. By knapping, they may connect with a vague ancestral heritage, but call up much more forcefully some of the values we assign to the past: careful craftsmanship, understanding of the natural world, survival skills, familiarity with weapons, freedom from oppressive bureaucracy, individuality, and fellowship.

1. Errett Callahan's "Tyrannosaurus Rex" fantasy knife. The two separate blades are knapped of obsidian with embedded quartz "eyes," and the handle was carved by Ron Myers. Now in Jean Auel collection. Photo ©Weyer of Toledo. Courtesy of Errett Callahan.

2. An array of points by modern knappers: Central biface: Jim Hopper (Texas Georgetown chert, 1994). Other bottom layer points, clockwise from top left: Jim Spears (Alibates chert Scottsbluff, 1999); Frank Stevens (Flint Ridge chert Snyder, 1998); Woody Blackwell (Wyoming Tiger chert Clovis, 1995); Jeff Gower (Burlington chert Thebes, 1996); Carl Doney (corner notched point, 1990); Don Kyleberg (Texas chert, 1999); Dale Cannon (Gerzean knife, 2001). Top layer points, clockwise from center: Jim Hopper (jasper lap-knapped fluted point, 1991); John Whittaker (Burlington chert Scottsbluff, 2002); John Whittaker (novaculite Scottsbluff, 2001); Miranda Warburton (Glass Buttes obsidian, 1997); Greg Nunn (jasper Scottsbluff, 1996).

For cost reasons, this photo section has been produced in black-and-white in this printing. The color version can be viewed at the book's page on the Press's website, www.utexaspress.com.

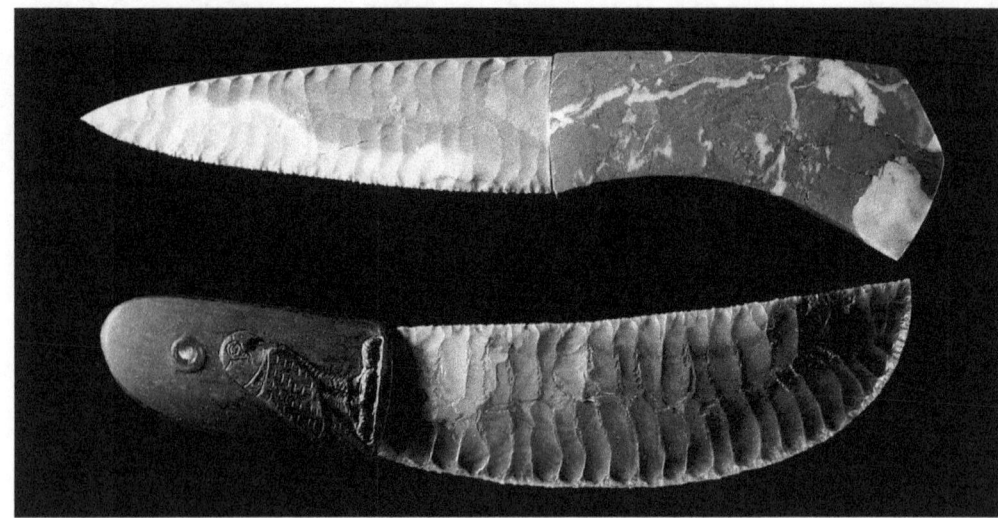

3. A contemporary stone knife by Dale Cannon (2000) and a modern take on the Egyptian Gerzean knives by Bob Keiper (2003). Photo by McLean Design at www.mcleandesign.com

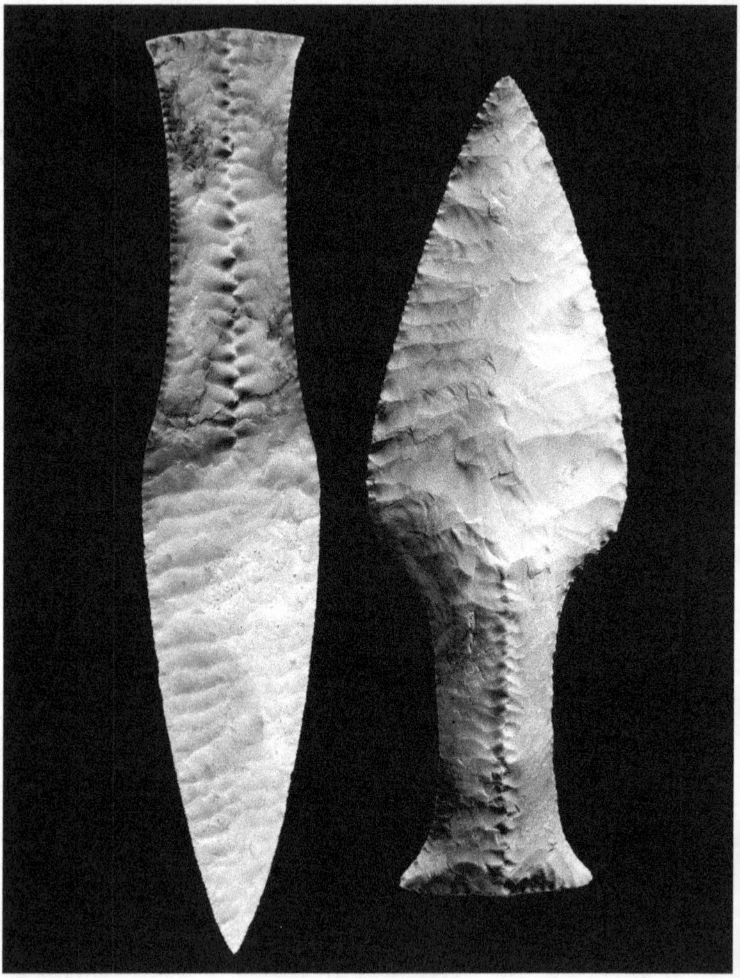

4. Danish Neolithic daggers by Mike Stafford (Flint Ridge flint, 2001) and D. C. Waldorf (Burlington chert, 2000). Photo by McLean Design at www.mcleandesign.com

5. Fluted points by different knappers. Top to bottom: Bruce Bradley (Spanish Point agate Folsom, 2002); Jim Regan (Paiute agate Clovis, 2001); Joe Miller (Alibates chert Clovis, 2003); J. B. Sollberger (grey Georgetown flint Folsom, 1990s); Cole Hurst (brown Paiute agate Clovis, 2002). Photo by McLean Design at www.mcleandesign.com

6. More fluted points. Left, top to bottom: Dan Theus (Mook jasper, Australia, Clovis, 2001); Bob Patten (Hartville Uplift chert Folsom, 1999); Dan Long (Alibates chert Folsom, 2001); Matt Trout (fossil palm wood, 2000). Right: Marty Reuter (Dover chert Cumberland, 2001). Photo by McLean Design at www.mcleandesign.com

7. Paleoindian point forms. Left to right: Joe Miller (Imperial jasper, Mexico, Scottsbluff, 2003); Bob Patten (Glendo agate Scottsbluff, 2001); Bob Patten (Hartville Uplift chert Hells Gap, 2001); Bruce Bradley (porcelainite Eden, 2002); Bob Thompson (Tecovas jasper Scottsbluff, 2002). Photo by McLean Design at www.mcleandesign.com

8. A selection of Dalton (Early Archaic) points by Fort Osage knappers. The variation reflects both variation in the prehistoric points and how different modern knappers choose to copy and interpret the originals. Clockwise from upper left: Roy Motley (Burlington chert, 1997); Steve Behrnes (2002); Bill Morton (Burlington chert, 1990); Bob Hunt (Burlington chert, 1993); Bob Hunt (1994); Dick Grybush (Hixton quartzite, 1994); Jim Redfearn (Burlington chert, 2001); Jeff Gower (Burlington chert, 1996). Photo by McLean Design at www.mcleandesign.com

9. Large Archaic/Woodland point forms commonly made by Midwestern knappers. Top left to right: Jim Redfearn (Hardin Barbed, 2000); D. C. Waldorf (Archaic E-Notch Thebes, 2000); John Mondino (Harvester Burlington chert Snyder, 2001). Center: Dan Long (Burlington chert Thebes, 2001). Bottom left to right: Roger Warmuskerken (Flint Ridge chert Dovetail, 2002); Mark Bracken (Hillsborough, 2000); Roy Miller (Flint Ridge chert Dovetail, 2002). Photo by McLean Design at www.mcleandesign.com

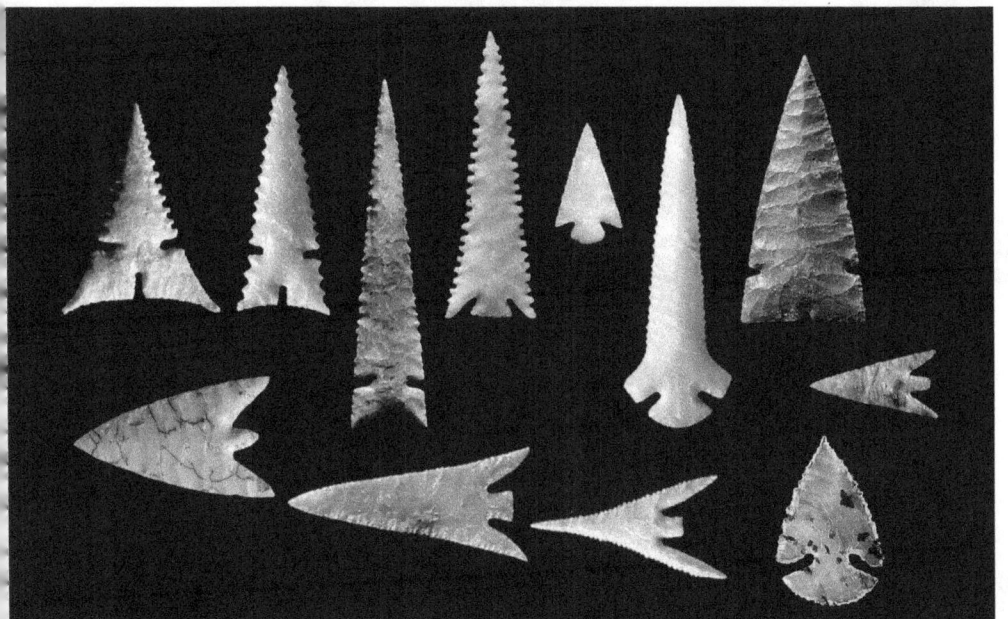

10. Small late prehistoric arrow points. Top left to right: Steve Behrnes (2000); Gary Merle (2000); Roy Motley (2000); Marty Schemp (2000); Craig Ratzat (2000); Dave Ediger (pink novaculite, 2001); Ron Fuller (jasper from India, 2001); Charlie Shewey (2001). Bottom: Ron Fuller (Australian dendritic opal, 2001); Ken Kurfurst (2003); Steve Alley (2003); John Siderio (2003). Photo by McLean Design at www.mcleandesign.com

11. A few pieces with unusual forms. Top left to right: Derek McLean (chert from Israel, cross, 2003); Dan Theus (Alibates chert, giant Pinetree, 2001); Bob Thomas (ring, 2000). Bottom left to right: Robbie Robinson (Flint Ridge chert Pinetree, 2002); Jim Miller (obsidian fish, 2003); Marty Reuter (agate scorpion, 2001). Photo by McLean Design at www.mcleandesign.com

12. Exotic materials. Top diagonal left to right: James Howell (millefiori glass, 2002); Craig Ratzat (silver fiber optic glass, 2000); Martin Schemp (silver fiber optic glass, 2001); Doug Kreis (2003); Doug Kreis (quartz crystal, 2003). Bottom diagonal left to right: Ron Fuller (Contra Luz glass, 2001); Dan Theus (Australian Mook jasper, 2001); Roy Miller (Flint Ridge chert, 2002); Bruce Bradley (Brazilian agate, 2002). Photo by McLean Design at www.mcleandesign.com

STATUS AND STONES

If you ask someone at a knap-in to describe a fellow knapper, you are likely to get something like: "Oh, you don't know X? Well, he's that guy from Alabama, wears glasses, real good knapper and a nice guy. Makes those big, flat Clovis points." Odds are good that descriptions of other knappers will include a judgment of skill or something characteristic about their knapping. It is not really surprising that craftsmen know each other by their skills and that they use skill to assign prestige within the group. It is, however, somewhat contradictory to the expressed ethos of the knap-in. Fort Osage knappers frequently say and write (Behrnes 1991; Regan 1991; Van Arsdale 1995) that knap-ins should be noncompetitive, a place for fellowship and sharing, respecting everyone regardless of skill or orientation toward differing views of knapping. They dislike the idea of formal organizations, rules, and authorities (Blake 1991). There are organizers for the knap-in, but they have little power over who comes and what they do. The knap-in is supposed to be completely egalitarian in structure. Nevertheless, within the knap-in community, there are individuals who are important to the knap-in, individuals whose opinions matter, who are looked up to and respected. Although there are a number of possible ways to gain status within the knap-in community, the most common and obvious is through knapping skill. In this chapter, I want to discuss the relatively overt expressions of equality and inclusion and the more contradictory and subtle manipulations and expressions of differential status.

The Knap-in as Egalitarian Event

The Fort Osage knappers value highly the egalitarian nature of their event. Perhaps the strongest indication of this is the intentional lack of structure and hierarchy. Bob Hunt and the other organizers make the arrangements for the knap-in, and organize volunteers to set up and take down the main tent, and clean up the area after the knap-in. They see to it that the facilities provided by the park are left in good shape, and provide a central source of information about the knap-in, but they do not provide much overt direction during the knap-in. Knappers who have come before and are on the mailing list receive an announcement and map, but this is not an exclusive invitation. The knap-in is widely publicized in newsletters like *Chips* and on the Internet, and anyone who hears about the knap-in is welcome to come and set up. There are occasional mutterings about certain individuals who make themselves obnoxious or are suspected of such misdemeanors as theft, but there is no way to ban anyone.

All the formal rules are dictated by the park. In the early years, knappers were expected to simply write their name and address on a list at the visitor center and pay a park entry fee of five dollars. In 1996, a registration form was provided, which listed a number of rules (Appendix B): Register, wear name tags, park in lot and not on grass, no alcohol. All of these had been understood previously, and most had always been loosely enforced if at all. Although nothing really became any stricter, once the rules were down on paper and knappers had to sign on to them, some were heard to grumble about how there were getting to be too many rules and restrictions at knap-ins nowadays. Two other rules may have actually underlain much of the grumbling: "Vendor names will be furnished to Missouri Department of Revenue upon their request," and "participants will abide by Federal and State laws concerning the sale of antiquities." I will discuss economic issues later; but much of the exchange at the knap-in, as in all hobbies, is informal, unrecorded, and untaxed. While various laws forbid the sale of artifacts (and their collection) from most federal or state lands, legal action is actually quite rare, partly because it is difficult to trace most artifacts back to their origin. Nevertheless, the unscrupulous collectors who loot sites and the more paranoid collectors, who see any regulation as a threat, have produced a lot of dishonestly slanted propaganda about "arrowhead police" and laws that will make it "impossible to collect at all." A surprising number of collectors are willing to believe this. In any case, the sign-in rules had no real effect on anything, and I haven't heard anyone complain about them lately.

The Fort Osage Knap-in has little formal structure. Knappers, vendors, and visitors show up when they wish, and knap, sell, watch, or participate according to their own desires. The park designates the knap-in area, but locations within it are not officially assigned or reserved. Many people bring their own chairs, tables, and tents. Some make a point of being under the large shelter, especially if they have displays they do not want to get wet, and many, like myself, simply stake out a chair or a piece of a picnic bench by putting their knapping kit there. Despite the informality, there are some distinct regularities in who sets up where and some traditional claims on particular spots. Knappers like myself who do not have large displays may move around from day to day, but larger setups are generally felt to have established a claim to their location for the duration of the knap-in, even when the owner packs his or her goods away for the night.

As we have seen, some knap-ins incorporate a sequence of events: raffles, auctions, drawings, demonstrations, knapping competitions, award ceremonies. Fort Osage has none of this.

Atlatl and archery competitions seem to be gaining ground and linking themselves to a number of knap-ins, including Fort Osage. At the spring knap-ins in 1995 and 1997 there were archery and atlatl contests, but the organization of this was an individual effort by Virgil Hayes rather than the knap-in organizers, although they encouraged it. It attracted a number of competitors and some audience and was deemed a success. Virgil provided targets and made up the rules. Each contestant was asked to provide an object "worth $10," which would then be used as a prize, with prizes to be claimed in order of score. Most of the prizes were thus points or other knapper paraphernalia, and all contestants ended up with something. The informal nature of this competition was reinforced by the participation of someone's young son, eight or ten years old. He was coached by a couple of the more experienced archers, encouraged by the crowd, and eventually lined up with the adults to claim a stone hatchet as his prize. Since 1998 the atlatl competition has become a regular adjunct to the knap-in. It is sponsored by the World Atlatl Association and the Missouri Atlatl

Association and organized by Ron Mertz and Ray Madden, who are not knappers. Although some people, like myself, participate in both, the atlatl competition is attached to the knap-in, rather than part of it. Archery remains unorganized.

The unstructured nature of the Fort Osage Knap-in reflects an extreme of the almost universal belief that knap-ins should be informal and egalitarian. The competition at the Genesee Valley Knap-in is discussed elsewhere; the organizers state repeatedly that it is intended to be a "non-competitive" competition, serving only to promote the art of knapping. The Fort Osage knappers in general dislike the idea of even so low key an event. Many of the knap-ins were organized by a local group of knappers who had met and started knapping together and decided to expand. A few of these groups have organized themselves more formally as clubs with officers, occasional activities, and dues. The Missouri knappers who started the Fort Osage Knap-in never felt a need to do so, nor do most of the other groups of knappers. Many are downright allergic to the idea of formal organization.

Errett Callahan, Ray Harwood, and D. C. Waldorf have in the past attempted to organize knappers' guilds that would be formal organizations with rights, duties, and some sort of written code of behavior. When D. C. started the *Chips* newsletter in 1989, he proposed that it should be the newsletter for a new "Flint Knappers Guild International." Even at the time he proposed a society without much structure: "The election of officers and the ranking of members according to their ability and all of the politicking that would follow would only serve to stratify the members and destroy the fellowship and spontaneity that has marked our past events" (Waldorf 1989b). He and Val, as editors of *Chips,* would be "acting" president and secretary and disseminate news, but the idea was simply to help knappers find and communicate with each other. However, almost no one was interested in the idea of a guild, even a very amorphous one. By 1994 the Waldorfs had given up on the idea, and D. C. admitted, "Who wants to work with an organization that doesn't want to organize?" (Waldorf 1994c, 1). *Chips* continues as a successful attempt to promote communication, but the Guild never got off the ground.

Errett Callahan had a similar experience. At about the same time as the Waldorfs' attempt, he was promoting an even more formal guild. He envisioned an organization with a board of directors, membership by application, and an ethical code. The guild was to "promote professional responsibility and ethics among flintknappers, to promote the legitimate sale of flintknappers' products and services, and to serve as a liaison between flintknappers, the professional community [meaning archaeologists] and the public" (Callahan 1989). Callahan was taking a strong stand against "passing off unsigned replicas as ancient originals, and offering authentic Indian relics for sale," and trying to promote knapping as art and part of experimental archaeology, rather than faking, or what he calls disdainfully "folk-knapping." We will discuss such ethical questions at length later; for the moment it is enough to note that Callahan and the knappers he aimed at are in a minority, and, as it turned out, not even the knappers who agreed with Callahan's goals were sufficiently motivated to form a guild.

Callahan's efforts then focused on the Society of Primitive Technology, which he and others founded in 1989 (Callahan 1996b; Watts 1991). The SPT has much broader concerns than just flintknapping, but knapping is well represented in the membership and in the articles in *Bulletin of Primitive Technology*. Other than the board, the "Society" does not meet or act as a body, but the *Bulletin* contains a statement of philosophy and ethics that reflects many of Callahan's concerns.

The literature produced by the knappers, including those from Fort Osage as well as those who have never been there, repeatedly expresses the ideals of unity, sharing, and equality. In all the newsletters, on the Web pages, and in conversation, the usual response to complaints about someone's behavior, arguments, or attempts to limit discussions is twofold. First, very few want any kind of organization or individual with authority over them. Second, there is a strongly held ethos of "live and let live." If you don't like someone's opinion or actions, you can avoid him, but should not interfere. Arguments should be friendly, and even if some feel that a topic is not interesting or relevant, it is usually not desirable to try to exclude it from a newsletter or discussion. Beyond that, knappers are expected to hold to the creed that while different people have different skills and knowledge, all have something to contribute. This is, of course, a philosophy common throughout American culture, whether or not it is actually acted on.

Among the knappers this philosophy seems to be particularly important. I think this is partly because the knap-ins are expressly intended to be educational, in the sense that they spread knowledge of knapping techniques among knappers and expose the public to prehistoric technology. Both are considered important goals. Many knappers want to educate the public in part because they wish be recognized as artists and distance themselves from the aura of artifact faking that they feel still clings to knapping; others are more interested in building a market. Knap-ins are important to many enthusiastic knappers who are interested in enhancing their personal skills and learning new tricks. Many speak with disapproval of the "old days," when some commercial knappers would not let anyone see how they knapped because they considered their tricks "trade secrets." Knappers who are ungracious about teaching beginners or letting others watch them are not liked. Accordingly, a diversity of techniques, skills, and knowledge is desirable at knap-ins; the more different ideas are floating around, the more you can learn.

Errett Callahan, who is not a Fort Osage knapper, but is well known as an extremely skillful commercial knapper and primitive skills teacher with academic credentials as well, considers himself a spokesman for "serious" knapping, both for the purposes of experimental archaeology and in the service of knapping as an art. He maintains a strong "purist" stance, arguing that knappers should begin with the basics and progress through a sequence similar to the technological development of stone tools through prehistory (Callahan 1996a). He also speaks out frequently against the use of modern tools such as copper billets (1995a). As a result of his purist stance and ethical statements, many of the Fort Osage knappers consider him arrogant and elitist. These arguments are often featured in letters and editorials in the *Bulletin of Primitive Technology* and other newsletters. Errett stands out as a minority "purist," at least in his view that knapping as a whole should be more traditional, although there are others who have similar ideas about their own personal knapping but are less willing to criticize others. The majority opinion is closer to that expressed in a letter on the subject by J. Harrison, who argued that knappers should knap in whatever way pleases them: "One of the greatest strengths this country has to offer is its acceptance of diversity. We allow each to contribute, effect change, and produce according to his individual initiative, the result being a blend of interests living fairly peacefully with one another. . . . Let's just enjoy one another, appreciate individual perspectives, and share our individual talents as part of one multicolored multiflow hunk of social rock" (1995, 9).

Ooga-Booga, a Ritual of Inclusion

Knappers celebrate their unity and express their communal identity in a number of ways. One of the most elaborate is a mock rite of passage, the Ooga-Booga initiation ceremony.

I was still feeling a bit the outsider at my third Fort Osage Knap-in in September 1991. Although I had made some friends and met a fair number of people, I had not yet been coming to the knap-in long enough to be considered a regular, and as an undistinguished knapper and an academic, I was aware that I had a ways to go before being fully integrated. I was a bit taken aback when I was told one evening that an initiation was being held, and several others and I were to stay in the garage until called for.

Outside on the gravel of the parking lot, a bonfire had been built and ringed with chairs. From inside the darkened garage we acolytes could hear repeated chants of "ooga-booga, ooga-booga," rising to a crescendo and a roar of laughter and applause each time one of us was led out and processed through the ceremony. When my turn eventually came, part of the ceremony involved swearing not to reveal the secrets, so I will have to be vague as to details. Suffice it to say there was a friendly "ordeal" involving some public harassment and a mild practical joke.

The structure of the Ooga-Booga ceremony was that of initiations everywhere. Anthropological theorists have noted a common pattern to "rites of passage" that all cultures use to symbolize and effect a change in social status (Turner 1969; Van Gennep 1960). Initiates are commonly removed from their old social roles and mainstream society and held in isolation, in limbo. During this period they are often taught things they need to know in their new roles. They then go through a ceremony that transforms them into a new social being, often with symbols of death and birth, indicating the end of one status and the beginning of another. Usually there is some kind of ordeal, and shared suffering is supposed to create bonds of "communitas," or unity, among those who have passed through the ritual. Rites of passage can take minutes or months and can be simple or elaborate, multipart ceremonies. They are common in all societies, probably because they are psychologically effective. Fraternity initiations, birthday parties, college graduations, and military induction and training are all rites of passage in American society and follow roughly the same patterns.

As an Ooga-Booga initiate, I was isolated from those in the know, ceremonially introduced to them as a potential new member, briefly instructed in the ideals of the society, subjected to an ordeal, and incorporated into the body of the elect after successfully passing the ordeal. The ceremony itself could have been adapted to any group; here it was made a knappers' ceremony by the use of knapping symbols. The "chief" and other leaders were masked and appropriately attired in "primitive" gear, and, not surprisingly, some of the ceremonial artifacts were flaked stone points.

Any ritual that defines a group and acts to incorporate individuals into a group necessarily excludes others who are not part of that group. When you are an Ooga-Booga, you are slightly different, you know something others do not. However, the purpose of the Ooga-Booga ceremony at the knap-ins is not to create an elite, but to include as many as possible and create ties among them. Anyone present who wishes can be initiated, knapper, spouse, vendor, or friend. The ordeal is not such as to drive anyone away or separate out those who cannot endure it. At the Ooga-Booga ceremony at the Genesee Knap-in in 1996, a number of wives and children were initiated, as is common. Some of the kids were rather young, but the crowd shifted from harassing to encouraging comments. However, the last couple were far too young, only five or six, and did not even understand what was going on, but were rather frightened. Larry Scheiber, the officiating "chief," began to balk and the little girl began to whimper. At this, there was a hasty consultation among the officers with audience participation, the ceremony was truncated, and the little girl was applauded until she smiled and then was hastily passed on to her parents. One knapper commented to me that he had been reluctant to participate, as he had gone through other initiations and had not enjoyed them, but was "really tickled" that the Ooga-Booga ceremony was so benign and friendly rather than a trial. After a ceremony, everyone sits around the fire companionably and tells stories, bringing the evening to a friendly and familiar close.

A few knappers choose not to be initiated, either because they disapprove of initiations and hazing and feel that secret societies are exclusionary and undesirable, or because they think the Ooga-Booga ceremony is silly. It certainly is humorous, and intentionally so. In fact, by mocking more serious initiations, the Ooga-Booga rite expresses the nonserious, inclusive, and friendly ideals of the knap-in. It succeeds on some level both in its overt goal of creating an in-group of initiates bonded by common experience and ritual, and in subverting this goal by expressing the good fellowship of an open and egalitarian knap-in community.

The Ooga-Booga Society has spread like a new religion and serves now as an additional bond between different knap-ins. It apparently began as a family joke among friends of Robbie Robinson, a Texas knapper. As near as I can tell he introduced it to the knap-ins at Flint Ridge in 1991 and took it on to Fort Osage, where I was initiated, and other knap-ins. The original name seems to have been "The Ancient Iroquois Ooga-Booga Society," but it almost immediately became "The Secret Ear-o'-Corn Ooga-Booga Society," which was an amusing and atrocious pun, and less likely to offend anyone. Robbie Robinson and friends of his, including Larry Scheiber, who is renowned for picturesque and even outrageous behavior at knap-ins, took the Ooga-Booga on the road to any knap-ins they attended. It rapidly swept the knapping community, with regular announcements by Scheiber and others in *Chips* of initiations held and members recruited, until ceremonies had been held at most of the major knap-ins. In the second year, Scheiber, who has regular cartoons and humorous comments in *Chips,* had a T-shirt made, with a large-nosed cartoon primitive encircled by the name of the society. These T-shirts are now one of the identity-marking items worn by some knap-in folk (Figure 6.1).

Typically, the Ooga-Booga Society remains a cobweb organization. Although Robinson, Scheiber, and several others have proselytized enthusiastically and estimate (or more likely overestimate) the membership at up to ten thousand, the society only operates as a group at knap-in events. Several of the instigators claim humorous titles: in 1997 Bob Hunt was "National Secretary" or "National Treasurer," depending on context; Robbie Robinson was "National President"; Larry Scheiber, the "Lone Wolf," was "National Vice President"; and Jim Woodring (a Pennsylvania knapper) was "Exalted National Janitor." However, while all the above are enthusiastic participants and initiation leaders, they are not really officers. Any initiated member with enough talent as a showman and a couple of supporters can run an initiation. There is considerable variation in details and feeling from ceremony to ceremony; Dana Klein told me that when he officiated, "it was a little more reverent than Lone Wolf's." Dane Martin has married at least two couples at knap-in ceremonies followed by Ooga-Boogas

Figure 6.1. Larry Scheiber's Ooga-Booga T-shirt design.

(Martin 2002), as has Joe Hewitt in New York (Van Arsdale 2000). Ten years after its beginnings, the Ooga-Booga Society is still going strong, with enthusiastic new chiefs like Dale Cannon and plenty of willing initiates.

Does such a headless society and playful ritual work for knappers? It seems to. Knappers ask each other if they are Ooga-Booga members and share reminiscences of initiations. In an early note in *Chips* (Scheiber 1992a), the "Lone Wolf" gushed: "It was a real thrill for me to share with you [Bob Hunt], D. C. [Waldorf], [Jim] Spears, and the other knappers whose points are ten times better than mine. I guess it just goes to show that, in the end, we're all equal." Jamie Ollinger (1993), also in *Chips*, explained his experience and exhorted others: "The Ooga-Booga Society thing with knappers is to welcome new people into the fold. I'm no 5/1 knapper [referring to width/thickness ratio as a measure of skill] but I'm an 'Ooga-Booga.' I'm accepted, and I *feel* accepted. Don't ever be afraid to become a member; it will put you right up there in the same class with the 'big boys'!" Both knappers sound the same key theme: regardless of level of skill, knappers are kin. For many, Ooga-Booga membership is a symbolically important part of being one of the knap-in insiders.

Status and Competition in Knapping

Even in rules of etiquette the noncompetitive ideals of the knap-in are enforced. Knappers are expected to be modest. If you ask a knapper how his point is going, he is likely to respond: "I'll break it in a minute." The most he is likely to admit to is "Not too bad. I'm trying to get around this flaw here" or "I got a good flake scar pattern on this face, but over here I had some trouble." It is good form to praise another's work, but very poor manners to boast about your own. One top knapper at Fort Osage has a bad reputation for arrogance and conceit because he talks in glowing terms of pieces he has made. To be fair to him, he also waxes enthusiastic about other knappers' works, so it is not all conceit, but he violates the rules of knap-in behavior when he praises his own work too much. Similarly, while it is normal to criticize another knapper's point to his face, most knappers are polite in doing so, and carefully point out good features, too. Criticisms of points when the maker is not present may be less restrained, but the good fellowship of knap-ins requires respect of others regardless of their skill, at least while talking to them. Likewise, gossip and comments about other knappers are frequent, some friendly and admiring, some not so. And a good thing for me: gossip is an indispensable boon to the anthropologist.

Although knap-ins emphasize an egalitarian worldview, there are, of course, differences in status and prestige among knappers, and there is a good deal of competition, usually unacknowledged. It is not surprising that the most important route to prestige and respect among the knappers is knapping skill.

There are other routes to prestige, other things a knapper can do to become seen as an important part of the knap-in. Knap-in organizers gain some status just by being hosts, although to be successful they usually have other admirable traits such as organizational ability, lots of local connections and good networks among knappers, and a charismatic or at least gregarious personality. Some individuals make notable contributions to the knap-in as an event, organizing competitions, bartering sessions, Ooga-Booga ceremonies, or presentations. Some shape the knap-in because they are witty, good storytellers, striking characters, or especially knowledgeable about artifacts or archaeology. Some regulars, not always knappers, provide needed services by selling stone, knapping tools, or raw materials for other crafts.

Although individuals may make important contributions to the knap-in and even become key participants without being expert knappers, most of those I had in mind as I wrote the paragraph above are also highly regarded for their knapping skills, and many knappers whose other contributions to the knap-in are small may still be admired and important simply as top knappers. Knapping skill is an important way of ranking people, and easily visible, because knapping at knap-ins is so public.

As I explained earlier, the action of knapping at a knap-in is meaningful in many ways. It is a means of exchanging knowledge about knapping, a public demonstration of your identity as a knapper, and an expression of skill that affects your standing among knappers.

Knappers consider public knapping to be important because knappers should share knowledge. Secrecy is frowned upon. Public knapping also demonstrates that you are a knapper, worthy of membership in the circle. As Tony Romano, a Minnesota dentist, put it, "Knapping is like dentistry. You can read all the books and talk the theory, but at a certain point you have to get down and *do* it, and if you can't, everyone knows it was just bullshit." Arrowheads are less sensitive than teeth, but the point remains true.

Public knapping allows an individual's skill to be assessed by others, which is the aspect I wish to consider here. Public knapping is more or less of a performance, depending on the knapper. Many knappers work in a cluster of friends, watching each other and exchanging gossip and comments on the knapping. Almost everyone wanders around the knap-in from time to time and stops to watch and chat with other knappers; you never know who will be looking over your shoulder. Often a knapper will respond to a question or comment from a bystander by explaining what he is doing, demonstrating a technique, or pointing out a problem he is trying to overcome. Some knappers also make a point of knapping where they can be seen.

Although most knappers like to see and be seen, and knappers of any level will watch and talk with beginners and experts alike, there are some distinct patterns. Even an outside observer with no knapping experience might eventually figure out who some of the top knappers were by watching who accumulates audiences when they knap. Certain knappers, and certain kinds of knapping, are considered dramatic, interesting, unusual, or especially skillful. People notice and stop to watch when Bob Hunt tackles an unusually large piece; as we will see, large pieces have high esthetic value, and making them is a dramatic process because it is risky. Watching Bob work on an 18-inch biface has some of the same appeal as stock car racing—there is always the potential for a spectacular disaster. Fluting is similar. Anytime someone flutes a point, other knappers will stop working to watch, and cameras and video recorders will be pointed. Again, a difficult feat provides a dramatic tension between reward and failure. Fluting is not done by everyone, and when a jig is used, the process of setting up a point for fluting is highly visible, notifying potential audiences. The whole process, however, does not take too long, five to ten minutes, so many people are willing to interrupt other activities to watch.

A few knappers will have an audience no matter what they are mak-

Figure 6.2. Jim Spears knapping with an audience. Fort Osage, 1994.

ing. Jim Spears is one example (Figure 6.2). Jim is a commercial knapper and fur trader who began knapping some thirty years ago. He is a handsome man of middle height with a fine mustache, soft spoken and articulate. He is famous among the Fort Osage knappers for his ability to make outstandingly thin large bifaces, and because he insists on working only with stone and antler tools. He was once described to me by another knapper as "the finest technical knapper alive," not just because of his knapping skill, but because he is unusually good at explaining what he is doing while knapping. This, of course, is also a highly valued trait, conforming to the knap-in ethos that skills should be taught and knowledge exchanged. In any case, when Jim sits down to knap, he is sure to have a group of other knappers standing around him, including other top knappers as expert as he. This, too, is a sign of a top knapper, that other experts will watch him. They are not as likely to learn something new as less skillful knappers, but are there to participate in the flow of information and for the pleasure of watching another good performer.

Audiences and performances can be more formally structured as well. There have been a number of occasions at Fort Osage when word spread through the crowd that a demonstration was in the offing. Usually a knapper with an unusual skill had been asked by someone to demonstrate, and others who heard of it considered the event interesting enough to spread the word. Three examples give a good feel for the patterns.

I first saw Jim Hopper at the May knap-in in 1991. I believe this was the first time he had come to Fort Osage; it was the first time I and many of the others had seen someone doing what is now called lap knapping or flake over grinding. People had seen some of his perfectly pressure-flaked points, and some also knew the work of Rick Warren, who did similar flaking over ground surfaces, but not many knew how it was done, and when it became known that he planned to demonstrate in the evening, many people stayed late.

Electric lights had been plugged in all over the garage, and Jim had set up his electric grinder on a table against one wall. There was a large audience crowded around, and Jim began by saying that he had been a little reluctant to show his techniques because if Warren had come he might have caused a scene. Richard Warren, I learned later, was a secretive man with a reputation for paranoia (see Chapter 2). He felt that this grinding technique was his personal trade secret. He died a year or two after this. Jim said he had figured out his version of the technique from examining Warren's points.

Working from a small cut blank of obsidian or other fine colorful material, Jim carefully ground it to a perfect lanceolate form with a biconvex cross-section, and prepared platforms along both edges on one face by grinding. With a small pressure tool he then removed a single series of perfect pressure flakes from one face, prepared another set of platforms, and repeated the process on the other face, as meticulous and precise as a Swiss watchmaker (Figure 6.3). When he was finished, the ground surfaces had been replaced by a perfect rippled pattern of narrow pressure flake scars.

The reactions of the watching knappers ranged from awe to disdain. A few felt that this was cheating rather than proper knapping, and I heard a couple joking about the "poor Indians" trying to grind a point by dragging it behind a horse. However, more knappers were distinctly intrigued. Hopper demonstrated again the next night, before an equally large audience, and spent some time letting others try, or preparing blanks for them to flake. There were a lot of detailed questions, and several knappers went away muttering about getting lap-

Figure 6.3. Lap-knapped points by Jim Hopper, 1991. Photo by Sarah DeLong.

idary grinding equipment for themselves. I left convinced that next season I would see a lot of imitators. As it turned out, this was not the case. The technique is not as easy as it looks, and it takes a lot of practice to achieve Hopper's level of perfection, not to mention the expensive cutting and grinding equipment. It took several years for the technique to spread, and Hopper is not the only one responsible. For instance, Scott Silsby had apparently given a similar demonstration at the Fairview Heights Knap-in in 1987 (Cresson 2001). Although a number of knappers do lap knapping consistently, it remains a minority technique, most popular among some of the art and commercial knappers.

At the same knap-in, Mike Stafford asked D. C. Waldorf to show him how he does the "stitching" on the handles of Danish Neolithic daggers. Mike provided a roughed-out dagger blank of Danish flint for D. C. to work on. This was a less public demonstration. Mike was the main audience, although others were welcome, and D. C. often attracts a crowd when he knaps. Mike knew I was interested, so he forewarned me and several others, and we all watched for a while. Other knappers would drift by and stop to watch, too, but the whole process took three hours and no one but Mike watched the whole thing. This is a fairly common format for demonstrations. One individual instigates a demonstration, often providing the material and asking for a specific lesson.

I saw a structurally similar, but more dramatic, demonstration by Jim Spears, in May 1994. Don Kyleberg, a Texas knapper who frequently attended the Fort Osage Knap-in until he died later that year, had asked Jim to show him how he fluted Clovis points by direct percussion. Don had provided two preforms for Jim to work with, and Jim prepared the first for fluting, isolating a nipple platform and grinding heavily. He uses an unusual motion, pressing his antler billet hard against the platform several times, then striking a very quick blow. This time he produced an adequate flute on one face and a weak one on the other.

This was on Sunday, toward the end of the knap-in, and most of the serious knappers who were still there watched at least part of Jim's demonstration. He thus had an unusually good audience, including D. C. Waldorf and a couple of other top knappers. At this point he put down his tools and announced dramatically:

> I am going to show you all one of my kept secrets. I do flute things this way, but now I'm going to show you how I really do most of them. Only two people in the world know about this, and they are sworn to secrecy. I've been a commercial knapper all my life, you see, but now I don't feel right trying to keep this a secret after Don asked me to show him what I do. So I'm going to open the little green bag and show you a trick I figured out from looking at the broken Folsoms from Lindenmeier when Joe Ben Wheat showed them to me. I noticed the tips are squared and ground, and that means an anvil technique.

Jim proceeded to show us his secret: a set of moose antler supports, in several sizes. He bound the point to the right-sized support, with the tip of the point resting on a shelf and the antler in turn held against a cobble anvil on his leg. His "trick" helped support the point and prevented it from breaking under the stress of removing a large flute by percussion. Jim kept saying that "anyone can do this," which may explain why he was originally reluctant to reveal it. The audience opinion was that not very many actually have the confidence and accuracy to do percussion fluting, even with his clever support system. It is also fair to say that by the time I saw this demonstration, fluting was no longer a valuable commercial secret, although a decade ago his trick might have given him an edge over some of the competition. Now there are far too many knappers who flute excellently, by a variety of methods. At the time, everyone was impressed and thanked Jim for showing us. By 1998, Frank Stevens's Great Lakes Lithic Supply Company was advertising "Hand held antler fluting jigs—another Jim Spears special!"

These three typical events show how some of the best knappers use the knap-in to show their skill and build or reinforce a reputation. By participating as audience, other knappers in turn express admiration and partake of the ethos of sharing and learning that is the ideal of the knap-in. To some extent, how members of the audience participate also reflects status. The demonstrator generally interacts with anyone who asks a question, but often tends to address more remarks to other knappers of high status. Mike Stafford, a young archaeological knapper who is well liked and was considered an "up and coming" knapper in 1992, was the instigator of several demonstrations when he asked people to show him their tricks. Even when the demonstration was not his doing, knappers tended to make sure that if he was interested, he got a good seat and was included in the discussion. I felt my own status change: as I became a better knapper and my book was published in 1994, and people at the knap-ins came to know me, top knappers were much more likely to address technical comments to me during a demonstration.

Talking with Stone: Ritual Exchanges and the Expression of Status

Knappers exchange goods and knowledge all the time at knap-ins—that is one of the obvious purposes of the occasion. What is less obvious to most is that some of these exchanges are not mere commercial transactions or even learning opportunities, but serve also to express relationships among the knappers. They are not ritual in any religious sense, but in the anthropological sense of a repetitively structured act intended to convey meanings to an audience. Part of the "message" behind many of the exchanges of stone points, raw material, and information is the relative status of the knappers involved.

Near the end of the May 1992 knap-in I was sitting near Bob Hunt as he tidied up his kit. He handed me a small piece of "mozarkite" and said, "Here, you can make a bird point out of this." (Mozarkite is a fossiliferous chert variety from Missouri, and Bob had a good source. A bird point is what knappers and collectors call any small arrow point.) The piece of stone was a blunt triangular flake with the edges trimmed, ready to be worked further. I said, "It's all started," and thanked Bob. I handled it awhile and laid it on my box. Later that morning I worked it into a pretty corner-notched point. Don Dreisoerner, who was talking to me as I worked, admired it. I took it off to show to Bob, saying, "here's your bird point," and he and Larry Kinsella pronounced it good. Actually, it was only average by knap-in standards—it was pretty stone, symmetrical, adequately thin, nicely notched, with no major mistakes, but not parallel flaked or unusual. They gave it back, and I turned around and gave it to Don, saying, "Here, this is for you." He thanked me and praised it, said he was making up a frame and would include mine with my name on it. I said if he had something he liked, I'd like a specimen of his work, and he gave me a nice little tri-notched point. He had earlier given me a rough biface of novaculite and a thick novaculite flake that he said was good for grinding platforms. This, in turn, grew out of his shyness when I asked him to do a formal interview. He initially said, "Well, let me think about it" and "I'm honored but . . ." and he hemmed and hawed but about an hour later came up to me and said, "I'm ready anytime you want." We had a good talk, and a long discussion of general archaeology after.

It was only thinking about this set of exchanges later that I realized I was seeing a kind of ritual, in the form of structured exchanges that reflect relationships among knappers. Appropriately enough, the primary medium of expression in these exchanges is stone. Many of the exchanges are structured by the relative status of the knappers and express their opinions of each other. It will be useful to discuss four kinds of exchanges, which express a variety of relationships.

One typical form of exchange is for a higher-status or more skillful knapper to give a piece of material to a less skillful knapper for him to "try something new." This is a friendly expression of superiority, and sometimes comes with a technical tip, or is in response to something the giver has noticed about the other knapper. When Bob Hunt gave me the mozarkite he was responding to my repeated inquisitiveness about different materials and his observation that I tended to make smallish points. Material in such exchanges is rarely of the highest quality; the mozarkite flake was too small for Bob to be really interested in it, although he had worked on it a bit.

In the exchange with Bob Hunt, the appropriate response was nonmaterial. I admired his gift, made something out of it, and showed the result to Bob to demonstrate that I appreciated it. I also used the occasion to demonstrate my ability to perform at a particular level, which, as we have seen, is part of a knapper's persona. Had I botched the point, the exchange was not important or public, and I would not have lost much status. Since the point turned out well, the appropriate cycle of material exchange and response was completed, and the finished point went on to play a part in a second, related kind of exchange.

Despite being one of the organizing core of the Fort Osage Knap-in, Don Dreisoerner always remained rather in the background. This is partly because he seemed rather shy and also because he is not one of the top knappers, but I wanted to interview him because he was one of the organizers and in previous conversations had always been friendly and observant. On his part, he is more interested in archaeology than many other knappers and wanted to pick my brains on archaeological subjects. Our mutual exchange of information and goodwill was further expressed by our material exchange: one knapper's point for another's. Our point exchange was on a more-or-less equal level, although since Don had watched and discussed my knapping as I made the point, and considered me the better knapper, my gift to Don was in some ways similar to Bob's gift to me. Points are usually exchanged between equals or acquired by less skillful knappers from those they admire. The most skillful knappers tend not to collect points from others, although there are lots of exceptions to this, as the status relationships are complicated by the collecting motives of many knappers, including myself. Those who, like myself, are collecting points (either for fun or investment, or to illustrate articles) mostly buy them, but it is still true that the flow tends to be from better knappers to less skillful, or from knappers to non-knappers.

Disregarding the more commercial exchanges, gifts of points usually reflect the high status of the giver. The first time I watched George Eklund knap, for instance, he noticed my interest, and without really knowing me at all, spontaneously gave me the point he made. I have seen him give away more points than any other knapper. There is usually an audience, and such spontaneous generosity carries a complicated message. It expresses the encouraging example that a skilled knapper should set for others, and it also demonstrates that making points is easy and fast for George. Even though he earns a living through knapping and related activities, he is skillful enough not to care about making a profit on each and every point.

A third important kind of exchange is the reciprocal gifting of materials. At the May 1992 knap-in, I brought with me a nodule of Partridge Creek rhyolite for John Reynolds, the state archaeologist for Kansas and one of the few archaeologists who regularly attended knap-ins. At the previous knap-in he had given me a sawn slab of obsidian from Guatemala. As we were packing up our tents, Earnie Jones asked me, "Did you get any of the Georgetown that guy was selling?" I said no, so he gave me two nice small nodules. In return, I said, "Here, try something different" and gave him my other nodule of the Partridge Creek rhyolite, which was small, and I apologized for a flaw in it. These exchanges are very typical. Most knappers like to try new materials, and exchanges like this are a primary means of obtaining small amounts of material to experiment with. They also express mutual goodwill and often long-term relationships that may pass into correspondence and contacts outside the knap-ins, or may simply be continued and renewed from knap-in to knap-in. This neatly conforms to the proper anthropological model of reciprocity—the exchanges tend to be between social equals, the material exchanged is roughly equal in value, the exchanges can take place over long time spans, and the expression and formation of social relationships are more important than any economic motive (Sahlins 1972).

Lower-status knappers also give material to higher-status knappers in a fourth kind of exchange. This is usually in the context of "show me how you do something" and sometimes develops into the kind of public demonstration described above, as when Mike Stafford provided a flint biface so that D. C. Waldorf could show him how he does the stitching on Danish dagger handles. Some more commercial transactions also take this form. A purchaser can "commission" a particular piece from a knapper he admires and often provides the raw material. For instance, I watched Roy Motley pressure flake a point for Ken Dempsey out of a piece of green agate that Ken had bought from someone else. Roy commented as he worked that it was rather scary, because the material was expensive as well as thin and fragile, and he would have taken more chances had it not been a commissioned piece.

In the end he finished it nicely and Ken paid him for it. The expensive and rare material added to the prestige and "manna" of the point, as did its manufacture by a well-known and skillful knapper. Being asked to make a piece is also a mark of regard for a knapper's skill.

This format is so well established and recognized that the knappers even play with it. On one occasion, Bob Hunt had started a large biface and made it into a nice blank when he discovered a serious crack. He took a marking pen and wrote a price on the blank in such a way that it not only looked like the other blanks he had for sale, but the price concealed the rather obvious crack. He then found a stooge, who publicly "bought" the cracked blank from Bob and took it to Roy to ask him to make something. Bob had delicious visions of Roy taking a preliminary whack at the blank and dropping his jaw when it shattered, but unfortunately decided he had to record the joke on his video camera and asked Roy to wait while he got his camera. In the interval, Roy discovered the crack and figured out the plot.

Table 6.1 summarizes the meaningful material exchanges. The overall pattern is that knappers of equal status tend to make reciprocal gifts. When knappers are unequal, a gift of stone is usually framed in the context of teaching. This too reflects a core knap-in value, and being regarded as a teacher confers status. It can also be said that in exchanges between unequal knappers, stone is generally exchanged for information. In one case, a knapper may be trading stone for a lesson, but when a higher-status knapper assumes the role of teacher and says "try this" as he gives a piece of material, the proper response is information. The higher teaches the lower, but the lower-status knapper should demonstrate his appreciation and learning. Unequal exchanges can also be regarded in some ways as challenges. To maintain his status, the teacher must teach, and to show a better knapper that you can do something, perhaps even make a better point than he expected, improves your standing in others' eyes. In fact, exchanges not only express perceived relationships, they can be used to create them. As Sahlins puts it, "if friends make gifts, gifts make friends" (1972, 186). If I go to a knapper I admire with a piece of stone and a request for instruction, he will usually feel some obligation to accommodate me; the ethos of the knap-in expects that all knappers will deal fairly and make an effort to teach others. A novice can thus create a teacher-learner relationship with a higher-status knapper, even one he does not know well. If both knappers are satisfied, the relationship may continue.

Table 6.1
Meaningful Material Exchanges

Receiver	Giver	
	High-Status	Low Status
High-Status	Reciprocal gifts of material; rarely points	Material "for demonstration" or "thank you"
Low-Status	Material "try this"; points	Reciprocal gifts of material or points

Exchanges of points and stone, like demonstrations and public knapping, allow knappers to create and express relationships. They especially reveal the covert competition to be recognized as an expert knapper. Few knappers would describe exchanges as reflecting status, however skillfully they use them to do so, and exchanges do not violate the knap-in ethos by setting up overt hierarchies. Whether or not they dislike a "competitive atmosphere," all knappers constantly rank other knappers by skill and compare themselves with others. This behavior is generally kept under cover, and even the few open claims for status are not much regarded. I have never seen anyone of the Fort Osage group make much of winning an award. The names of the few who have participated and won in the New York knapping competition are hardly on the tip of every tongue. While the idea of a competition was hotly debated, no one except D. C. Waldorf, who was describing how the competition worked, argued about the winners and their relative merits. I found this especially notable in a crowd where the fortunes and qualities of national sports teams and athletes, and personal hunting trophies, are frequent topics. Knappers are not uncompetitive, they have simply defined knap-ins as places where competition is to be kept under the tarps.

Art, Craft, or Reproduction: Knapper Esthetics

One of my first friends at Fort Osage was Mike Ash, a cheerful Kansan about my age with a startling head of ash blond hair. Mike's booth features a large glass jeweler's display case, and Mike usually has something new in it each year. Once it was a Remington revolver, realistically carved out of wood. Other times it has been eagle feathers carved of antler or gourds painted in perfect imitation of Southwestern pottery. Always there are knapped points, too. Mike tends to make finely pressure-flaked small to medium points of exotic stone. His favorite form is a basic corner-notched arrowhead, immaculately done, which he mounts with silver wire as pendants or earrings. Mike's background is in art, and he owns a small stained glass studio. A few years ago, Mike began mounting his points as small sculptural pieces, set in polished driftwood, geodes, or other material on a hardwood base with a brass title plate. In 1998 he started using a simpler presentation, matting and framing select points (Figure 7.1). The example illustrated is a "Lost Lake" point of heat-treated Burlington chert. Like most of Mike's points, it is an idealized specimen of the type, rather than a replica. It is "artistic," and putting it in a frame is a statement. A frame says "this is art," and it is a peculiarity of the modern world that imitations of prehistoric tools can now be framed.

Archaeologists, like other scientists, are sometimes thought to be cold and unemotional toward the objects they study, regarding them only as information, data. In fact, we often promote that view with our

Figure 7.1. Mike Ash's point becomes framed and titled art, 1998. The stone is purplish, with a red corner. The title plate reads "'LOST LAKE' Point, 2,500–1,500 B.P."

deadly serious writing. Furthermore, we quite reasonably worry about how too much artistic appreciation of artifacts might bias our interpretations. Even quite savvy archaeologists find themselves slipping into unjustified assertions based on the assumption that ancient hunters had the same esthetic response to artifacts as we do. For example, George Frison and Bruce Bradley (1999, 57) consider some of the Clovis points from the Fenn Cache as so elegant that "we question whether they were ever intended for use." Their book is a fine piece of readable archaeology, but perhaps it is not a coincidence that it is also an art book describing artifacts owned by a prominent collector. Similarly, museums have always tended to display the "best" artifacts, meaning those that are the prettiest, rather than those that are most typical.

I would never suggest that prehistoric stoneworkers had no regard for the beauty of some of their products. Surely they did, and many stone tools have been worked far beyond what was necessary for mere utility. Likewise, all the scientists I know also have, and often express, a deep appreciation of the objects they study as things of beauty and wonder, whether these be mountain ranges or chemical compounds, mathematical formulae or blind cave insects, tropical flowers or prehistoric tools. I don't know any archaeologist who doesn't enjoy holding a finely crafted pot or doesn't mutter "beautiful!" under his or her breath while examining a really nice specimen. We differ from some of the public, who accuse us of coldness, not because we lack an appreciation of beauty, but because we consider the possibility of learning something about prehistoric people more important, while to archaeologists, collectors seem to value the beauty of an object, but all too often have little or no appreciation for what it can teach us about other ways of life. However, it is also true that for many of us, one of the personal rewards of being an archaeologist is that you get to study, handle, and understand some marvelous artifacts. We are a very object-oriented science, and however much we emphasize the informational value of the objects we work with and the need for care in unbiased interpretations of them, we are usually capable of enjoying them as objects, too.

To be specific, I study stone tools not just because they are informative, but because I *like* them. My reasons are hard to define, but I find them intrinsically fascinating and often beautiful. The other Fort Osage flintknappers feel the same way. Many knappers talk about knapping as an "art," and not just in the sense that any tricky skill can be spoken of as an art. The "stone tools" we make are fundamentally art objects. A few knappers make them for income, a few others hunt with them, but the overwhelming majority of stone tools made today exist to be appreciated as objects of beauty. It is perfectly possible to make a stone tool with no thought beyond its usefulness or salability. Many prehistoric points may have existed only to make an arrow sharp. The wretched things that are currently being made in Mexico by the millions and sold in rock shops and airport boutiques across the United States as "Indian arrowheads" are probably made without appreciation—they are certainly cranked out without much care (Figure 7.2). However, even these can be considered beautiful by someone. After all, the tourists who buy these "Indian arrowheads" are not intending to put them on an arrow and kill game.

All the knappers I know have strong ideas about beauty and express them frequently in describing and evaluating stone tools. Although

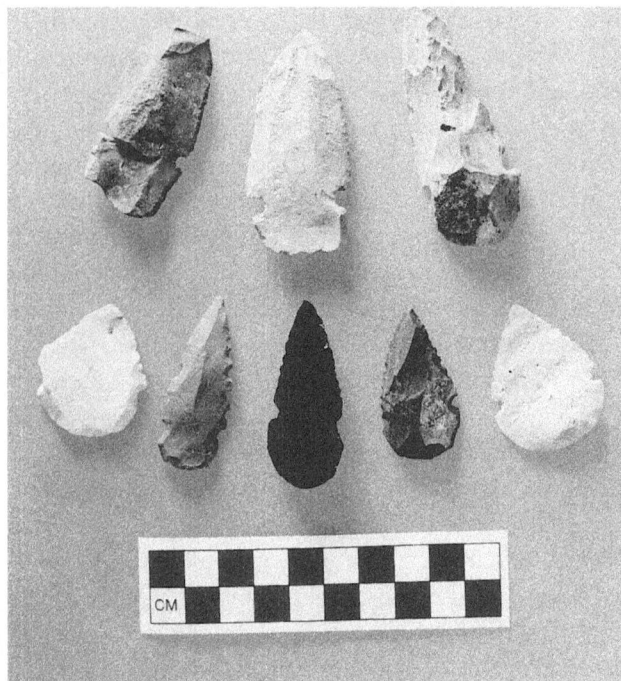

Figure 7.2. Mexican mass-produced arrowheads. Bottom five bought in Phoenix airport 1984, top three in Denver 2001. Notice how they are made with minimum labor by slightly trimming flakes, and the notches on the top three are cut with a grinding wheel instead of flaked. So bad you have to laugh! Photo by Sarah DeLong.

there are differing tastes and opinions, many of these ideas are held in common, a "canon" of esthetic rules defining what is a good point. Rare as unanimity is, I would confidently say that all of the Fort Osage knappers despise the Mexican tourist points. They are the opposite of what a good point should be. They are irregular, minimally worked, unevenly flaked, asymmetrical, small, and thick, conforming to no legitimate prehistoric type of point. These are overt rules, but there is a deeper emotional sense that the Mexican points are made without care, without feeling: they fail as art.

Stone Tools as Art and Folk Art

I will discuss only briefly the esthetic theories of art historians and folklorists, a literature I find painful to read. Art historians are interested in the transmission and history of art forms and motifs, sometimes their meanings, and in artistic merit. The rules by which they judge objects for artistic merit and meaning are usually based on their own culture, and, while they sometimes assume those rules to be universal, historians (and their rules) are often fatally ethnocentric. However, some art historians do concern themselves with the esthetic judgments of other cultures and the meaning of art and art motifs within the culture that produced them. Folklorists are generally interested in the culture of "folk," the nonacademic and informal manifestations of groups that are often subcultural in nature: minorities, ethnic groups, occupations, and the non-elite. They tend to study cultural products: performances like song and poetry, artifacts like folk art and houses. Anthropologists tend to focus on culture and society, the rules and ideas shared by groups of people, and the way people interact and organize themselves. Material objects and immaterial performances are often most of interest to anthropologists as evidence of the underlying structures of culture and the interactions of the human members. However, anthropology also includes the interests of some folklorists and art historians. Performances and material culture, and esthetic judgments and the meanings of art within any culture, are of interest in their own right. This, by the way, is why I hold the academically ethnocentric view that my field is superior. By being so inclusive, anthropology allows me to indulge my curiosity in many ways.

Most of this book has focused on the knappers rather than their products, yet it should be evident that the knappers themselves focus a lot of interest, effort, and emotion on small bits of stone. What, then, can we say about stone tools as art? First, while avoiding esoteric arguments about the nature of art, I want to make the case that both the folklorist and the art historian should find stone tools worthy objects of study according to their own definitions.

Modern knapping is clearly a folk art in the sense used by folklorists. It is a craft that embodies tradition, both an ancient tradition that it emulates and a shorter, more recent tradition as a historic craft. Knapped stone artifacts are produced by a social group that forms a distinct subculture or community of practice. Stone tools are embroiled in performance and symbolic manipulation. As art, knapping follows well-defined esthetic rules, as I will show in a moment. However, it is certainly not a product of the usual academic or high-culture art world, and had its origin as a largely functional craft. Thus, while the folklorist should embrace modern knapping, the art historian might be expected to regard stone tools with disdain.

An example shows where stone tools reside in the art historian's view. The Gerzean knives made at the end of the Predynastic period in

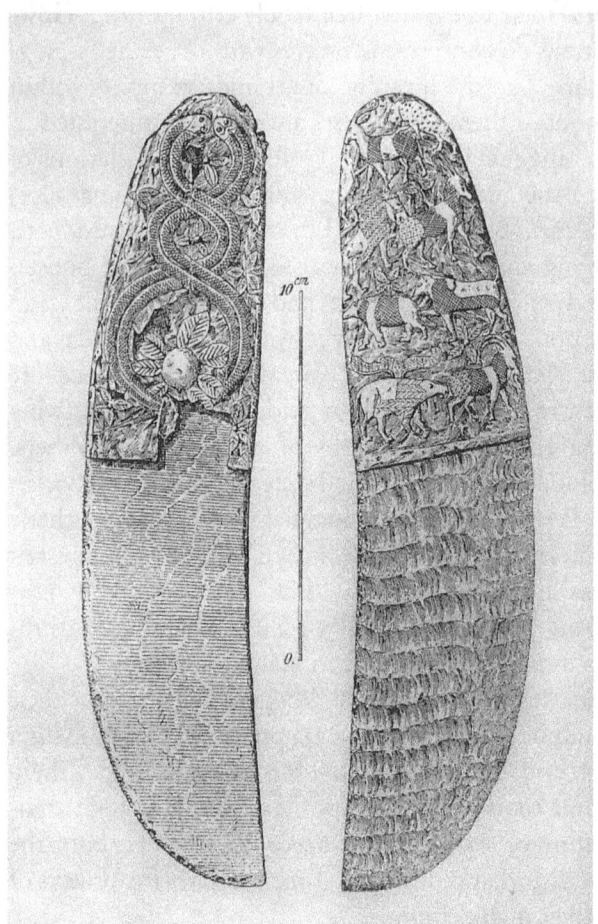

Figure 7.3. Predynastic Egyptian flaked knife in its handle of wood covered in gold leaf. From de Morgan 1926, 144.

Egypt are some of the finest flaked stone objects ever produced (Figure 7.3) (Bradley 1972; Hoffman 1979, 1987; Kelterborn 1984). Some were mounted in handles of carved ivory or gold-sheathed wood. When art historians discuss early Egyptian art, the handles are often illustrated, even if the blade is missing, but the blades are usually not illustrated unless they have been retained by a handle (e.g., Aldred 1965, 35). The handles are art, the blades merely craft. However, just as some folklorists, such as MacDowell and Dewhurst (1980), have used the theories of art historians to argue that some folk art can be treated by the same criteria as "high" art, I would argue that stone tools can also fall under the same light.

According to MacDowell and Dewhurst,

When a body of material folk objects has been located, then the tools of the art historian could be used to sort the objects into three categories: object-types, craft-types, and art-types. Object-types would be those handmade items which show no evidence of a discernible craft tradition or sense of aesthetic values. Craft-types would encompass those objects which exemplify the continuation of a traditional creative expression with no effort at infusing the object with innovation or personal vision. Art-types would include those objects, functional or non-functional, that adhere to the accepted cultural definition of good aesthetics. Presently, any traditional craft-type item may be viewed as art if (1) there was a conscious effort on the part of the maker to construct a pleasing arrangement of form, color, and texture, and (2) if the larger societal definition of beauty coincides with the arranged result. (1980, 57)

These definitions are a good example of why I do not like the art theory literature. It is hard for an anthropologist to imagine any artifact whatsoever that has no evidence of tradition or esthetic values. Even a paper clip can be made in party colors, or become an animated computer icon, or decorate a teenager's earlobe. But let us ignore the absurdities of these definitions to continue the discussion. Ordinary replica projectile points certainly fit the second class, and many modern and prehistoric stone tools unquestionably conform to cultural definitions of esthetics, were carefully made to please the eye of the maker, and even appeal to the larger society, stimulating collectors and connoisseurs to offer huge prices. However, to continue quoting MacDowell and Dewhurst, "Often a reigning societal definition will capriciously neglect a medium of production, although the summation of its components falls within the dictated canons of taste" (1980, 58). In other words, some things don't attract enough attention or are not recognized by the art authorities—true enough in the case of stone tools. At the moment, I am inclined to consider neglect by the art authorities a compliment. After all, in recent years these authorities have awarded prestigious art prizes to self-absorbed twerps for exhibits of dirty beds, bottled feces, and small lights blinking in empty rooms. Or perhaps that just shows how hard it is to define art, but the cry of "Don't criticize what you can't understand" often seems to mean "Shut up, my scam is working."

Perhaps it is also the language we use that hinders the recognition of stone tools as art. Tools of any kind are rarely seen as art, and the general terms for the objects we make mostly imply a functional origin or intent: stone tools, projectile points, arrowheads. While many folklorists and some art historians would allow functional items to be considered art, others would disagree. Art must rise above mere craft or tool. It must be individual and emotionally expressive.

To follow our folklorists (MacDowell and Dewhurst 1980) once again, we can quote the widely known opinion of Leo Tolstoy: "To evoke in oneself a feeling one has once experienced and having evoked it in oneself, then by means of movements, line, colors, sounds, or forms expressed in words, so to transmit that feeling that others experience the same feeling—this is the activity of art" (1953, 123). Tolstoy goes on to claim that good art is "infectious," that is, emotionally stimulating and communicative. Infectiousness depends on three traits. The more "individual feeling" a piece of art embodies, the more strongly it speaks to the viewer. "Clarity of expression" communicates effectively and is readily interpreted. Good art is "sincere," in that the artist is impelled by an inner need to express his or her feelings.

Not to belabor the point, it should be clear from what we have already heard knappers say that their stonework attracts and communicates considerable emotion, impels them (sometimes obsessively), embodies both individual and cultural definitions of what is beautiful, and follows traditions while allowing innovation.

When D. C. Waldorf titled his manual *The Art of Flint Knapping*, he surely meant "art" both in the sense of a skill to be learned and an expressive esthetic; this is how knappers think of knapping. Knappers talk constantly about flintknapping as an expressive art and describe prehistoric finds the same way. As Jeff Gower told me, hunkered over the debitage at Fort Osage, "I want my Daltons to look the best they can, that's the goal of every flintknapper, in my mind, to excel to the best of their ability. You look at a piece that is a piece of artwork that Native Americans did, or even a modern flintknapper, and that creates the mindset for that point type. That's why I do the things I do—a fluted Dalton is more attractive to me than a nonfluted Dalton." Jeff is entirely typical. He is a commercial knapper, who makes his points as replicas of prehistoric types, but he is still knapping for art, and he considers the prehistoric and modern examples he uses as models "artwork."

There are now enough knappers at such a level of technical expertise that many feel knapping can and should be going beyond replicating prehistoric forms. Woody Blackwell expressed in print what I have heard from him and a number of others. In a column in *Chips* (Blackwell 1996), he wrote that the "golden age" of knapping is here. We are no longer bound by the relatively limited repertoires of any individual prehistoric culture, but can replicate points from any of them. We have access to new tools and materials from all over the world. We are not bound by the necessity to produce an efficient tool. "Most of us knap to create things that please the eye and gratify the hand. Indeed, many of the words used to define fine sculpture are equally valid for well knapped pieces, words like quality of line, rhythm, symmetry, balance, and proportion. We are becoming more aware of the artistic potential of knapping" (Blackwell 1996, 5).

In promoting knapping as art, Woody is perhaps more radical than most knappers. He would like to see knappers go beyond the normal bifacial forms and try multifacial work. "I expect to see sculpture that incorporates knapping . . . we are about to see the birth of sculpture in the medium of flintknapping" (Blackwell 1996, 5). On one occasion, Woody and I talked about not merely incorporating knapped pieces into multimedia sculptures, but sculpting by knapping, and combining knapped surfaces with carved and polished surfaces on the same piece of stone.

Errett Callahan expresses a similarly radical view of the future of flintknapping (Callahan 1990, 1992, 1999). Callahan makes and sells stone knives (see Figure 9.5) that regularly win "Art Knife" and "Fantasy Knife" awards at knife shows, but is ambivalent about calling his work "art." While he uses the term frequently, and his catalog contains numerous comments about the creative and expressive nature of art that certainly apply to his knapping, he prefers to emphasize craftsmanship and technical perfection. At one point he describes the artist as "one who works at the limit of his ability" (Callahan 1999, 34), but then goes on to say rather contradictorily, "I'm not interested in 'art.' I'm interested in craftsmanship. What I want to do is make the best crafted stone knives of which I am capable, taxing myself to the limit of my ability. . . . I like good traditional design and I like exotic design, and if someone wants to call that art well let them. But if it's not well done, then I don't give a hoot, no matter how clever the design. In other words, the better the craft, the better the artistry." Callahan also emphasizes "tradition" as part of his art, at the same time as he promotes innovative pieces such as his "Dinosaur Series." These large knives with eccentric stone blades set in handles carved in the shape of dinosaurs are anything but traditional forms. For Callahan, the traditional aspect of such work is in his techniques, which he calls "Neolithic," insisting that he uses only antler and stone percussion, antler and some copper pressure flakers, and hand grinding (Callahan 1999, 10–11, 39). This esthetic of "tradition" combined with "taking knapping to its limits" is one we will return to, as many knappers share it in one way or another.

No one I know has yet gone very far in experimenting with completely nontraditional knapping such as sculpture. The use of knapped elements in sculptural arrangements is becoming more common. Mike Ash's work is one example; others do similar things at various levels of quality. In 1998 I noticed a couple of knappers starting to incorporate knapped glass points into stained glass panels, and Callahan is also experimenting with this form (Callahan 1999, 32). The most elaborate sculpture-related knapping I have seen so far are Richard Warren's "teleolithic" arrangement of bifaces and a piece, advertised by Callahan in his *Piltdown Productions Catalog,* which he describes as "A floral arrangement of razor-sharp colored glass slivers. Prismatic blades of ruby red, golden amber and emerald green glass unfold amid a pool of blue percussion flakes on a mirror surface" (1999, 70). It is notable that both these examples, like the simpler pieces of Mike Ash and others, attract admiration partly by crossing borders, creating the unexpected. They all use recognizably traditional knapped forms in unusual sculptural or artistic settings, or to look at it the other way around, the traditions of sculpture, framing, and other artistic conventions are made to incorporate forms that most people have not previously thought of as art.

Much art knapping works through the elaboration of traditional forms as much as by the creation of new forms. Stone whimsies fall in this category. Flaked rings, jewelry, and letters were made by the nineteenth-century English gunflint knappers (Forrest 1983; Whittaker 2001b) and are occasionally produced today. There was a short vogue at Fort Osage for points that were knapped with their tips still attached to the parent nodule so that they seemed to be embedded in the stone, or growing out of it. "Eccentrics" imitating or inspired by ancient Maya pieces are being made by a number of knappers. Other eccentrics, like

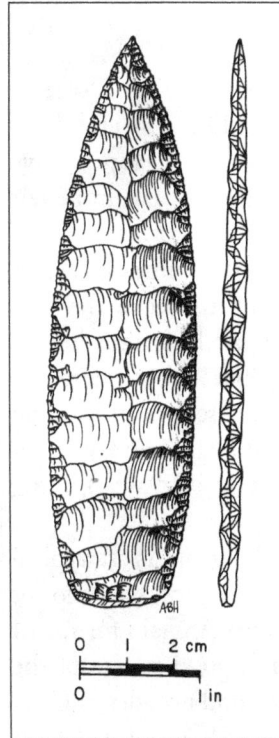

Figure 7.4. Finely flaked blade by Scott Silsby. Drawing by Amy Henderson from Lithic Casting Lab cast.

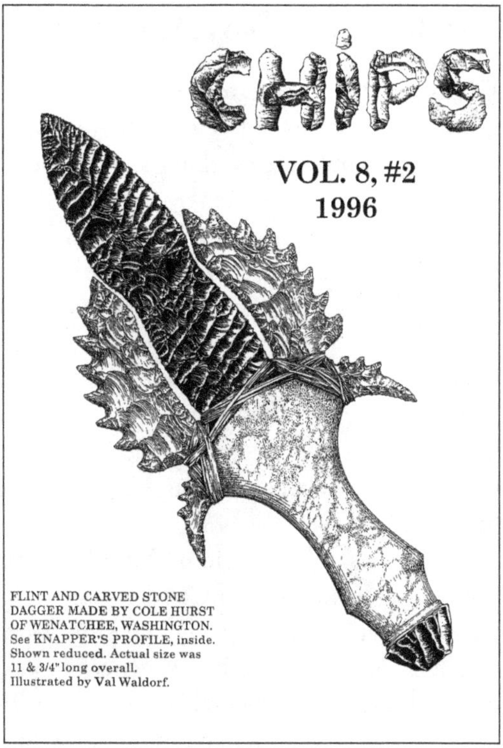

Figure 7.5. Cole Hurst's fantasy knife from the cover of Chips 8 (2), drawing by Val Waldorf. Courtesy of Val Waldorf, Cole Hurst.

the ones once sold as antiquities by Mack Tussinger, owe more to a tradition of decorative elaboration of points and a display of knapping virtuosity. Superbly controlled patterned pressure flaking, often over ground surfaces (Figure 7.4), is now common, both on points and on larger pieces that can be used as fancy knife blades. Many knappers who make knives are hafting finely flaked stone blades in carved handles of stone, antler, or wood. Some of these are elaborate multipiece fantasies, like Cole Hurst's stone-handled dagger (Figure 7.5) or Callahan's creations.

Although many knappers speak of knapping as art and sympathize with visions like that expressed by Woody Blackwell, there is also some ambivalence among knappers about what they think they are doing.

Two Knappers, Two Attitudes

Sitting under a side tent on a hot September day at Fort Osage in 1994, I was one of several people watching Mike Ash and John Mondino, who were working side by side. Both these knappers have characteristic, and extremely different, styles. Mike works from cut blanks, making almost exclusively small to medium corner-notched points. They are a stereotyped "arrowhead" form, very symmetrical and carefully done, with nice regular pressure flake patterns (see Figure 7.1), and usually made of some exotic and pretty material. This time, he was working blue glass. Mike's preferred point style reflects his background as a jeweler and stained glass artist, and the way he uses points in small art pieces and jewelry. I have not seen him knap at knap-ins very often, but this time he was showing his style to Art Bibby, who was filming him at work.

Right beside Mike, John Mondino was making his most typical product, a Turkey Tail of Cobden chert (Figure 7.6). John sells a lot of reproduction points, mostly the large Midwestern Archaic forms, of which Turkey Tails are his favorite. He also has a good source of the material used for many prehistoric Turkey Tails, round nodules of Cobden chert with distinctive banding. As John and Mike finished their points, someone in the group teased John, saying, "Why don't you do pretty flaking like Mike's?" Although John and Mike had been admiring each other's work, John immediately replied with considerable force: "I'm making reproductions, not artwork!"

John and Mike are two typical knappers, both considered quite skillful, but reflecting a major division within knapping esthetics. Both points intended as art or jewelry and those made as reproductions of prehistoric tools embody esthetic judgments. Some judgments, such as how closely a point follows a prehistoric prototype, can only be applied to some points, but other ideals are sought in all points. What, then, are the esthetic qualities that knappers seek in their work?

The Ideal Point: Common Esthetic Rules

Listening to what knappers praise and strive for, it is easy to abstract the general rules of esthetics. The ideal point looks good, and looks right. More specifically, a good-looking point is large, thin, and well flaked, symmetrical, with good lines, and is made of attractive materi-

Figure 7.6. Two typical points by John Mondino, a Hardin and a Turkey Tail of Cobden chert (1994), flank a small arrow point by Mike Ash (1990). Photo by Sarah DeLong.

al. Many points, especially those that are intentionally replicating prehistoric forms, embody all of the above, but do not look "right" unless they conform in appearance and style to the appropriate type.

Technical mastery is a large part of the esthetic of knapped stone, and many of the general rules that are heard everywhere and universally understood have to do with technical excellence. The three most obvious are size, thinness, and quality of flaking.

In general, the larger the dimensions of a stone tool, the more desirable it is. Collectors see prehistoric points in this light; not only are the larger forms of more interest than the smaller, but the larger specimens of any type are more valuable, all else being equal. Many modern points are giants by prehistoric standards. Desirable size is limited only when a point is being judged by its authenticity as a replica. Large points gain prestige because they are visually imposing, but also because they are technically difficult. Flint is extremely hard, but quite inflexible. The longer a point is, the more likely it is to vibrate or flex beyond its endurance when it is struck or even if it is gripped too hard. "Bending fractures" are a common and easily recognized disaster in both prehistoric and modern knapping (Whittaker 1994; Callahan 1979a). Desirably thin and fragile points are, of course, the likeliest to be broken by a minor error.

Small points are generally devalued. Beginning knappers may admit that they only make "bird points," and small ordinary points are just not seen as very interesting. Even the finely flaked examples of Cahokia points and similar "bird point" forms do not attract a lot of attention, although some top knappers make and sell them. However, making extremely small points can also be technically difficult. George Eklund, Errett Callahan, and Mike Cook (a Michigan knapper, not at Fort Osage) are among those who sometimes make miniature points, less than a centimeter long. Although they are well flaked, using a needle or similar tool, and usually made of exotic materials, these tiny points are a novelty that few knappers are interested in making, and I would guess that they are too small and too unconventional to be much in demand among collectors.

Even relatively large pieces may be unimpressive unless they are properly thinned. On the other hand, extremely thin points, even if they are not oversized, are considered attractive. Obviously, this is partly a matter of technical difficulty. Thin pieces are easy to break, and it is difficult to set up good platforms on thin edges to further thin a biface. As a biface gets thinner, the surfaces tend to get flatter, and it becomes difficult to maintain a regular flake pattern and avoid ending flakes in ugly steps.

Knappers even quantify thinness. A ratio of width to thickness is commonly used in describing points and as a knapping goal. A W/T ratio of 5/1 makes a good normal point and 10/1 is outstanding. Beyond 10/1, knappers begin to joke about points that disappear when you look at them edge on (Blackwell 1995), and make poetic comparisons to paper and potato chips. Thinness is even more important on large bifaces than on points. The skill of knappers like Jim Spears and Bob Patten is admired partly because they are reputed to make thinner bifaces than almost anyone else (Figure 7.7).

The concept of good flaking is more nebulous than thinness. A well-flaked point has a pleasing regularity of flake scars, even if it is not parallel flaked (Figure 7.8). Regular flake scars produce an attractive pattern on the surface and also demonstrate mastery of the material.

Figure 7.7. Large, thin bifaces by Jim Spears, Jim Hopper, and an unknown knapper. The last was bought at an auction in Iowa, in a case marked "Hardin County." It is much too thin and finely flaked for a normal point from the Midwest, not a normal type, unpatinated, made of Danish flint, and so obviously modern that I was the only one interested in it. Photo by Sarah DeLong.

On a point knapped by traditional methods, producing a perfect final series of flakes, rhythmically spaced, without step termination or other irregularities, requires thinking like a chess master. A well-planned strategy from start to finish, brilliant tactical innovation to overcome unforeseen problems, and perfect execution at every step are needed, because a flaw anywhere in the process may prevent a perfect endgame. Most knappers admire parallel pressure-flaked points, also referred to as pattern-flaked or ripple-flaked, and part of the admiration recognizes the mental discipline, the intangible thought, behind the solid flint.

Most knapped pieces which aspire to high art are pattern-flaked, which is why lap knapping is popular. Grinding a perfect surface avoids all the intermediate knapping steps where problems may crop up and makes it easier to produce a perfect final pattern. This, too, is why many knappers do not admire flake over grind pieces as much as they

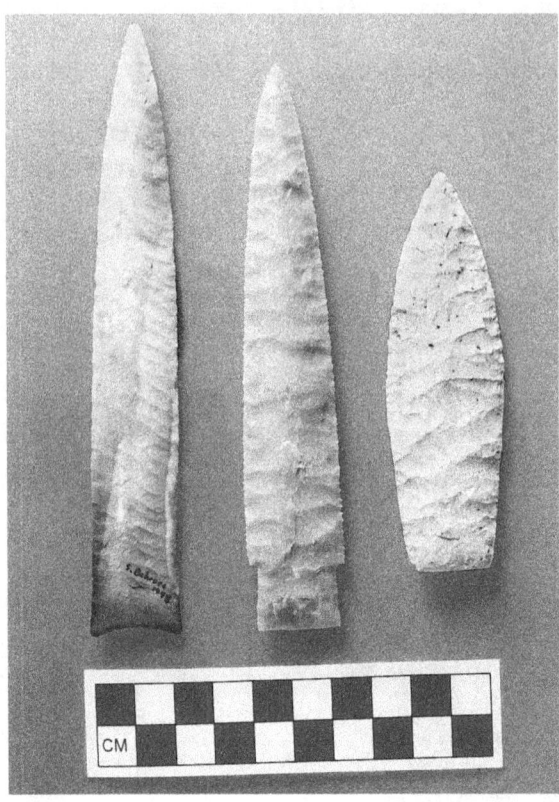

Figure 7.8. Regular flaking patterns on points: Left, extremely regular diagonal patterned pressure flaking over ground blank (Steve Behrnes, 1998). Center, moderately patterned collateral pressure flaking (John Whittaker, 2001). Right, unpatterned but careful flaking (Dick Grybush, 1996). Photo by Sarah DeLong.

do points that are finely knapped by "abo" (aboriginal or traditional) techniques. The input of skill is seen, justly or not, as being less.

Ordinary points are more randomly flaked, especially if they are realistic replicas of most prehistoric point types. Here, good flaking means avoiding errors. Terminations should "feather" out smoothly; hinges or steps leave abrupt lines and high spots on the point which disrupt the visual surface. Remnant areas of cortex or the surface of the original flake blank indicate that the knapper failed to run flakes all the way across the piece, and may not have thinned it effectively, either (Figures 7.9, 7.10).

A good piece of knapping is not just technical mastery. I have, in fact, seen some work that was at a high level of skill, but left me cold. At one knap-in I visited, there was a knapper whose name I never learned who had a whole table of extremely thin points. Although their thinness was impressive, no one seemed to consider them very attractive. They had begun as slabs and been so obsessively thinned that they

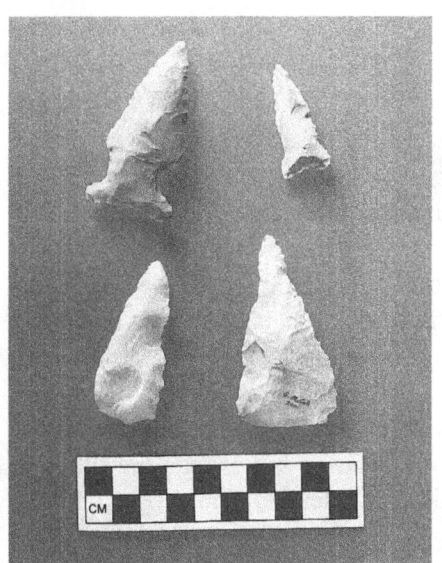

Figure 7.9. Everyone starts like this: first points by Grant McCall, 2001, showing typical beginners' errors: failure to thin, irregular flaking with step terminations, remnant flake surfaces, asymmetrical forms and edges.

Figure 7.10. Three contemporary Mexican commercial points. The two to right were bought in 1996 in Mexico City, and the long biface at Teotihuacan in 2002. These represent rather careless percussion thinning. The long biface is not too bad, but note the ground area in the center where the knapper failed to remove a thick spot and ground it off. Compare to the really well-done thin bifaces in Figure 7.7. Photo by Sarah DeLong.

Art, Craft, or Reproduction

were very flat. A good point should have at least a slightly biconvex cross-section, so that it looks like a "traditional" point. As a result of the thinness and exceedingly flat cross-section, the retouch finishing the edges was rather steep, and the edges had a beveled look rather than a more pleasing smooth contour. In addition, the outline shape of the points tended to be rather squared-off and mechanical-looking. My overall impression was that the knapper had mastered a particular skill at some cost to other considerations.

Good form in a point thus plays a major part in its artistic impact. There is, of course, some variation in esthetic judgments of this sort; some knappers prefer straight lines, others more curvilinear forms, and so on. Nevertheless, everyone would agree that a good point should be symmetrical, with clean lines and a pleasing balance among different parts. Details like notches should be well defined, and edges should be straight and sharp.

A few other rules apply less generally. Attractive material is one. Attractive material to a knapper usually means stone that flakes well with smooth fracture surfaces. Even more important, it should be colorful. The most desirable materials are those that have patterning or color variation within the piece. Most knappers also prefer material that looks natural. Few do much work in glass, even though some gaudy colors can be found. Occasionally an exception is made. Fiber optic glass is flaked by a few knappers. It has an odd metallic look, definitely not natural, but it is still considered attractive by many and is also valued because it is a novelty. At first it was also very expensive, which added to its prestige.

The Rules in Action: Knapping Contests

Anthropologists who are interested in the rules that organize societies and human activities often have to learn them by observation, and derive a sort of an abstract that is partly their own interpretation. We all learn many of the rules we live by this way and often know whether something is right or wrong without being able to explain why. Language is a perfect example; most people recognize good or bad grammar, but often cannot list the rules that determine their judgment. Modern Americans, living in a society that is literate and has a complex formalized legal system, are used to the concept of explicit rules. We have legislation, grammar books, guides to etiquette, and so forth. Becoming a knapper and a member of the knap-in community involves learning the esthetic rules by observation and osmosis. Most knappers could explain them in much the way I have, and in fact, I, like most knappers, picked up much of the esthetic rule system by listening as other knappers criticized my work and discussed each other's. As knap-ins became larger and more formalized, it was inevitable that someone would come up with the idea of knapping contests. Contests, after all, are common in almost every aspect of American life. The development of knapping contests is an interesting social trend in knap-ins, and contests also imply formalized rules by which performance can be judged. In contests, the esthetic rules the knappers absorb around the debitage piles are made explicit and set down for posterity.

The first knapping contest seems to have been in 1993, at the Genesee Valley Flint Knappers Association Knap-in in Castile, New York. Few of the Fort Osage knappers had been to New York, so I heard little about the Genesee knappers until the next year. At Fort Osage in September of 1994, Gene Stapleton told me he and a number of others had been at the New York Knap-in. He mentioned the contest, but was not at all interested in it and dismissive of what he felt was a competitive atmosphere.

Early the next day, I was sitting in the shed, chatting with Bob Hunt and several others as people drifted in. D. C. Waldorf mentioned that he had just been at the New York Knap-in, and I asked him about the contest. He immediately waxed enthusiastic. "Knapping contests are the wave of the future," he said. "They are going to grow, and we should consider laying some ground rules and organizing them so they are fun and promote good knapping." Waldorf, one of the most expert knappers, confident and proud of his abilities, felt that contests are fun and not really competitive. They publicize knapping in general and raise public interest, and inspire younger knappers and get them recognition. This is the view promoted by the Genesee Valley Knappers and expressed in the statement of philosophy attached to their contest rules (Appendix C). However, not everyone sees contests in that light. While D. C. described his experiences, the other knappers present listened politely. As soon as he had left, Bob Hunt, who had been conspicuously silent and knapping intently throughout, looked up, and the guy next to me looked up, and everyone exchanged glances. Several started shaking their heads, and then Bob burst out, "Well, now I know it's time for me to find a new hobby!" Although a couple of those present defended contests, most of the others agreed that they did not like this competitive idea. They felt it would bring back bad feelings and undesirable practices such as keeping "trade secrets," and there was enough competition, politicking, and tension anyway. There was a general feeling that contests were contrary to the noncompetitive atmosphere of sharing information and good fellowship that they liked at Fort Osage, and someone even said, "I thought I wanted to go to the New York Knap-in, but now I know I don't."

More moderate feelings about contests are probably typical of most knappers. In a letter to *Chips,* Scott Van Arsdale, one of the New York knappers, wrote that contests were fine if not overdone, but "the greatest things about knap-ins are the camaraderie, learning opportunities, and just plain fun. Contests create losers as well as winners. As knappers we should respect each other's work regardless of ability" (Van Arsdale 1995).

As we have seen, there are undeniable rivalries and competitive aspects to knapping, but they often exist covertly within an ethos of egalitarianism. It is common in all cultures for the overt rules of social behavior to be partly subverted by less obvious rules that may not be openly expressed or admitted. Our own society is a case in point, and the conflict we see in knapping reflects a wider social contradiction in America. Our cultural ideals, and our legal system, express again and again the rule that "all men are created equal" and that everyone should be treated equally, and equally valued as a person. Of course, we know that there are many reasons why our society does not often live up to this ideal. There are other rules that we all know, but as a society do not like to admit: that traits such as wealth, birth, gender, race, and social status affect how one is treated and what one is allowed to achieve. Similarly, the knappers say frequently that everyone is supposed to be equal, regardless of who they are or what they do. This ethic is necessary oil for the smooth functioning of a knap-in, with its emphasis on fun, camaraderie, and sharing of knowledge. Nevertheless, knappers judge and rank themselves and each other, assign status in the group on the basis of skills, maneuver for position and influence, and clamor for recognition.

I will return in a moment to consider how the competitions seem to work out socially, but first, it will be useful to look at how the knapping contests express the rules of knapping esthetics.

The Genesee Valley Knappers Association Competition

It turned out that Waldorf had been asked to enter a Danish dagger in the first New York contest the previous year, and having won a prize, he felt it would be more appropriate for him to judge the 1994 contest. D. C.'s account of the judging (he also published much the same in *Chips,* Waldorf 1995b) gives some idea how the esthetic criteria discussed above are used, and also some of the difficulties in judging points and knappers.

Contestants entered in three levels: "Lamoka" (beginners with five years' or less experience), "Meadowood" (intermediate, five to ten years' experience), and "Clovis" (master, ten or more years of experience). The names reflect New York point types. Points were entered in three categories. The judges apparently cooperated on all categories, but each was assigned the lead for one. D. C. judged the "Stone Mastery" category, based on technical quality, considering things like how well the knapper carried out his intentions and how difficult the attempt was. Gary Fogelman, who edits *Indian Artifact Magazine,* judged the "Typology" category, scoring points on trueness to type: did the points use the right material and have correct proportions and flake patterns for their type? Gail Liscomb, an artist with no knapping experience, judged a "Free Form" category based on artistic merit, looking for pretty stone, regular flake patterns, and an attractive overall appearance.

D. C. and others (Van Arsdale 1995) felt that there were problems with the rules. In the first place, knapping skill did not correlate well with length of experience, so that particular attempt to even up the comparisons did not work well. D. C. also felt that in judging quality of flaking, it was difficult to compare points flaked in traditional style with those that were "lap knapped" to obtain perfect flake patterns. In judging two lap-knapped points in the intermediate knapper class, Waldorf awarded the prize to a corner-notched point by Don Kyleberg because it not only had "the most perfect parallel flaking you ever saw on both faces," but also had notches that expanded into the point, difficult to flake without breaking off the corners of the point. The other piece was a fluted point by Steve Behrnes. While one flute went off the tip, the other was less long. This made the point not fully symmetrical, and D. C. felt that full-length flutes on both sides had been the knapper's intention, so it was judged less technically successful.

Waldorf had also entered a large Thebes point, which he disqualified himself from judging. When the points were considered for trueness to type, its rival turned out to be a Turkey Tail by Robbie Robinson, "the prettiest Turkey Tail I've ever seen." Fogelman apparently found them hard to judge, as they were "both right on the money," but after some discussion about whether Thebes points should be that large, split the prize. In retrospect, Waldorf noted that his Thebes might have been eliminated because most such points, when made of high-grade Burlington chert, were not heat treated.

As a result of discussions among the organizers, the judges, and others, the competition rules evolved. When I attended the Seventh Annual Genesee Valley Flint Knappers Association Knap-in in August of 1996, the rules provided for seven categories of entries, one based on skill level, the other six on forms and materials (Appendix D). The different levels of knappers, which had proved problematic, had been eliminated except for a "Lamoka" category for beginning knappers. There were four "Traditional" categories of types of points: Fluted, Paleo Non-Fluted, Archaic, and Woodland/Formative (later points). The points entered in the four "Traditional" categories were expected to be technically excellent and conform to the standards of their prehistoric type. Although they should "ideally" be made with traditional tools, modern equipment was allowed. A sixth category, "Modern or Art," was explicitly nontraditional, "where flint knapping has room to grow and break free of the constraints of the past." The seventh category was "a celebration of New York State lithic sources, restricted to materials used in New York." Presumably the points entered in this category should also be appropriate New York types.

There are several other interesting aspects to the rule sheet as provided by the knap-in organizers. The rules specify what can be entered, but not how they will be judged. This may be in part because the team of judges differs from year to year, and their standards may be expected to differ. It may also be that the three general criteria of technical merit, trueness to type, and artistic merit are considered obvious and essentially universal.

The philosophy of the contest is expressed in similar words in two separate places: "Competition is used only in the sense that awards are presented. All events are designed to promote the preservation of the art of flint knapping, to educate the public about lithic art, and to facilitate sharing among knappers of various experience levels." And again:

"This competition has no winners and no losers. Recognition awards are presented to serve as inspiration to lithic artists of all skill levels, and to promote the preservation of ancient art forms." What is most notable is the emphasis on knapping as art and on the noncompetitive nature of the contest.

I attended the 1996 New York Knap-in partly because I was interested in seeing how the contest worked, but did not do very well at achieving that particular goal. Throughout the Sunday morning there were loudspeaker announcements that knappers should get their entries in for judging, and although I managed to see some of them, the points were not publicly displayed as a group before judging. Meanwhile, I got distracted by other matters. I had bought my first atlatl from Bob Berg the day before and was engaged in a friendly contest with Mike Stafford and Kristian Pedersen, who were also beginners. By the time I caught up with the knapping contest, the award winners were being announced. Dana Klein, one of the organizers of the knap-in, was master of ceremonies, and the contest awards were part of a series of presentations that culminated the knap-in. Most, but not all, of the knappers attending, plus some of the other craftsmen and spectators, wandered over and stood under the main tent for the ceremony. They clapped cheerfully as awards were announced. My impression of the contest was that it worked very much as the organizers intended. It was quite low key and noncompetitive; knappers were pleased if they got a certificate, but there was nothing much at stake. There were only eighteen entries, so not everyone was interested, but there was no pressure one way or the other. The awards ceremony was quiet and friendly, a pleasant final event, but perhaps not the attention-catcher the organizers hoped. People went in and out, and other activities continued. The collection of contest points that the Genesee Valley Knappers Association is accumulating will be a nice representative group of good knapped art, and displaying it at knap-ins will attract some attention and perhaps help inspire other knappers. In any case, the negative feelings of the Fort Osage knappers, most of whom had not seen the contest, seemed a bit overheated. However, the comfortable feel of the New York contest is partly due to the personalities of the Genesee knappers, who have already developed a reputation among the knappers I know for hospitality and friendly enthusiasm. At other knap-ins, the scene could be quite different.

The Texas Cache Competition

A much more formal competition is represented by that at the "National Artifact and Flintknappers Show of Texas," sponsored by *The Texas Cache,* an artifact collectors' newsletter.[1] This was held for the first time in October 1996, and I was not able to attend, but got some accounts from those who did and obtained the official competition rules.

The show had two halves, run in parallel. One was an artifact show, for authentic artifacts only. Artifact shows are like county fairs, with artifacts being displayed and judged instead of melons and cherry pies. It has always seemed a bit odd to me that prizes are awarded merely for possessing an object which the owner neither made nor found; at least it takes some skill and effort to grow prize-winning vegetables.

In the artifact competition, ribbons were awarded for best artifact of various types, and best frames, or groups of types. I was a little surprised to see that stone tools received an overwhelming emphasis, with twelve award categories, while pottery and "engraved pieces—bone, shell, and stone" formed the other two categories.

The knapping contest categories were similar to the stone tool categories in the artifact show competition, and there were two separate subcompetitions. One was for premade points in six categories: Paleo-Fluted, Paleo-Unfluted, Archaic-Dart Points, Historic-Arrow Points, Blades [meaning large bifaces], and Eccentrics. There were to be first-, second-, and third-place ribbons in each category, plus a "best of show" award and a "people's choice" award. Knappers accumulated points in these toward a "Texas Cache Knapper of the Year Award." The second subcompetition involved points made on-site. Knappers had two hours to complete points of a type named by the judges at the start. They were to furnish their own preforms; heat-treated preforms were allowed, but nothing was said about slabs, and there were no apparent restrictions on tools. These points were to be judged by audience ballots. First place was to receive two hundred dollars and a trophy, second fifty dollars and a ribbon, third place twenty-five dollars and a ribbon.

Points were to be judged "for accuracy in replicating an authentic point type," with an exception: "in the eccentric division, let your mind run wild!" According to the "Official Score Sheet," each entry was to be scored one to ten points on each of seven criteria, as follows:

Length; Normal to maximum lengths accepted; Too large or small for the type will count off.

Width; Normal to maximum widths accepted; Too large or small for the type will count off.

Thinness; Exceptional thinness scores the most.

Flaking; Normal flaking patterns for the point type. Flaking patterns not found on certain types will be a deduction.

Symmetry; Any piece not symmetrical will have a deduction.

Without Damage; (Natural occurring imperfections in the stone is acceptable unless it causes obvious damage to the piece).

Material; (materials score depends on color, translucency, hardness).

None of this is very surprising. I have listed the important rules to demonstrate the wide acceptance of certain esthetic standards in stonework. They come from an appreciation among knappers for what is difficult and from decisions by collectors about what is rare and valuable. The Texas Cache scoring system derives from earlier grading systems used to describe and value points in collector books and sales catalogs. The criteria for a ten-point grading scale for prehistoric points are described in Overstreet's series of arrowhead identification and price guide books (Overstreet 1995; Overstreet and Peake 1991) and are very similar to the rules above. The only major difference in emphasis seen in judging old and new points is that new points are expected to be undamaged, while for ancient points, the amount of damage is a focus of the grading system.

The Texas Cache competition is much more formalized than the Genesee Valley Knap-in because this sort of competition has a long tradition in artifact shows, and for that matter in related art, gun, agricultural, and other American shows. Not only is modern knapping easily fit into the standard show format, the traditional rules by which collectors judge artifacts apply equally well to modern pieces.

Imitation as Esthetic Goal

Partly because the Texas show originated with artifact collectors, there is an emphasis on making points that look "authentic." "Trueness to type," one of three equal criteria in the New York competition, dominated the Texas show. This is a kind of esthetic judgment that has so far remained in the background of our discussion. The knapper who says, "I am making a reproduction" is judging his piece by its conformity to a prehistoric standard as well as, or perhaps more than, its success under more general esthetic criteria. Some knappers, in fact, eschew the normal esthetics, at least in part. A good replica is not too large, too thin, or too regular. Mark Moore, in a *Chips* article detailing the replication of Elko points, discusses why he deliberately mismatches the notches: "I find the resulting points to be better replicas of the old points, and less visually redundant when seen as a group, and hence more pleasing to the eye. . . . The slight asymmetry of the finished specimens speaks of an elegant 'desert aesthetic' mostly forgotten by our modern era" (1993, 10). Not only does he feel he is making a more realistic replica, but like a number of knappers I have heard, he comes to feel that the prehistoric people liked their points less perfect than we do. Whether or not this last is true, the criterion of close imitation of a prehistoric model is certainly an esthetic judgment.

If art is creative, expressive, and innovative, as the general public as well as expert opinion would declare, then a criterion of close replication may reflect an esthetic, without being truly "artistic." However, it is really much more complicated than that. What is the model being replicated? In most cases, it is not the average point found in a cornfield. It is, in fact, usually an abstracted and ideal model, derived from prehistoric points selected for their esthetic qualities along the lines discussed at length above. Note that in the Texas competition, while points that were "too long" or "too short" scored lower because they did not replicate their prehistoric models, there was no restriction on thinness. A close replica of many point types would not really be as thin as some modern knappers make them, but thinness is such a highly valued mark of technical skill that it overrides the criterion of "authenticity."

Point Types and Artistic Choices

As an archaeologist at the Fort Osage Knap-in, I soon realized that some types of points are favored and others neglected. (For descriptions of point types see Justice 1987; Waldorf and Waldorf 1987; Perino 1985; Morrow 1984.) You see lots and lots of generalized "arrowheads" that are not especially true to any prehistoric type, but when

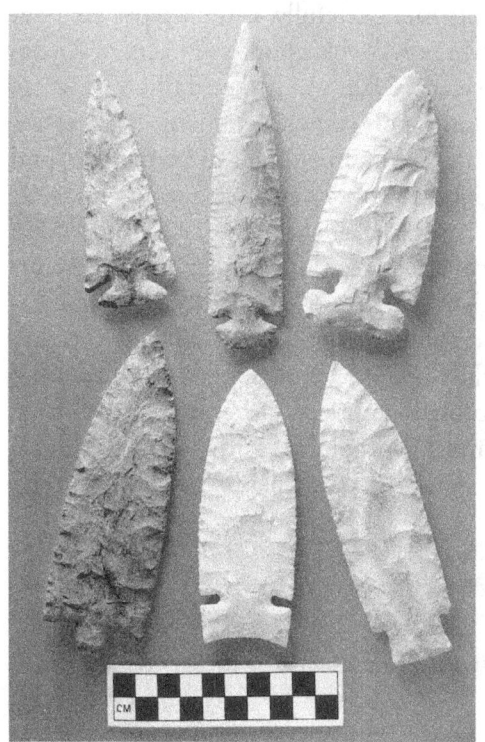

Figure 7.11. Large Midwestern Archaic point forms made by modern knappers. Top: Jeff Gower, 1996; Tim Dillard, 1997; Ted Frank, 1997. Bottom: Mark Bracken, 1999; Dave Schorn, 1996; Glenn Leesman, 1997. Photo by Sarah DeLong.

Figure 7.12. Fluted points. The two upper left are casts of ancient points: a Clovis from the Kimmswick Site, Missouri (Lithic Casting Lab), and one of the Folsom points from the Lindenmeier Site, Colorado (Denver Casts). The other four represent ordinary modern fluted points. Top: Bob Hunt, 2001; John Whittaker, 2000. Bottom: Jeff Gower, 1997; Dick Grybush (Hixton), 1994. Photo by Sarah DeLong.

Art, Craft, or Reproduction

knappers try to replicate points more carefully, certain types are definitely favored. The large Midwestern Archaic points (Thebes or Archaic Bevels, St. Charles or Dovetails, Daltons, Turkey Tails, Etleys) are probably the most common targets of Midwestern knappers; they are well-made and attractive points, common enough to be familiar, and much desired by collectors (Figure 7.11). There are thus good models and a ready market for both replicas and fakes. A couple of early and middle Woodland types such as Snyders are similar. Fluted points (Clovis, Folsom, and their relatives) are also popular for the same reasons, and have a bit more prestige because fluting is difficult and dramatic (Figure 7.12). Because fluted points are older and rarer than other types, prehistoric specimens bring high prices. Other large points, such as Calf Creeks, Scottsbluff, and Eden points, Hardin Barbed, Adena, and Waubesa, and so on, are made by some knappers sometimes, and

Table 7.1
Popularity of Reproduction Point Types according to Berner (2000a, 12)

Point Type	%
Clovis	22.0
Dovetail/St. Charles	18.4
Hardin Barbed	11.3
Agate Basin	8.7
Thebes	8.0
Daltons	7.0
Cumberland	4.8
Adena (various)	4.5
Scottsbluff	4.2
Turkey Tail	3.5
Calf Creek/Smiths	3.4
Folsoms	2.7
Pinetree/Kirks	1.5
TOTAL	100.0

even favored by a few individuals, but are overall much scarcer. Many of the smaller, cruder types, which actually dominate the archaeological record, are not replicated at all, or only rarely. John Berner (1998b; 2000a, 12), who writes for collectors and has handled thousands of ancient points and modern fakes, gives a breakdown of popular reproduction types from records he kept of points he examined over several years (Table 7.1).

I have not tried to quantify point types at Fort Osage. I would say they agree in general patterns with Berner's observations of points, with some differences. I think Clovis is over-represented in what Berner sees because it is a high-value point often faked and often sent to experts like Berner for authentication. Dalton points (an early Archaic form) are very popular among the Fort Osage knappers, probably in part because the distribution of Dalton points centers around Missouri, and they are well known and desirable points for Midwestern collectors. Among knappers there are individual preferences, and many like to make points from their own region, but everywhere, the types copied are selected on the basis of the general esthetic criteria discussed earlier. Types that are usually large, well flaked, and made of high-quality stone are considered interesting; others are neglected. Moreover, it is the better-quality examples of all types that serve as the models, not the average point.

At one knap-in, I had a long discussion with Charlie Shewey and Gene Stapleton about Scottsbluff points. The Scottsbluff is a late Paleoindian type, with square shoulders and a squarish stem (Figure 7.13). These points tend to be rather diamond-shaped in cross-section, and often have very regular large collateral flaking. They are thus large, old, and difficult to make, but although they are sometimes replicated, they are not that common. They happen to be one of my favorite types, and I was speculating on why they were not made by more knappers. My best guess is that a preform that has been worked well enough to finish as a Scottsbluff is also ideal for a fluted point, and many knappers prefer to make the fluted forms. In any case, the conversation turned to the traits typical of prehistoric Scottsbluff points. Charlie, the old collector, owned several, and was also very savvy and interested in typological details, as is Gene.

Charlie's dictum on Scottsbluff points was that "real" ones have the base thinned from the margins, rather than from the base up. Furthermore, the flakes on the base continue the sequence and rhythm unbro-

Figure 7.13. Scottsbluff points, modern replicas and casts of prehistoric specimens. Clockwise from left: John Whittaker, 2001; Saskatchewan (Denver Casts); Matt Graesch, 2000; Finley Site, Wyoming (Du-Pla-Cast); Horner Site, Wyoming (Du-Pla-Cast); Jim Spears, 1999. Photo by Sarah DeLong.

ken, despite the break in the point's outline at the shoulders. Charlie had been showing Gene his frame of Paleo points, because Gene was interested in making his "right." Gene did, in fact, start making Scottsbluff points in large numbers. Typically, he made a virtuoso performance of them. Like his Clovis points, which are a long-term focus, his Scottsbluff points were gigantic, made on premium heat-treated material (Figure 7.14). He ground the blanks in preparation, then removed a final series of extremely large and regular pressure flakes. Gene's Scottsbluff points, like his fluted points, were larger, finer, and more regular than any prehistoric examples, but they incorporated the rules that Charlie and Gene believed defined a proper Scottsbluff. In particular, Gene emphasized how the base had been correctly thinned, with an unbroken flake scar pattern.

This particular detail of Scottsbluff typology seems to originate with Charlie Shewey, whose vast experience gave him great authority. I heard it from him a couple of other times in evaluating knappers' points or

Figure 7.14. Giant Scottsbluff point by Gene Stapleton. Photo courtesy of Gene Stapleton.

discussing those in his collection. I have heard it also now from other Fort Osage knappers. In fact, when I made a Scottsbluff form and showed it to Bob Hunt, his immediate comment was that it was pretty good, but the base should have been thinner and worked more from the margins; I relied too much on thinning from the base up.

Examining collections of Scottsbluff points from archaeological contexts, Bruce Bradley and Dennis Stanford (1987) discussed typological and technological details at length. In Scottsbluff and Eden points from the Claypool site and other sites, "transmedial" thinning of the bases, as prescribed by Charlie, was common, but so was basal thinning. In fact, some points even have one technique used on one face and the other on the second face. Flake scars are also very variable in pattern and quality (Bradley and Stanford 1987, 426) and do not always display the regularity desired by Charlie and Gene and others in a "really good" Scottsbluff. Many Scottsbluff points are, in fact, not large points at all.

I have discussed these typological details at length to show how they are used by knappers. In this instance, and many others, details are selected as important when they conform to existing standards of

Art, Craft, or Reproduction

knapping esthetics. These standards are then applied back to the prehistoric record and may determine not only what is considered a good example of a prehistoric point, but whether or not a specimen is judged authentic or fake. Archaeologists are not immune to this kind of thinking either. Although we work more often with groups of points rather than individual specimens, and thus ideally consider a fuller range of variability, we undoubtedly favor the "nicer" specimens in our illustrations and type definitions, and this can hardly avoid influencing archaeological thinking as well.

Replicas and the Art of Knapping

Knappers are strongly influenced by their esthetic rules, so a good replica is not merely a copy of any point, it imitates a "good" point. Most of the replicas made by the Fort Osage knappers would be considered unusually nice specimens of their prehistoric type, even the ones where the knapper is trying not to get too fancy. Some replicas are at or beyond the limits of the prehistoric model (Figure 7.15). Foot-long fluted points made of heat-treated red jasper, with perfect parallel flaking and nine-inch flutes, cannot be mistaken for prehistoric Clovis points. Such points combine the perceived traits of the prehistoric type with the ideals of point esthetics to create an interpretation of a prehistoric type that approximates what the modern knapper thinks the prehistoric knapper would have wanted if he could have done it. In this sense, even some "replicas" are creative, innovative, and expressive and can be considered more "art" than imitation. Some knappers whose esthetic focus is on creating a close replica would judge these idealized points "too pretty." All knappers would, however, recognize them as quality knapping.

The esthetic rules used by knappers can be summarized under the categories of the early New York knapping competition: technical mastery, artistic merit, and trueness to type. Aspects such as thinness, large size, regular flaking, and details of specific types such as long flutes or narrow notches all reflect technical mastery. Some level of technical mastery is also implicit in artistic merit. Without regular flaking, good lines, and crisp details, a point does not look attractive. Artistic merit also resides in the ability to perform the basics unusually well. Artistic considerations also go beyond technique, considering such things as attractive, appropriate, and high-quality material; symmetry and regu-

Figure 7.15. Jim Redfearn with oversized obsidian Clovis point. Fort Osage, 2001.

larity of form; and a pleasing balance of proportions. Trueness to type involves a somewhat different set of ideals. For some knappers, it means a close replica of existing prehistoric points. For others, it can be extended to include points which adhere to the defining traits of a point type, but carry the technical mastery and artistic qualities beyond what is seen in prehistoric specimens.

All points that a knapper would applaud embody more than the sum of these criteria. Knapping is an expressive, creative act, often an emotional outlet. Fine stonework provokes an emotional response in the knapper because it is imbued with a sort of panache. Only a confident knapper can do really good work. Hesitation, indecision, and blurry ideas of what one is making usually result in mistakes: platforms that are poorly prepared cause irregular or poorly terminated flakes, and failures to plan ahead result in a misproportioned piece and errors that have to be overcome at the expense of design. This is why some points are more desired than others. They are more difficult to do well, riskier. Fluted Clovis and Folsom points embody the panache of knapping better than most other types. Fluting is a relatively risky step in the production of a point, usually late in the process when a lot of effort has been invested. If fluting succeeds, it leaves the immediately recognizable mark of a difficult feat. The risk, the struggle, the triumph visible in a good point reflect technical mastery, but true skill is not just technical, but also spiritual. In admiring a piece of knapped art, a knapper appreciates the interaction between man and material, mind and stone, plan and obstacle, ideal design and tangible artifact.

8

Can't Never Have Too Much Flint: The Lore of Stone

It *should probably be obvious* that stone is central to the craft of knapping. Not only is it necessary raw material, and thus economically important, it is also endowed with meaning and social value and becomes a central metaphor in the knapping world. I have already described how stone can be used in meaningful exchanges among knappers. Such a use is possible because of the multiple values, economic, social, and symbolic, that are assigned to stone.

Part of what you learn as you become a knapper and frequent knap-ins is what one might call the lore of stone. Knappers use "stone," "rock," "flint," and sometimes "chert" as general terms for workable material, but distinguish dozens of named stone types. At Midwestern knap-ins, the three most common materials are Burlington chert, various Texas cherts, and obsidian. They will serve as examples of knap-in stone lore.

Burlington chert is a Midwestern native, occurring in limestone formations of Middle Mississippian age in Iowa, Illinois, and Missouri (DeRegnaucourt and Georgiady 1998; Holland 1992; Morrow 1984; Meyers 1970; Ray 1985). It is usually collected by knappers from secondary deposits, where the hard siliceous chert has eroded out of the limestone and can be found either loose in stream courses or embedded in clays or other soft sedimentary deposits (Figure 8.1). Prehistoric knappers would have exploited such sources also. Modern knappers sometimes get cherts out of limestone quarries or road cuts, where it is still in primary context in its original limestone matrix, but removing

Figure 8.1. The author and friends collecting Burlington chert from the clays at a construction site near St. Louis, 2001. Left to right: Don Jay, Mike He Crow, Steve Owens, John Whittaker, Tom Harvey.

the chert is often difficult, and in such situations it is sometimes disappointingly shattered by blasting or cracked by frost. I have already described digging for flint at Flint Ridge; we used steel tools, but other than that we did pretty much what a prehistoric flint miner would have done in the Ohio woods a thousand years ago. There are some extensive prehistoric quarry areas where Burlington cherts were dug in the same way as the Flint Ridge material.

Burlington chert is widely used because it is relatively plentiful, occurs in fairly large pieces, and is often of very good quality. Much Burlington chert is white or cream in color, but there are numerous colorful variants, with tan, grey, yellow, pink to red, and black-striped or mottled. Some Burlington chert also has fossils in it, most often crinoids, which can either enhance the appearance, or wring bitter curses from the knapper if they interrupt smooth flaking.

Burlington is one of many cherts that can be effectively improved by heat treating. Heat treating requires slow heating and cooling, and temperatures between 300 and 900 degrees Fahrenheit. In prehistoric times, chert was heated in pits under a strong fire. Modern knappers occasionally heat treat with fire, but more often use ovens or turkey roasters for lower temperatures, and kilns if they need high temperature and careful control or treat large batches. Heat treating usually intensifies the colors of stone and brings out more reds and yellows, as well as improving the gloss and flaking quality of the stone. Heat-treated stone is thus prettier and easier to flake, although more fragile for tool use.

Prescriptions for heat treating stone are part of knapping lore, and sometimes hotly argued. For Burlington cherts, Waldorf (1993, 13; 1998, 17) recommends temperatures between 550 and 675 degrees Fahrenheit, but Burlington cherts are quite variable, and others prefer lower temperatures or push them even higher. Chert nodules collected from rivers have absorbed iron and other minerals from the water and can develop especially strong color changes. Many knappers feel that heating a stone longer at low temperature improves the color.

Knappers use a number of names of specific locales as subtypes of Burlington or as chert types in their own right. Crescent, or Crescent Hills, or Crescent Burlington, chert comes from Missouri and has both white and colorful forms. There are well-known prehistoric quarry areas for Crescent Burlington near St. Louis (Ives 1984; Holmes 1919, 195). The High Ridge housing development near St. Louis, Missouri, was the source for a much-liked and very colorful variety of Burlington. Bob Hunt remembers taking truckloads out of there when the development first opened, and I visited it with him in 1994. As the development is all built and occupied now, the chert is largely under lawns and houses, but we were delighted to find one plot still under construction. The raw cut for the foundations and basement had exposed large irregular blocks and nodules of chert in the clay, and the workers did not mind if we got them out of their way. Other named types of Burlington include Avon, Noix, Hinkson Creek, and Grimes Hill. Harvester is a slightly grainy variety that is usually mottled light brown and tan. Mozarkite, which some knappers consider a form of Burlington, is often mottled with interesting patterns of greys and white.

Texas cherts or flints are also plentiful and much used by Midwestern knappers and supply as well a large knapping population in their home state. They illustrate a common knap-in argument: is it flint or chert? Chemically and structurally the two rocks are the same. The technical distinction most often used by archaeologists is that flints form in chalk, and cherts in limestone, but this is not a very useful distinction, and most knappers and archaeologists use either term inclusively (Whittaker 1994, 70; Luedtke 1992). However, knappers like to argue about it. On one occasion at Fort Osage, Steve Behrnes brought out a large nodule of Texas chert, 60–80 pounds at least. He loudly proclaimed, "I'm gonna show you some good flint! There's no bad stuff on this, it's good all through." He then proceeded to "spall" it, breaking it up with a sledge into large spalls, or macroflakes. Everyone gathered around to watch, and he sold the spalls at a dollar a pound, not weighing them, just guessing generously. He sold a bunch of spalls, put the rest in a bucket, and left the debris. Meanwhile, a discussion about chert versus flint had started with someone saying, "Waldorf says Georgetown and White River are the only true flints in the U.S." These are both Texas varieties out of chalky deposits. Others sneered at that and discussed the issue, ending with a dogmatic statement by Steve, which met with general agreement: "Flint is microcrystal, chert is macrocrystal." He was making the common knapper distinction that flint is finer-grained and better quality than chert and demonstrated by breaking up his nodule further. "Here," he said, tapping the outer layers of smoother material with his billet, "is flint, and this," pointing to the grainier inner material, "is chert." This distinction also does not seem very useful to most archaeologists or geologists.

Texas cherts come in even more varieties than Burlington and from several geological strata. It will suffice here to list only the most common. Edwards Plateau chert is usually grey and often massive, sometimes grainy but responding well to heat treatment. Bob Hunt, who likes to make large things, is fond of working "sidewalk chert," a variety of Edwards Plateau that occurs in huge tabular sheets about the dimensions of a square of sidewalk. Pedernales chert is usually in the form of nodules from the Pedernales River and adjacent drainages. It is derived from several strata and is thus quite variable. Most of it is brown, tan, or grey, but there are also pink and purple pieces, and the quality varies from excellent to mediocre. Georgetown is a nodular flint from chalk beds. Under a white cortex, the flint is clear grey and usually very good. Alibates is a particularly colorful chert from the Amarillo area, which was used for some fine Paleoindian points (Banks 1990). "Cowpie" is another kind of large, nodular Texas chert. "Rootbeer"

Texas chert is very fine and nodular; you can guess the color from the name.

Obsidian is natural volcanic glass, mostly from relatively recent geological contexts (Skinner and Tremaine 1993). It varies in texture from completely glassy to rather grainy and can be transparent, translucent, or opaque. The most common color is black, but obsidian can be clear, brown, red, greenish, or mottled with any of these colors. In the United States there are obsidian sources scattered around the Western states, in California, Utah, Arizona, New Mexico, Wyoming, and Oregon. There are also important sources in Mexico, and some imported material reaches the knap-ins, by way of rock shows like that at Quartzite, Arizona. The best-known single source of obsidian for American knappers is Glass Buttes, in Oregon, and much of the obsidian seen at knap-ins comes from Glass Buttes.

Unlike most cherts, obsidian is usually given descriptive names rather than being known by source. Knappers are likely to call it pumpkin or mahogany obsidian if red or brown, silver or gold sheen obsidian if it sparkles with those colors in reflected light, and peacock obsidian if it has greenish or purplish iridescence. Ordinary black obsidian is not as desirable and is more likely to be referred to by source. Source names for obsidian may be more a part of Western knappers' lore than they are among the Midwestern knappers. It may also be that because obsidian comes from many sources, and is often similar from source to source as well as variable within each source, source names would convey less information about the stone itself, which is what most interests the knappers. Actually, archaeologists often make visual as well as chemical distinctions between named obsidian sources (e.g., Lesko 1989), so I am not sure why the Midwestern knappers do not.

Knappers tend to have strong opinions about different materials, and obsidian is no exception. Many of the Midwestern knappers, who work with tough cherts, dislike obsidian because it is too fragile and because it produces lots of sharp little splinters that get in your clothes and on your hands. Obsidian is so sharp that even small pieces can give you bloody cuts before you know what is happening. Other knappers prefer obsidian over cherts. It is easy to work, requiring less force and producing less wear on tools than most cherts, and allowing very precise work, especially in pressure flaking.

The Mystique of Stone

Esthetic considerations figure in the sometimes passionate feelings knappers have about stone. Obsidian has glossy surfaces that show flake scar patterns well in reflected light, and internal color patterns that are attractive when you hold the point up and look at the light through it. On the other hand, I have heard a number of knappers who agree with a message on the Internet "Knapper" mailing list:

> Obsidian is almost too easy and gets boring really fast. I know there are many colors and all that, but real knapping skills are developed working true flint. The shiny look of glass is not desirable to me. A case full of obsidian points to me has always been ho hum, so what, they all look the same. The real beauty within flint can only be revealed by breaking it open.... I look at a case of flint points and I see all the colors of the rainbow.

Obsidian enthusiasts are quick to defend the beauty of vivid reds and browns, translucent patterning, and exotic sheens.

The argument above is repeated in many contexts and around different stones. Many knappers develop a sort of flint chauvinism for their favorite material, which is usually something found near their home base. If it is unusually fine stone, they are proud of that. If it is difficult to work, that is a source of pride, too. Jim and Dick Grybush, two knappers from Wisconsin, are among the few knappers who work Hixton silicified sediment, or Silver Mound quartzite. This material comes from a well-known source in west-central Wisconsin that was heavily exploited throughout prehistory. Hixton quartzite is composed of welded quartz sand grains and has a sugary texture and sparkle. It is attractive, but tough, and because of its less homogeneous structure, flakes tend to step fracture and platforms to crush if the knapper is not careful. The Grybushes have explored the sources extensively and worked with the material for years; it is their particular baby. Like the New York knappers, the Grybushes complain about the difficulty of their material, but there is an element of bravado, of boasting, in their complaints; they can challenge the stone and win.

Knappers seem almost animistic in their beliefs about stone. Sometimes the stone "cooperates." At other times one struggles against a perverse piece that refuses to let any flake go where it should. It is amusing to hear a knapper exult, "Hah! take that!" when a difficult problem is resolved, or swear at the stone as "you dirty piece of concrete!" I do it myself, so I am entitled to laugh. Some knappers tend to see the stone as an opponent to be overcome, consistent with the "challenge" that they find in knapping. Others prefer to talk in terms of a more harmonious relationship. "I'm making a Clovis, if the stone will let me" is a common sort of remark. Bob Hunt once showed me a frame of Dalton points he had been making for a customer. He said he did not usually try to make Daltons (probably because they are too small for his taste), but "if that's what the stone wants, that's what I make."

D. C. Waldorf was reminiscing one time about a visit to Denmark and walking on beaches where all the rock was nodules of flint. Trying to convey his awe at the endless flint he said, "It was hard to find pieces with a dagger in them, but you walked over thousands of pieces with a good Clovis in them." More than one knapper in my presence has borrowed a trite line from sculpture, saying, "you just chip away everything that doesn't look like a point." The implication is that there is a point inherent in a good piece of stone.

Obviously, different knappers will "find" different points in the same piece of flint, but the notion of "finding" expresses the necessary ability to foresee what a nodule will make and how it needs to be worked. Carl Dowell, a Missouri knapper, is one of those who is fond of saying, "Every piece of stone has an arrowhead in it!" The story goes that he was preaching this gospel at the Pine City Knap-in while demonstrating what could be done quickly with a variety of pieces. A small boy who had been watching wandered off into the woods and came back with a lump of granite. He held this totally unsuitable material out to Carl and asked, "Hey mister, can you make me an arrowhead out of this?" The other knappers laughed heartily as Carl had to explain that, after all, some rocks just don't make arrowheads.

The ability to make a point out of "any" piece of stone is an expression of mastery of the craft. Bob Hunt often sells buckets of Burlington flakes that result from his work and are large enough for points but too small for the things he likes to make. A fellow knapper criticized some of his material, and Bob told him, "If I can't make a point of it, it wouldn't be in the bucket." He then bet the other knapper that he could prove it. Bob would make a good point out of any piece the knapper wanted to select from his bucket. The resulting Dalton was a pretty point, and Bob thought it was one of the more authentic-looking Daltons he had made; he sold it for $15. This kind of test of skill on a difficult piece of stone is not uncommon (e.g., Martin 1995).

Most knappers, like Bob, partake of both the antagonistic and the cooperative view of their stone, depending on how well it is working and the circumstances, as well as their personalities. Complaining about problems with the stone and personalizing it are good ways of being humble. Even if a point is going well, you can seem modest by predicting that the treacherous stone will put one over on you before you finish or by pointing out a flaw that you are not sure you can overcome. Of course, if you do succeed, the previous deprecation and the problems you pointed out add to the luster of your achievement. You should not remind the audience of this, but the alert watcher can then praise you for your ability to make the stone do what you want.

The Qualities of Stone

Stone is most praised for two qualities, its workability and its color. Flawless stone is avidly sought after, but even more desirable is beauty. Some knappers will choose colorful stone of lesser quality over finer but less attractive material, and some fine knapping stone types are not as popular as one might expect because they tend to be monochromatic. Obsidian is one example, as reflected in the quote earlier. Even bright single colors are not as desirable to most knappers as multicolored or patterned pieces. The statement quoted earlier also reflects this, referring to "all the colors of the rainbow" as one of the superior qualities of cherts over obsidian.

A piece of flint is also a mystery. In a very true sense, you never really know what will be inside it. Although a nodule is partly predictable (that is part of the skill of knapping), it also conceals a mysterious interior whose qualities will largely determine what you can make. As you knap the stone, you open it up and expose new ways of seeing it with each stroke. You encounter obstacles and are rewarded by unexpected streaks of color or fossils formed with impossible beauty. You not only create a work of art from a piece of stone, you bring to light surfaces, forms, and colors that not only were invisible for millions of years, but in some sense did not exist without the intervention of the knapper. It is no accident that knapping appeals to some of the same people who hunt artifacts or do archaeology.

Exotic colorful materials have an especially strong allure, and the expense and rarity of some stones add to the "manna" of a point made from them. Knappers admire such points for the beauty of the stone and, to some extent, for the daring that went into risking a piece of expensive material. At one knap-in, Sharon Mondino was passing around an enlarged photograph of a small point. It was a nice, symmetrical little Northwestern form, but the color was all wrong. The whole point was spots and streaks of red, orange, yellow, blue, green, and purple, and you could hardly see the flake scars. It turned out to be a photo by Pete Bostrom of a point made by Jim Hopper and owned by Charlie Shewey. It was said to be one of two made out of a piece of synthetic opal and sold by Jim before he knew what the stone was worth. Charlie acquired it sometime thereafter and said he had been offered thousands of dollars for it since; he wished he knew what became of the second of the pair. Other knappers I know have worked opal that they bought at $250 an ounce. I never did find out whether they sold the resulting points for enough to make a profit.

Another exotic stone that became popular a few years ago is fiber optic glass. Held one way, light goes through a point of fiber optic glass, but at a different angle, the surfaces are highly reflective and look like polished metal, except that the flake scars seem to have extra ripples and the whole thing glitters. At first it was quite scarce and expensive. A small cut slab suitable for a small point cost around $25 in 1995. Eventually the lapidary market, more than the knapping market, spurred production of fiber optic glass for craft work, and it is now much more common and cheaper and is sold as different-sized blocks in a variety of colors. When it was still a novelty, it stood out almost shockingly amidst normal stone. Craig Ratzat told me that he liked to have a couple knives of fiber optic glass when he displayed at knife shows and other events, because lots of people would stop to ask what it was. He had a nice pendant point made out of it, too, and claimed that it was good for getting the ladies to come up real close to take a look. His neighbor's comment was "I got to get me a belt buckle of that stuff."

The Quest for Stone

If you hang out with hunters, you hear hunting stories. If you spend time with fishermen, you hear about the one that got away and the ones that didn't. If you go to knap-ins, you swap lies about the size of the nodules you couldn't carry back to the car. You can even hear combined knapping/hunting stories, when knappers show off stone-tipped arrows they used to kill deer, wild pig, or even bear (for published versions see DeSimone 1991; Berg 1995).

Many knappers also hunt and fish, look for arrowheads, collect mushrooms, or are rockhounds, if not all of the above. At knap-ins, I hear stories about all of these hobbies. There is a general similarity between all of these pursuits and the quest for stone, and many of the stories start to sound the same, too. They also serve some of the same purposes: social exchange based on common interest and experience, display of personal qualities, and transmitting information about how to do a craft and where to find the resources. Like mushroom hunters and fishermen, knappers have some favorite sources that they try to keep secret, but some sources, especially the larger ones, are common lore.

Knapping a point is a matter of technique, and although each piece is unique in some way, there is so much similarity that narratives about the making of any single piece are not common. Collecting raw material, however, is a less frequent activity, usually requires a special expedition, and may be an adventure. Although some sources of material are easy to access, and some collecting expeditions mundane, by and large the quest for flint is well suited to tale spinning.

A couple of examples of flint hunting tales will suffice. Paul Schilkofski told me about collecting Harvester, a Burlington variety, with George Pelfrey and George's old truck.

> We kept digging it up, and piling it in the truck, until I noticed the tire was really low. George looks at it, says, "That's the good one." We walked around the truck, and the other tire was down on its rims. So we had to unload it all, take the truck into town and pump as much air as we could into the tires, it's a wonder they didn't blow out. Then we went back and loaded up again. With the flint in the back, the headlights shone straight up in the air, and it was pouring rain, and the front tires barely touched the pavement, so we were just floating along. And George is doing seventy, saying, "Don't worry, it rides just fine." And all I remember is the headlights shining on the telephone wires over the highway.

Dick and Jim Grybush, the Wisconsin-dwelling Hixton-knapping brothers, tell how they went to the knap-in at Fort Hood in Texas to get some good stone. Jim had borrowed a trailer from a neighbor, and with a third knapper, they loaded it with "three tons" of flint. As they roared along the highway, with Jim pushing the speed limits and the others praying, another car overtook them and honked urgently. They pulled over and discovered that the weight on the trailer was so extreme that the axles had bent until the tires tipped in at the tops and rubbed against the sides of the trailer, sending up a cloud of black smoke. A blowout would have been serious—"We would have lost all of that flint!"—and they plainly could not go on. They tried unloading some of the flint, but that did not help, and it was late Sunday in a small town in Arkansas, so they couldn't find anyone to fix the trailer. Dick was worried because the next night he was supposed to be inducted as president of the Wisconsin Archaeological Society and had important business on Tuesday. He tried to find a car to rent, but there was only one at the airport, and the car rental agency would not let it go out of state. He tried to find a flight out, but the times were bad and the price outrageous, so he gave up. Meanwhile, Jim finally saved the day by finding someone who had a trailer that they were willing to swap for the damaged one plus $300. This they did and made it home with part of their flint. Their neighbor was a bit startled to find that he had lent one trailer and got another back, but agreed that it would be all right if the Grybushes put fenders on it. "But somebody will be pretty surprised someday to find a big pile of fine Edwards Plateau flint sitting in a back lot in a small town in Arkansas."

When I told Dick that I was going to put his story in my book, he added to it: The trailer fiasco briefly soured relations between the two brothers, who ordinarily communicate at least once a week. Dick told his wife, "I'm really angry and I'll never go collecting with him again." After a couple of weeks, Jim called and Dick immediately started to give him a piece of his mind. Jim listened quietly. A few minutes passed, then Jim, having made no comments, said, "Let's go to Hixton next weekend." Dick paused, and the brothers were off again.

Flint hunting stories are hunting tales and treasure yarns. The major themes are repeated again and again: companionship with other quirky characters, the difficulty and perhaps danger of the quest, sometimes the romance of doing what our ancestors before us did, and always the prospector's joy of "striking it rich" with a find of stone. Examples abound in the talk at knap-ins and even in the newsletters (e.g., Moore 1989a; D. Waldorf 1991, 1994a, 1994b; Blake 1992; Klein

Figure 8.2. Disappointed flint hunters. Cartoon by Larry Scheiber, Chips *10 (1): 24, 1998. Courtesy of Val Waldorf, Larry Scheiber.*

1994; Boudreau 1995; Martin 1998). It is not too much to say that knappers dream about flint. D. C. Waldorf even went so far as to write a sort of knapper's daydream, a short story about a fictional expedition on a sailing boat to Denmark to trade washing machines for flint (D. Waldorf 1996).

The underlying theme of all these stories is the length to which knappers will go to get flint. Knappers are well aware that much of the world thinks their hobby is a bit odd, and they make many jokes about the absurdity of their obsessions with knapping. Stone is a perfect metaphor for this, because to most people, a stone, a rock, means something worthless and often ugly. It takes a knapper to recognize other qualities in stone and to desire it like a miser lusting after gold (Figure 8.2).

"At one knap-in, this knapper had a big load of flint in his truck, and he was just backing out of the knap-in driveway when a car on the highway rammed into the side of his truck. The driver of the car got out screaming 'My car, my car!' but the knapper got out yelling 'My flint, my flint!'" The first time I heard this story, Jim Regan told me it happened in Texas. I heard it a couple of other times, and a parody of a news item about the New York Knap-in appeared in *Chips* with a version ("Lance Free" 1994). Dana Klein also told me it happened at the New York Knap-in. He added that when the dust settled, the car driver became intrigued by the strange guy with the truck full of rocks, started going to the knap-in, and became a knapper. So strong is the lure of flint!

Whether the details of that story are true or not, knappers are peculiar about stone. They hunger for it, seek it, collect it, and hoard it. They devote large areas of their yards to piles of rock and build barns to shelter their stone. They spend hours and fortunes acquiring exotic material. Time and again, knappers who admit that they have enough material to last their lifetime will shake their heads sheepishly as they recount another expedition, or fork over a handful of bills for a bucket of stone. "You can't never have enough flint."

The obsession with stone may seem petty and sound exaggerated, but a few figures will give some idea of the demand for stone and the magnitude of the knappers' quest. I have not been able to make really accurate estimates, but at the average knap-in at Fort Osage, tons of stone change hands. Dickson (1996) estimated at least twenty pickup trucks, each carrying between 1.5 and 2 tons of material, at one knap-in. I think this is an overestimate. I see usually six to ten major loads, typically a ton or so each, plus many smaller lots. Ten to 20 tons of stone is probably a reasonable guess for a normal Fort Osage Knap-in.

At the Fort Osage Knap-in in May 1997, probably the largest knap-in up to that time, I tried to make rough estimates of material as each new knapper arrived. I considered only material for sale, not personal supplies, and made rough visual estimates of quantity based on my own experience: a bucket full of stone weighs about 50 pounds, and spalls, blanks, and preforms such as are commonly sold can be estimated at 1 pound each. Twenty-two knappers had major amounts of stone for sale, but my total estimates were 11,950 to 15,700 pounds, or 6 to 8 tons. I regard this estimate as conservative, more likely to be much too low than too high.

A few specific examples from 1996 illustrate stone consumption. At the New York Knap-in, Craig Ratzat had a trailer that he said had about 6,500 pounds of obsidian in it. He said he had collected 8,000 pounds in Oregon and hauled it to a Texas knap-in, where he sold some before going on to New York, where he expected to sell another 1,500 pounds or so. I saw it again, further diminished, at the Flint Ridge Knap-in the next weekend. After that he hoped to sell much of what remained to Mike Stafford for use in classes, then dispose of the rest in rock shops before heading home. While Craig sells knapped pieces and two instructional videos on knapping (Ratzat 1994, 1996), he said much of his business is in stone. He had four rock saws and sold much of his stone as slabs. He also preferred working slabs, partly because that conserves material; you can get several more workable pieces out of a nodule if you saw it than if you spall it. He estimated at the New York Knap-in that maybe 15 percent of his obsidian was debitage and cutting scraps that he had to throw away, about 200 pounds of waste a week. If this is accurate, he processed an average of over 1,000 pounds of stone a week, or better than 25 tons a year. On a later occasion in 1997 he estimated that he used 10 tons of stone a year and sent about 150 pounds a week to the dump as small waste. This was only the really worthless stuff; Craig tried not to be wasteful, spalling out the cutoff ends of nodules and bagging good flakes from his debitage pile for sale. In the 1990s, Craig was getting much of his material from Bureau of Land Management land at Glass Buttes in Oregon, where there was a fairly liberal attitude about collecting stone. Recently the policy has tightened up, allowing only noncommercial collection of 250 pounds per person, so Craig is exploring other sources.

Advertisements from *Chips* give a good idea of the range of stone available and relate closely to knappers I know at Fort Osage (Table 8.1). In 1997 eleven individuals, some doing business as small companies, were advertising stone as their primary product. A couple more advertised stone among other products, and several who do not advertise stone also sell it. This does not count the many individuals who sell stone at knap-ins, or even through the mail, but do not advertise in *Chips*. The most common stones for sale were obsidian and Texas cherts, but the list gives some idea of the available variety, and much more was available if you knew where to ask. Quantities were not indicated by most of the ads, but two imported lots of stone were so impressive that the quantities were announced and spread by word of mouth at knap-ins. Eric's Rocks and Such, based in Indiana, was

Table 8.1
Advertisements in Chips, *1997, with Some Information Added from Personal Observations (Comments)*

Name	State	Products	Comments
PRIMARILY STONE			
C. Ratzat, "Neolithics"	OR	Obsidian and dacite, knapping class, videos *Caught Knapping, Lap Knapping,* stone points and knives	Much material as slabs, fancy modern knapping, eccentrics
J. Mondino	IL	Dongola, Cobden cherts, moose antler billets	Also sells books and points at knap-ins
"Eric's Rocks and Such"	IN	Indiana Hornstone nodules $2/lb, or slabs, butterstone $2.50/lb, catlinite, alabaster, soapstone, other carving stone, ocarinas, 45,000 lbs Brandon flint $2.65/lb	Also fossils
"Nemec Stone Company"	TX	Texas grey nodules + Texas river cobbles $1/lb, Tortilla nodules + Georgetown blue pancakes + Amoeba flint nodules $2/lb, large Tortilla nodules $3/lb	
B. J. Shelden	CO	Black Mesa slabs, WY jasper, obsidian, flint knives, pipestone Stone-handled knives also sold by Lowrey	
M. Condron	FL	Florida fossilized coral, opal, flint knives, antler handles	

Name	State	Products	Comments
PRIMARILY STONE			
L. Harms	MO	Obsidian preforms, slabbed chert, agate, and jasper	Also sells grinding supplies
J. Distefano	TX	Central Texas Edwards Plateau chert, spalls $1.50–5.00/lb, nodules (20–40 lbs) $0.60/lb	
R. Lowrey, "White River Supply"	CO	Alibates, Fredericksburg Rootbeer, Ft. Hood–Hyner Lake flints, Colorado sugar quartzite, obsidian, dacite, various colors pipestone, antler for handles and billets, moose hide	Lots antler, lots stone, more variety than most in choice nodules and slabs, stone knives by other knappers
G. Hardy	OH	Flint Ridge flint, $3/lb	Lives near source
M. Trout	TX	Mexican rainbow obsidian $3.50/lb, Texas Brazos R. chert cobbles $0.75/lb, obsidian and heated chert slabs, fluted point replicas	
PRIMARILY KNAPPING TOOLS			
J. Regan	MN	Copper knapping tools, heated agate slabs	
T. Richter, "T&J Copper Supply"	TX	Copper knapping tools, 50,000 lbs Belize chert	
D. Herbort, "Elkhorn Mountain Neolithics"	MT	Sinew, antler billets, knapping kits	

Name	State	Products	Comments
PRIMARILY POINT REPLICAS			
V. Tonn	TX	Parallel-flaked Paleo point replicas, arrow points, antler-handled stone knives	
W. Blackwell	VA	Fluted point replicas, video *Making Fluted Points with the Sollberger Jig*	
G. Eklund	OK	Hardin, Dalton point replicas 3–4" $15, flint axes	Many other point replicas, blanks, stone, antiques
OTHER MISCELLANEOUS			
M. Bracken, "Bracken Bows"	GA	Moisture meter for bow makers, diamond scribes for point marking	Bow staves, bows, artifact collector cards, points, arrows
R. Berg, "Thunderbird Atlatl"	NY	Several models of atlatl, atlatl kits, darts, raw materials	
R. Otteson, "El Inca del Peru"	FL	Peruvian wool blankets, coffee, pots, jewelry	
B. Metcalfe	TX	Video *Introduction to Flint Knapping*	Stone, point replicas, beads
D. Thompkins	CA	"Your arrowhead mounted" with silver for jewelry	
C. Spear	IN	Book and video *The Illustrated Knapper*, newsletter *Flint Knapper's Exchange*	

Can't Never Have Too Much Flint

Name	State	Products	Comments
OTHER MISCELLANEOUS			
D. Martin	WA	Waldorf videos, books, *Chips* newsletter, moose antler billets	Waldorfs' W. Coast distributor
D. and V. Waldorf, "Mound Builder Books"	MO	Waldorf books *Art of Flint Knapping* and *Story in Stone*, newsletter *Chips*, videos *Caught Knapping* and *Knapping Obsidian*, Clovis commemorative mugs	Also point replicas, original drawings
"Red Willow Primitive Skills"	MO	Primitive skills classes and outings	
"Tugaloo Environmental Education Center"	SC	Primitive skills classes and outings	
D. Wiley	PA	Ooga-Booga T-shirts	
C. Mulka	CT	"Dealer buying well made points for resale"	

Not all ads ran in each issue, but many were repeated. Company names are given in quotation marks. Prices for stone and points given if advertised. Almost all of these vendors have been at Fort Osage at least once.

---

importing 45,000 pounds of British Brandon flint, to be sold mail order at $2.65 per pound. Brandon flint is familiar to most knappers, even if they have not worked it; it is a fine, hard, black or grey flint, from which gunflints were formerly made. Tom Richter, whose T&J Copper Supplies sells mostly copper knapping tools, imported 50,000 pounds of chert from Belize to sell at a similar price. The Belizean stone is also very high quality, but much less familiar than Brandon flint, so Richter circulated a few samples. The Waldorfs mentioned this in *Chips* and praised the stone, and Craig Ratzat was showing samples to his obsidian customers at the New York Knap-in in 1996. According to Tom and knap-in rumor, this was a particularly difficult import. The Belizean government, which is trying to protect its national heritage from looting, would not let nodules with more than a couple of flakes off them go out for fear they might be artifacts. The U.S. government required that all the stone be washed to ensure that no foreign dirt was imported, potentially bringing organisms dangerous to American agriculture. The hassles of uncertain airline travel, explaining to farmers why Tom wanted their rock piles, and dealing with customs officials made this enterprise a super rock-hunting yarn.

Not many of the *Chips* advertisements listed prices, but those listed give a pretty good idea of what is typical, both for mail order and at knap-ins. The knapper literature also contains information and advice on buying stone (Potter 1993; V. Waldorf 1999), and occasional complaints about the expense of stone are met by comments from sellers about how much work it is to obtain and prepare quality material.

Most stone is sold by the pound, either as raw nodules, in which case it may be a bit cheaper, or as spalls or flakes, which may cost more per pound—depending on whether or not they are heat-treated, how big they are, and how much effort the seller puts into selecting them—but of course include less waste. The usual price for many ordinary kinds of stone is $1.00 to $2.00 per pound. The range is about $0.50 for some Burlington at Fort Osage, where large amounts can be brought in cheaply, to $3.00 or $5.00 for some of the scarcer desirable nonlocal stone like Knife River flint or the best Georgetown (Texas) pancake nodules. The seller's price also depends, of course, on what he has to do to get the stone. Imports or stone that has been purchased elsewhere costs more. I have already mentioned exotics like fire opal that sell for startling prices, but these are the exception, available only in small amounts and used by relatively few knappers. The basic price of $1.00 to $2.00 per pound for common stone has been stable for the last few years.

Stone may be processed in several ways before selling, which also affects the price. A lot of knappers prefer to sell stone that they have "spalled" (knapped into large flakes) or "blanked" (worked into rough bifaces). Spalling and blanking remove waste material and eliminate some flawed pieces, reducing transportation problems for the seller. The work of the seller reduces the work of the buyer, and the price rises accordingly. Blanks in particular are priced by the piece ($2–15 depending on size, quality, and material), or even by the inch, like points, and the price varies somewhat depending on how refined they are. Sold by the inch, the price is usually $2–3 an inch (compared to points at $6–15/inch). Mail-order sales are most often blanks or spalls, which reduces weight and waste, but adds labor in addition to mailing costs. Some of the more commercial knappers prefer to work with blanks from other knappers because, although they are more expensive, it is still cost-effective to finish them as points rather than start from scratch.

Slabbing and heat treating are also commonly performed by stone sellers. Not all knappers have the equipment to process large amounts of stone. Rock saws are especially expensive and bulky, so relatively few knappers own them. Knappers who like to work slabs can buy them from others or provide material to be cut either for a price or a percentage of the stone. Slabbing is a good way to conserve stone, producing less waste than ordinary knapping of blanks, but not all knappers like to work slabs. Unless they are knapped properly, they tend to have flat cross-sections, unflaked sawn surfaces, or hinge terminations. However, it is not that hard to deal with them, and for many knappers, starting with a slab also reduces the amount of work that goes into a point. Slabs of flint and other hard stone typically sell for around $0.50 a square inch, and slabs of obsidian $0.30 a square inch.

Most stone sold as blanks or slabs is heat-treated, unless it is obsidian or other material that does not need it. Heat treating is another process that is most efficiently done on a large scale, in a kiln. Some knappers learn to do particularly well with certain stones, through experiment and experience, and some sellers have reputations for providing stone that is heat-treated just right.

It should be evident from the amounts of stone and the prices discussed above that there is a lot of money and stone moving in the knapping marketplace. However, the labor and other costs of getting, processing, and moving stone, as well as the somewhat limited market, mean that only a few people are actually making much of their living at it, even though many deal in stone in a small way or use it to cover some of the cost of their knapping hobby.

Decreasing Resources

The large market for stone, and the many knappers and rockhounds it supplies, must have an effect on the resources of knappable stone. Although this is hard to document in any reliably quantified way, it is undoubtedly the case.

I hear many complaints at knap-ins that certain sources of stone have now been wiped out or so picked over that only poor material is left. When I asked knappers on my survey if they saw trends in knapping they did not like, various concerns about stone supplies were mentioned by eighteen, of whom eleven specified waste or depletion of sources. Knappers are also expressing this worry in articles in *Chips* (Mondino 1993; Trotta 1996) and on the Internet. A related worry is that some sources will become inaccessible. Occasionally a source is covered or destroyed, as was the High Ridge Burlington chert source when the development project was finished. Some sources are on public land, and knappers are aware that with increasing population and more knappers exploiting sources to meet a growing demand for material, a time may come when they are no longer freely accessible. Increased restrictions at Glass Buttes (Higgins 1994) and other public land sources are another concern.

The depletion of resources also puts a strain on some aspects of the knap-in ethos. Knappers are becoming increasingly cagey about their sources and less likely to freely inform others. Some knappers grumble about beginners who waste good rock instead of learning on less-valuable material. Prices will inevitably rise, making knap-in trips less economically feasible for some knappers, and increasing the commercial aspects for others. One response is an increase in the use of sawn slabs. With the increase in lapidary knapping and rock sales in general, more knappers have rock saws, and there are also frequent comments that slabbing saves stone resources.

At the moment, the depletion of materials is by no means a crisis, but it is something that knappers are beginning to worry about. Trends in stone use are hard to quantify. Some of my impressions come from ten years of watching scavenging behavior and the waste pile at Fort Osage, and it seems to me that wastage decreased at first but is on the rise again. Knappers in general seem less prodigal of material than in the first couple of years that I went to Fort Osage. I was new to the scene, and my eyes bulged at the huge pile of flakes and debris around George Eklund and some others, debitage that they were not bothering to salvage and sell or use. However, a lot of this debitage was not ultimately wasted. I immediately became one of many scavengers, and I continue to retrieve stone from the waste pile established at the edge of the knap-in.

The first few years I was at the knap-in (1991–1993 or so) were marked by relatively careless use of stone resources. After that, I began hearing more and more complaints about depletion of collection sites and rising prices, and the wastage slowed down; few knappers were to be seen at the knap-in spalling their way through a ton of stone. The Fort Osage Knap-In moved out from the museum garages, and a debitage pile was established on the tarmac at one edge of the parking lot, where everyone's waste was dumped at the end of the event. By the time the next knap-in came around, visitors and Boy Scouts had considerably reduced what the scavenging knappers had left. As the knap-in grew, demand for stone inspired new sources, especially relatively plentiful Burlington, and with more knappers, the pile began to outstrip the scavengers. Around 2000, I began to notice that the quality and size of the waste was going up again. Although good stone was more expensive, the market and the knappers wanted large points. I also suspect that the proliferation of new sources, with many types of stone coming from long distances, actually increases wastage, as knappers who want to try new material are sometimes less successful with unfamiliar stone. Rathje (Rathje and Murphy 2001) has identified a similar pattern in food waste. It also seems to me that, increasingly, knappers who want to sell points are unwilling to spend time working the problems out of difficult pieces.

I remain one of the dedicated scavengers, because I have a practical use for lots of small flakes as practice material for my students and because I often make relatively small pieces. Furthermore, I just can't bear to see stone wasted! The etiquette of scavenging is that one should not collect flakes from under a working knapper without asking permission, as he may intend to collect them himself. Once they have been abandoned, they are fair game. At the end of the Fort Osage Knap-in, whoever is helping clean up rolls the tarps and dumps the waste stone (with cigarette butts and other small debris) into a wheelbarrow. When the knap-in was behind the visitor center, there was a small gully on the edge of the woods that was gradually being filled. Now there is a frame of railroad ties at the edge of the parking lot where the debitage is deposited. In both places, it was further picked over, both by knappers before leaving and by other visitors to the site during the year.

To some extent, scavenging reflects status as a knapper. The highest-status knappers usually do not scavenge; they tend to make large pieces, and they tend to have access one way or another to choice material. Knappers who are less experienced or less integrated into the knap-in are more likely to be working small points or just experimenting with flakes, and may not have good stone sources or be willing to pay much for material. There is no real stigma attached to scavenging, but some other knappers will assume that you are willing to settle for smaller, less prestigious points and lower-quality material.

I am also among the knappers who feel a moral commitment to scavenging and other means of conserving material. Collection and consumption of stone are such an important part of the knapping world that few knappers seem willing to make any active effort to conserve, but there are a few practical actions that are widely advocated (e.g., Mondino 1993; Trotta 1996). Some, like slabbing, are adopted by knappers unconcerned with conservation, because they offer other advantages.

Slabbing is frequently discussed as conserving material. Working a slab also reduces the amount of work to make a point. A typical nodule that might make one large point and a few small ones by traditional knapping can be cut into several slabs that will yield large points. Careful knapping also reduces waste. If the same nodule is spalled into large flakes, rather than reduced bifacially to make one large point, it is also more productive, although less so than if the nodule is sawn. Heat treatment is also viewed by some as a conservation measure, in that it makes poor-quality stone more knappable and expands the range of what knappers consider good stone.

The knappers' lust for high-quality raw material wars against the developing need for conservation. Good knappers are usually reluctant to use low-quality material; it is less fun, and produces less-attractive (and -salable) points. Accordingly, although many knappers grumble that beginners should work glass or other low-value stone, and suggest that all knappers ought to use the lesser stone as well as the prime (e.g., Trotta 1996), only a few knappers express a personal desire to do so. However, many beginners are reluctant to spend too much money on material they know they will spoil, so market forces do push some knappers in the direction of conservation. Similarly, the increasing number of beginner knappers has created a market for a certain amount of smaller flakes, and many knappers who work large material salvage at least the best of their waste and sell it in buckets or by weight to others.

The economy of stone is affected not just by supply and demand, but by the symbolic value of stone and the esthetic rules of the knap-in. As we have seen, stone is a medium of exchange among knappers, and not just a raw material to be bought and sold, but a lore to be learned, a language to communicate status and knowledge, and a symbolic as well as an economic good. The modern knappers' quest for stone and the economy that it creates in the knapping world extend beyond the knap-in and beyond the purely material. Points and other equally charged, but even more complex knapped art will be the next aspect of the knap-in economy and ethos to be discussed.

Modern Stone Age Economics

"**I'm thinking of quitting my job** and just knapping," a young knapper was telling Gene Stapleton. "Do you think I could make it as a pro?" "Well," Gene growled around his pipe, "that depends. Do you want to own a house and have a family, or would you rather be a drunken, drug-using bum living out of the back of your van?" Gene went on to explain forcefully that knapping is not an easy way to make a good living, and the knapping itself is not as much fun when you have to crank out point after point every day to make ends meet. Nevertheless, the ebb and flow of money, like the tide on a rocky coast, moves the knap-in world, floating some enterprises and nourishing a wider fringe. The market for points and other bits of the knapping world is brisk, and a surprising number of people support themselves as knappers or entrepreneurs in knapping-related goods.

One of the reasons for knap-ins is to facilitate the economic flow of the knapping world. For a few knappers, the commerce is their main reason to be there; for many others, the opportunity to sell stone and points makes possible their trip to the knap-in. Even most of those for whom this is not true participate some in the economic flow, at least by buying material and tools.

As my survey suggested, most modern knappers are hobbyists, even though many sell points and other things as part of the hobby or to support it. Mentally counting people I know at Fort Osage, I can come up with ten to twenty whose primary source of income is knapping related. There are several possible strategies among them. We have already discussed the Waldorfs, who represent a mixed strategy, but are also unique in their position as promoters of knapping. Other knappers like George Eklund rely primarily on their knapped products, focusing either on the fake and replica markets or the "art" market, or both. Several small businesses sell tools, stone and other raw materials, books, videos, memorabilia, or some combination.

Frank Stevens, Knap-in Entrepreneur

I first met Frank "Moose" Stevens at Flint Ridge in 1996, when he was just beginning his company Great Lakes Lithics Supply. A stocky young man with short red-blond hair stood behind a table piled high with deer and moose antlers. I like to use antler, and it is not always easy to find, especially the desirable heavy moose. Frank also liked antler billets and told me he started sales partly because he, too, had a hard time finding antler. When I pointed out that this made him a minority among the copper-using modern knappers, he said, "I've got that covered, too," and showed me a stock of copper tools for sale as well.

Frank said he had been a chef, but now, with a working wife and new child, he wanted a job where he could mostly work at home, but didn't need to rely on his job for the family's complete income. Accordingly, he started small, concentrating on knapping tools, but became increasingly sucked in as he succeeded. At first he sold little stone, but soon saw the potential in the stone market, and he bought slab saws so he could buy premium stone in bulk and sell it as more profitable and transportable slabs. He took up books and videos, and some knives, points, and other knapped art. He added sinew, pine resin glue sticks, rawhide, and carving stone. Ultimately, he outfitted a trailer with shelves so he could transport all this to an expanding round of knap-ins, where he sets up a large sheltered booth with tables of tools and books, and crates of stone around the perimeter.

As well as the tools, materials, and products of knapping, entrepreneurs like Frank also sell the kind of memorabilia and ephemera that attach to many hobbies. Knap-in T-shirts and bumper stickers become more plentiful every year. Val Waldorf produces commemorative mugs. In 2000 Derek McLean began to produce a yearly calendar that lists the dates of knap-ins, as well as public holidays, and, more importantly, features an array of finely photographed points by a different knapper for each month. Better than a *Playboy* centerfold. Knappers vie for the honor, and the calendars have been a great success. One can also buy posters of point types drawn by Val Waldorf or photographed by Pete Bostrom, who also produces artifact postcards and superb casts of prehistoric points.

Frank's interest in knapping increased with his business, which gave him access to the highest-quality material and made him known to all the knappers. His own skills improved, and he began to collect points by other knappers. For a while Frank had a "project bucket" of his very best stone that he used to entice top knappers to make a point for him.

Frank is happy to combine hobby interests with his small business, but it is still a lot of work. He attends many knap-ins and has also found a receptive market with a somewhat different range of goods at primitive-archery meets. He sells a lot by mail order, advertising on a Web page and in newsletters like *Chips*. He maintains a presence on The Tarp mail server, largely for fun, but also to beat his own drum and steer knappers to his products. Frank spends a lot of time processing orders and material—running slab saws, grinding antler to billet shape, refining resin, packing and mailing. He conducts a certain amount of business by barter—he can exchange some of his material for other goods and make a monetary profit further down the line. Accordingly, Frank keeps busy at his booth and making deals and doesn't get to knap much at knap-ins, although he is an enthusiastic participant. As we sat around the evening fire at Fort Osage one evening, chanting and initiating new Ooga-Booga members, Frank was so worn out that he dropped off to sleep in his chair, a wad of smoldering sage incense in his fist. Those of us nearby watched with some anticipation to see if he would enliven the proceedings by setting his pants on fire, but he never did.

Frank is also quick to defend knapping vendors like himself from the occasional grumbles about prices, both at the knap-in and in messages on The Tarp:

> It is hard to recoup thousands of dollars invested into supplying such a small group. Whether it be material, videos, calendars, equipment . . . whatever. The initial investments are enormous compared to market size. Add on top of that operating costs and eventual losses. I know I've seen some ferocious

winds at Ft. Osage eat many an EZ-UP shelter. Imagine if it tipped over a table full of slabs or points. Books and calendars can get wet if a quick rain comes up. Dust is always a problem. I'm on my second vehicle motor in five years. You get the idea.

On another occasion we discussed knap-in economics. "I wonder how much money actually leaves the knap-in or comes in from outside, and how much just goes around and around here. Lots of guys buy a slab from me, make a point, and sell it to another knapper." I pointed out that there is a certain amount of profit in some of these transactions, which the knapper may use outside the knap-in, and after the knap-in ends, everyone goes away and takes his money off to other markets. "Yes, and of course visitors and dealers come here and buy points, but still a lot of the action is just inside the knap-in." This is an aspect of the knap-in world for which I can give no figures, but the knap-ins are just part of a wider, and probably very large, hobby economy that includes untraceable barter and other informal exchanges, as well as business enterprises like Frank's. A visit to the rock show at Quartzite, Arizona, gave me some taste of one part of this and showed how knapping extends into and interconnects with other hobbies. Primitive archery, black powder shooting and rendezvous, and outdoor survival skills groups would be other examples of the informal hobby economy.

A Trip to Quartzite

The economy of knapping extends far beyond the commercial transaction and far beyond the boundaries of any individual knap-in. A visit to the appropriately named town of Quartzite gave me a good example of the diversity and wide reach of the knapping economy.

The town of Quartzite, Arizona, hosts what it claims is the world's largest gem and mineral show in February each year. Quartzite's only other claim to fame is that Hajji Ali, known as Hi Jolly, is buried there. He was a Syrian Arab who came to the United States in the 1850s as the manager of a load of camels, part of a short-lived attempt by the army to use camels in exploring and subduing the American Southwest. The camels apparently performed well in the Southwest, but the cavalry horses and pack mules had fits every time they came near, perhaps an example of early trade unionism. In any case, the army abandoned the project and the camels, leaving them to roam the desert for some years thereafter. Hi Jolly settled down and became a local character until he died in 1902, according to the pyramid-shaped stone monument erected over his grave sometime later. I had to tell this story because it is the only romantic or picturesque thing about Quartzite, which is surely one of the least attractive towns in America.

Picture a strip of two-lane highway with dirt shoulders, running about four miles, with an exit to the Interstate on each end and a stoplight where another highway crosses in the middle. Quartzite sprawls along this road, with the usual nasty fast food places at one exit, a few other dingy restaurants, a couple of stunted groceries, a few other small businesses, and a handful of permanent residences. The rest of the town is completely made up of huge vacant lots filled from time to time with swap meets and gem and mineral shows, and other huge vacant lots filled somewhat more of the time with "motor homes," trailers, RVs, and other mechanized abominations of the American road. According to the Chamber of Commerce, Quartzite claims a population of 2,005, plus a million or so visitors in the winter. The warm climate is the main attraction, although when I visited in January 1997, it was around 60 degrees at noon. A howling wind was toothed with dust from the barren, vehicle-abraded trailer parks and swap meet grounds. Other than the climate, the only attractions are the presence of dozens of old folk who share a mobile lifestyle, and the shows.

I was there for the gem and mineral show because I had heard from a number of my friends at Fort Osage that knappers came there to buy stone and to sell their work. There are actually several shows or swap meets, two of which ("Cloud's Jamboree" and the Quartzite Improvement Association "Annual Pow Wow") are primarily gem and mineral shows. The others have some rock-related stuff, but are more swap meet-, antique-, and souvenir-oriented. The City of Quartzite sold 1,800 permits for booths in 1997.

I covered all the shows, a martyr for science. Among the tons of stone, and the tables full of fossils of all kinds, mixed with petrified wood ashtrays and tabletops, agate bolo ties, crystal earrings, and sardines canned in sandstone, there were a few knappers, and a surprising number of dealers who had points for sale. The disgusting Mexican "arrowheads" made on trimmed flakes, which can be found in every tourist trap in the Southwest, were common, of course. There were also quite a lot of rather poor points made on cut slabs of obsidian being sold as jewelry or loose points, or hafted on antler handles. I met a total of twelve knappers and heard that a couple more I knew had been there but left. Three of the knappers I talked to were friends from Fort Osage and other knap-ins, and they can serve as an example of the more sophisticated knapping and related activities at Quartzite.

Right beside the road, where the stream of traffic could see him easily, Jerry Calvert had set up some tables, a tipi, and a large sign reading "Knap-in." He was in a stretch of booths along the road, with the owners' mobile residences parked farther in. Jerry and his friend Mary Webster live year-round in a converted bus that they drive from place to place. As both are retired, this is a relatively cheap way to live, and they enjoy the life on the road. Knap-ins and rock shows offer an occasion to socialize with other craftsmen and to supplement their income by selling their crafts. On the roadside tables, Mary's antler carvings were on display with Jerry's points. Ron Fuller, another knapper, and his friend Mo, one of the few female knappers I have met at Fort Osage, were set up with them, too. Ron and Mo were about to leave, hitching his trailer full of stone to his pickup full of gear and saying their good-byes before heading to the gem and mineral show starting the next week in Tucson.

Jerry, a tall, grey-bearded man wearing an Ooga-Booga T-shirt, introduces himself as "Nine-Fingers," having lost most of his left thumb. This was not a knapping injury and does not seem to slow him down. He said he had done quite well in the couple of weeks they had been at Quartzite. With his roadside display, and the interest he creates by sitting there and knapping, quite a few people stop and buy points, blanks, copper knapping tools, and books and videos by Waldorf and Ratzat. He also had blowguns, atlatls, a couple of old guns, bows and bow staves, and some other primitive craft items out for sale. He had had to run his small electric kiln several times to keep up his supply of heat-treated rock and was spending a lot of his time blanking out nodules of Texas chert before heating them. He said he had sold 200 inches of blanks to a dealer at $2/inch, his nonbulk price being $3/inch. There was an almost bare space on his table that he said was formerly filled with points, and he had another customer who wanted a bunch of knives, at $7/inch. The customer planned to haft the knives for resale, so Jerry needed to make these in the next couple of days. A stone knife blade Jerry sells for $15 to $25 will be set in an antler handle and sold for $35–75, and if it is mounted in a frame or a shadow box, not only will it then bring $100 or more, but flaws can be concealed on less than perfect pieces. Nine-Fingers grumbled that he knows a guy who buys a few knives and casts them in resin; once they are mounted behind glass no one will handle them, and if they look good, who cares? This is obviously less good for the knapper, but as Jerry said, "What can you do?"

Jerry's points find several kinds of buyers. The dealers who buy batches of blanks will resell them to other knappers, make finished points themselves, or have someone else finish them. Many of the resulting points will eventually be sold as fake antiquities. I encountered only one dealer at the show who was obviously selling fakes. He had a number of trays of genuine artifacts, some bone tools from Alaskan sites, a couple of Mississippian pots, and a couple dozen frames of points. Some were obsidian points currently being made for the tourist trade around Teotihuacan, and most were ordinary rough prehistoric field finds from the Midwest, but he also had two frames of nice, complete large Archaic and Paleoindian forms. These are rare; when you see a bunch of perfect specimens all together, you should be suspicious. These were certainly made by modern Midwestern knappers. There were a half dozen more obviously modern points of exotic materials; these he pointed out to me as "new," while claiming "all the rest are old."

I encountered more modern points, sold more honestly, in a booth at Cloud's Jamboree later that day. Cloud's is the second of the Quartzite shows that features primarily "gem and mineral" and related crafts. Janet LeRoy and Steve Wall have a gallery in Colorado. Janet creates paintings on turkey feathers. Laying them flat in a frame, with some beads or other gewgaws, she paints a variety of "Western" scenes on them, ruins, Indian portraits, and so on. Steve bills himself on their card as "Mat Wizard" and does the frames. They also frame selected modern points with multicolored three-dimensional matting, a title, and sometimes the name of the knapper. A couple of nicely made art points that originally cost $30 to $50 apiece will sell for a couple of hundred as nice wall art in a handsome frame. Steve was attracted to knapping a couple years previously after seeing knappers at Quartzite and was soon making competent points himself. Their frames included "The Nine-Fingers Collection" and points by Craig Ratzat, Virgil Tonn, and Jim Hopper. They also had quite a few by Stan Norgard, another regular at the Quartzite shows. Stan and his wife had a booth over in the main Pow Wow, and were also selling modern points as framed art, as well as single art points by a number of modern knappers. They buy mostly from the knappers, at Quartzite and other shows, but rarely go to knap-ins.

A lot of stone is available at Quartzite. The various rock dealers cater more to rock hounds and lapidary workers than to knappers, but much of the stone that lapidarists find attractive is also knappable. The dealers are aware that they sell some stone to knappers, and some bring stone especially for that. The various people I talked to, knappers and dealers, had the impression that knappers were getting more common at such shows. In any case, there were literally tons of obsidian, jasper, glass slag, and other materials that knappers would buy, at about the same prices as I have seen at knap-ins, both in bulk and as slabs. Ordinary cherts and flints were not very common; most of the knappable stone was colorful and exotic, and desirable to others as well as knappers. Jerry had brought with him a lot of Texas chert that he had collected and was selling that, but he was there as a knapper rather than a stone dealer and selling to people interested in knapping and points rather than lapidarists. Ron had bought some stone and also a few large multicolored glass beads. He has discovered that a large, flat "butterfly" bead can be knapped to produce a very pretty small arrowhead, which some of the dealers and jewelers will buy to make pendants.

Meanwhile, Jerry was spreading the gospel of knapping. While we chatted, he demonstrated percussion to a group wandering by, who had "always wanted to know how arrowheads were made." A bit later a car peeled off from the bumper-to-bumper traffic stream and stopped in front of Jerry's tables. A young man got out, saying he had been there the previous day and had bought a "copper bopper" from Jerry. He was a beginning knapper from Alaska and had some problems he wondered if Jerry could help with. Jerry sat him down, and he showed us his tools and some points he was working on. When I left he was getting an extensive lesson on basic platforming tricks.

The shows in Quartzite thus represent a kind of event that is distinct from knap-ins, but which draws knappers and is part of the flow of stone and knapped art. It is evident that the public is becoming more aware of knapping; there have always been points at these shows, but the consensus was that there are more and more modern knapped pieces being sold as curios, jewelry, and art, as well as the understream of fake and real antiquities. Knappers like Jerry, who perform at shows as part of their advertising and to pass the time, also attract public interest. If, like Jerry, they make an attempt to draw people in, offer to teach them, and project the image of knapping as a friendly hobby, they have even more effect and are expressing some of the core values of the knap-in.

The gem and mineral shows at Quartzite also cover most of the kind of things that are relevant in the knap-in market. Stone is there in abundance, and some knappers go there to get materials they cannot collect themselves, especially exotic gem-quality stone. The peripheral goods are there, too. Lapidary equipment like rock saws that are used by some knappers were of course available. Knappers like Jerry were selling knapping tools, instructional books and videos, knapping kits, and other primitive crafts. Primitive crafts in general were not as well represented at Quartzite as at most knap-ins, but you could buy leather, carving stone, exotic woods, and antler. There were several antler dealers, selling antler mostly for buttons, pipes, carvings, knife handles, and hideous furniture, but they were aware of knappers and a couple had some pieces explicitly intended for sale as billets.

Points and other knapped work were also for sale. As we saw in Chapter 3, the modern point market is part of a long tradition of commercial knapping. Today the market can be divided into several parts, which are, of course, interconnected. As at Quartzite, some modern knapping is sold honestly as modern replicas or art, some as fake antiquities. The way knappers sell their work is not only a market decision, but a matter of ethics and worldview. The market in points provides further insight into the knapping ethos, and affects archaeology as well, a topic that I will also cover in Chapter 10.

Market Knapping

When Gene Stapleton warned the young knapper not to rely on knapping as a profession, he had in mind a particular kind of professional knapping. The other knapper was quite competent at producing replicas of prehistoric points, for which there is a good market, but as Gene pointed out, this market does not always work to the advantage of the knapper.

Jeff Gower, Marty Reuter, and Jim Spears are three of the better-known commercial knappers at Fort Osage. They make primarily replicas of prehistoric points and have slightly different orientations and styles. Jeff is a modern copper user, with an unusual backhanded pressure technique. Marty and Jim use only antler and stone tools, and are very interested in experimenting with prehistoric techniques of knapping and comparing the results to archaeological evidence. Marty uses indirect percussion with antler or ivory punches to do a lot of things most knappers would do with a copper billet. Jim is an older knapper who has been knapping professionally since the 1970s. He sells hides and has some other enterprises as well. Marty and Jeff are very focused on knapping and turn out hundreds of points a year. All three knappers make primarily the Paleoindian and large Archaic Midwestern points, and while they all sell at knap-ins, much of their income comes from dealers who buy the bulk of their work. Although these knappers are perfectly aboveboard in making and selling replica points, as these points move through the market, many of them will become fakes, often modified to look older and sold dishonestly as antiquities by someone in the chain of owners. In Chapter 10, I will discuss fakes and the market for them in more detail. Here it is enough to say that ancient stone tools command surprisingly high prices in today's antiquities market. A knapper like Jeff, Jim, or Marty sells a good replica point for $20 to $150 dollars, depending on its size, type, quality of stone, and difficulty of flaking. As antiquities, the equivalent point types in perfect condition can fetch ten times those amounts, and the top end of the best and rarest points more than that. The knapper, of course, sees little of the profit when someone else turns one of his points into a fake.

Meanwhile, the economic realities of making points can be harsh. One full-time professional knapper who sells most of his work to dealers told me that he regularly makes ten to fifteen points a day, or seventy-five to a hundred per week, which is more than any of the knappers who responded to my survey. A couple of others who knap mostly for sale but are not full-time knappers said they try to average three points a day, or at least thirty per month. An average point takes roughly an hour to make, with some more elaborate ones requiring a lot more time. A knapper thus has to keep up a rigorous production schedule and sell a lot of points to produce an adequate income. This requires considerable stamina as well as skill.

Of course, the net is reduced by expenses for tools and raw material, especially if the knapper buys the high-quality materials prized by the market or must acquire the particular stone correct for a certain type of point. Some knappers complain that the explosion of knapper numbers in the last few years has increased competition and reduced the prices they can ask for points.

And there are physical disadvantages, too. The silica dust produced in flaking is very hard on the lungs. British gunflint knappers who worked long hours in enclosed and poorly ventilated rooms often died young of lung ailments. Modern knappers are much more aware of dust as a health problem and try to ensure good ventilation, but still some risk remains. Repetitive use of muscles and tendons with great force is also a health hazard, and many knappers complain of arthritis, carpal tunnel syndrome, and the like. Marty Reuter arrived late one evening at Fort Osage and immediately began comparing injuries with Jeff Gower. Jeff had been having problems with his left hand. He took it to the doctor and had it X-rayed. The doctor told him he had broken the thumb sometime in the past, and that was healed, but now the finger tendons were inflamed. When he explained what he did for a living, the doctor told him he ought to lay off pressure flaking, where a constant fierce grip was required, for at least a while. Accordingly, at that knap-in he did mostly percussion work. Meanwhile, Marty had cut his finger pretty severely and also had a painfully overused wrist. He showed us a brace he had made for it, which at first glance was just a strange homemade device of straps and bars. Closer inspection showed that it was partly made of antler. We thought it was pretty funny that he would carry his preference for primitive tools so far as to make his medical aids out of antler, and when someone teased him about using nylon cordage to tie it up, he promised to make a proper leather strap.

Most of the knappers who live off point production value independence over security and high income, and many of them are young. The strains on personal life, especially with travel to knap-ins, can be great, and the strains on the body are also considerable. Although some of the full-time point knappers seem to making an adequate living, others appear to be pretty much hand-to-mouth.

Art Knapping

An alternative strategy for some knappers is to aim at a different market, which I will distinguish as the art market, although, as I have said, most knapping is "art" on one level or another. A few people have always bought fine knapping for its own sake, but until very recently there has not really been much market. For years, Charlie Shewey was practically the only collector amassing large numbers of modern points by the best knappers. Most artifact collectors disdained all modern work as fakery or simply failed to appreciate that modern points were equal in artistry and interest to prehistoric pieces. As modern knappers became more visible and united, more skilled and less underground, and as a few of them tried to promote knapping as modern art and create a collecting market, a few collectors began to get interested.

I first saw Carolyn Johnson and Larry Alexander at Fort Osage in 1997, shortly after they had begun collecting points. Larry was interested in collecting modern work from the first, while Carolyn started by collecting old points. They are now familiar figures at Fort Osage and other knap-ins, where they seek out the finest work by top knappers. Larry says he prefers the best replicas, made with unheated stone of the right type, using antler, while Carolyn is more attracted to "arty" points, colorful stone, and lap-knapped pieces. However, they are interested in anything that is high-quality and have a number of knappers they buy from regularly. Larry has also taken up knapping himself.

Hershel Harper and his wife also came to my attention about the same time. Longtime Texas artifact collectors and dealers, they more recently branched out into modern work and now display trays of points by each of a couple of dozen of the better-known knappers. Several other collectors have entered the scene, mostly with an interest in the top-end pieces, and the prices the top knappers can ask have risen in the last couple of years.

While many who would call themselves art knappers concentrate on points of unusual quality, others avoid some of the ethical problems of knapping replicas by intentionally making pieces that cannot be considered replicas of prehistoric forms. Several knappers say they intentionally use materials that would never have been used for a particular point type, and a number of the more expert knappers talk about their work as "pushing the envelope" or "taking knapping beyond artifacts." Nevertheless, the distinction is blurry: much of the art knapping is actually inspired by prehistoric pieces, and far and away the majority of "art" pieces are points. The ground and pattern-flaked points made by Hopper, Behrnes, Kylberg, and others are very finely worked and often do not conform well to any particular type, but they are still "arrowheads."

Figure 9.1. Gene Titmus experimental replica of a fancy Maya eccentric. Although Gene used obsidian, most large prehistoric Maya eccentrics were made of fine chert. Photo courtesy of Gene Titmus.

A few knappers make "eccentrics," that is, nonpoint forms, which usually have the edges flaked with elaborate notches, barbs, or even silhouettes of heads or animals. Some of these are inspired by prehistoric Maya pieces, which are spectacular enough to be pictured in popular publications like *National Geographic* (Stuart 1989, 492), although archaeological analyses are hard to find (Iannone 1992; Meadows 2001; Woods and Titmus 1996). Some Mayan eccentrics are more than 30 cm high and elaborately shaped. A thin biface that size is difficult enough to make; working intricate notches into it vastly increases the labor and the likelihood that it will be broken in the process. I have only heard of a few knappers making eccentrics on the Maya scale of size and difficulty (Figure 9.1). Gene Titmus, one of the early amateur archaeological knappers, was known among the early knap-ins for his "Titmus lace," small eccentrically flaked point forms made of obsidian (Figure 3.10; Titmus and Callahan 1980). More recently, he and archaeologist James Woods have been experimenting with replicating full-size Maya eccentrics (Woods and Titmus 1996) and offered a few for sale through a gallery created to support Maya research in the Mirador Basin of northern Guatemala (Hun Ahau Gallery 1996). Among the knappers who come to Fort Osage, Bob Thomas and Larry Langford make Maya-like and other eccentrics, usually small, and Craig Ratzat and several others make eccentrically flaked point forms, often to haft as knives. Dan Theus made several refined versions of a specimen cast by Pete Bostrom and illustrated on the cover of my *Flintknapping* (Whittaker 1994). Dan's eccentrics were partly instigated by a request from Carolyn Johnson, one of many examples of how collectors can affect the work of knappers.

A few knappers make what I call whimsies. The most common of these are point forms that are not detached from the rock and seem to be either driving into, or growing out of, the parent flake or nodule. George Eklund, Roy Motley, and a few other Fort Osage knappers made these for a while in the early 1990s, and Errett Callahan offered them in one of his catalogs (1993), but they seem to have died out now. Many knappers experiment playfully with odd forms, such as George Eklund and his "Danish scrapers" (Figure 9.2). Dave Schorn presented me with a business card written on a flint flake. Others make stone rings, letters, or animal effigy forms from time to time, but none of these are common or made regularly, and there does not seem to be a large market for such pieces, although outline effigy buffalo, eagles, and turtles turn up in collections from the early days of knapping to the present. George Eklund, Jim Miller, and a few others sometimes make miniature points, less than a centimeter long, flaked with a needle or other small tool. Although they say they sell some, these are difficult to display and appreciate, so I expect the market will be very limited. Errett Callahan and Payson Sheets have attempted to create a medical market for obsidian blade scalpels (Bowman 1997; Callahan 1999; McIlrath 1984).

The most profitable market for art knapping at the moment appears to be knife collectors. Knife collectors pay thousands of dollars for some steel knives; stone knives are an attractive novelty, and gener-

Figure 9.2. "Danish Scraper" by George Eklund, 1993. It conforms to no prehistoric type, and a knapper recognizes the joke: a scraper is ordinarily a simple flake with a steeply sharpened edge, one of the simplest of stone tools. George has given this a grotesquely long handle, elaborately flaked with zigzag "stitching" on the ridge like that on a Danish dagger handle. Compare Figure 9.6. Photo by Sarah DeLong.

ally cheaper. Errett Callahan has been instrumental in stimulating this market (Callahan 1990, 1993, 1999) and encouraging some of his students to use it as an ethical and profitable outlet for their knapping talent. The knife magazines have increasingly featured work by Callahan and others (Callahan 1997; Dickson 1992; Kelley 1990; Lang 1990; Shackleford 1987; Warner 1986), and several knappers of my acquaintance have begun to focus on knife production (Figure 9.3).

Dale Cannon and Stone Knives

Dale Cannon is a good example of the art knapper who works the knife market. He specializes in one thing and does it well, but has come up with several innovations. I first met him in the rain at the Pine City Knap-in in 1996, a tall, skinny man with a grizzled beard and tattoos from an earlier rock band career. A Minnesotan, he began knap-

Figure 9.3. Two stone knife craftsmen in Dale Cannon's "Future Artifacts" booth, Fort Osage, 2000. Dale (left) holds a lap-knapped Gerzean knife in its display box. Bob Keiper makes knives with distinctive carved handles such as the "Celtic Horse" in his hand.

ping after finding an arrowhead and getting some help from his brother, then came to the Pine City event around 1992 or so and was hooked. He started making pressure-flaked points on small cut obsidian slabs, but when he saw a frame of Jim Hopper's work that Jim Regan was showing off, he knew what he wanted to do. Dale had been a vending route driver and machinist, with photography and music as artistic outlets, but realized right away that knapping could be a good career, although his wife supported them for a while until he got established. Dale considers Jim Hopper the greatest influence on his knapping style, although it was some years before he sought Jim out and thanked him for the inspiration. By the time I met Dale in 1996, he had developed a distinctive lap-knapped style of knife and a successful marketing strategy.

Dale's knives are usually either symmetrical dagger forms or bowie-like pieces, and his earlier work shows influence also from Mike Stafford, who Dale says convinced him knife-making was the best way to package his knapping for sale (Figure 9.4). The blades are ground and pattern-flaked, and he prefers obsidian, although he uses other pretty stone, too. He cuts and grinds a simple modernistic handle out of marble or other soft stone with attractive patterns, cuts a socket in the end with a Dremel tool, and epoxies the flaked blade in. At first he left a decorative bead of epoxy around the junction of blade and handle, but now finishes with a band of silver wire. The forms are harmonious and attractive, but Dale considers his best idea to be the little wooden cases with a glass front that he mounts them in. "People were afraid to buy a stone knife, 'cause they're breakable. You put it in a box, and they can see it and handle it, and hang it on the wall, and it's safe." A little brass label says, "Future Artifacts, by Dale Cannon" and carries his symbol, which also goes on the knife handle. Dale also makes large lances and some points, but his only interest in replicating prehistoric tools is a recent exploration of Egyptian Gerzean knives, which were made with the same kind of grinding and flaking that he uses, and which are also showy artifacts that almost no one else is making.

When I talked to him in 1996, Dale had only recently decided to make knives full-time, and he is still enthusiastic about being a pro. He calls himself "a production knapper," meaning that he emphasizes the commercial aspect of his craft. In 1996 he was producing three or four knives in a ten-to-twelve-hour day, but it was on his own time, with breaks when he wanted. He was selling them then for $100–150 for single large knives and $150 for a couple of frames with two smaller knives in them. Today the prices have gone up considerably, and he produces

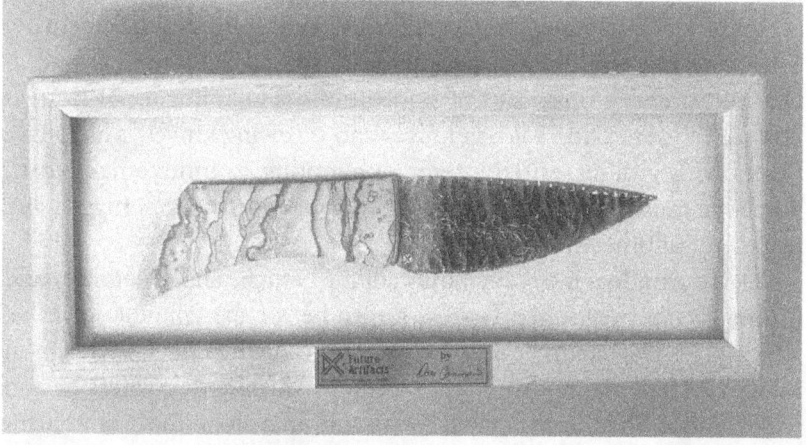

Figure 9.4. Dale Cannon knife (1996) in its display box. Photo by Sarah DeLong.

fewer knives and feels less forced to "turn things out." His ultimate goal is to get into the really high-end markets. "I did eighteen knap-ins or shows last year. I'm fifty years old now—can I do this another twenty years? Can a seventy-year-old do what I do? I want to get more money for my knives, because I've got to think about the future—maybe get some up into the thousands of dollars, who knows?" Meanwhile, Dale's knives are not only cash income: "Five knives to get my house painted, a knife a year for all the videos I want to watch at the local video store."

Dale is unusually good at the promotional side of his business. He is a very visible presence at knap-ins, where he sets up an elaborate booth with knives on display in their boxes and in the grip of primitive ceramic figurines. Overhead waves a deerskin banner proclaiming "Future Artifacts—Tomorrow's Artifacts Today." One of Dale's roles at the knap-ins is as an enthusiastic Ooga-Booga chief who also occasionally entertains the late-night knappers with banjo music and knapping songs. Beyond the knap-ins, Dale sells knives through several art galleries. "I find them on my knap-in trips, just pick the highest-end gallery I can find and walk in. Ninety-five percent of the time I win, 'cause I give them a good price and the quality is top."

Dale also got some good publicity in lapidary and knife magazines (Selbert 1996) and set about convincing large knife companies to carry his knives. Smokey Mountain Knife Works, the largest mail-order knife company in the United States, sold them for a short while, but the company wanted a more standardized and cheaper product than Dale likes to make. However, the influence of Dale and others like Errett Callahan on the higher-end knife market has raised the visibility of stone knives among knife collectors, and SMKW now regularly offers cheaper and less-artistic knives by several knappers, as well as cheesy cast epoxy imitations of stone knives. The influence of stone is also seen in some steel folding knives and throwing knives, which have blades with ground patterns feebly attempting to imitate flake scars. Someone must think that a bogus stone tool appearance is rugged and primitive, or otherwise appealing.

Dale's grandparents were Potawatami, French, and Cherokee, and his grandfather registered Dale as a member of the Potawatami tribe, which gives Dale another useful connection. At the Pine City Knap-in in 2001 he had just returned from a trip to Washington, where he and Mike Stafford had been invited to consult on a stone tools exhibit for the new National Museum of the American Indian. Mike, who is an archaeologist at the Cranbrook Institute of Science and one of the few archaeologists attending knap-ins, advised them on archaeological aspects, and Dale was to represent modern knapping. Dale considered it rather flattering to be used as the endpoint of thousands of years of technological evolution in stone tools, and hopes to do demonstrations and a video for the museum and get more into the educational aspects of knapping. Meanwhile, Dale has also produced a video on his techniques (Cannon et al. 2000), in which he is interviewed by Dane Martin and waxes enthusiastic about the kind of knapping he does:

> This is like taking the training wheels off your Harley—all of a sudden you've got all this freedom. Not like beating on a rock. I've done it. I choose not to at this point because I'm way way too busy with what I'm doing. Maybe sometime I'll slow down on knives and learn percussion techniques and become an all-around knapper, but this has overtaken me and I have no room for anything else. I just jump on that Harley and take off. There's no rules in this art work. I can make what I want, and nobody has to tell me it's wrong or right. It is what it is.

To me he says, "I love the knap-ins, they're just *fun*. Like a family reunion, and more fun each time." They provide a social life centered around people who appreciate his craft. "I'm in it for the money, sure, and for art, and gratification—people show off my work, they're proud of it, I'm proud, every artist needs that feedback."

The knife market is a good niche for a number of knappers. Errett Callahan supports himself partly by making knives, which he sells at knife shows and through his catalogs. He makes a variety of forms, ranging from fairly normal knives with wooden or antler handles to parallel-flaked blades in scrimshawed handles. His fanciest works are a suite of eccentric obsidian blades hafted on antler or wood carved and painted as dinosaur busts (Figure 9.5). These "fantasy knives" he makes as "limited editions" and sells for a couple of thousand dollars. In a 1997 letter Errett told me he makes between thirty and seventy-five knives a year. "I sell about as many knives in a year as I make. But not always the same ones. Virtually all the knives I make go to knife and art collectors (few knappers buy), except for my research pieces, which are primarily Danish daggers. I also make a lot of other tools for research, teaching, demonstrations, etc. Knapping is a half-time job for me. It's not recreation; but I happen to love knapping feverishly."

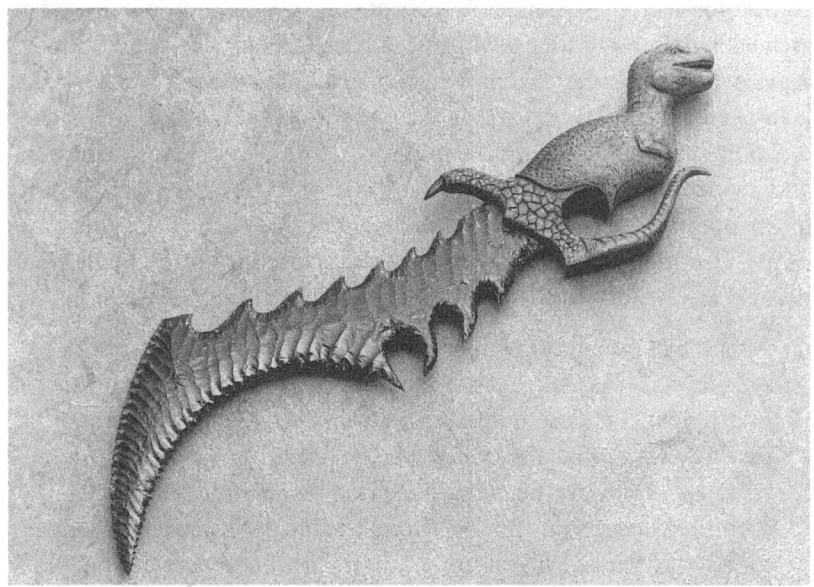

Figure 9.5. "Velociraptor II" fantasy knife by Errett Callahan, "the most challenging and elegant of the series," which won the Best High Art Knife award at the Shenandoah Valley Knife Show in 1998. Handle carving by Ron Myers. Photo by Jim Weyer, courtesy of Errett Callahan, ©Weyer of Toledo.

Errett's marketing strategy has been to interest the knife shows and knife magazines; he has won prizes at the former and been featured in the latter, and this has probably helped create a market for other knappers as well. Errett promotes his knives at knife shows, but disdains Fort Osage and similar knap-ins, where, as I have mentioned, he feels in conflict with the nontraditional knapping. He produces detailed catalogs (1990, 1993, 1999), which promote stone knives as both art and functional tools and feature slick photographs, information, and opinion about knapping along with testimonials from collectors and other knappers.

Dale, too, is something of an innovator, and his strategies make a good example of how new ideas and styles spread in the knap-in community. About the same time Dale was starting out, Ron Lowry began selling stone and other knapping items as White River Supply. Ron is an entrepreneur rather than a knapper, an oil geologist who still receives much of his income from oil properties, but he has a good understanding of the knapping market. He specializes in raw material and carries a wide variety of choice stone, as well as antler, copper knapping tools, videos, and books. Ron also sells stone knives, at several levels of quality and price. He says they make up about half his business. He buys the blades from knappers and either sets them in handles himself or has someone else do it to his order. His most distinctive knives when I met him at the Evergreen Lake Knap-in in 1996 had lap-knapped blades by Billy Joe Shelden, a Colorado knapper, set in handles of cut yellow mudstone with woodgrain patterns from Wyoming, which were made by an associate in New York. Ron later told me that putting his knives together involved a lot of mailing back and forth.

Less than a year after I met Ron, his knife inventory had changed. At the May 1997 Fort Osage Knap-in he had even more knives, with blades made by several different knappers. He had more fine work and fewer of the cheap, small obsidian knives of mediocre workmanship hafted in antler or fox jaws, which are what you commonly see in "Indian Art" and tourist shops in the West. Most notably, many of his knives now had polished marble handles and were being sold in small boxes with glass fronts and a brass label, directly copied from Dale Cannon's knives of a year earlier. Right next to Ron Lowry, Ron Martis had a display including points similar to Craig Ratzat's (whom he learned from) and knives inspired by Dale's. He also makes blades for Ron Lowry, favoring slightly more complex forms than most of the other knife makers. When I asked Dale how he felt about others using his ideas, he just grinned and said, "Imitation is the sincerest form of flattery" and admitted that, in fact, he had got the idea for the form of his knife handles from a knife Mike Stafford had made with a wooden handle a couple of years previously. By the 1997 knap-in, it was apparent that other knappers had been impressed by Dale's work, and stone-handled knives appeared to be taking over from wood and antler as the "wave of the future." Dale was investigating collaborating with a woman who could scrimshaw some of his marble knife handles, an idea he picked up from several other knife makers who prefer antler handles.

In a competitive market, innovation sells. Errett Callahan has his dinosaurs; Bob Keiper, who works more for fun, but has sold a few knives, makes carved wooden handles with Celtic reflections; Bob Patten imitates the famous Maya and Aztec knife handles; and I have seen antler snakes, eagles, and alligators, wooden totem poles, and exotic wood, including cholla stems, and all sorts of animal parts used as han-

Figure 9.6. Danish Neolithic dagger replica by Mike Stafford, 1996. This is a good replica of the most elaborate stone tools made in prehistory, requiring advanced skill in making percussion bifaces, using indirect percussion to shape the handle, and different pressure flaking techniques to finish the blade with parallel flaking and the handle with "stitching," all executed in very tough stone. Photo by Sarah DeLong.

dles. However, creativity is not merely a selling point, but the mark of a good knapper, and new forms, well executed, earn the respect and imitation of others. Some of the art knapping is, in fact, best appreciated by other knappers. Only a few knappers make really good Danish daggers (Figure 9.6). Errett Callahan, D. C. Waldorf, Mike Stafford, and Dave Schorn are the ones I know best. Mike says that knife collectors are not very interested in the daggers—only a knapper can really appreciate how difficult they are and how many different knapping techniques are involved (Stafford 1998). Publications and interest by D. C. and Errett have made them familiar to most knappers and created such market as exists, but while Danish daggers are widely admired by knappers, they are not in great demand. In the United States they are art knapping, and both Waldorf and Callahan mostly use materials other than Danish flint. Mike Stafford, who does his archaeological research in Scandinavia, says there are knappers there who make daggers for sale as fakes.

The problem of stone tools that resemble prehistoric artifacts affects the archaeologist directly and involves the knappers in some of their most difficult ethical issues. This is a further aspect of the knap-in economy that will be considered in Chapter 10.

Knappers, Collectors, Archaeologists: Ethics and Conflicts

The first time I came to Fort Osage, I wandered anonymous and fascinated among the knappers and sat on a bench with some other knappers watching George Eklund make a point. He had a nice, thin chert biface roughed out, and while I watched, he pressure-flaked it to final form. He worked fast, as he always does, strong hands armored in surgical tape, taking off large flakes with rapid movements of his short pressure flaker. It was a nice Thebes point, roughly triangular with corner notches and a beveled blade. While he worked, he exchanged jokes with his audience, and we asked occasional questions. George did not know me, but noticed my interest and pointed out what he was doing and why a couple of times. When he had demonstrated notching and put the final touches on the flaked bevel, he frowned and said, "Looks too fresh." Reaching down to his workbox, he took out a can of Old English furniture antiquing stain and, soaking a rag, wiped stain over the light grey chert, dulling it to a dirty grey-brown. I soon learned that this is a common practice; the antiquing brings out the color patterns of the stone, makes it look old, and accentuates the flake scars. George was not satisfied, however. He picked up an old piece of rusty iron and, exclaiming "Here comes the plow!" dragged it across the surface of the point, leaving a streak of rust and a small nick on the edge. Everyone laughed; George then buffed the point on a dirty blanket for a final touch.

Was George making a fake antiquity, or giving an antique appearance to a modern point, just as furniture is "antiqued"? George said he always antiques his points, because otherwise "they don't look right." This is one of the esthetic choices made by some knappers, and in fact I have seen George and others use the Old English on whimsical pieces that resemble no prehistoric artifact at all (see Figure 9.2). That first time I watched him, he gave the point to me after I watched him make it, but under other circumstances, with other knappers, with successive owners, what would happen? The issue of fakes is a complex one.

Replicas, Fakes, and Art

Modern knapped stonework divides rather uneasily into three major categories: replicas, fakes, and art. All of these overlap one another, and many knappers also are difficult to categorize in terms of which they make, but some basic distinctions are useful here. Replicas and fakes resemble prehistoric specimens. The difference is in intent: replicas are to teach, experiment, or display, while fakes are intended to deceive someone. Art knapping is not intended to reproduce a prehistoric form, but to be appreciated simply as art. Those are the easy definitions; some problems should already be obvious.

Replicas come at all levels of quality and fidelity to the original. Some archaeologists (e.g., Callahan 1995b; Coles 1973, 1979; Crabtree 1966) take a strict view that only a few kinds of experiments are useful, preferring to reserve the term "replica" or "replication" for experiments that conform as closely as possible to the archaeological evidence for manufacturing techniques, raw material, and waste products, as well as the form of the artifact. In my opinion (Whittaker 1996a, 1996b) such distinctions are matters of degree. Much can be learned from experiments that conform to archaeological evidence only in limited ways, from failed experiments, and even from replicas that are incorrect. A replica that was not manufactured with primitive techniques or materials may still be a useful representation of the original artifact that conveys our understandings of it and stimulates hypotheses about manufacture and use. In any case, here I use the term "replica," in its most general sense, to mean a copy of the form of a prehistoric specimen.

Fakes are usually replicas, in the sense of conforming to an original prototype, but are made to fool someone, usually a buyer, into believing that they are authentically ancient. However, some pieces sold as fake antiquities are either poor replicas or not replicas at all. Grey Ghosts and some other knapped pieces that have been commonly sold as prehistoric "finds" do not resemble authentic points very closely. As I have said, some other modern points resemble prehistoric forms but are far too large or finely flaked. These may be made as art, but they, too, are sometimes sold as antiquities.

Art knapping is intended to be sold and appreciated as modern work, and it often intentionally does not follow prehistoric forms. When it does, it often blurs the lines among the three categories of replica, fake, and art. For some knappers, like George, above, looking "old" is part of the esthetic appearance of real antiquities, fakes, and points that are never intended to be mistaken for ancient finds.

Fakes, Replicas, and Ethics

Far and away the majority of knapped pieces today do resemble prehistoric points. This is mostly because the majority of knappers came into knapping because of an interest in prehistory, Indians, and arrowheads. The fact that there is a ready market for points is also a factor. As my survey showed, most knappers can be considered hobby knappers (71 percent of survey respondents). Another fifth of the respondents were either professional knappers (7 percent) or heavily involved in selling their work (14 percent), and the rest were "archaeological" knappers, who knap mostly for experimental purposes. A majority of knappers (on the survey 58 percent, not counting "archaeological" knappers) sell at least some points.

I will discuss the size and nature of the market for stone points in a bit. For now, it is enough to know that there is a very large market for both antiquities and fakes, and increasingly, for modern art points. The amounts of money involved in the antiquities trade are quite sufficient to stimulate faking. Selling points is considered normal and unexceptional; the way points are sold is, however, a bone of contention.

Ethics involve defining a group's rules in a very explicit way. Although there are moral rules for all kinds of behavior, the biggest ethical issue among knappers is the question of faking.

Murmurings at the Knap-in

At Fort Osage, in the warm September of 1998, problems with the commercial side of knapping were heating up. A bunch of us were crowded into Steve Behrnes's trailer, where Charlie Shewey was holding court, sitting on a bed in his undershirt with moths wheeling around the overhead light. The conversation ranged from anti-Clinton diatribes to a debate about religion and on through the more immediate issues of the knapping economy. Several of the more commercially oriented knappers were complaining that prices were down—too many good knappers making good points, including some knappers that no one knew, the rising Internet, and the death of a major dealer who was reputed to have bought five thousand points a month from various knappers. Charlie was particularly incensed that a certain individual was being seen at the knap-ins again after an arrest for stealing artifacts out of a museum. He was more of a collector and dealer than a knapper and had a bad reputation for dishonesty and obnoxious behavior. "What's he doing out with just a pat on the wrist?" asked Charlie heatedly. "An informer!" muttered another knapper. What no one wanted to say to Charlie's face was that one of his friends also had some knappers on edge.

David DeTar Newbert is another knowledgeable collector of big-money artifacts. He had recently become a friend of Charlie's, and at a couple of previous knap-ins, Charlie had been introducing him around. He is also a federal prosecutor and writes for collector magazines like *Prehistoric American,* a glossy quarterly featuring high-quality photos of prime artifacts. The articles are a mix of archaeological information about artifact types with the "how I found it" or "how I bought it" stories about specific pieces that dominate the collector literature. There are also frequent articles about fakes, and the most recent issue was no exception. David DeTar Newbert's article (1998) was entitled "Selling Counterfeits Is a Crime," and was accompanied by a two-page color spread of "Twentieth century Reproductions/Fakes," with captions, and an editorial "Advice for New Collector/Investors" by editor John Berner (1998c, 1998a). Another article on fakery by Harmer Johnson (1998) of the Appraisers Association of America followed. The knappers in Behrnes's trailer were able to identify makers of some of the points pictured.

The articles in that issue of *Prehistoric American* expressed the collector view of knappers: Knappers are fakers, getting rich from dishonest profits, and the fakes damage the great hobby of collecting, scare off new collectors, and diminish the investment value of collections. Knappers hear this all the time if they also move in collector circles or read the collector literature and email lists. Newbert's article particularly grated for several reasons. First, it seemed to imply that any replica must be a fake, and anyone making modern stone tools must be a faker. I didn't think he was saying that, but knappers were reacting to the hostility common among some collectors. Second, he made a pointed comparison to some fake Picasso prints, which had recently been produced by one dealer for sale as fakes by others. This implied that knappers likewise are accomplices to the dishonest dealer when they sell points that become fakes. This cut close to the bone for many knappers. A lot of knappers who would not sell a point dishonestly know full well what will happen when they sell to some dealers, even though the knapper may deplore faking and complain that he has no control over what is done with his points. Newbert also suggested that the dishonest dealer was unlikely to report taxable profit on points he bought cheaply from knappers and retailed for many times their cost as valuable antiquities.

And finally, and worst, David DeTar Newbert was a federal prosecutor who was now being seen at knap-ins. The more paranoid knappers regarded this as probable spying, while the more generous interpretation was that Newbert intended the article as a friendly warning. In any case, the market knappers who make primarily replicas of prehistoric points are especially sensitive, but most knappers are aware that collectors and archaeologists often distrust them as fakers. In the conservative and often antigovernment milieu of the knap-in, the specter of government intervention and oppressive legal action seems to loom. But worse was to come in the next knap-in season, for the Woody Blackwell affair was about to hit.

Woody's Dreams and Knappers' Nightmares

At the Society for American Archaeology meetings in April 1999, and from knapper friends, I began to hear rumors and stories about a fraud involving lots of money and large numbers of Clovis points. People knew I was interested in the archaeological problem of fakes because Mike Stafford and I had written an article, "Replicas, Fakes, and Art: The Twentieth Century Stone Age and Its Effects on Archaeology," which had come out in *American Antiquity* just that month. *American Antiquity* is the major U.S. journal for academic archaeologists, but I sent or gave copies to many of my knap-in friends, and reactions to that article figure in this story.

Figure 10.1. Left, Clovis point made for me in 1995 by Woody Blackwell. Right, Lithic Casting Lab cast of one of the points from the Fenn Cache. Woody's point is just a very fine fluted point, not a replica of any particular Clovis. Photo by Sarah DeLong.

At Fort Osage in May of 1999, the Woody affair was on every tongue, and friends buttonholed me to discuss it and to praise or criticize the *American Antiquity* article. The basic story, of which I did not get all the details at the time, was that Woody Blackwell had created a dozen fine Clovis points (Figure 10.1), which he had aged and then provided with a story about their being a "cache" that had been found long ago but left languishing in an attic for years. Through an intermediary, he sold them to Forrest Fenn, a rich collector in Santa Fe.

Fenn already had a well-known collection of Paleoindian points, which included another group of Clovis points and tools reputedly found as a cache in the West many years ago, and widely known as "the Fenn Cache" (Frison and Bradley 1999). Fenn also had enough connections in both the collector and archaeological worlds to organize a large public conference, "Clovis and Beyond," in Santa Fe (in 1999, after Woody's fraud had been exposed). Fenn was said to have paid a total of about $100,000 for Woody's points. Fenn said, "the asking price was $150,000" (Fenn 2001, 40); Woody told me in 2002 that he had actually been paid $15,000–16,000 for the first three, with a price of around $80,000 still being negotiated for the last nine when he decided he couldn't go through with the deception. In any case, it seemed a shocking amount of money for stone tools.

However, as Fenn showed his new acquisitions around, a few people became suspicious. Ken Tankersley, an archaeologist, took a close look and discovered that the points had been artificially aged by tumbling and oxidizing with potassium permanganate. Some were coated with red ochre and some merely with reddish soil, and two quartz crystal points were apparently made of Brazilian crystal, difficult to accept for prehistoric Clovis material (Fenn 2001; Fogelman 1999; Preston 1999; Tankersley 2002). At the same time, a couple of other collectors had bought several other points for prices in the thousands of dollars. By the Fort Osage Knap-in in May, Woody had confessed and much of the story was out. He says his conscience couldn't take it anymore, and he spontaneously called Fenn; the collectors say they confronted him and legal action was looming. He returned the money to Fenn and a couple of others with written confessions, and they kept the points, while Woody avoided prosecution.

I had first met Woody at Fort Osage in May 1991, but did not get to talk to him much until a year later. He was an impressive knapper, and when I got to know him a bit, I found him articulate, friendly, and interested in all sorts of things, so I did a formal taped interview. We went off to the side of the knap-in and sat on the wall around the old cemetery under some shade trees, where the din of the knap-in was not so disturbing. As usual, I asked Woody how he got interested and started knapping, and learned that he had only been to his first knap-in, in Texas, in April 1990. This was humbling, because he was already far more skillful than I and plainly going to be a top knapper. At that point he was making very large Clovis points in the style of a cache found near East Wenatchee, Washington (Gramly 1993). He fluted with a lever jig, and already other knappers were forming an audience around him when he worked. His style of knapping and preference for Clovis points fluted with a jig reflected the influence of Joe Miller and J. B. Sollberger, from whom he learned (Figure 10.2). When I commented on how fast he had progressed, he said, "Well, I go at it hammer and tongs, generally almost every day, a couple of hours every day

Figure 10.2. Woody Blackwell knapping at Fort Osage, May 1996. Behind him are Charlie Shewey and Joe Miller. Note the knapping T-shirts: "Folsom New Mexico" on Woody, and "J. B. Sollberger Clovis Factory" on Joe.

and weekends a lot of the time both days for six or eight hours." Part of our conversation was in retrospect ironic:

JW: So, what do you do for a living, air force?
WB: Yeah, major in the air force. [He was soon to retire.] Got a bunch of guys who work for me and we do criminal investigations for the military.
JW: Well, that should suit you for an archaeological career.
WB: I don't know, I hope not. Don't run into many dopers and murderers in archaeology!
JW: Well, I was thinking more in terms of thinking about evidence and stuff.
WB: Yeah, that might be.

JW: So what do you do with your flint work? Do you sign your pieces?
WB: No, I don't sign them, uh . . . yet. It's kind of a chintzy cop out. I haven't signed them just because I haven't bought an engraver. There are guys who are buying my stuff and I'm about probably 99.99 percent certain that they're dirtying them up, beating them up and passing them off for authentic. One side of me says, caveat emptor, if anybody is dumb enough to bite on it, well a fool and his money are soon to be parted anyway. Another side of me says I don't like the unscrupulous people out there. I don't know. Selling a few points lets me buy more material to feed this habit of mine. I don't know. I think there are more guys out there who are willing to buy them and pass them off as genuine than there are guys who are willing to buy them because they are nice to look at and they would like a piece of my work.
JW: I wonder about that too, that's one of the things I'd like to know more of.
WB: Yeah, it's pretty shady. And if you find many folks who'll talk to you about it, I'll be surprised. They might talk to you about it, how honest they'll be, I don't know. I don't know.
JW: I've heard the ethic expressed several times that "Well, you know if they don't ask me I won't tell them but if they ask me I'll tell them I made it."
WB: Yeah, I don't know. It's kind of unethical, I think.
JW: Well, I like seeing people signing points, partly as an archaeologist who doesn't want the record contaminated. But partly because it's a craft. The *artist* is interesting to me and that's why I'm doing this.
WB: Well, the super fine pieces which I try to make, I'm not always successful, in fact I'm rarely successful in making a super fine piece. Just because they're super fine is probably telltale that they're not old. Because of our tools, the high quality of the stone that we have. Because they are not subjected to use and wear, I think generally the products we're making now are far superior to most aboriginal pieces.
JW: They're certainly above the average.
WB: Yeah. Of course, there are a few exceptional pieces out there that are authentic. Sweetwater biface, the Wenatchees, the pieces from the Fenn Cache. I don't know if we'll ever successfully duplicate some things.

For much of the rest of the interview we talked with enthusiasm about how modern knappers were eventually going to be able to do anything that was done in prehistory, but we both agreed that this poses problems for archaeologists of the future and that already collections are contaminated by modern points accepted as ancient. We went on to discuss possible future directions for knapping, especially its expansion into more pure art (see Blackwell 1996).

In an email (January 2003) Woody told me,

> At that time I'd been knapping for two years (I began April 1990.) My work was far from art quality. But as with all beginners, it had an aboriginal look to it; it was good enough to approximate the form of old pieces and was also unintentionally crude enough to mimic old techniques. For all intents and purposes, the art market did not yet exist. Charlie Shewey was the only collector of modern pieces, and he was not then interested in my crude work. At that time, my work was bought by other knappers, some of whom occasionally dealt in artifacts. If I sold five or six points at a knap-in, it was a major event for me. The standard price was $20 to $25 for the best point I was capable of making, although the majority of my work was traded: I received other knappers' work and/or raw material.

I don't intend to imply from the interview that Woody had plans for fraud at the time. To me, the real moral of the interview lies in the power of the marketplace to corrupt. All knappers are aware of the potential for fakery, and most speak out against it. But like Woody, many knappers who say repeatedly that they deplore fakery may be sucked in. I have less access to the world of dealers, collectors, and authenticators, but I suspect from what I hear that many of them are similar: they hate fakes and try to keep them out of their own collections, but the opportunity to make easy money is too much for some.

Over the next few years, I talked with Woody a lot—he was one of the more thoughtful observers of the knapping world and, increasingly, a knapper of great reputation. He became known for superb Clovis points and large pieces as thin as anyone could make them. He was a knapper whose advice was sought on difficult problems and who always had an audience at knap-ins. Although he did a lot of research, especially in private collections, and was interested in the way prehistoric points were made and in duplicating the details of their appearance, he remained a copper knapper, perhaps better known for virtuoso work that was too good to pass as prehistoric. As a few more collectors of modern knapped work began to enter the market, and as his skills increased, Woody started to develop a clientele of collectors interested in fine pieces by Blackwell, including Charlie Shewey at Fort Osage. He produced two good videos on knapping (Blackwell 1995, 1996) and articles for *Chips* (Blackwell 1994a, 1994b, 1997a,b,c,d). He publicly positioned himself as a top art knapper with a serious interest in the archaeology of stone points. Nevertheless, when he retired from the military, he ran into financial difficulties, and the temptation to cut out the middlemen who make replicas into fakes was too strong.

As the story unfolded in 1999 I was one of several knappers contacted by the *New Yorker* for information about the knapping world. It seemed that Douglas Preston was writing about Woody and the knappers. Preston is a journalist whose articles for the *New Yorker* frequently focus on archaeology, especially controversial aspects (Preston 1995, 1997, 1998). He also writes novels such as *Thunderhead* (Preston and Child 1999), a lurid supernatural thriller with archaeological themes. I sent a copy of the *American Antiquity* article at the request of a researcher, but never got to talk to Preston himself. Although I screwed up my courage to broach a difficult topic a couple of times, I was also unable to contact Woody, so I did not hear his side of the affair at the time, except indirectly.

I was most interested in watching the reactions in the knap-in world and among collectors. Unfortunately, I spent the fall semester of 1999 in London and could not get to the Fort Osage Knap-in, so I had to follow developments through email and published accounts. Douglas Preston's article "Woody's Dream" (Preston 1999) came out in November and catalyzed commentary on the Woody affair.

Preston's article was a fine piece of writing and a gripping story, although there were some careless little archaeological errors. However, it suffered from a number of imbalances that infuriated many knappers. To quote the header under the title: "Nobody knew how the ancient Clovis hunters created their brilliant artifacts—except for one man, and nobody wanted to believe him." This, of course, is simply nonsense—there are a number of knappers who can and do make Clovis and other Paleoindian points at an equal level of skill, including some who are archaeologists or working with archaeologists. However, Preston gave a good dose of journalistic hype to Woody's undisputed skill, repeatedly quoting Fenn and others describing the perfection of the points. As Preston and Blackwell tell it, Woody sort of slipped into forgery almost accidentally, learning to duplicate the minute details of authentic points, experimenting with patination under different conditions, and then falling on hard times. The knappers and collectors see it differently, pointing out that the fraud focused on known collectors, was inspired by famous earlier finds, and resembled them. Woody produced not just points but false documentation, and was successful partly because of his skillful replications, but also because he was trusted (Fenn 2001; Taylor 2000a, 2000b). Fenn and Jeb Taylor, two of his victims, glorified Woody's points to Preston and wrote articles after the affair to explain why they, the expert collectors, were taken in and to boast that they won in the end.

Meanwhile, many knappers felt betrayed by Woody, offended by Preston, and vilified by the world in general. My *American Antiquity* article did not help, either, although Mike Stafford and I discussed positive sides of the knap-in as well as negative. Knappers felt that once again they were all being portrayed as fakers or potential fakers, and the actions of a few would damage all. An unwelcome window was opened into the dark "black market" corners of the knap-in. Those who actually participate in faking, mostly by knowingly supplying points that others would use to defraud, but others less innocently, were very unhappy to have any official attention focused on knappers at all. A few of the more paranoid knappers actually worried that there might be attempts to legally ban knapping. This is quite absurd. While the collector literature often calls for more legal action against fakers, the knowing sale of modern points as antiquities is already fraud and covered by existing laws. It is no more possible to ban the making of replica points to prevent fake Folsoms than it is to ban cabinetmaking to prevent the sale of fake Louis XIV chairs.

As long as there is a market for some limited collectible, fakes will be produced, whether they be points, pocket knives (Witcher 1997), or fine art. No one is surprised to hear about counterfeit coins, fake faience, or ersatz icons, and there are enough fakes in great museums that they can set up entire exhibitions and publish books about them (Jones 1990). Some other fakes might surprise you. Steve Owens, one of my knapping friends from Iowa, tells an illuminating story. Steve worked for years for Maytag, maker of washing machines and other appliances since the early 1900s. Maytag was one of several early washing machine companies in central Iowa, including one in Grinnell, and there are, of course, collectors of antique washing machines. Steve was a collector of Maytag-related material and owned some rare washing machines, including a 1919 model that ran on a small gasoline engine whose fuel tank was a Mason jar screwed upside down on the top of the engine, so you could easily see the fuel level. A glass fuel tank attached to a hot and vibrating machine was actually not such a good idea, and a spate of laundry-shed fires soon convinced Maytag to discontinue this model, so they are rather scarce. Soon after Steve acquired his, someone else took one apart, cast the parts, and began selling fake versions. That was bad enough, but Steve lost his collecting zeal when someone turned up at a Maytag collectors' show with nice glass jars that had "Maytag" embossed on them, upside down—plainly the gas tank to go with the machines. Unfortunately, it seems Maytag never made any such jars. They were fakes, but like all good fakes, made sense and played to collectors' expectations and hopes (Whittaker 1992). This may seem like a story from Podunk, Iowa, but I assure you that for any object you can name, someone collects it, and if there are enough collectors to create a market, and it is physically possible, someone is also faking it.

How bad a problem is this for archaeology? There have, of course, been some famous scientific fakes, like the supposed "Dawn Man" of Piltdown, England, "discovered" in 1912. Here the motive was probably personal advancement or embarrassing the establishment, depending on who you think was the perpetrator. A more common incentive to faking is economic. Antiquities that fetch high prices on the international art market spawn a web of deceit (Tubb 1995). High value stimulates plundering of archaeological sites, and also faking, and between the two crimes, we sometimes do not really know how some artifacts developed, where they fit in the lives of the ancient people, or even which pieces we can use as evidence (Gill and Chippendale 1993). One would think that fakes would only be made in numbers if there was a good market for the originals, and it was a surprise to me, when I entered the knap-in world, to learn that there is, in fact, a huge market for both ancient stone tools and modern replicas and fakes.

Fakes and Archaeology

When I started going to knap-ins, I had no idea how many nonacademic knappers there were, or how many points were being produced, or what the market for old and new stonework was like. Very few archaeologists do. Archaeologists who work with stone tools may be knappers, even very skillful knappers, but only a small minority have any involvement with the knap-in world. Archaeologists respect the contributions to archaeological knowledge made by knappers like Don Crabtree from outside the academic world, and by knapping experiments in general: without knappers of all sorts, we would not be able to interpret stone tools. However, most archaeologists are uncomfortable with anything connected to the buying or selling of antiquities. This is because, despite the denials of collectors, many of whom do not, in fact, themselves destroy sites, the market for antiquities is what spurs a lot of looting. The stronger the market for particular artifacts, the more sites that have them will be ravaged, and the more artifacts will be faked to meet the demand. This is one place where the knapping world meets and is often in conflict with other interests, and the Woody story is just a small part of this scene. There are a number of ways in which modern stone tools and knapping affect the archaeological record, both for archaeologists and for collectors, and it is useful to consider these issues here before returning to the Woody story to see what the knap-in world thinks about it all.

I have already loosely characterized three kinds of modern stone tools: replicas, fakes, and art. The art lithics are usually distinct from prehistoric points and pose no immediate problem for the archaeologist, although they may be confusing in the farther future. But I'm willing to let archaeologists of the twenty-seventh century worry about that. If they are any good, they will be able to figure it out, even in the likely event that this book does not survive as a classic for the ages. Modern flints made to look like prehistoric ones are the problem, and that, of course, is what most knappers make. How big a problem is it, and why? Mike Stafford and I started exploring this question a few years ago (Whittaker and Stafford 1999), but there have been some changes since.

The problems of fakes go way back into the roots of knapping history, as we saw in Chapter 3, but after some comments in the early days of archaeology, the professional literature contains only a few mentions of fake stone tools. This is probably because archaeology in general became less interested in collecting artifacts from unknown sources, which have no context to make them useful for interpreting past cultures. Thus the threat of contamination that fakes posed to archaeological knowledge of stone tools seemed less. Many early fakes also were not very good. Often they were crudely made, with bizarre forms, and could be easily detected as archaeologists became familiar with the expected types of genuine artifacts. However, as archaeologists were losing interest in fakes, but not yet very interested in replicative experiments, nonacademic flintknappers were increasing in numbers and skills.

Collectors, who continued to be interested in unprovenienced finds, were more worried by the prospect of nonauthentic stone tools than were archaeologists, and many of the older knappers have heard artifact collectors express hostility toward knappers (Scheiber 1992b; Waldorf 1980). Roy Motley told me that he knapped for years before letting anyone but close friends know about it, since he felt that other collectors who learned that he was a knapper would then be suspicious of anything that passed through his hands. This exact sentiment was expressed by a prominent collector: "The best advice on how to make Indian arrowheads is: 'Don't!' Never even try. If someone comes along and finds you endeavoring to turn out a crude arrow, the rumor will get out, 'He makes his arrowheads. His collection consists mainly of fakes.' The only exception to this is if you are an Indian. If an Indian makes arrows and spears, the work is modern, not fake" (Russell 1962, 162). Although the collecting world has found ways of coping with the knappers, as we shall see, some collectors still hate them.

As the scale of modern knapping grows, so does its impact on collectors and archaeology, but assessing the numbers of knappers and their productivity is difficult.

Counting Knappers and Points

When you go to Fort Osage or another knap-in and see a couple of hundred knappers flaking in din and dust, with crowds milling around tables laden with stone tools, tarps covered with raw material and heaps of debitage, and parking lots full of beat-up vehicles with "FLINT" or "KNAPPR" on the license plates, you are obliged to realize that there are quite a few knappers. There are certainly more than I ever expected and probably many more than most archaeologists realize.

Mike Stafford and I were unable to come up with a way to make an accurate census of knappers, but we made some educated guesses. Many hobby knappers are still unconnected to the informal knapping network, and some commercial knappers are still secretive. It is not even easy to count academic knappers. The main academic lithic journal in this country, *Lithic Technology*, had some 300 subscribers in 1997, according to the editor, George Odell. Many of these are lithic analysts rather than knappers, but many knap, at least at some level, and many academic knappers are not subscribers. Errett Callahan, who was one of the editors of the newsletter *Flintknappers' Exchange*, which ran from 1979 to 1981 and was oriented toward archaeologically involved knappers, told me it had some 700 subscribers at its peak. Perhaps 300 to 500 is a reasonable conservative guess at the numbers of academic knappers in the United States.

Nonacademic knapper numbers are similarly hard to specify. Between 1991 and 1994 Jeff Behrnes edited a second flintknapping newsletter aimed at non-archaeological knappers, *The Flint Knapper's Exchange*, and compiled a list of over 1,300 names, mostly knappers, with some related craftsmen and small businesses. The current newsletter *Chips* has around 1,000 subscribers, according to editors D. C. and Val Waldorf. The *Bulletin of Primitive Technology* recently reached 2,907 subscribers (Callahan 1996b), and while many of them are more interested in other pursuits, Callahan feels that most of them knap at least some. The Waldorfs, whose first edition of *The Art of Flint Knapping* came out in 1975, are now selling a much expanded fourth edition (Waldorf 1993). In 2002 they estimate that they have sold more than 70,000 copies over the years, mostly the fourth edition. My book *Flintknapping: Making and Understanding Stone Tools* (1994) has sold over 16,000 copies, and Bob Patten also seems to be doing well with his *Old Tools—New Eyes* (1999). These books, although oriented toward teaching knapping, are still a poor way to count knappers, as sales are spread out over long times, and many non-knappers also buy them. There are enough knappers to support a couple of newsletters, several Web pages, and half a dozen small businesses selling stone and knapping tools. An estimate of 5,000 more or less active nonacademic knappers seemed reasonable and conservative when we published it in 1999. None of my knapping friends considered us likely to be too far off.[1] Now, after a couple more years of changes, particularly the networking made possible by the Internet, I suspect 5,000 is an underestimate, but it will serve for discussion here.

How many points do 5,000 knappers make? Again, we can only estimate. My survey of 90 knappers who go to the Fort Osage Knap-in and 70 knappers who do not is not really a random sample of knappers, but I think it gives a pretty accurate picture.

Remember (Chapter 4) that a wide range of age and experience was represented and that a high proportion of the respondents considered themselves beginners or were relatively new knappers. This reflects the way the craft has been growing and bolsters my feeling that there are many more new knappers now, eight years later.

Responding knappers included 12 "academic" knappers, who work in archaeology either as a profession or vocation. (I didn't include myself or Mike Stafford in the survey.) Only 4 of the academic knappers said they ever sell points. We considered 11 knappers (about 7 percent) to be professional knappers, who made most of their income from knapping-related activities. Another 23 (14 percent) we considered "heavy commercial knappers," estimated to sell over a hundred points or over $1,000 worth of knapping-related material a year. Some of these have an even more substantial economic involvement in knapping, but it is not their primary source of income. The rest (114, 71 percent) are essentially hobby knappers, working stone for their own amusement, although 47 of these sometimes sell points, often as a way to defray costs of their hobby. Almost half of all the knappers (not counting academic knappers) in the survey (67, 42 percent) said they never sell points. We suspect that a slightly higher proportion of knappers sell points than admitted it on the survey. Many hobby knappers who do not actively market their work will sell it if they have the chance, even though they consider themselves as "not selling points."

Even knappers who work purely for fun may produce lots of points. Knappers frequently joke about their "obsession" or "addiction," and the average response to the question "about how many hours total do you knap in a month" was 24.5 hours per month. This average includes many who knap only a few hours a month, but also 10 knappers who said they knapped 100 hours a month or more; 5 of these were hobby knappers.

The questionnaire asked, "How many pieces do you make in a month (best guess)?" Knappers were also asked whether they sold points, and if so, to estimate how many per year. Obviously, these figures are going to be approximate, but they are fun to play with. One hundred and forty knappers (out of the 160 respondents) estimated their monthly production, ranging from "don't knap much now" (counted as 0) to "a couple" to 250 pieces; the average per knapper per month was about 25 points. Nine knappers claimed to make 100 pieces a month or more; 4 of these were professionals, 4 were considered heavy commercial knappers, and 1 claimed not to sell points at all. The total claimed by all 140 knappers for a month's production was 3,448. Multiply that by twelve months, and we can estimate that 140 knappers produced some 41,376 points in a year. If we accept our estimate of 5,000 active knappers, averaging 25 points a month, some one and a half million points are being made every year.

My eyes bulged the first time I made this calculation, but Stafford and I think it is reasonable, and there are several lines of evidence that support it. Individual stone tools do not take long to make. Small points require 15 to 30 minutes, larger points up to a couple of hours. The extreme high end of the scale is represented by Danish flint daggers, which may take from 8 to over 20 hours of work (Stafford 1998), and some of the very fancy art knives mentioned earlier should be similar. Few knappers make anything that complicated; the overwhelming majority of knapped products to be seen at knap-ins are medium to large points, most of which can be readily made in an hour or so. Comparing the hours/month to the points/month estimates of the knappers confirmed that they feel 1 hour/point is a good average. In any case, a dedicated knapper working only the average of 24.5 hours a month would have no trouble making 294 points a year.

A few detailed individual records are available. We have already encountered Errett Callahan, who knaps for both commercial and scholarly purposes. He keeps records of his production and informed us that he made 8,515 pieces from 1976 through 1996, an average of 405 a year. The "limited edition" knives that Callahan makes as part of his output are exceedingly complicated. Between 1984 and 1990 he produced 352 knives, or about 59 a year (Callahan 1990, 13). Another professional knapper who also does some complex work and keeps records told us that he currently averages about 300 pieces a year. In 1989, D. C. Waldorf interviewed Jim Spears for *Chips*. Waldorf estimated that he himself had made 10,000 pieces in some 25 years of knapping, and Spears responded that his own production was similar (Waldorf 1989c,

5). One full-time professional knapper who mostly sells to a dealer told me that he regularly makes 10 to 15 points a day, or 75 to 100 a week, more than anyone on the survey. Another said 3 to 4 points per day, or about 1,300 per year, was his normal output. Two part-time knappers who do not earn all their income from knapping, but knap mostly for sale, both said they try to average 3 points per working day, or at least 30 per month. I have more than once seen a couple of the more efficient knappers make 7 to 10 points a day over a knap-in weekend.

What all this means is that I have no doubt that there are many knappers who make hundreds of points every year. Of course, most knappers are not nearly so prolific. The average of 25 points per month within the survey sample takes account of the many knappers who only make a few points, as well as the full-time workers. It is fair to point out that the voluntary survey may over-represent the dedicated knappers, and under-represent the majority, who consider themselves knappers, but actually knap only sporadically or with little result. However, whether we accept the estimate of a million and a half points made a year or prefer to be superconservative and cut it in half, a staggering number of new stone tools are being created.

Markers, Again

I have already discussed the market for knappers, mostly from the point of view of the knappers themselves and emphasizing art knapping. Now I want to consider the rest of the market, from the outside.

Many modern stone tools go directly to a flourishing market for antiquities and modern replicas. The survey asked knappers to estimate the number of pieces they sold in a year. These estimates totaled precisely one-third the estimated number of points made. As I have said, the art market is a bit different from the point market, although they overlap. I can't completely separate the two in my survey figures, but most of the knappers in the survey produce replica points, some of which would not pass as antiquities, but most of which might.

The American market for antiquities of all sorts has been strong in recent years, but the existence of a powerful market for stone tools is surprising to most people, who think of arrowheads as small and ordinary. In fact, huge numbers of modern and prehistoric points are gobbled up, and the trade in both seems to be expanding. *Prehistoric Antiquities Quarterly and Archaeological News,* for example, is a collectors' magazine that, despite its title, is really little more than a catalog where thousands of artifacts are illustrated and listed individually for sale in each issue, along with ads for auctions where 500 lots or more may be offered. Although all kinds of artifacts are included, points dominate the offerings. In the May 2001 issue, seventy-two different auctions, sales, and artifact shows were listed in the calendar of events in the half year between May and December. Considering only dealers offering pictured individual points or groups of points, thirteen different dealers offered 698 points at prices ranging from $100 for 25 common points to several thousand dollars for some of the individual points. EBay is another place to see the extent of the market. On any given day in 2001, some 700–1,000 "arrowheads" are on offer. Not all of these are ancient—many, if not most, are fakes, and some are honestly sold as modern, but there is also a separate category for "Flint Knapping Art," which generally has a couple of hundred items. As others have pointed out (Bruhns 2000), eBay has opened huge new markets among people who were not previously interested in antiquities, and also manages to sell some inexpensive items that were not much in demand before. This makes selling easier for the less-skilled knappers and also makes it profitable to loot sites having only artifacts that no one would have bought before.

Collectors complain about some reduction in the availability of prehistoric artifacts, due to the destruction of sites and such factors as the trend away from deep plowing in agriculture. If anything, scarcity contributes to the demand and prices are rising. Overstreet's *Indian Arrowheads: Identification and Price Guide* is a standard collectors' book, often seen at knap-ins. It is illustrated with numerous photos of points organized by type, gives some dating and distributional information, and emphasizes the joys of collecting and the monetary value of points. Price ranges are given for each specimen based on recent sales of similar pieces. Between the second edition (Overstreet and Peake 1991) and the fourth (Overstreet 1995), the estimated prices of the same Clovis points, to give one example, doubled or tripled, and even point forms much less in demand have appreciated in value similarly, although a number of knappers have told me that Overstreet's prices are somewhat inflated. However, a recent auction boasted the highest price recorded for a single point: $77,000 for a large Hemphill, a long notched Archaic point, made of colorful stone (Arbeiter 2000). This is not even one of the types most eagerly sought by collectors.

The point of the information above is that whether or not you approve of the market in antiquities, it is a major economic force. The effects on knapping are predictable. First, there is a growing demand for honestly modern replicas, both to fill out a collection with examples of hard-to-find types and because some collectors like nice stone tools of any origin. Second, there is a strong incentive to fake antiquities when a well-made modern point commands only a fraction of the price of a prehistoric specimen. To be specific, a nice modern Clovis point commonly sells at a knap-in for $50–100, maybe more if it is especially fine work by a knapper of reputation. Dealers can retail the same point as a modern replica for somewhat more. A similar prehistoric point, if available, will bring from several hundred up to several thousand dollars. Forrest Fenn was buying 12 of Woody's Clovis points for $95,000–150,000—sold as modern points, they might have made Woody a couple of thousand dollars.

The World of Collecting

To understand the scale of the market, it helps to know a bit about the ethos of collectors. I generally use that term to mean artifact collectors, while recognizing that a lot of different motives and positions are included. Here I want to generalize even more: artifact collectors and flintknappers are only part of a much larger phenomenon.

Russell Belk (1988) surveyed and interviewed a large number of collectors with diverse interests and suggests a number of fundamental traits common to most collectors. As he cites estimates that one out of three Americans collect something, most of us, however grudgingly, will recognize themselves in his discussion, which it will be useful to briefly summarize. In particular, much of what characterizes collecting behavior also applies to most knappers. Even if they are not artifact collectors, they usually collect something, be it their own pieces, other knappers' work, stone, knapping tools, or knapping literature, and exhibit some of the compulsive behavior typical of many collectors.

Belk notes that collections often begin serendipitously through a gift or random acquisition. An extraordinary number of knappers and artifact collectors begin with the chance find of an arrowhead. Collectors, and those who know them, often describe collecting as "addictive," "obsessive," or "compulsive." As we have seen, knappers use the same words when they talk about knapping. Many collectors are willing to expend vast resources of energy, time, and enthusiasm, as well as money, to amass a large and complete collection, even to the point of uncontrollably running up debts or alienating friends and family (Belk 1988; Muensterberger 1994).

Completion is a common goal with collectors, but rarely achieved; even if you collect limited categories of manufactured goods such as the loathsome Precious Moment figurines, it is always possible to branch out to related items. Most collectors do, in fact, branch out, in part because completing a collection means ending the exciting quest for objects. Moreover, the goal of making a complete or systematic collection helps raise the pursuit from mere acquisitiveness to art or science and legitimizes the collector, the collection, and the activity of collecting.

As Belk notes, whatever may be collected becomes sacred to the collector, separated from its mundane meaning, uses, and values, and placed on display like an art object or a scientific specimen. Sacred value is often attached to objects by some significant association—belonging to a famous person, having been present or used at a historic occasion, or representing personal memories. This sacred dimension is very visible among artifact collectors, with their worries about authenticity.

Ancient pieces are valuable not just for their esthetic qualities, but because they bear what I think of as "manna," that is, magical power derived from association with something. The knowledge that a point could have been carried by a hunter stalking mammoths along the edge of the glaciers gives it a power, a connection to the past, that a modern replica does not have. By finding or owning the ancient object, you capture some of this magic, touch it, and transfer something of it to yourself. However, as Cornelius Holtorf and Tim Schadla-Hall (1999) point out, this manna (they call it "aura") is not inherent in artifacts. The "authenticity" of any object, which is what gives it power in our minds, is determined by its cultural context and presentation, "negotiated" by people with different understandings, sources of information, and goals. To a knapper, for instance, authenticity may mean that he has made his point resemble as closely as possible a prehistoric type. To the artifact collector, this is not good enough—the point must actually be ancient. But how is its age determined? By the evidence of archaeological context, if any, and the argument of experts, who often have contrary opinions. If the consensus, or even one trusted opinion, decides that a valued point is a fake, it falls from grace and may be discarded or destroyed. It has lost not only monetary value, but also its manna, which explains some of the emotional impact that these arguments have on some collectors.

Similarly, a modern point successfully passed as an antiquity may become a treasured relic, imbued with all the associations of the ancient world. To this extent, as Holtorf and Schadla-Hall put it, "if the past is not a renewable resource, then at least it is a reproducible one," at least for some objects and some people. Reproductions authentic in the sense of being accurate may be very useful in conveying information about the past, as in museum displays, or providing a good experience for students, museum visitors, or collectors. However, a real origin in the past is necessary if, as an archaeologist, you wish to use an object as accurate evidence for studying prehistory. Accordingly, the determination of authenticity is a serious business for both collectors and archaeologists, for somewhat different, but overlapping, reasons.

Collecting is also an important expression of self, of wealth and the ability to obtain things, of taste and knowledge about them, of control over one dimension of a largely uncontrollable world. Many collectors specialize in something with a symbolic connection to family, occupation, or other aspects of their identity (Belk 1988; Belk and Wallendorf 1994). Collectors receive praise and recognition from the world around them if their collections are defined as important, but even less prestigious objects have fans who form groups of collectors with similar interests. Collectors often worry about the future of their collection. Passing a collection on to a relative or another collector, or having it accepted by a museum, validates the worth of the collection in the eyes of the world and provides a sort of immortality for the collector. Loss of a collection is a real injury to the collector's person and sense of self-worth (Muensterberger 1994; Akin 1996).

All of this is visible among the artifact collectors who create the market for art, fakes, and replicas in the knapping world. There is a great deal of prestige attached to accumulating a fine collection and being knowledgeable about it. This is as true among Missouri arrowhead collectors as it is among London connoisseurs of Greek vases or famous New York art museums. Collectors like Charlie Shewey are highly valued among the knappers as patrons, arbiters of taste, and sources of knowledge about artifacts. Charlie and others get lots of acclaim and attention at knap-ins.

In their own way, collectors are at least as obsessed as flintknappers.

For many collectors, a single example of a type or of an individual artist's work is not enough. Among the knap-in regulars are collectors like Charlie Shewey who have bought dozens or even hundreds of pieces from a single knapper, just because they like his work. In the antiquities market, the competition to have the "best" cache of Clovis points or to outbid another collector jacks up the prices of points to extraordinary levels. Artifact collectors hold shows and conventions and offer prizes, build display rooms in their houses, and worry about the security of their homes when they own valuable collections.

As the quest for authenticity, manna, completion, and self-expression collides with market forces and the limits of the archaeological record, collectors have adopted a number of poses that are irritating to archaeologists, and sometimes to knappers. It is fashionable to claim that "we don't dig sites" and that most artifacts on the market are surface finds or out of old collections. Surface finds might be destroyed by erosion or plowing anyway, and for that matter, sites are often destroyed by development. There is some truth in all of this, and many archaeologists, myself included, are not necessarily hostile to surface collectors, especially the ones who are sincerely interested in archaeology and make an effort to record the location of finds so that the information will stay with the artifact and be useful to archaeology. However it is hypocritical at best to claim that $77,000 points don't inspire some people to go out and loot sites or take up a billet and a piece of flint with fraud in mind. This kind of market creates its own enemies. Most archaeologists admit that some sort of antiquities market is inevitable in a free society, and it is probably not possible or even a good idea to attempt to crush it, but reputable archaeologists try not to participate in it, because market forces are behind the archaeological evils of faking and looting.

Holtorf and Schadla-Hall (1999, 234) are among a number of archaeologists who suggest that large numbers of fakes should debase the market for antiquities and reduce the mining of sites for artifacts. I don't think that is true for points, and probably not for other artifacts; the market seems bottomless. The demand for real and faked antiquities has led to some interesting social developments among the knappers, including some ethical issues that I avoided discussing in the earlier chapters.

The Woody story was a scandal at Fort Osage because the knappers' ethos, expressed at knap-ins and repeatedly voiced on the survey, is that faking is dishonest and bad (Table 10.1). Similar sentiments appear often in the knapper literature (e.g., Merlie 1989a; Waldorf 1990; Martin 1996), and the Society of Primitive Technology includes an ethical statement in its *Bulletin of Primitive Technology* condemning faking and promoting the marking of modern artifacts. Many knappers say that marking modern points to prevent their being passed as old ones is both ethical and important to them as artists. They want the recognition and perhaps higher prices that producing signed art brings. A few, looking forward from their interest in the past, want to leave a permanent trace that will survive as long as the relics of ancient people. What many support in theory, relatively few actually do. Among the knappers in the survey, 54 percent said they did not sign points, 27 percent said they marked points "sometimes," and 19 percent said they always did. It is not that hard to remove even an engraved mark from most points, and many knappers who say they deplore faking give this as a reason for not signing their work.

The majority voice among knappers is against faking, in part because many of them are also artifact collectors or work with collectors and dealers who are very concerned about the authenticity of their artifacts. A few are concerned about the effect on archaeology or the unsavory ethics of faking, and some begrudge the ability of dishonest dealers to turn an enormous profit on points sold honestly by a knapper who sees only a fraction of the money. I think only a few of the knappers I know actually sell with the intent to deceive. However, many knappers sell points to dealers, and many points pass through several hands on the way to collections. There are thus many opportunities for them to acquire false pedigrees and to be scuffed up, stained, patinated, or otherwise "antiqued." I am told that modern points are sometimes inserted in old collections being sold at auction, or even planted for someone to find, and then purchased from the finder who then is willing to vouch for the points' antiquity. Woody is not the only one to have "found" an old collection with points wrapped in out-of-date newspapers or accompanied by a yellowed letter from a long-dead finder. However, such elaborate schemes are not usually necessary. Many or most points sold as ancient have only the last owner's statement as evidence of antiquity. Dealers and collectors alike rely on individual reputations and expertise.

Table 10.1
Answers to the Question "Do you see any trends in knapping that you do not like or approve of?"

55	Disapprove of passing or selling modern points as antiquities
	10 mentioned "aging" or "patination" or similar
	10 mentioned not marking or signing points
	6 disapprove of selling to middlemen
	4 use the word "fake" or "fraud" or "counterfeit"
	2 worry about contamination of sites or stimulating looting
	2 worry about contaminating collections or museums
	2 dislike dishonesty
	1 fears fakes "give us all a black eye"
40	Gave no answer to the question
19	Say "No" or "Nothing"
24	Have concerns about raw material
	7 mentioned depletion of resources
	4 blame commercial rock collecting
	3 "waste"
	3 "high flint prices"
	3 worried about limited access to sources
	2 complained about damage to prehistoric quarries
	1 worried about health problems from chemically treated rock
	1 angry about bad material sold as good by ignorant merchants
7	Concerns about the economics of knapping
	4 excessive prices charged by knappers
	1 knappers selling work for less than it's worth
	1 "watch out for IRS"
	1 fears competition from cheap Mexican labor
	1 "buying and selling"
19	Mentioned the conflict between tradition and modern knapping
	11 mentioned "mechanical" or "non-traditional" techniques
	8 "slabs, slabbing"

        8 "grinding" or "lapidary"
        4 "copper"
        3 "levers"
        5 "too fancy" or "not correct" points
        3 "abandoning tradition" or "getting too modern"
25   Social problems with knapping or the knap-ins
        7 "commercialization"
        7 "competition"
        3 specify "contests" at knap-ins
        4 "prima donnas" or "big egos" or "elite"
        1 "not helping new knappers"
        1 private exclusive knap-ins
        3 low moral standards
        1 theft
        1 dishonest trade
        1 accusations
        1 "playing Indian"
        1 "too much regulation"
        1 "people"
        1 "too many knappers"
        1 "too many knap-ins"
4   Miscellaneous problems
        2 lack of connection to archaeology
        1 pothunters
        1 quantity rather than quality
Total: 193 answers on 160 questionnaires

Numbers are the number of responses that include a particular element, and subcategories don't necessarily add up, as some knappers used only generalities or made more than one comment.

Authentication

The craft of the faker supports the business of the authenticator. A number of experts, usually experienced collectors and often dealers themselves, will "authenticate" a point, providing an informed judgment and a certificate for a fee. I interviewed Roy Motley in his house not far from Fort Osage. We sat in his collection room, a den decorated with a variety of unique antiques and a nice small collection of prehistoric material and some frames of modern points.

Roy used to have a large collection of points, but sold much of it, partly because it was too valuable and too easy to steal. Roy is one of the few authenticators who is also a knapper, which he says is a great advantage to him in spotting fakes, since he not only knows how points are made and antiqued, but recognizes some knappers' work. Roy started learning to knap almost forty years ago, as a teenager, but his primary interest was in collecting. He was one of the founders of the Fort Osage Knap-in, but says others who knew him as a collector were astounded when he first knapped a large point. He had kept quiet about his skills for years because if other collectors knew he knapped, it would cast suspicion on his collection, and he "didn't want to spoil good points," that is, damage their reputation and value as genuine antiquities.

A few years ago Roy fell out of a hunting stand and was severely injured, which cost him some of his knapping strength and forced him to retire from his job with Missouri Gas Energy, where he trained local offices. Having retired, Roy set himself up officially as an authenticator. He had started authenticating on the side almost by accident, after other collectors began asking his opinion and finding him reliable. They began requesting written opinions and photos, and he decided he should charge a fee. As well as relying on his experience as a knapper and collector, he has a home laboratory with microscope and black light, and some other tricks he does not reveal. He says business is good, in fact backlogged all the time, and he gets to see a lot of fine artifacts. And a large number of fakes. At Fort Osage in May 2001, Roy said in the year since he started his authentication business he has "papered" over seven hundred good points and seen over eight hundred fakes. This is perhaps the most shocking estimate of the extent of faking that I have heard—that over half the points circulating as ancient are not, and I hear it from others as well. Greg Perino, an old and widely respected authenticator, has reported that not only are points faked, but some faked points are now being sold with forgeries of his authentication papers (Perino 1996). Despite the desire of collectors for authentic pieces and their faith in testimonials, expert opinion, and oral histories of a point's provenance, there is widespread agreement that collections and the market for ancient points are peppered with modern fakes.

Modern points are often difficult to distinguish from their ancient prototypes. Many of the best knappers, both commercial and hobby, are knowledgeable typologists and use the correct materials and flaking style for particular point types. Because most modern knappers use at least some copper flaking tools, which often leave marks on the stone, and some knappers "antique" points with furniture polish and other modern materials, many modern points are easily recognized as such. However, it is also easy to scuff a point up with a bit of dust and grit or to tumble it in sand to dull flake scars and remove obvious copper marks. On many points, there is little or no evidence of modern manufacture, and an appearance of age cannot be trusted. As a result, the evidence of collections being contaminated is hard to confirm, non-quantified and largely anecdotal.

Among the knappers and collectors that I know, there is an undercurrent of disquiet about fakes. Arguments about ethics and marking of points are common in the knapper literature, as are discussions of faking and the detection of fakes in the collector literature (Berner 1984, 1997a, 1997b, 2000a; Hothem 1992; Maus 1997; Miller 1997). Stories about the difficulties of authenticating points are a strong thread in the oral folklore at knap-ins. Knappers are an ornery lot, and many have an ambivalent view of experts in general and the archaeological profession in particular. I hear a lot of stories about how the famous So-and-so was taken in and how Museum X displays a group of modern points as ancient. The same ambivalence applies to authenticators. Several, like Perino, are widely admired for their knowledge and their opinions frequently quoted. At the same time, stories are told about modern points that have been passed with a "COA" (certificate of authenticity) from the same experts. At least two knappers have admitted in my hearing that they bought or almost bought (as antiquities) points that they themselves had made a few years previously. Points for which big money was paid, or which may be documented as found by a particular collector at a particular site, or "authenticated" by experts, are sometimes later publicly acknowledged by a knapper as his own work. More than once I have sat in a group at Fort Osage, passing around the latest Overstreet price guide or another collector book, while knappers scoff at some points, and occasionally someone says with a touch of pride, "I made that one!" Many collectors, and knappers who collect, admit that it is often impossible to be really sure if any point is ancient.

Some authenticators are more confident, and indeed the market value of many items depends on the collectors' confidence in the judgment of such experts. Roy Motley told me, "If you had a hundred points right now, I could get them all right, with maybe one I wasn't sure about. Ninety-nine-point-nine percent of fakes are easy to tell. In fact, I love Old English and lazy fakers." Roy feels that it would be very difficult to fool him or several of the other top authenticators, although he is about the only one who is also an expert knapper. However, he complains about two things. Some authenticators are sloppy, or "dirty," and will paper all sorts of stuff either because they don't know or because they are dishonest. In fact, as I finish this manuscript, my email lists are hinting at another large-scale fraud involving authenticators making and passing fakes. Roy says authenticating also involves him in unpleasant "politics"—arguments about whose judgment you can trust. He says quite a few people are unhappy about paying to hear him say that a cherished buy is actually a modern fake, and if they accept his judgment, he may become involved in disputes between the collector and whoever sold the point.

The responses to this situation of uncertainty in separating the old sheep from the new goats are complex. Some knappers who collect points say they no longer buy them and collect only what they find themselves. Some collectors are interested in quality rather than pedigree and now concentrate on modern work or acquire pieces they like regardless of origin. Older commercial knappers say that the artifact collecting organizations were once extremely hostile to knappers, regarding them all as "fakers." Some of them still do, but others have realized that they have to deal with the existence of knappers whether they like them or not.

Several of the big artifact shows have recently invited knappers to demonstrate or to sell, and one, the Texas Cache Artifact and Flintknapper's Show, divided the show in half and offered parallel prizes for prehistoric and modern pieces, as we saw in Chapter 7. In part, this seems a strategy of containment: if modern knapping is in the open, it is less likely to get mixed in with the antiquities. The style of some individual knappers becomes known and recognizable, and therefore safer. However, when Mike Stafford and I discussed this with our sources, it seemed even more to us that the world of commercial collecting has simply decided that on one level, the faking doesn't matter anymore. Collectors write fervent and angry articles about how fakes scare off newcomers to the hobby. More importantly, when suspicion is cast on a particular artifact, its value drops dramatically. This is partly market demand—there are lots of modern points, more made all the time, and only a few ancient ones. It is also partly that collectors value the intangible magic of holding an ancient point that might have slain a mammoth or whistled through the aspen leaves as it sped toward an enemy a thousand years ago. A modern point lacks this manna, and authenticity attracts both emotion and dollars. Nevertheless, in a more general sense, it is possible to continue collecting complacently. Opinion in the collecting world seems to be that even the most expert collector is going to be fooled sometimes, but with enough experience, you can detect most fakes. The market for ancient points is stronger than ever, prices continue to climb, business is good, and there are lots of points to be collected. For those who want ancient points, there are still some being found, old collections being sold, and lots of undetectable fakes that sell just as well to all but the most expert buyers. All in all, the world of artifact collecting and commercial dealing has adapted easily to the increasing number of modern stone tools.

Archaeological Impacts of Modern Knapping: Collections

Collectors can probably live with fakes more easily than can the archaeologists. This is especially true because archaeologists are mostly less knowledgeable about the knapping world and much less practiced at recognizing fakes than authenticators and some collectors. As a knapper and an archaeologist, I love the knap-in world, but worry about it a bit because it has serious short-term and long-range effects on the archaeological record and how we interpret it. The most immediate and obvious effect is that collections of artifacts are being muddled. Unsystematic collections are not much use for many of the current fine-grained archaeological questions. More interesting archaeological problems can be studied with artifacts from good provenance. Provenance means origin, and to an archaeologist, good provenance means that we know where an artifact came from, not just which site, but where on the site, so that we can use information about what it was found with to interpret it. An arrowhead in a grave tells us something different from one in a trash pile or on a house floor. This is why archaeologists are distressed by uncontrolled and unrecorded digging—once an artifact is out of context, much of its value to inform us about the past is lost.

In the collector world, provenance often just means whose collection a piece has been in previously. This is often enough to establish that it has been around a long time and is thus less likely to be a fake, but is of absolutely no use archaeologically. However, many collectors also have records of where artifacts were found, and this is more useful. If we know what site an artifact came from, then amateur collections and old surface finds can be important to regional surveys attempting to locate and date sites or establish time spans, distributions, and cultural sequences in a region (e.g., Amick 1994; Dorwin 1966; Dunbar 1991; Faulkner 1961; Farnsworth 1973; Lepper and Meltzer 1991; Tankersley 1989). Studies of the variation and distribution of particular artifact types may also depend heavily on amateur collections (e.g., Amick 1995; Brennan 1982; Luchterhand 1970; Pitblado 2003; Rolingson 1964; Tankersley 1989).

Most projects that use collections rely heavily on the collectors themselves for provenance information. At this point, I should also clarify the term "collector." I use it loosely, and it actually covers a lot of variability, from individuals who pick up what they find around them on their land or a local territory to enthusiasts who collect through the markets on a regional, national, or even international scale. The amount of information associated with a collection can also vary enormously. Some collectors enjoy acquiring objects, but care little about their archaeological meaning or origins. At the other end of the scale are some collectors who are extremely knowledgeable amateur archaeologists and keep detailed and useful records.

Archaeologists working with collections are generally aware of all this and of the possibility of encountering fakes, and others have sounded a warning note in the archaeological journals (Hester 1999; Howard 1994). However, I believe that few archaeologists, especially those who have never seen a knap-in, realize how numerous and plausible the fakes have become.

Considering what I know of the knapping world and its history, I would worry about any non-archaeological collection made after the 1930s. Especially in the Midwest and Texas, where large and attractive Archaic and Paleoindian points are common and desirable finds, and have consequently been widely copied, I would not feel comfortable using any recent collection for archaeological interpretations without definite provenance information, preferably from the finder. Even then, humans are mortal and memory fallible. As collectors die and collections change hands, provenance information rapidly becomes less reliable, and the chance of contamination greater.

In fact, even better-documented finds may include problem pieces. I know at least one reliable amateur archaeologist who almost published a fake that was planted on him by friends as a joke. At least two major finds are currently considered suspicious. Howard (2001) suggests that the Angus, Nebraska, fluted point once considered the first artifact found associated with a mammoth is actually an early fake by an unknown knapper. It was excavated in 1931. Sandia Cave in New Mexico (Hibben 1941, 1946; Hibben and Nichols 1978) produced unusual points that the excavator, Frank Hibben, claimed were as old as Clovis or older. Unfortunately, the site is rife with contextual problems, the points are not found elsewhere, and some archaeologists distrust Hibben, as well as the circumstances of the find (Haynes and Agogino 1986; Preston 1995). I look at the Sandia points and think that putting a shoulder on an old point is an easy way for a poor knapper to make a distinctive new point type that looks old; other archaeologists are also suspicious. Howard (1988) published a short article on the points before he developed his current interest and techniques for authenticating points (1994); reexamining them in 1998, he says many illustrated pieces have "disappeared" and the remainder are apparently old but a "collection of oddities," with one modern point shouldered by grinding.

A more insidious problem with fakes in collections is that they have perhaps already influenced our views of typology and point type distributions. Even among collectors and authenticators, who rely on their expertise, "the trained eye has probably been trained on fakes" (Bruhns 2000, 15). At the knap-ins there is a further loop. Existing typologies and collections influence what is made today. Knappers use their knowledge of collections, published sites, and illustrations in typologies and price guides as models for their work. As a result, a desirable rare form may become much more common, as much because knappers like to make it as because of market demand. And, of course, some of the models for modern points are themselves modern fakes accepted as ancient. Similar problems exist with other kinds of artifacts, including the Cycladic figurines discussed by Gill and Chippendale (1993) and Chinese ceramics (Holtorf and Schadla-Hall 1999).

Over the long term, collections will become even more unreliable.

As they change hands and finders die or sell off their collections, what provenance information exists is often lost, or at least can no longer be relied on. Furthermore, although the majority of points made by the hobby knappers in the survey may not immediately enter the market, eventually many of them will, when, in time, the knappers die or change hobbies. The points made by archaeologists learning to knap, performing experiments, or just enjoying a craft may (or may not) be carefully labeled and kept from circulation now, but in the end, they, too, may be separated from any knowledge of their origins and pass into the confusing archaeological record.

The Creation and Destruction of Sites

Modern knapping is also affecting the archaeological record on the ground. A few archaeologists (Dickson 1996; Tunnell 1979) have noted that the activities of modern knappers deplete some stone sources, contaminate sites with modern debitage that is often indistinguishable from old material, and create entirely new lithic sites that may confuse the archaeologist. Again, the scale of modern knapping is such that these problems are larger than most archaeologists realize and are bound to increase.

A vast amount of raw stone material is extracted, moved, and consumed by modern knappers. In Chapter 8 I discussed some estimates. Hundreds to thousands of kilograms of material are likely to be exchanged at a knap-in, depending on its size and location. This necessarily puts a strain on some lithic resources, and triumphant flint-hunting stories are now matched by tales of woe about emptied creek beds and picked-over quarries.

It is difficult to specify how much debitage is produced, but we can guess at the scale of consumption. A large flake or sawn slab suitable for making a Clovis or other medium to large point weighs roughly 500 grams (about 1 pound). Some points are much smaller, but some are larger, and producing the flakes and blanks also creates waste. If we use our estimate of 1.5 million points per year and guess that each produces an average of 0.5 kg waste, the total is 750,000 kg, or about 375 tons. Again, we can offer a few specifics to support this. Three prominent knappers interviewed by Callahan twenty years ago estimated that each used 500 to 2,000 pounds of stone a year, consuming especially large amounts in the early years of their career when they were learning

(Sollberger and Callahan 1978; Bonnichsen and Callahan 1978; Titmus and Callahan 1980). I have already mentioned (Chapter 8) Craig Ratzat's estimates of obsidian consumption and the import of large amounts of British and Belizean flint to meet demand.

Much of the debitage from knap-ins and modern knappers goes into landfills or other contexts where it can do no immediate harm. Some knappers have huge piles in their yards or work areas or in a convenient drainage or pit nearby. Such large deposits, which include dozens of different foreign materials, are also not likely to confuse the modern archaeologist. It is at the source areas that knappers are likely to damage the archaeological record. Many prehistoric sources are being exploited for stone, as well as collected for artifacts, and sometimes prehistoric debitage and blanks are treated as raw material. The tendency of many knappers to at least test stone on site, and often to make "spalls" or "blanks," has undoubtedly contaminated many prehistoric quarry sites and, as Dickson (1996) reports, begun to create entirely new lithic workshop sites.

I have discussed the problems of faking and stone use at length from the archaeologist's point of view, as well as that of the knapper worried about dwindling resources and damaged reputations. As members of both camps, Mike Stafford and I published the *American Antiquity* article to alert the archaeological community. Although we focused on aspects of knapping that we worry about and dislike, we also wanted to convince our archaeological colleagues that our knap-in colleagues have something to offer. The knapping community includes many people who are interested in protecting archaeological resources and exchanging information with the archaeological profession. Most importantly, knap-ins offer the archaeologist a common ground to communicate with an interested public, some of whom can perhaps be won over to a more archaeological view of prehistoric sites. If more archaeologists attended knap-ins, they would know more about the public view of archaeology, and more members of the public would see archaeologists as pleasant people with whom they share a common interest, despite sometimes differing goals and viewpoints. The shared interest in stone tools and knapping, and the ethos of a "community of practice" centered around the knap-ins, often overcome prejudices, hostilities, and disagreement, at least temporarily. And that is the final note in the story of Woody's fakes.

Epilogue: Sin and Society

The story of Woody Blackwell's fall from grace did not end with his confession and the *New Yorker* article. Reactions continue today. Some of them were a bit surprising, at least to me. First, there was a period when it seemed the knapping world was covering its eyes. As the story was breaking in Spring and Summer 1999, and I kept up with the FlintForum email listserver, there were almost no comments at all. After Preston's *New Yorker* article came out in November, there were a few comments, and a couple satires of the article—its sympathetic slant toward Woody irked some knappers. With a handful of exceptions, the email knappers declined to discuss Woody's Clovis fraud or even the wider problem of faking.

Another organization I had started watching was The Pack, which presented a listserve and Web page for collectors and dealers of artifacts who were worried about fake arrowheads on eBay auctions. There were two things that interested me in the short time that I followed The Pack. First, it confirmed my sense that the market for stone artifacts, including eBay, was riddled with fakes. Second, some of The Pack members did not much like archaeologists and really hated knappers. The Pack.net maintained a "Be Aware Board," where attention was called to specific eBay items and issues argued at length. A couple of examples present the dominant point of view (reproduced with original spelling and grammar):

> Let me say this to all you Knappers you people are counterfeiting art. I have never been taken by one of you, for you people hide behind oh we are just knappers that make art this is balogna. I am a collector and it is time people should open there eyes up to you money making so called Knappers you have tried to ruin our hobby with your junk I for one will be happy when the day comes that it will be against the law for you counterfeiters to make your **FAKES**.

Occasionally after comments like that, a couple of knappers who collected artifacts and also belonged to The Pack list would respond to defend knapping, usually setting off more rants. George Pelfrey, one of the Fort Osage knappers, defended a group of modern points that were offered on eBay, explicitly labeled as "look good, sell good, but not old," and on July 15, 1999, got this among the responses:

> George, the knapper of these points "MAY" not intend to defraud an unsuspecting buyer, but I can guarantee that the buyer will. Sooner or later they will end up in someones collection as real. If the modern stone age is to be practiced than I think they should be hung on the knappers wall for him to admire. You see George, knappers are the carriers by which the disease of fakery is spread. No knappers, no fake points.

This writer then cited the number of points estimated in our *American Antiquity* article and the "36 ebay pages with about 40 on each page, × 2 a week" and closed by stating that if knappers make points for themselves it is "Kinda like VD, spread it by doing what you enjoy." Another added:

> If us collectors don't condemn this unanimously, then we deserve to get screwed by the fakers. How can any honest collector condone flint knapping?

Nevertheless, as the Woody story unfolded The Pack remained silent. Several messages noted the *American Antiquity* article, and our guess of 5,000 knappers and 1.5 million modern points per year rapidly became quoted as established fact. Surely the collectors on The Pack would have read *Indian Artifact Magazine,* where Fogelman gave the first more or less complete account of Woody's fakes in late July. No comments appeared on The Pack. By the time Preston's *New Yorker* article came out in November, The Pack was in the process of changing hands and falling apart. Perhaps the knappers on The Tarp hated to spread the disgrace of a knapper any further in public, and the collectors on The Pack did not want to talk about how badly they could be taken. It was not until early 2000, after The Pack had gone, that accounts and commentary really began to appear in the collector literature that I was seeing (Berner 2000b). The Pack and other pressures did have one real effect on the antiquities market—at the request of a group of knappers, eBay created a new category for "Flint Knapping Art" to separate modern points from ancient. Nevertheless, most of the points sold as antiquities on eBay today are still more or less obvious fakes.

At the same time, in early 2000, a new sentiment was sweeping The Tarp, this time expressed in many messages. It began with a few Tarp messages neutrally mentioning Woody as a great knapper and then in

March developed into a full-scale rehabilitation. Derek McLean wrote:

> Hey, I heard that Woody Blackwell would like to join the Tarp but is hesitant because of his previous indiscretions. I say . . . Woody come on down. I would be a fool if I let something like that hold back my thirst for knowledge. Maybe others feel different, but I would welcome any input from such a seasoned and accomplished knapper.

There followed a series of messages, almost all of which agreed, offered "he who is without sin should cast the first stone" morals, and asked Woody to join The Tarp and share his knowledge. There was even a certain sentiment in some messages that big-money collectors and authenticators had got what they deserved, best expressed by Gary Merlie:

> While I am sure there are those in the collector community that would consider Woody a goat, I praise him as a hero. He exposed the scam that is being pulled on the collectors, that of the so called "Authenticators." Both commercial authenticators (Greg Perino and Calvin Howard) blew it and passed Woodys cache. I was told from a reliable source that at one point last year, one of these authenticators had 2200 artifacts in their possession to authenticate, that 30–40 were arriving each day, and they were being "looked at" for $15–$20 each. Run the numbers and you will see that it is not the knappers that are getting rich. As for Woody Blackwell, I would welcome him here. I would also be proud to knap with him and would take him rock hunting anytime.

Shortly after this, Woody began contributing comments and advice on The Tarp. Among other things, he was asked to explain how he makes such thin bifaces, and responded with a teaching specimen with prepared but unstruck platforms that John Cianfarani cast and distributed among The Tarp knappers. Woody has pretty much been welcomed back to the knap-ins, too, although there are a few hard-liners who say they will have nothing to do with him.

There are probably a good many morals one could draw from this whole saga. The collectors will mostly see Woody's crime and rehabilitation as proof of the corruption of all knappers. Douglas Preston, the journalist, found in "Woody's Dream" the story of the knappers' obsessive search for a connection with the past. His final paragraph tells of Woody dreaming about walking up to a band of Clovis hunters sitting around a campfire and yearning to join them. "Every Clovis point I've ever made, I wonder if this will be the price of admission, the ticket to let me go back and sit with those guys." John Berner (2000b), writing for the collectors, titled his piece "Their Real Dream Is to Fool the Experts," which pretty much covers what he had to say. I think they both got it partly right, but the whole story speaks to me even more profoundly about the meaning of being a knapper.

As most knappers would see it, Woody ought to be forgiven. He sinned, he was shamed, and now he should be welcomed back, because he obeys much of the best of the knap-in ethos. His skill is admired, he is friendly and willing to share, he advances the art of flintknapping. What of his sin? Yes, he transgressed, and all agree, at least on the surface, that faking and deception is bad, and he justly suffered for what he did. But it was partly his admirable skill and obsession with the past that led him to "a brief criminal career," as he puts it. Moreover, in his sin, he also did what many knappers not so secretly wish to do: he blacked the eye of the experts—authenticators, collectors, and archaeologists—often seen as enemies of the knapper.

Even more importantly, Woody is a *knapper*, a member of the community. Corresponding with me in January 2003, Woody said,

> For some people, an enormous amount of ego, vanity, and jealousy is evident in this craft, but fortunately that is a tiny minority of knappers. Many others have shown enormous compassion and understanding. I am struck by two things: how good people can be and how many there are of those people. It's worth noting that not a single person has ever directly spoken negatively to me about the incident. A few people have written negatively about it, but they stand in great contrast to the many folks who have personally offered support. They include knappers, collectors, and dealers. I don't believe their kindness is influenced by any knapping ability I may have; I think they are genuinely good people with big hearts and open minds. I can't ever thank them enough, although I am thankful for them every day.

The knap-in world takes care of its own, and the rules of the knap-in are sometimes more important than the rules of the outsider. The inevitable jealousy over skills and successes, the personal promotion and competition for prestige and markets, these things are influential in the knap-in world, but are suppressed as much as possible. In a small community with a lot of personal interaction, it is very difficult to turn your face away from a friendly member of the group, however much you may disapprove of him in the abstract. As in all societies, expressions of social disapproval, scowls and slighting comments, newsletter articles and Tarp messages help keep members in line, but they are minimized at the knap-in itself. The maintenance of harmony, honesty, egalitarianism, and solidarity is necessary to keep the knap-in running smoothly, and like most communities, the knappers mostly prefer forgiving and rehabilitating errant members to damaging the community with too much conflict. The common interests, the friendships, the sense of belonging, of community, are what makes the knap-in so important to knappers. Several further developments remain to be explored.

Silicon and Society

It was a predictable development in 1995: knappers began to communicate on the Internet. After all, mail lists and Web pages for any kind of specialized group or unique individual you can imagine sprang up like mushrooms, even while nobody was really sure where electronic communications were headed. As someone said at the time, "All known knowledge is on the Web, but even God can't find it."

Computers are the most modern technology; stone tools the most ancient. The use of computer-based communication by flintknappers reflects and intensifies trends in the rest of the knapping world.

As a not-very-adept computer user in 1995, I began to hear rumors about a knapping Web page, but of course, at knap-ins, no one could remember the proper string of letters to connect with it. My computer at the college had Internet capabilities, and I had even "surfed" a couple of times, but had no idea how to find anything in particular. Finally, Richard Sanchez, who had been trying to organize a knappers' club in the Dallas–Fort Worth area and had seen my book (Whittaker 1994), emailed me addresses for Jamie Boley's Knapper mail list and Tim Rast's Knappers Anonymous Web page. The computer knapping network at the time was somewhat peripheral to the Fort Osage Knap-in, and only a few of the people who appeared on it were Fort Osage knappers. I remember wondering if I should bother to keep track of it, and then deciding that the Internet was a new resource that just might grow in importance for knappers.

Today my early naïveté and fumbling attempts to use computers seem incredible and would be even more astonishing to some of the younger knappers who have grown up with computers. Electronic media have had a galvanizing effect on the knapping world. By 1995 I was smugly feeling that after working hard at learning names and faces, I knew who most of the influential knappers were, even if I hadn't met them all. Now I see on the Internet so many new knappers at all levels of skill that I know I am rapidly losing ground. Electronic media have added a new dimension to the knapping culture and permitted the society of knappers to grow far more than anyone expected.

Silicon Connections

The first of the email listservers, Knapper, was started on January 21, 1995, by Jamie Boley. He got interested in flintknapping by reading an article about it in one of his knife magazines (he used the nom de computer "Stiletto") and, despite having little knapping experience, set up a successful communication network for knappers. It grew fast, from some 44 members early in July to 128 late that month when I signed on. By September 2, Richard Sanchez reported that 154 individuals were receiving the mail list messages, including at least 2 in Australia. By late October there were 177 members on four continents, with many of the states represented.

In 1994 I did not know about email listservers; by 1996 probably every literate American did. However, if anyone cares to read this in another ten years, it is likely that the computer world, which changes faster than I type, will have moved on, so a brief explanation may be useful here. An email listserver is an address that serves as a node; messages sent there are forwarded to all members on the subscriber list. This results in some peculiarities. Messages come with the computer name and address of the sender. These are often highly revealing, or at least colorful, but as only some messages are signed with real names, it is not always easy to know if the "Stiletto" whose message you read is someone you know off the computer or not. Anyone may reply to any message (or say anything for that matter), but replies often come days after the original message, depending on when someone reads his or her email or is inspired to answer it. One way to keep message and reply connected is to use the command "respond" or some other action that sends all or part of the original message, followed by the reply. Of course, if you are replying to an answer to a response to a comment, and it all gets forwarded each time, the message begins to grow like a fungus. You are supposed to trim messages to only the relevant material, but list members are often lazy or ignorant about editing text. This is considered bad "netiquette" and draws angry messages from other users who find themselves with pages and pages of repetitive email. Others then respond to the angry messages or write to say they agree, and another mass of irrelevant email accumulates. Computer users, like knappers, are developing a distinctive culture of esoteric information and rules for behavior.

Knapper ended in September 1997 and was replaced by Flint FORUM, run by Richard Sanchez. At the time, Richard had recently been introduced to knapping by his father-in-law. Richard lives in Texas and occasionally refers to himself jokingly as the "Mescan Ishi." Richard told me (in an email, naturally),

> When I closed the FORUM I got a number of letters comparing me to a DC Waldorf. The comments made were that I was like DC who brought knapping to a wider audience through his book, videos and magazine. I brought Knapping to the Masses via the Internet. Funny thing is I never imagined it would grow so much. Nor did I ever want to attain any "status." At the time I started all these online endeavors I had Nothing to Offer the Knapping World. I was a beginning Knapper but I knew the [computer] Technology. So since I could not offer any Knapping Advice I offered what I could which was my Tech Knowledge.

Richard promoted FlintFORUM via Web sites, search engines, flyers, and word of mouth among knappers and built it up to 650 members. However, there were some strains:

> The first year was Hellish. I had spent all this money on software and hardware to run a List from my home, only to get blasted repeatedly by Knapper's for petty stuff like, Why does the list have rules? Why am I getting so much mail, I don't want to click twice, etc. It was a daily thing. Most of the Emails DEMANDED I correct something and when I did few offered thanks. It was then I determined that if I was going to grow this Online Knapping that I might as well give up being

Silicon and Society

thanked for it. Funny thing is that this kind of stuff continues even today. I helped to start the First Knapping Web page on the Internet. Knapper's Anonymous. I bought the guy the software to build it with, searched for tons of Links, did my Reports for him and other items. It was very fun to be the First on the Web. When it finally hit Production for All to See it was something. I closed the FORUM when one knapper from New York decided he wanted to start his own list. He concocted a story and proceeded to email all who would hear. I started getting email from these people who got his email asking me why I had done such a thing. He was telling people I had deliberately deleted his email. This was bogus but some believed it. It was too strange. I had run the FORUM for 4 years never breaking even monetarily, sent thousands of emails daily, helped countless people learn the Online Ropes. And yet this guys bogus claim was causing some people to believe what he said was true. The guy claimed that I was making SO Much money from the FORUM that I had even bought a TRUCK. [Richard had asked subscribers for donations to cover his costs.] Man what a joke. But to this day some people really believe that I bought my truck with FORUM money. That's too distorted. The combination of this guys threats and emails from others asking me why I had done this was too much. I got fed up with the Thankless Job and started TheTARP.

FlintFORUM was replaced by The Tarp, also created by Richard, in early 2000. A group of moderators who had the power to remove anything really offensive or irrelevant remained anonymous and behind the scenes to avoid some of the acrimony of FlintFORUM. The Tarp was as popular as its predecessors, and the contribution of email lists to the growth of knapping is plainly visible. As of August 2001, there were some 450–460 members on The Tarp, and 594 by January 2003. Richard says:

> The FORUM and TheTARP have launched New Vendors, videos, calendars, Knap-ins, and Knapper's into Cyber-Stardom, which becomes Knap-in stardom. A number of knapper's were never known until joining these lists. Now their names are as common as Waldorf, Callahan and others.

Several other knapping listservers have come and gone or are current at this writing, but The Tarp is the one I have followed and seems similar to others.

The Tarp promotes itself as an "online knap-in," and in fact, the conversations entered into there are remarkably like those at a knap-in. You can't actually watch anyone knap, but with the addition of a Web page (under Yahoo.com) where knappers post pictures of their work, tools, finds, and techniques, some of the performance aspect of a knap-in is captured as well. In 2002 Richard Sanchez offered the following cyberknapper's vision of the future:

> With wireless technology becoming more readily available this will open up an even greater avenue of information sharing. In the future It will not be uncommon to see knapper's walking around with Laptops and Wireless streaming camera's capturing all the sites and sounds of a Live Knap-in. No longer will online knapping be limited to words on a monitor. It will be rich with the sites and sounds of lithic production. With one mouse click you'll be able to take a guided tour of a knap-in as it occurs and watch the Lithic Legends you have read about online live via Webcast. This will open up a KnapperNet with live broadcasts of knap-ins and classes all over the continent. Our knap-in circle would have grown to encircle the globe . . . provided they have Internet Access.

This has not happened yet. A lot of the listserve interchange is the same kind of personal chitchat that goes on at knap-ins or at any social gathering—greetings, jokes, invitations, queries about health and friends. In a public forum, the gossip about third parties is muted. In fact, an ethical debate that has appeared more than once concerns the propriety of posting complaints when a deal with a vendor goes sour. The consensus seems to be that such problems should usually be private, but in grievous cases, the victim has the right and maybe the obligation to warn other knappers. General announcements of knapping-related events appear often, as do requests for information about times and places, and responses providing this information, sometimes not as accurately as needed.

More interesting are the topics of direct or less-direct relevance to knapping, some of which become exchanges lasting a week or more. Tools, techniques, and raw materials are all discussed time and again, as are ethical issues of selling points. There have been several long "threads" of comments about prehistoric copper knapping tools, and the arguments about copper versus antler and traditional versus modern knapping that we have already discussed. Every now and then someone describes material he has recently knapped, asking what people thought it was and where it came from, or where you could get more of it. There have been discussions of synthetic materials and the possibility of creating a man-made knapping stone better than glass, and as beautiful as flint, but cheaper and more plentiful. The flintknapper as alchemist! There are frequent tips on hide glue, scrimshaw, and heat treating. At one point the old misinformation about how Indians made arrowheads by heating the stone and dripping cold water on it was brought up, and several suggestions as to how this dumb idea got started appeared. This entwined with some of the heat treating discussion and also with burnt rock middens and a series of comments on stone boiling and cooking in baskets. A comment on the possibility that stone knives were used for circumcisions in biblical times (which someone found on a Web page devoted to knives) led to some vague reports about modern surgery with obsidian, mentions of injuries, and complaints about getting off the subject of knapping. One example of a "thread" that I remember as particularly characteristic is in my notes as "the great mammoth debate."

The great mammoth debate, if I may inflate it a bit with such a title, grew out of a dialog between one of my Fort Osage friends, Jim Oyler ("Old Jim"), and Jim Pfaltzgraff. Old Jim was proposing some theories of culture change and wondered about the effect of the bow and arrow. Jim Pfaltzgraff responded that the bow and arrow might reflect a shift toward hunting smaller game and mentioned the theory that human hunters may have been responsible for the extinction of some of the Pleistocene big game like mammoths. This is a hotly debated topic. The argument for "overkill" of Pleistocene megafauna by Clovis hunters is based on the finds of kill sites where Clovis points are found with mammoth and other bones, and the evidence that the Clovis culture spread rapidly across the continent at the same time as mammoth, mastodon, horse, camel, ground sloth, and others became extinct. The other side notes that this is not direct evidence that humans overhunted the megafauna, and that the climate was also changing drastically at this time (Martin and Klein 1984; Grayson and Meltzer 2003).

Once the can of fauna was opened, the debate rapidly expanded. Russ Brownlow, an archaeology grad student, immediately weighed in with the skeptical view that small bands of hunters armed with spears were not likely to have had much effect on elephant populations. Pfaltzgraff defended the theory, citing a "Stanford paper published during the 80s [he probably meant Frison's 1989 experiments using spears on elephant carcasses]" and the slow rate of reproduction of large mammals. Further arguments pro and con cited the difficulty of overhunting without guns, the effectiveness of atlatls, and the possibility of mass kills, driving animals over cliffs. Several wrote to defend the power of the atlatl, citing Callahan's experiments on dead elephants (Callahan 1994), or personal experience with throwing spears or watching atlatls in action. Once the atlatl was brought up, others followed with links to Web pages with atlatl information, requests for information on atlatls, descriptions of atlatls and darts, and regrets that hunting with atlatls is not yet legal in most states. There was further discussion of hunting technology and animal behavior, modern extinctions and whale hunting, Native American worldviews, and Pleistocene climatic changes. After four days, members were beginning to argue about whether the discussion had strayed too far from knapping, the purported topic of the mail list. About half wanted to keep to knapping, the other half thought related archaeological and cultural matters were interesting. Some of the main players claimed to be ready to quit arguing about mammoths, but often were needled into "just one more" comment. Russ Brownlow ended one of these communications with "Die Megafauna, Die!"

The email listservers graft together parts of the knapping and computer worlds. Several knappers in the early days of the list commented on how many of the list members had some sort of high-tech or computer-oriented work, and thought it was symbolically interesting that both computers and flintknapping use silicon-based raw materials. Some wondered if this indicated a spiritual kinship between the crafts or some predilection among the high-tech silicon professionals to pursue the low-tech silica craft as well.[1] More likely, the relatively high numbers of high-tech workers who found the lists early related more to the kind of people who were interested in computer-based communication and had access to a computer, since the knapper community includes people from all sorts of occupations. In any case, the language on the mail lists soon came to reflect both rock-knockers and computer geeks. One message, for instance, referred to both "newbies and old flakes," new and experienced knappers, blending computer language and lithic reference. "Newbies," a piece of computer slang, was adopted by many of the new knappers entering the list to describe their level of knapping skill.

The email lists tend to be dominated by relatively small groups of members. A few of the more knowledgeable, enthusiastic, or garrulous knappers appear frequently, and the computer now serves as an important medium for teaching and displaying knowledge. Many other members are "newbies" who want information as they start a new hobby, which means some of the advice gets repeated frequently. However, the Web is now one of the most important recruiting devices; people find out about making stone tools from Web pages, connect to the email lists, and almost immediately can establish personal contacts and sources of information that took ages to find when I was learning. Over time, the Net becomes less important to some, as they go to knap-ins and meet other knappers face to face or decide they have better things to do than smash rocks and cut fingers. For others, email lists and Web pages become even more important as an easy way to maintain friendships, collect information, or advertise oneself. For some, it is plain that a visible presence on the email list, even if it takes the form of mostly personal greetings and irrelevant comments, is a way of expressing involvement and membership, just as is attending a knap-in.

Two other Internet forms have had a major influence on knapping. I have already mentioned eBay, the most important of the online auction services, which makes selling to a much wider audience vastly easier for many knappers. Web pages are the second.

Richard Sanchez told me in November 2002:

> Years ago I did a search for "flintknapping," on what was then the biggest search engines on the web. I got maybe a dozen hits but the results were not fruitful in helping me learn more about the craft. I found term paper reports, and some archeological info but I did not find the heart of knapping.
>
> Recently I did the same search on what is now the biggest search engine and I got 3,750 hits.
>
> As I perused through the search results I could see that all the hits could be placed into 3 categories.
>
> 1. Web sites that teach and promote the craft of knapping.

2. Web sites that sell Finished Knapped Products or Supplies.

3. Web sites that showcase a particular group, or personal web page.

The majority of hits fall into the first 2 categories.

The two Web sites that have had the most influence are Knappers Anonymous and Knapper's Corner, both essentially electronic newsletters. Knappers Anonymous was begun by Tim Rast in the early spring of 1996 as a project for a "Computer Uses for the Archaeologist" class at the University of Calgary, going through incarnations at several sites and under different people before perishing sometime in 2002. In September of 1996, Phil Hellerman set up a commercial Web site for the Waldorfs and Martins, The Knapper's Corner, which was still going strong in January 2003.

The two Web sites had similar features, but some differences. Both included some basic explanations of what flintknapping is and the prehistory of stone tools. Both had numerous links to other sites with stone tool or primitive technology material, and lists of addresses and some personal profiles for other knappers. The Knapper's Corner resembles the Waldorfs' newsletter *Chips*, with an extensive posting of knap-in times and contacts, and many commercial ads. Knappers Anonymous featured relatively detailed reports on knap-ins and a "Gallery" of photos of points by modern knappers, with a section of information on photographing points. Later, The Knapper's Corner began posting articles from *Chips*, and both sites increasingly included information on commercial vendors, heat treating recipes, and the like. Ultimately, such Web pages may compete with knapping newsletters, and it will be interesting to see if *Chips* and others can maintain some kind of a competitive niche. Knappers and vendors of knapping material like Frank Stevens of Great Lakes Lithics quickly developed their own Web pages to advertise and sell the same things they sell at knap-ins and through newsletter advertisements.

Forming and Breaking

It is often believed that societies maintain stability by balancing the internal conflicts of members and factions within them with patterns of crosscutting memberships (Gluckman 1956; Eggan 1950). Multiple ties of kinship, religious affiliation, and social participation among individuals mean that while they may be opponents in some circumstances, they are likely to be allies in others. However, this need not be the case. My colleague Doug Caulkins, studying small communities in Norway, a society with an unusually good record of harmonious relationships and political stability, argues that, in fact, most of the church, athletic, literary, and other social group memberships follow preexisting lines of polarization between conservative fundamentalist and liberal factions. Nevertheless, overt conflict is restrained by a strong ethos of cooperation and respect for individual rights and dignity (Caulkins 1998).

Knap-in society works somewhat the same way. Knapping brings together individuals with diverse other interests and affiliations, who bear with them the current religious and political polarizations of America. Knapping does promote friendships between individuals who would probably not meet otherwise and who continue to think, vote, worship, and associate with very different factions outside of the knapping world. Perhaps this helps in a small way to maintain stability in American society. However, more importantly, the knap-in is a loose-knit and temporary society. People can and do come and go, join and leave, sit with friends, avoid rivals. Rather than reducing polarization, the knap-in ignores it. The shared interest in knapping, the ethos of shared passion and equality of all members, and the common goal of having fun for a weekend temporarily overwhelm all the normal differences that separate individual knappers.

Jon Andelson, another colleague here at Grinnell, suggests the relevance of his work with what he calls "intentional communities," more often called "utopian communities," such as the Amana Colonies and modern communes. Among other things, he studies how they form, coming together "intentionally" as a result of common goals and interests, a process he calls "sociogenesis" (Andelson 2002). One of the important aspects of sociogenesis is that people who are brought together through a single interest, or even accidentally, are likely to form other bonds. Those who come to a knap-in because of an interest in prehistoric crafts, or even as spectators, may be incorporated and united by further ties of interest in prehistory or collecting, common friends, shared experiences at the knap-ins, or created rituals like the Ooga-Booga. Sociogenesis entails increasing the number of bonds and the complexity of relationships to hold a community together. The electronic media reflect the sociogenesis of the knapping community very well, as email lists produce enduring friendships and economic partnerships, as well as brief exchanges. They also reflect the other side of the coin, which Jon, following Bateson (1972, 1979), calls "schismogenesis," or the process of breaking up.

Communities break up for a variety of reasons, and Bateson and Andelson seem most interested in the structure of relationships within a community as it breaks up. For my purposes, I think of schismogenesis more as reasons some members leave a group. It is also useful to consider reasons some individuals never join or remain only partly integrated, since these reasons are often similar.

Membership in any group entails costs as well as benefits. These costs are often felt as restraints on behavior, subordinating personal desires for the group good, or the necessity of meeting expectations of the group. The ethical issues already discussed are good examples among knappers. The potential conflicts between archaeology and collecting, between replication and faking, between egalitarian ideals and the commercial value of being a top knapper, may overcome shared interests in stone tools or ancient lives. Commercial knappers may thus flee some knap-ins, antler-using purists avoid the "copper-bopper" events, and many archaeologists shun the whole knap-in world.

On the other hand, the decision to accept a group's ethics, to behave as expected, is a strong expression of membership, and serves to bond you to other members. One reason The Tarp and other email groups form, change hands, shift membership, and redefine themselves frequently is probably because the cost of both joining and leaving is low. When electronic exchanges begin to create other relationships, these are likely to be the stronger bonds, and parting shots like this are common on The Tarp:

> Date: Thu, 18 Oct 2001 02:16:09 -0000
> From: B_____
> Subject: Goodbye . . .
> As much as I hate to say it, I have drifted from knapping. Between school, family, social life, and work, I have no time to sleep, let alone knapp. I have watched The Tarp turn from an informative learning ground to nothing more than a pissing match. I have to deal with too many pissing matches at school, work, and at home. I don't need them on my computer as well. Some of you have been great friends, and I plan to keep in

touch with you. R_____ has been my greatest asset on here. He and I talk every day, not only about knapping, but everyday things. Something that is obviously not permitted on here. V_____ has been another good friend. At my one and only knappin he and I beeing newbies helped eachother and exchanged ideas. I plan on keeping in touch with both of you, as well as a few others. Most of the rest of you have gotten too skilled at this for your own good. Some of you are so wrapped up in how good you are that you absolutely REFUSE to help others, affraid they might show you up if you do. I can name a few offhand . . . [he did]. The point is I am tired of being shunned by the "Big Wigs" for being a newbie, for not having the experience they have. I plan on continuing to knapp in what little free time I DO have, and like I said, I will keep in touch with those of you I feel worth keeping in touch with. That is all I have to say. Goodbye.

B____

I removed the names, but the point is clear: the important relationships here outlive the cheap email membership, as does the interest in knapping. However, the knapping community failed to incorporate this knapper effectively, and he felt that it fell short of the knapping ideals of egalitarianism and sharing, although his farewell message was shortly followed by a whole series of responses with contrary views.

The email lists seem to suffer from this kind of openly expressed disagreement and lack of cohesion more than the knap-ins themselves. Messages go out to a wide public, and you are never sure who will be reading them, so some of the gossip about individuals that is common in more controlled face-to-face conversations at knap-ins is restrained. However, the facelessness of the computer and the relatively low investment that many members have in the computer group, seem to promote incivility and the willingness to quickly respond to offense with angry messages, or by dropping out. It seems to me that the email server groups are more openly acrimonious and much more fragile than the knap-ins.

As they grow, email groups become more active, new people become interested and sign up, more messages are sent and replied to. Those joining are connected by a common interest in knapping, but often come at it from different backgrounds (knives, black powder, lapidary, archery, hunting, survival skills, artifact collecting) or have different goals (selling goods, beginning to learn, making friends and connections, finding knap-ins, socializing). The more members there are, the surer it is that not all will be interested in all the same things and that some messages will displease some of the audience. Perhaps there is a maximum effective size for a computer mail list before the number of messages becomes overwhelming and the squabbling gets unbearable. More importantly, the same processes are obviously at work in the knap-in as well.

It often appears that central aspects of a community may both hold it together and tear it apart. The celebration of knapping skill, as we have seen, also creates the potential for a hierarchy that is loathed by many knappers and disdained by the expressed ideals of the group, but which inevitably will be manifested. However, individuals who accept the hierarchy too readily, push to organize others, or promote their own place at the top too enthusiastically risk driving off other knappers. The goals of differing factions may even be the same, but they may dispute the means. For example, knappers widely agree that promoting knapping art is a good thing, but argue bitterly over whether competitions are a desirable way to do it. Similarly, the successful growth of the knapping community may turn some members away from it. Those who prefer an eccentric hobby, who value their uniqueness and individualism above other things, increasingly find knap-ins too large and complex, too organized, too hierarchical.

The Future

So what is the future of knapping? To use an appropriate metaphor, I have no crystal ball, but some trends are clear. Interest in prehistory and primitive skills ebbs and flows, but is currently surging upward, as are collecting of all sorts and the market for antiquities. Perhaps as important, Americans seem to be seeking membership in small, comfortable, comprehensible groups. Church memberships, some kinds of clubs, and hobby groups are all reported to be on the rise. Our media are full of expressions of a desire for a social setting that is manageable in scale, that makes sense to individuals, that allows them to be the individuals they wish to be. We see this desire in journalistic lists of "the best small towns in America," nostalgia for the "good old days" of neighborhood, the angry reaction of traffic-jammed drivers, the ostentatious displays of eccentric movie stars, and the territorial graffiti of the gang. Some of the nostalgia and political posturing may be more words and fantasy than spurs to action, but participation in voluntary activities and organizations like the clan of knappers is one way to find a congenial community and express a sense of self among others who appreciate the same things. The knapping ethos itself builds on the desire for a better world. Stone tools symbolize a past of community, skilled craft, appreciation of beauty, respect for the individual—the "Good Old Days."

Knap-ins and the electronic communications media have created new ways for knappers to learn, get together, and spread the knapping ethos to new recruits. For the immediate future, I think the knapping world will continue to grow.

Richard Sanchez suggested one possible futuristic direction when he found Harold Dibble's Web site offering a flintknapping simulation program (published in Dibble, McPherron, and Roth 2003). The simulation allows you to vary the shape of the core, the platform angle, and the position of the blow and see how these variables affect the resulting flakes, a model based on work Dibble and I did some years ago (Whittaker 1994; Dibble and Whittaker 1981). You can then take the resulting virtual flake and shape it by retouch into various kinds of tools. The simulation is only capable of relatively simple "knapping," but Richard saw wider possibilities:

> I am confident that this method of teaching is just the begining for the flintknapping world. I can see when there will be software that will prompt you to select the type of point you wish to manufacture. Once you select the Point Type you will then be prompted to select the type of Tools that you use. Then you'll need to decide whose Style or Method you would like to use. You selections will be several of the better known knappers. Once you make your selection, You can then print detailed instruction how this type of point should be manufactured using your type of tools in the style and method of the knapper you selected. While this may seem far fetched the technology is there to create such a program.

Richard's enthusiastic commentary reflects once again important elements of the knapper ethos with which I began this book: Flintknapping is an art, an esoteric and beautiful skill practiced by admirable experts. Teaching this art is a key value, and learning it a shining goal. The point types are part of the knowledge that a member of the knapping community learns, knowledge that also connects you to the heroic past, even as you sit at a keyboard. Point types, tools, and individual skills represent the fascinating texture of variation in the knapping world, variation that is valued by the egalitarian ideals and that makes the experience of being a member novel and exciting.

Although the sort of cyberknapping envisioned by the simulation and Richard's further extrapolation can be a useful teaching aid, and fits readily into the knapping world, it will never be more than a small part of it, irrelevant to most knappers. Computer knapping, like so much of the world we see through the pixellated lens of a computer screen, is a pale abstraction. It can never capture the delight of striking just the right spot, hearing the ineffable sound of a perfect flake, feeling the grit between your fingers as the flake drops from your hand to fall musically on the debitage pile.

I have talked at great length about the commercial side of knapping, a great moving force in the knapping world and a battleground of conflicting ideals and motivations. The ability to earn money by knapping, and the market forces of the trade in antiquities, replicas, and artistic products, will continue to shape the knapping world for as long as I can imagine it lasting, just as it did in the early days of faking and archaeological experimentation, and just as trade moved stone and shaped tools in the prehistoric past.

Perhaps a greater motivation for most individual knappers, and certainly for the formation of knap-ins and related groups, is also lacking from the computer simulation. The social aspects of knapping have been my focus throughout, and the ethos expressed by most knappers also emphasizes the importance of being a knapper among knappers.

Many knappers think that the knap-ins are becoming more cliquish and disunified. I think we are seeing a certain amount of factionalization. As the knap-in world gets larger and more densely populated, more knappers feel the need to define a distinct identity within it. Being "a knapper" is not enough for many, and some feel a need to separate themselves from others, often because of some issue like the ethics of reproduction and sales. The usual response seems to be to create subgroups—The Tarp, the Society of Primitive Technology, a local club, an informal group of friends, a symbolic distinction between lap knappers and purists. In the past, most attempts at formal groups with hierarchy and sets of rules have failed, and the groups forming now are still weakly structured and informal.

The Tarp seems typical of small groups within the wider knapping circle—a loose group of people whose email communications are the basis for relationships. They have expanded the social possibilities of the electronic media, making attempts to meet face to face at knap-ins and developing some symbolic markers of membership like T-shirts. A few events have developed—for instance, a Tarp-organized knap-in in Texas, which was not exclusive to Tarp members. There have been gift exchanges conducted over the email list. Interested members give their names to an organizer (Richard Sanchez or Derek McLean in the recent past). Participants are then paired off to exchange knapping-related items by mail. There follows a week or two where many Tarp messages are devoted to commenting on the gifts and thanking partners, which, of course, serves to publicize generosity, skill, and membership. Such events are also good examples of the ad hoc leadership of informal groups. A few members are recognized as leaders by virtue of knowledge, skills, charisma, or a desire to participate and organize, but there is no formal head or hierarchy.

Beyond the splits and arguments, the cliques and factions, rivalries and differing motivations, there is the common interest in knapping. This shared interest and the collective activity of the knap-in serve as bonds between diverse groups and contending individuals.

One of the traditions of the Pine City Knap-in is a communal dinner in a local steak house and bar. Many of the knappers have left by Saturday evening, but at least twenty knappers and wives generally come. In June 2001, Pat Romano made reservations as usual, and we all sat at a single long table in a noisy, smokey barroom. It had been a hard year for the Minnesota knappers. In August 2000 Jim Regan died suddenly of a heart attack, and soon thereafter Dave Plankers was diagnosed with cancer, and his death in April was still fresh in everyone's mind. Jim had been the mentor of many of the Minnesota knappers and, with Tony Romano and Gene Altiere, had founded the Pine City Knap-in. Dave Plankers was an expert archer and bowyer and more recent knapper, but Jim and Dave were also the main forces, with Tony Romano, behind arranging and setting up the knap-in. After the knap-in, Art Magruder, who stepped in as one of the primary organizers, wrote a message on The Tarp and in *Chips* (Magruder 2001).

Whew! We made it through our first Knap-in without our guide and mentor, Jim Regan. As many of you know, Jim Regan along with Tony Romano and Gene Altiere started the MN Knappers Guild. When Jim passed away last August many of us were concerned that the Minnesota knap-in tradition may go by the wayside. Many of us looked to Dave Plankers to help keep the group together. Dave and Tony told us that we must keep things together or all of the work that had been done would be for nothing. Fate struck again when Dave was diagnosed with cancer not long after Jim died. Dave continued to be a force with the MN knappers until his death in April of this year. The whole group stepped up to fill those big spaces. Kevin and Jeff Plath beat the bushes at various functions. They found a bunch of new knappers. I am happy to report that this years Knap-in was bigger than ever before. We registered over sixty knappers. Many of them are folks new to knapping.

At Pine City, both Jim and Dave were sorely missed and very much present in spirit at the knap-in. Their pictures and points were displayed by several friends, and we spoke of them often. Both Pat Regan and Lynn Plankers came to the knap-in with their sons. Pat and Darren sold some of Jim's cache of stone and the last of the copper tools that he was famous for, and Bob Plankers sat with Tony and me and began to learn to knap.

After going to knap-ins for ten years, I had finally convinced my wife Kathy to come with me to one, see what they were like, and meet some of my friends. We sat at the long dinner table, conducting shouted conversations about flint, artifacts, knap-ins past and future, food good and bad. We remembered absent friends, teased old friends, learned more about new friends, and had a lively good time in each other's company. At one point Kathy leaned over to me and whispered, "Well, I'm not sure I find knapping real fascinating, but I guess I know why you like going to knap-ins." Here were twenty-some people, from all kinds of backgrounds, most of whom I would never have met in my ordinary academic and hometown circles, but all of whom are truly friends. Of course, we like making stone tools, exchanging stone, admiring artifacts, discussing archaeology and knapping techniques—a common bond of interest. But these superficial bonds soon grow into

Figure 11.1. Group photo of the knappers at the Pine City Knap-in, 1996.

something more, a feeling of unity that holds even the non-knapping relatives of some knappers. They have become part of a small culture, a circle of friends, a family even, and just as Pat and Lynn will always have connections to the knapping world, I know that I can travel anywhere in the country, introduce myself to a knapping stranger, and have an instant bond.

The worn bumper sticker on Bob Hunt's tool chest says, "Only the Rocks Live Forever." Henry David Thoreau (1906) said much the same thing in his journal for March 28, 1859:

> Time will soon destroy the works of famous painters and sculptors, but the Indian arrowhead will balk his efforts and Eternity will have to come to his aid. They are not fossil bones, but as it were, fossil thoughts, forever reminding me of the mind that shaped them.

Knappers may feel that fragments of flint they have shaped provide a personal monument as eternal as the relics of antiquity, but it is not just individuals who leave their mark on the stone. The knap-in society, like all cultures, is stronger than any individual member. Hobbies come and go, rise to become fads, sink to obscure eccentricities. For the near future, knapping is on the rise. We cannot say how long that will last, but it is unlikely to become a lost art again in our lifetimes. The people that have revived the ancient craft will pass, but the knap-in world should pass on the traditions of knapping for some time to come (Figure 11.1).

Appendix A

Knapper Mail Survey Questionnaire

John Whittaker   Anthropology Dept.
Grinnell College
Grinnell, IA 50112

Dear Fellow Knapper,

I *have been coming* to the Fort Osage and other knap-ins for several years now, and as you may know, I am interested in writing about knap-ins and the knapping world today. This questionnaire is designed to give me some basic information about who we are as a group, why knappers learn a difficult and unusual craft, and what knapping means to us. Your cooperation is greatly appreciated, and I hope to share this information with you all in the future. Your individual responses to this questionnaire will be confidential—I will not use anyone's name with it, although if you write your name in it will help me because I am interested in the networks of learning and teaching. If you do not wish to answer some questions that is fine too. I have tried to keep the questions short, but please add anything you wish, and if you have questions or want to discuss things with me I would be grateful for your help.

Age: _____   Sex: M___ F___   State of residence:_____
Name (optional):

1. How long have you been knapping? _____
2. What got you started? _____
3. How did you learn? (number relevant items—1 = most important, 2 = next most important, etc.)
   ___ taught by friend(s)
   ___ paid for lessons
   ___ watched others
   ___ read books
   ___ looked at artifacts
   ___ figured it out by self
   ___ went to knap-ins
   ___ other (explain) _____
4. Who has influenced or taught you, and when? (in order of importance)

Who?	When?	What taught?

5. Do you knap with anyone regularly? Who?
6. Do you teach or have you taught anyone? Who?
7. What kinds of things do you like to make? Why?
8. What tools do you use? (rank 1= frequently, 2 = some, 3 = a little, 0 = don't use)
   ___ antler billet
   ___ copper billet
   ___ hammerstone
   ___ indirect percussion
   ___ lever device
   ___ short copper pressure tool
   ___ long ("Ishi" stick)
   ___ antler pressure tool
   ___ other (explain) _____
9. What materials do you prefer to work?
10. Where do you get material? (number in order of importance, 1 = most important, etc.)

    ___ collect at source
    ___ buy through mail
    ___ buy at knap-ins
    ___ exchange with friends
    ___ other _____

11. Rank your skill level
    ___ Beginner
    ___ Competent (capable of normal point replicas)
    ___ Skilled (large thin bifaces, fluted pts, etc.)
    ___ Expert
12. When and how much do you knap? (check boxes)

	1/week or more	1/month	1–5/yr	never
by yourself				
locally with friends				
at knap-ins				
other events				
demos for others				
other _____?				

13. About how many hours total do you knap in a month (best guess)?
14. How many pieces do you make in a month (best guess)?
15. What do you do that you consider different from other people, or typical of you?
16. Why do you knap? What do you like about knapping?
17. What other hobbies or crafts are you involved in?
18. Have you attended knap-ins?

    Knap-in   When?

    _____   _____
    _____   _____
    _____   _____
    _____   _____

19. What do you do at knap-ins? (1 = always, 2 = usually, 3 = often, 4 = sometimes, 0 = never)
    ___ Knap
    ___ Watch knapping

Knappers Mail Survey Questionnaire

___ talk to friends/others
___ film/photograph
___ buy material
___ sell material
___ buy points
___ sell points
___ buy other crafts/materials/tools
___ sell other crafts/material/tools
20. What do you like about knap-ins?
21. Other related interests?
___ read about archaeology
___ visit museums
___ collect prehistoric artifacts
___ collect other knappers' work
___ belong to archaeological society
___ take courses related to arch.
___ watch TV specials on arch.
___ have participated in arch. project or excavation
___ antiques
___ hunt/fish
___ black powder/rendezvous/reenactments
___ archery/bow hunting
___ collect knives
___ rock hound/lapidary work/jewelry
___ other _____
22. What do you do for a living? (if retired, what did you do?)
23. What is your educational background?
___ high school
___ college
___ advanced degree (MA, PhD, etc.)
24. Do you sign your work? Y____ N____ sometimes ____
How?
25. Do you sell your work? Y_____ N_____
Where? ___ knap-ins
___ through mail
___ rock shows
___ rendezvous
___ other _____
To whom?   ___ friends/other knappers

    ___ collectors
    ___ museums
    ___ a middle man
    ___ other _____

How many per year (best guess)?
Average prices?

26. What else do you do with your points?
27. Do you see any trends in knapping that you do not like or approve of?
28. Any trends you do approve of or would like to see?
29. Why do you think other knappers knap?
30. What qualities make a good knapper?
31. What else should anyone who wants to understand the knapping scene today know? What else should I be asking?

Appendix B

Fall 1966 Fort Osage Knap-in Registration

FALL 1996
KNAP-IN REGISTRATION

- KNAPPER NAME_____
- ADDRESS_____

_____

- DEALERSHIP NAME_____
- OTHER PARTICIPANTS ACCOMPANYING KNAPPER

_____
- _____
_____

- WILL YOU BE ENGAGED IN RESALE ACTIVITIES?
  YES____ NO ____
- WILL YOU BE STAYING OVERNIGHT ON PARK PROPERTY? YES___ NO ___
- All participants (including family members) must register prior to set-up. The fee for each participant is $5.00 for Wednesday, September 11, through Sunday, September 15, 1996.
- All participants are required to wear name tags at all times during public hours.
- Vehicles are required to be parked in designated paved parking areas. No parking on grass is permitted.
- Vendor's and participant's names will be furnished to the Missouri Department of Revenue upon their request.

- Consumption of alcoholic beverages is not permitted on park property during public hours. 9:00 A.M.–5:00 P.M.
- Participants stipulate that they are aware of all applicable Federal and State laws concerning the sale of antiquities and that they will abide by such laws.
- All property and equipment of each participant will be removed from park property by 5:00 P.M. Sunday, September 15, 1996.

AGREEMENT

I, the undersigned, agree that neither Jackson County Parks & Recreation Department nor its representatives are liable for any personal injury, damage or loss of exhibition wares, materials or personal property. I further understand and agree that I am participating in this event as a licensee and will abide by rules stipulated by the Jackson County Parks Department and its representatives. Further, that the County has full discretionary rights on approval of wares to be sold and on the appearance of display booths.

SIGNED_____DATE_____

Appendix C

New York Knap-in Contest Rules, 1994

Philosophy: Competition is used only in the sense that awards are presented. All events are designed to promote the preservation of the art of flint knapping, to educate the public about lithic art, and to facilitate sharing among knappers of various experience levels.

1. Artist may enter one item per year. All entered pieces will be judged in three categories. These categories (described herein) are diverse, and one piece may be better suited to one or the other. However, in the interest of expediency, to minimize competitiveness among people, and to focus on the art form, no artist category designation is permitted.
2. Entry is by invitation only. Unverified art work will not be accepted.
3. All entrees must be completed by 3:00 P.M. for 3:30 awards presentation.
4. All categories will have 3 entry levels:
Lamoka (1–5 years experience)
Meadowood (5–10 years experience)
Clovis (Masters 10+ years)
5. All pieces receiving awards become the property of the Genesee Valley Flint Knappers Association for future use in promoting lithic art and educating the public. All non-award pieces, at the artist's discretion, will either be returned to the artist or entered into the per-

manent collection of the GVFKA for future use in promoting lithic art and educating the public.

6. This competition has no winners and no losers. Recognition awards are presented to serve as inspiration to lithic artists of all skill levels, and to promote the preservation of ancient art forms. If this form of non-intense competition does not appeal to you, your participation is not required.

Typology

Art pieces to be evaluated as to trueness to form of classic point typology in material, flake pattern and form. This category is designed to promote an awareness of lithic materials, typology, and knapping techniques.

Free Form

To include exotics, effigies, unique materials, non-traditional lithic interpretations. This event is designed to promote the expansion of horizons of lithic art and to promote experimentation and scientific inquiry into ancient methodology.

Stone Mastery Award

Judged on width to thickness ratio, control of percussion and/or pressure flaking. This category is to showcase mastery of diverse materials and educate the public on conchoidal fracturing in different lithic materials.

Appendix D

NEW YORK KNAP-IN CONTEST RULES, 1996

Philosophy: Competition is used only in the sense that awards are presented. All events are designed to promote the preservation of the art of flint knapping, to educate the public about lithic art, and to facilitate sharing among knappers of various experience levels.

All pieces receiving awards become the property of the Genesee Valley Flint Knappers Association for future use in promoting lithic art and educating the public. All non-award pieces, at the artist's discretion, will either be returned to the artists or entered into the permanent collection of the GVFKA for future use in promoting lithic art and educating the public.

This competition is based on input from knappers around the country. It is different than last year, and we expect it to evolve over time with your feedback.

Winning entries receive a certificate of merit.

Any knapper can enter two points but not in the same categories. Categories 1 and 7 are restricted. All others are open.

1. *Lamoka—For beginning knappers 0–3 years experience only. Judged on best attempt at replication.*
2. *Traditional Fluted.*
3. *Paleo Traditional Non-Fluted.*
4. *Traditional Archaic.*

5. *Traditional Woodland or "Formative" with allowances by region.*

All Traditional entries, while ideally done with only hammer stones, antler billets and antler tine pressure flakes, will also be allowed with copper, phenolic, etc. tools. In the interest of promoting study various leverage devices for fluting are allowed. Slabbed material is allowed for the conservation of lithic material.

6. *Modern or Art Category*

You may use flake over ground surface ("lap-knapping") or Traditional with any kind of color of wild material create your own point type or eccentric or whatever. This is where flint knapping has room to grow and break free of the constraints of the past.

7. *This category is a celebration of New York State lithic sources restricted to materials used in New York. Deepkill, Onondaga, Normanskill, etc.*

This competition has no winners and no losers. Recognition awards are presented to serve as inspiration to lithic artists of all skill levels, and to promote the preservation of ancient art forms. If this form of non-intense competition does not appeal to you, your participation is not required.

This event is evolving into a consensus of what the knappers want. Attached are the four committees that are required to run this event. If the contest is not to your liking please sign on to the recognition committee and give us your input.

Bibliography

Videos

Alexander, J. E. "Swoose." 1997. *Parallel Flaking the Paleo Indian Way!* San Angelo: Texas Amateur Archaeological Association.

Blackwell, Woody. 1995. *Fluting Points with the Sollberger Jig.* Opposable Thumbs Productions.

———. 1996. *Welcome Back to the Stone Age: Beginning and Intermediate Flintknapping with Woody Blackwell.* Opposable Thumbs Productions.

Bradley, Bruce. 1989. *Flintknapping with Bruce Bradley.* Cortez, Colo.: INTERpark.

Cannon, Dale, Dane Martin, D. C. Waldorf, and Val Waldorf. 2000. *Flake Over Grinding with Dale Cannon.* Washburn, Mo.: Flintknappers Corner.

Crabtree, Don. 1992. *The Tools of Early Man Series with Flintworker Don Crabtree.* Idaho Museum of Natural History. (Original five films produced by Earl Swanson with Informational Materials Incorporated, 1972.)

Jacobs, Howard, and Alan Taylor. n.d. *Flint Knapping Made Easy.* Neosho, Mo.: IPB Video.

Klostermeier, David. 1993. *Rediscovering the Lost Art of Flintknapping.* Privately produced, St. Louis.

Lackey, Wade. n.d. *Two Hour Course on Making Arrow Heads.* Privately produced, Evant, Tex.

Martin, Dane, D. C. Waldorf, Val Waldorf, and Mary Martin. 1999. *Water Creek Knap-in,* 1999. Washburn, Mo.: Flintknapper's Corner.

Metcalfe, Bill. 1995. *An Introduction to Flint Knapping.* Branson, Mo.: Mound Builder Books.

Ratzat, Craig. 1994. *Caught Knapping: The Fundamentals of Flint Knapping.* Springfield, Ore.: Neo Lithics.

———. 1996. *Lap Knapping with Craig Ratzat.* Springfield, Ore.: Neo Lithics.

Redfearn, Jim. 1999. *Making the Hardin Point with Jim Redfearn.* Washburn, Mo.: Flintknapper's Corner.

———. 2000. *Making a Dalton Point with Jim Redfearn.* Washburn, Mo.: Flintknapper's Corner.

———. 2001. *Making a Clovis Point with Jim Redfearn.* Washburn, Mo.: Flintknapper's Corner.

Shelden, Billy Joe. 1997. *Knapping the Big One: Detailed Grinding and Flaking.* Folsom, N.Mex.: HGR Productions.

Spear, Chas. 1994. *The Illustrated Knapper.* Privately distributed.

Waldorf, D. C. 1992. *Caught Knapping.* Branson, Mo.: Mound Builder Books.

———. 1993. *The Art of Flintknapping Video Companion.* Branson, Mo.: Mound Builder Books.

———. 1998. *Roasting Rocks: The Art and Science of Heat Treating, with D. C. Waldorf.* Branson, Mo.: Mound Builder Books.

———. 2000a. *Novaculite—From Pit to Point with D. C. Waldorf.* Washburn, Mo.: Flintknapper's Corner.

———. 2000b. *Thebes Points and Their Variants.* Washburn, Mo.: Flintknapper's Corner.

———. 2001. *Getting Started in Flintknapping with D. C. Waldorf.* Branson, Mo.: Mound Builder Books.

Warmuskerken, Roger F. 2001. *Abo Knapping Techniques.* Privately produced.

References Cited

Ahler, Stanley A., and Phil R. Geib. 2000. Why Flute? Folsom Point Design and Adaptation. *Journal of Archaeological Science* 27: 799–820.

Akin, Marjorie. 1996. Passionate Possession: The Formation of Private

Collections. In *Learning from Things: Method and Theory in Material Culture Studies*, ed. W. D. Kingery, pp. 102–128. Washington, D.C.: Smithsonian Institution Press.

Aldred, Cyril. 1965. *Egypt to the End of the Old Kingdom.* New York: McGraw-Hill.

Amick, Daniel S. 1994. Folsom Diet Breadth and Land Use in the American Southwest. Ph.D. dissertation, University of New Mexico, Albuquerque.

———. 1995. Patterns of Technological Variation among Folsom and Midland Projectile Points in the American Southwest. *Plains Anthropologist* 40 (151): 23–38.

Andelson, Jonathan G. 2002. Coming Together and Breaking Apart: Sociogenesis and Schismogenesis in Intentional Communities. In *Intentional Community: An Anthropological Perspective*, ed. Susan Love Brown, pp. 131–151. Albany: State University of New York Press.

Arbeiter, Dennis. 2000. The Atlas Spear. *Prehistoric Antiquities and Archaeological News Quarterly* 20 (4): 4.

Bakken, Kent. 1993. Lithic Raw Material Resources in Western Minnesota. *Platform* 5 (1): 2–3; 5 (2): 6–7; 5 (3): 7–8; 5 (4): 7–8.

Banks, Larry D. 1990. *From Mountain Peaks to Alligator Stomachs: A Review of Lithic Sources in the Trans-Mississippi South, the Southern Plains, and Adjacent Southwest.* Oklahoma Anthropological Series Memoir 4. Norman: University of Oklahoma.

Barbieri, Joseph. 1937. Technique of the Implements from Lake Mohave. In *The Archaeology of Pleistocene Lake Mohave: A Symposium.* Southwest Museum Papers 11: 99–107.

Barker, Joan C. 1999. *Danger, Duty, and Disillusion: The Worldview of Los Angeles Police Officers.* Prospect Heights, Ill.: Waveland Press.

Bateson, Gregory. 1972. Culture Contact and Schismogenesis. In *Steps to an Ecology of Mind*, pp. 61–72. San Francisco: Chandler Publishing Co. Orig. 1935; *Man* 35 (199).

———. 1979. *Mind and Nature.* New York: E. P. Dutton.

Behrnes, Jeff. 1991. From the Editor. *Flint Knapper's Exchange* 1 (5): 11–12.

Belk, Roger. 1988. Collectors and Collecting. *Advances in Consumer Research* 15: 548–553. Reprinted in *Interpreting Objects and Collections*, ed. Susan M. Pearce, pp. 317–326. London and New York: Routlege, 1994.

Belk, Roger W., and Melanie Wallendorf. 1994. Of Mice and Men: Gender Identity in Collecting. In *Interpreting Objects and Collections*, ed. Susan M. Pearce, pp. 240–253. London and New York: Routlege, 1994.

Bell, Robert E. 1947. Trade Materials at Spiro Mound as Indicated by Artifacts. *American Antiquity* 12 (2): 181–184.

Berg, Robert S. 1995. A Wild Boar Hunt at Cold Brook: An Eolithic Adventure. *Chips* 7 (3): 4–5.

Berner, John. 1984. Artifact or Artifake? *Central States Archaeological Journal* 31 (4): 186–188.

———. 1997a. The Authenticators. *Prehistoric American* 31 (4): 10–11.

———. 1997b. Is It a Reproduction or a Fake? *Prehistoric American* 31 (3): 21.

———. 1998a. Advice for New Collector/Investors. *Prehistoric American* 32 (3): 3.

———. 1998b. Popularity of Reproduction Styles. *Prehistoric American* 32 (3): 10.

———. 1998c. Twentieth Century Reproductions/Fakes. *Prehistoric American* 32 (3): 16–17.

———. 2000a. *American Indian Artifacts: Genuine or Reproduction.* Roswell, N.Mex.: American Antiquities Inc.

———. 2000b. Their Real Dream Is to Fool the Experts. *Prehistoric American* 34 (1): 19.

Binford, Lewis R., and Jacqueline Nichols. 1979. Problems/Solutions: Interview with Lewis R. Binford. *Flintknappers' Exchange* 2 (1): 19–25.

Bird, Caroline F. M. 1993. Woman the Toolmaker: Evidence for Women's Use and Manufacture of Flaked Stone Tools in Australia and New Guinea. In *Women in Archaeology: A Feminist Critique*, ed. Hilary du Cros and Laurajane Smith, pp. 22–30. Canberra: Australian National University.

Blacking, John. 1953. Edward Simpson, alias "Flint Jack": A Victorian Craftsman. *Antiquity* 27: 207–211.

Blackwell, Woody. 1994a. Making Fluted Points with the Sollberger Jig, Part I. *Chips* 6 (2): 6–8.

———. 1994b. The Sollberger Jig, Part II. *Chips* 6 (3): 4–6.

———. 1995. Knapping the Montell Point. *Chips* 7 (3): 5–8.

———. 1996. The Golden Age Is Here. *Chips* 8 (3): 4–5.

———. 1997a. Billets and Bad Attitudes. *Chips* 9 (3): 2–4.

———. 1997b. Knapping the Pine Tree Point. *Chips* 9 (4): 12–13.

———. 1997c. Making the Scottsbluff II. *Chips* 9 (2): 9–11.

———. 1997d. Some Thoughts on Folsom Culture. *Chips* 9 (1): 12–13.

Blake, Mike. 1989. Untitled letter. *Chips* 1 (2): 2.

———. 1991. Fort Osage Knap-in. *Flint Knapper's Exchange* 1 (4): 13–16.

———. 1992. Back in Time. *Chips* 4 (4): 6–7.

Bloom, Stephen G. 2000. *Postville: A Clash of Cultures in Heartland America.* New York: Harcourt.

Bodio, Stephen. 1984. *A Rage for Falcons.* Boulder, Colo.: Pruett Publishing Company.

Bonnichsen, Robson, and Errett Callahan. 1978. Craftsman: Rob Bonnichsen. *Flintknappers' Exchange* 1 (2): 16–24.

Bordes, François, and Don Crabtree. 1969. The Corbiac Blade Technique and Other Experiments. *Tebiwa* 12 (2): 1–21.

Bostrom, Pete. 2003. Mack Tussinger's Oklahoma Eccentrics, ca. 1921. Lithic Casting Lab Web page, http://www.lithiccastinglab.com.

Boudreau, Jeff. 1995. Flint Hunting in Denmark. *Chips* 7 (3): 10–12.

Bowman, Rex. 1997. Obsidian Scalpels Are Prized. *Richmond Times-Dispatch,* October 23, 1997.

Bradley, Bruce. 1972. Predynastic Egyptian Flint Implements—An Inductive Technological Sequence. *Newsletter of Lithic Technology* 1 (3): 2–5.

———. 1978. Hard Hammer—Soft Hammer: An Alternative Explanation. *Flintknappers' Exchange* 1 (2): 8–10.

Bradley, Bruce A., and Dennis J. Stanford. 1987. The Claypool Study. In *The Horner Site: The Type Site of the Cody Cultural Complex,* ed. G. Frison and L. Todd, pp. 405–434. New York: Academic Press.

Brennan, Louis A., ed. 1982. A Compilation of Fluted Points of Eastern North America by Count and Distribution: An AENA Project. *Archaeology of Eastern North America* 10: 27–46.

Brown, Dee. 1970. *Bury My Heart at Wounded Knee: An Indian History of the American West.* New York: Bantam Books.

Brown, James A. 1966a. *Spiro Studies vol. 1: Description of the Mound Group.* Norman: University of Oklahoma Research Institute.

———. 1966b. *Spiro Studies vol. 2: The Graves and Their Contents.* Norman: University of Oklahoma Research Institute.

———. 1971. *Spiro Studies vol. 3: Pottery Vessels*. Norman: University of Oklahoma Research Institute.

———. 1976. *Spiro Studies vol. 4: The Artifacts*. Norman: University of Oklahoma Research Institute.

———. 1996. *The Spiro Ceremonial Center: The Archaeology of Arkansas Valley Caddoan Culture in Eastern Oklahoma*. Memoirs of the Museum of Anthropology. Ann Arbor: University of Michigan.

Brown, Linda Keller, and Kay Mussell, eds. 1984. *Ethnic and Regional Foodways in the United States: The Performance of Group Identity*. Knoxville: University of Tennessee Press.

Bruhns, Karen Olsen. 2000. http://www.plunderedpast.com. *Society for American Archaeology Bulletin* 18 (2): 14–15, 17.

Callahan, Errett. 1976. A Lithic Workshop Symposium. *Newsletter of Lithic Technology* 5 (1–2): 3–4.

———. 1978a. Editorial. *Flintknappers' Exchange* 1 (1): 2–4.

———. 1978b. Editorial. *Flintknappers' Exchange* 1 (2): 2–3.

———. 1978c. The Ginsburg Experience: A Mammoth Task. *Flintknappers' Exchange* 1 (2): 31–32.

———. 1978d. On Identifying and Documenting Replicas. *Flintknappers' Exchange* 1 (1): 10–11.

———. 1978e. Synthetic Billet Material. *Flintknappers' Exchange* 1 (1): 9–10.

———. 1979a. The Basics of Biface Knapping in the Eastern Fluted Point Tradition: A Manual for Flintknappers and Lithic Analysts. *Archaeology of Eastern North America* 7 (1): 1–180. (Reprinted 2000.)

———. 1979b. From the Editors. *Flintknappers' Exchange* 2 (3): 1.

———. 1979c. Review of *The Art of Flint Knapping*. *Flintknappers' Exchange* 2 (3): 11.

———. 1989. Dear D. C. *Chips* 1 (2): unpaginated letter inserted in newsletter.

———. 1990. *Piltdown Productions Catalog #4*. Lynchburg, Va.: Piltdown Productions.

———. 1992. Flintknapping, Elitism, and Fracture Geometry: A Cautionary Note. *Bulletin of Primitive Technology* 4: 16–19.

———. 1993. *Sword in the Stone Supplement to Our 1990 Catalog #4*. Lynchburg, Va.: Piltdown Productions.

———. 1994. A Pause for Thought: Traditionalism vs. Modernism. *Bulletin of Primitive Technology* 8: 9.

———. 1995a. A Pause for Thought: An Ongoing Discussion. *Bulletin of Primitive Technology* 10: 7–8.

———. 1995b. What Is Experimental Archaeology? *Newsletter of Primitive Technology.* 1: 3–5.

———. 1996a. A Review by Errett Callahan: *Flintknapping: Making and Understanding Stone Tools,* by John C. Whittaker. *Bulletin of Primitive Technology* 11: 82–85.

———. 1996b. State of the Society—The First Five Years, 1990–1995. *Bulletin of Primitive Technology* 11: 8–9.

———. 1997. Back to the Stone Edge: How to Identify and Use the Best Stone Knives. *Blade Magazine* 97 (May): 16–19.

———. 1999. *Piltdown Productions Catalog #5.* Lynchburg, Va.: Piltdown Productions.

———. 2000. What Is Traditional Flintknapping? *Bulletin of Primitive Technology* 20: 11.

———. 2001a. Craft or Art? *Bulletin of Primitive Technology* 22: 85–86.

———. 2001b. Regarding Bryon Rinehart. *Bulletin of Primitive Technology* 22: 5–6.

Callahan, Errett, and Robson Bonnichsen. 1978. Craftsman: Rob Bonnichsen. *Flintknappers' Exchange* 1 (2): 16–24.

Callahan, Errett, and Don Crabtree. 1979. Craftsman: Don Crabtree. *Flintknappers' Exchange* 2 (1): 27–34; 2 (2): 8–13; 2 (3): 22–26.

Callahan, Errett, and Jacqueline Nichols. 1979. The Wyoming Knapin. *Flintknappers' Exchange* 2 (2): 1.

Callahan, Errett, and J. B. Sollberger. 1978. Craftsman: J. B. Sollberger. *Flintknappers' Exchange* 1 (1): 12–17.

Callahan, Errett, and Gene Titmus. 1980. Craftsman: Gene Titmus. *Flintknappers' Exchange* 3 (1): 18–25.

Caulkins, Douglas. 1998. Norwegians: Cooperative Individualists. In *Portraits of Culture: Ethnographic Originals, Volume III,* ed. Melvin Ember, Carol Ember, and David Levinson, pp. 3–30. Upper Saddle River, N.J.: Prentice Hall.

Chagnon, Napoleon A. 1997. *Yanomamö.* 5th ed. Fort Worth: Harcourt Brace and Company.

Clements, Forrest E. 1945. Historical Sketch of the Spiro Mound.

Contributions of the Museum of the American Indian, Heye Foundation 14: 48–68.

Clements, Forrest E., and Alfred Reed. 1939. "Eccentric" Flints of Oklahoma. *American Antiquity* 5 (1): 27–30.

Cohen, Larry S. 1978. A Guide to Knapping Strategy. *Flintknappers' Exchange* 1 (2): 12–15.

Coles, John. 1973. *Archaeology by Experiment.* New York: Charles Scribner's Sons.

———. 1979. *Experimental Archaeology.* New York: Academic Press.

Cooper, Eugene. 1980. *The Wood-carvers of Hong Kong: Craft Production in the World Capitalist Periphery.* Prospect Heights, Ill.: Waveland Press.

Counts, Dorothy A., and David R. Counts. 1996. *Over the Next Hill: An Ethnography of RVing Seniors in North America.* Peterborough, Ont.: Broadview Press.

Crabtree, Don. 1966. A Stoneworker's Approach to Analyzing and Replicating the Lindenmeier Folsom. *Tebiwa* 9 (1): 3–39.

———. 1968. Mesoamerican Polyhedral Cores and Prismatic Blades. *American Antiquity* 33 (4): 446–478.

———. 1972. *An Introduction to Flintworking.* Occasional Papers no. 28. Pocatello: Idaho State University Museum.

Cresson, Jack. 1978. Further Comments on Hard Hammer Percussion. *Flintknappers' Exchange* 1 (2): 7–8.

———. 2001. The State of Flintknapping: Traditional or New Age. *Bulletin of Primitive Technology* 21: 8–10.

Cushing, Frank Hamilton. 1895. The Arrow. *American Anthropologist* 8 (4): 307–349.

Del Bene, Terry A. 1979. Untitled letter. *Flintknappers' Exchange* 2 (1): 4–5.

de Morgan, Jacques. 1926. *La Préhistoire Orientale, Tome II: L'Égypte et L'Afrique du Nord.* Paris: Paul Geuthner.

DeRegnaucourt, Tony, and Jeff Georgiady. 1998. *Prehistoric Chert Types of the Midwest.* Upper Miami Valley Archaeological Research Museum, Occasional Monograph 7. Greenville: Western Ohio Podiatric Medical Center.

DeSimone, Barney. 1991. Use Those Points. *Chips* 3 (3): 7–8.

Dibble, Harold L., Shannon P. McPherron, and Barbara Roth. 2003. *Virtual Dig: A Simulated Archaeological Excavation of a Middle*

Paleolithic Site in France. 2d ed. Boston: McGraw-Hill Mayfield.

Dibble, Harold L., and John C. Whittaker. 1981. New Experimental Evidence on the Relation between Percussion Flaking and Flake Variation. *Journal of Archaeological Science* 8: 283–298.

Dickson, Don. 1996. The Production of Modern Lithic Scatters and Related Problems. *Lithic Technology* 21 (2): 155–156.

Dickson, Jim. 1992. Stone Age Knives Today. *Gun Digest Book of Knives*, 4th ed., pp. 35–37. Iola, Wisc.: Krause Publications.

Dorwin, John T. 1966. *Fluted Points and Late-Pleistocene Geochronology in Indiana.* Indianapolis: Indiana Historical Society.

Dothager, Myrtle May. 1989. Flint Knapper's Dream. *Chips* 1 (3): 14.

Dubuc, M., and J. Nichols. 1978. An Experiment in Recovery. *Flintknappers' Exchange* 1 (1): 7–8.

Dunbar, James S. 1991. Resource Orientation of Clovis and Suwannee Age Paleoindian Sites in Florida. In *Clovis: Origins and Adaptations,* ed. R. Bonnichsen and K. Turnmire, pp. 185–213. Corvallis, Ore.: Center for the Study of the First Americans.

Eggan, Fred. 1950. *Social Organization of the Western Pueblos.* Chicago: University of Chicago Press.

Ellis, H. Holmes. 1965. *Flint-Working Techniques of the American Indians: An Experimental Study.* Orig. 1939; Columbus: Ohio Historical Society.

———. 1940. A Study of the Oklahoma Eccentric Flints. *Ohio State Archaeological and Historical Quarterly* 49 (2): 120–127.

Evans, Sir John. 1866. On the Worked Flints of Presigny le Grand. *Archaeologia* 40: 381–388.

———. 1872. *The Ancient Stone Implements, Weapons, and Ornaments of Great Britain.* New York: D. Appleton. (2d ed., London: Longmans, 1897.)

Farnsworth, Kenneth B. 1973. An Archaeological Survey of the Macoupin Valley. *Illinois State Museum Reports of Investigations,* No. 26.

Faulkner, Charles H. 1961. *An Archaeological Survey of Marshall County.* Indianapolis: Indiana Historical Bureau.

Fenn, Forrest. 2001. The Infamous Woody Blackwell Fakes. *Prehistoric American* 35 (1): 40–41.

Fleisher, Mark S. 1995. *Beggars and Thieves: Lives of Urban Street Criminals.* Madison: University of Wisconsin Press.

———. 1998. *Dead End Kids: Gang Girls and the Boys They Know.* Madison: University of Wisconsin Press.
Flenniken, J. Jeffrey. 1984. The Past, Present, and Future of Flintknapping: An Anthropological Perspective. *Annual Review of Anthropology* 13: 187–203.
Fogelman, Gary. 1999. Too Good to Be True: The Woody Blackwell Clovis "Cache." *Indian Artifact Magazine* 18 (3): 8–9.
Foley, Douglas E. 1995. *The Heartland Chronicles.* Philadelphia: University of Pennsylvania Press.
Forrest, A. J. 1983. *Masters of Flint.* Lavenham, U.K.: Terrence Dalton Ltd.
Frake, Charles O. 1964. How to Ask for a Drink in Subanun. *American Anthropologist* 66 (6, part 2): 127–132.
Frank, Ted. 1991. Edward Simpson, Alias "Flint Jack." *Flint Knapper's Exchange* 1 (2): 13–17.
Frederick, Terry. 1989a. Archaeology and Flintknapping in a Stormy California Winter. *Chips* 1 (1): 8–9.
———. 1989b. Ramblings from California. *Chips* 1 (3): 2.
"Free, Lance." 1994. Castile Knap-in. *Chips* 6 (4): 5.
Frison, George C. 1989. Experimental Use of Clovis Weaponry and Tools on African Elephants. *American Antiquity* 54 (4): 766–783.
Frison, George, and Bruce Bradley. 1999. *The Fenn Cache: Clovis Weapons and Tools.* Santa Fe: One Horse Land and Cattle Company.
Gero, Joan M. 1991. Genderlithics: Women's Roles in Stone Tool Production. In *Engendering Archaeology,* ed. Joan M. Gero and Margaret W. Conkey, pp. 163–193. Cambridge: Basil Blackwell Ltd.
Gill, David W. J., and Christopher Chippendale. 1993. Material and Intellectual Consequences of Esteem for Cycladic Figures. *American Journal of Archaeology* 97: 601–657.
Gluckman, Max. 1956. *Custom and Conflict in Africa.* Oxford: Blackwell.
Gmelch, George. 1971. Baseball Magic. *Transaction* 8 (8): 39–41, 54. Reprinted in *Anthropology for the Eighties,* ed. J. B. Cole, pp. 394–399. New York: Free Press.
Gmelch, George, and J. J. Weiner. 1998. *In the Ballpark: The Working Lives of Baseball People.* Washington, D.C.: Smithsonian Institution Press.

Goffman, Erving. 1959. *The Presentation of Self in Everyday Life*. Garden City, N.Y.: Doubleday.

———. 1971. *Relations in Public: Microstudies of the Public Order*. New York: Harper and Row.

Gonsior, Leroy. 1992. Lithic Materials of Southern Minnesota. *Platform* 4 (1): 5–7; 4 (2): 4–6; 4 (3): 5–6; 4 (4): 4–5.

Goodenough, Ward G. 1957. Cultural Anthropology and Linguistics. In *Report of the Seventh Annual Round Table Meeting on Linguistics and Language Study*, ed. Paul L. Garvin. *Georgetown University Monograph Series on Language and Linguistics* 9: 167–173.

———. 1961. Comment on Cultural Evolution. *Daedalus* 90: 521–528.

Gorman, Alice. 1995. Gender, Labour, and Resources: The Female Knappers of the Andaman Islands. In *Gendered Archaeology: The Second Australian Women in Archaeology Conference*, ed. Jane Balme and Wendy Beck, pp. 87–91. Canberra: Australian National University.

Gramly, Richard Michael. 1993. *The Richey Clovis Cache: Earliest Americans along the Columbia River*. Buffalo, N.Y.: Persimmon Press.

Grayson, Donald K., and David J. Meltzer. 2003. A Requiem for North American Overkill. *Journal of Archaeological Science* 30: 585–593.

Hamilton, Henry W. 1952. The Spiro Mound. *Missouri Archaeologist* 14: 1–276.

Harris, Harry. 1926. A Modern Artist in Flints. *Art and Archaeology* 21 (2): 68–70.

Harrison, Jack. 1995. Untitled Letter. *Bulletin of Primitive Technology* 9: 9.

Harwood, Joyce Ann. 2001. The Gray Ghosts of Gustine. *Bulletin of Primitive Technology* 21: 12–16.

Harwood, Ray. 1988a. *Orcutt, King of the Flintknappers*. Pamphlet privately distributed by author.

———. 1988b. Using the Ishi Stick. *20th Century Lithics* 1: 84–91.

———. 1989. The 1989 California Rendezvous. *Chips* 1 (3): 2.

———. 1991. The History of 20th Century Flintknapping in North America. *Chips* 3 (4): 4–5.

———. 1999. *History of Modern Flintknapping*. Distributed by author.

———. 2001a. Points of Light, Dreams of Glass: An Introduction into Vitrum Technology. *Bulletin of Primitive Technology* 21: 24–36.

———. 2001b. The Search for Ted Orcutt: Eugene's Journey. *Indian Artifact Magazine* 20 (1): 6–7, 72–74.

Haynes, C. Vance, and George A. Agogino. 1986. *Geochronology of Sandia Cave*. Smithsonian Contributions to Anthropology No. 32. Washington, D.C.

Heeringa, Irene, and Willard L. Elsing. 1960. *Treasure from a Pre-Historic Age: Part One, the Eccentrics of Oklahoma*. Joplin, Mo.: Oak Crest Museum.

Hester, Thomas R. 1999. Observations on Fraudulent Artifacts in the Borderlands. *La Tierra* 26 (3): 1–6.

Hibben, Frank C. 1941. *Evidence of Early Occupation in Sandia Cave, New Mexico, and Other Sites in the Sandia-Manzano Region*. Smithsonian Miscellaneous Collections 99 (23).

———. 1946. *The Lost Americans*. New York: Thomas Y. Crowell Company.

Hibben, Frank C., and Jacqueline Nichols. 1978. Comment on Point #3: Fluted Sandia. *Flintknappers' Exchange* 1 (3): 29–35.

Higgins, J. P. 1994. Letters: From the Puget Sound Knappers. *Chips* 6 (1): 1.

Hodder, Ian. 1982. *Symbols in Action: Ethnoarchaeological Studies of Material Culture*. Cambridge: Cambridge University Press.

Hoffman, Michael Allen. 1979. *Egypt before the Pharaohs: The Prehistoric Foundations of Egyptian Civilization*. New York: Dorset Press.

———. 1987. Late Gerzean Ripple Flaked Knife. Cast EG-2. *Lithic Casting Lab Catalogue No. 2*. Troy, Ill.: Lithic Casting Lab.

Holland, John D. 1989. Paleo Conference in Maine. *Chips* 1 (3): 3.

———. 1992. Burlington Chert. *Chips* 4 (3): 3–4.

Holmes, William Henry. 1891. Manufacture of Stone Arrow-points. *American Anthropologist* o.s. 4: 49–58.

———. 1919. *Handbook of Aboriginal American Antiquities. Part 1: Introductory and the Lithic Industries*. Bureau of American Ethnology Bulletin 60. Washington, D.C.: Government Printing Office.

Holtorf, Cornelius, and Tim Schadla-Hall. 1999. Age as Artefact: On Archaeological Authenticity. *European Journal of Archaeology* 2 (2): 229–247.

Horwitz, Tony. 1998. *Confederates in the Attic: Dispatches from the Unfinished Civil War*. New York: Pantheon Books.

Hothem, Lar. 1992. *Fake Chipped Artifacts: Some Considerations.* Lancaster, Ohio: Hothem House.

Howard, Calvin. 1988. Notes on Sandia Points. *Plains Anthropologist* 33 (122): 535–537.

———. 1994. Natural Indicators of Lithic Artifact Authenticity. *North American Archaeologist* 15 (4): 321–330.

———. 2001. Authentication Analysis of the Angus Nebraska Fluted Point. *Plains Anthropologist* 46 (177): 323–325.

Hun Ahau Gallery. 1996. *Catalog: Fine Mesoamerican Art.* Sun Valley, Idaho: Hun Ahau Gallery.

Iannone, Gyles John. 1992. Ancient Maya Eccentric Lithics: A Contextual Analysis. Master's thesis, Trent University, Peterborough, Ontario.

Iler, Jim. 1996. Oklahoma's Buried Maya Treasure. *Ancient American* 13: 3–6.

Imel, Ivan. 1989a. Folsom Fluting: An Overview of the Techniques Used. *Chips* 1 (4): 4–10.

———. 1989b. Making a Paleo Point Type Set. *Chips* 1 (3): 4–5.

Ives, David. 1984. The Crescent Hills Prehistoric Quarrying Area: More than Just Rocks. In *Prehistoric Chert Exploitation: Studies from the Midcontinent,* ed. B. M. Butler and E. E. May, pp. 187–196. Center for Archaeological Investigations, Occasional Paper 2. Carbondale: Southern Illinois University.

Jarvenpa, Robert, and Hetty Jo Brumbach. 1995. Ethnoarchaeology and Gender: Chipewyan Women as Hunters. *Research in Economic Anthropology* 16: 39–82.

Jelinek, Arthur. 1965. Lithic Technology Conference, Les Eyzies, France. *American Antiquity* 31 (2): 277–278.

———. 1982. Obituary: François Bordes, 1919–1981. *American Antiquity* 47 (4): 785–792.

Jenks, Albert Ernest. 1900. A Remarkable Counterfeiter. *American Anthropologist* 2: 292–296.

Johnson, Harmer. 1998. Antiquities. *Prehistoric American* 32 (3): 21.

Johnson, Lucy Lewis. 1978. A History of Flint-Knapping Experimentation, 1838–1976. *Current Anthropology* 19 (2): 337–372.

Johnson, M. 1978. Problems of a Journeyman Flintknapper. *Flintknappers' Exchange* 1 (1): 8–9.

Jones, Mark. 1990. *Fake? The Art of Deception.* London: Trustees of the British Museum.

Justice, Noel. 1987. *Stone Age Spear and Arrow Points of the Midcontinental and Eastern United States.* Bloomington: Indiana University Press.

Kamp, K., and J. Whittaker. 1999. *Surviving Adversity: The Sinagua of Lizard Man Village.* University of Utah Anthropological Papers Number 120. Salt Lake City: University of Utah Press.

Katz, Pearl. 1999. *The Scalpel's Edge: The Culture of Surgeons.* Boston: Allyn and Bacon.

Kehoe, Alice B. 1991. The Weaver's Wraith. In *The Archaeology of Gender,* ed. Dale Walde and Noreen D. Willows, pp. 430–435. Calgary, Alberta: University of Calgary Archaeological Association.

Kelley, Gary. 1990. 1990s, The Stone Knife Age. *Blade Magazine* 1990 (September–October): 44–47, 60.

Kelterborn, Peter. 1984. Towards Replicating Egyptian Predynastic Flint Knives. *Journal of Archaeological Science* 11: 433–453.

Klein, Dana. 1994. Great Chert Chase of 1993. *Chips* 6 (1): 6.

Knudson, Ruthann. 1982. Obituary: Don E. Crabtree, 1912–1980. *American Antiquity* 47 (2): 336–343.

Kroeber, Theodora. 1961. *Ishi in Two Worlds.* Berkeley and Los Angeles: University of California Press.

Lang, Bud. 1990. Flintknapping. *Knives Illustrated,* Fall 1990, pp. 16–19, 84.

Lave, Jean, and Etienne Wenger. 1991. *Situated Learning: Legitimate Peripheral Participation.* Cambridge: Cambridge University Press.

Lepper, Bradley T., and David J. Meltzer. 1991. Late Pleistocene Human Occupation of the Eastern United States. In *Clovis: Origins and Adaptations,* ed. R. Bonnichsen and K. Turnmire, pp. 175–184. Corvallis, Ore.: Center for the Study of the First Americans.

Lesko, Lawrence M. 1989. A Reexamination of Northern Arizona Obsidians. *Kiva* 54 (4): 385–400.

Lubbock, Sir John. 1890. *Pre-Historic Times: As Illustrated by Ancient Remains and the Manners and Customs of Modern Savages, Fifth Edition.* New York: D. Appleton and Company. Reprinted, Freeport, N.Y.: Books for Libraries Press, 1971.

Luchterhand, Kubet. 1970. Early Archaic Projectile Points and Hunting Patterns in the Lower Illinois Valley. *Illinois State Museum Report of Investigations* No. 19.

Luedtke, Barbara. 1992. *An Archaeologist's Guide to Chert and Flint.* Los Angeles: UCLA Institute of Archaeology.

MacDowell, Marsha, and C. Kurt Dewhurst. 1980. Expanding Frontiers: The Michigan Folk Art Project. In *Perspectives on American Folk Art*, ed. Ian M. G. Quimby and Scott T. Swank, pp. 54–78. New York: W. W. Norton and Company.

Magruder, Art. 2001. Minnesota Flint Knapper's Guild Pine City Knap-in, June 29 and 30, 2001. *Chips* 13 (4): 5–6.

Malinowski, Bronislaw. 1925. Rational Mastery by Man of His Surroundings. In *Science, Religion, and Reality*, ed. J. Needham. London: Sheldon Press; New York: Macmillan. Reprinted in *Anthropology for the Eighties*, ed. Johnnetta B. Cole, pp. 386–393. New York: Free Press, 1982.

Marsden, Barry M. 1983. *Pioneers of Prehistory: Leaders and Landmarks in English Archaeology (1500–1900)*. Ormskirk, U.K.: G. W. and A. Hesketh.

Martin, Dane. 1995. News from the Northwest Coast. *Chips* 7 (3): 3.

———. 1996. The Three R's. *Chips* 8 (3): 4.

———. 1998. Hunte'n Flint with D. C. or How I Broke My Body. *Chips* 10 (1): 18–21.

———. 2002. Stuff. *Chips* 14 (3): 20–23.

Martin, Paul S., and Richard G. Klein, eds. 1984. *Quaternary Extinctions: A Prehistoric Revolution*. Tucson: University of Arizona Press.

Maus, James. 1997. The Blacklight, a Useful Collector's Tool. *Prehistoric American* 31 (3): 7–8.

McCarl, Robert. 1985. *The District of Columbia Fire Fighters' Project: A Case Study in Occupational Folklife*. Washington, D.C.: Smithsonian Institution Press.

McIlrath, Sharon. 1984. Obsidian Blades: Tomorrow's Surgical Tools? *American Medical News*, November 2, pp. 29–30.

Meadows, Richard Keith. 2001. Crafting K'awil: A Comparative Analysis of Maya Symbolic Flaked Stone Assemblages from Three Sites in Northern Belize. Ph.D. dissertation, University of Texas, Austin.

Merlie, Gary. 1989a. More on Marking Points. *Chips* 1 (3): 1.

———. 1989b. Pressure Flaker. *Chips* 1 (4): 12.

Mewhinney, H. 1957. *A Manual for Neanderthals*. Austin: University of Texas Press.

Meyers, J. Thomas. 1970. *Chert Resources of the Lower Illinois Valley*. Illinois State Museum Reports of Investigations 18. Springfield: Illinois State Museum.

Miller, Frank. 1997. Facts on Fakes: Archaic Bevels. *Indian Artifact Magazine* 16 (2): 58.

Mondino, John. 1993. A Few Comments on Material Resources. *Chips* 5 (3): 3–4.

Mooney, James. 1896. The Ghost-dance Religion and the Sioux Outbreak of 1890. *14th Annual Report of the Bureau of American Ethnology for the Years 1892–1893,* pp. 641–1136. Washington, D.C.: Government Printing Office. Reprinted, Chicago: University of Chicago Press, 1965.

Moore, H. R. 1989a. Knappin Nomads: High, Wide, and Windy. *Chips* 1 (4): 3.

———. 1989b. Modern Tools for an Ancient Craft. *Chips* 1 (3): 6–7.

———. 1989c. Point to Point Contact: Here and There. *Chips* 1 (4): 11.

Moore, Mark. 1993. Replicating Elko Points. *Chips* 5 (2): 8–10.

Morrow, Toby. 1984. *Iowa Projectile Points.* Iowa City: University of Iowa Press.

Muensterberger, Werner. 1994. *Collecting, an Unruly Passion: Psychological Perspectives.* Princeton, N.J.: Princeton University Press.

Nelson, Larry Lee. 1968. The Effect of Annealing on the Properties of Edwards Plateau Flint. Master's thesis, University of Denver.

———. 2002. The Richard Warren I Knew. *Chips* 14 (4): 16–18.

Nelson, Nels C. 1916. Flint Working by Ishi. In *William Henry Holmes Anniversary Volume,* ed. F. W. Hodge, pp. 397–402. Washington, D.C.: J. W. Bryan Press. Reprinted, New York: AMS Press, 1976.

Newbert, David DeTar. 1998. Selling Counterfeits Is a Crime. *Prehistoric American* 32 (3): 25.

Nichols, Jacqueline. 1978a. Editorial. *Flintknappers' Exchange* 1 (2): 3–4.

———. 1978b. Editorial. *Flintknappers' Exchange* 1 (3): 3.

———. 1978c. A Staging Problem. *Flintknappers' Exchange* 1 (2): 25–26.

———. 1979. Alternate Knap-in Terms. *Flintknappers' Exchange* 2 (1): 35.

Olausson, Deborah. 1998. Different Strokes for Different Folks: Possible Reasons for Variation in Quality of Knapping. *Lithic Technology* 23 (2): 90–115.

Ollinger, Jamie. 1993. Ooga-Booga News. *Chips* 5 (2): 7.

Orr, Kenneth G. 1946. The Archaeological Situation at Spiro, Oklahoma: A Preliminary Report. *American Antiquity* 11 (4): 228–256.

Overstreet, Robert M. 1995. *The Overstreet Indian Arrowheads Identification and Price Guide.* 4th ed. New York: Avon Books.

Overstreet, Robert M., and Howard Peake. 1991. *The Official Overstreet Identification and Price Guide to Indian Arrowheads.* 2d ed. New York: House of Collectibles/Random House.

Patten, Robert J. 1978a. Cushioned Percussion. *Flintknappers' Exchange* 1 (1): 5–6.

———. 1978b. The Denver Series, Point #13: Eden. *Flintknappers' Exchange* 1 (1): 18–20.

———. 1978c. The Denver Series, Point #3: Fluted Sandia. *Flintknappers' Exchange* 1 (2): 28–29.

———. 1978d. "Push" vs. "Pull" Flaking. *Lithic Technology* 7 (1): 3–4.

———. 1979. The Denver Series, #5: Folsom Point from Folsom, New Mexico. *Flintknappers' Exchange* 2 (3): 16.

———. 1980. Folsom Staging: A Speculative Approach. *Flintknappers' Exchange* 3 (2): 7–10.

———. 1999. *Old Tools—New Eyes: A Primal Primer of Flintknapping.* Denver: Stone Dagger Publications.

Patterson, L. W. 1975. Lithic Wear Patterns in Deer Butchering. *Texas Archaeology* 19 (2): 10–11.

———. 1978a. Comments for Novice Knappers. *Flintknappers' Exchange* 1 (2): 10–12.

———. 1978b. Practical Heat Treating of Flint. *Flintknappers' Exchange* 1 (3): 7–8.

———. 1979a. Quantitative Characteristics of Debitage from Heat Treated Chert. *Plains Anthropologist* 24 (85): 255–259.

———. 1979b. A Texas Knap-in. *Flintknappers' Exchange* 3 (2): 2.

———. 1980. The Fineness Syndrome. *Flintknappers' Exchange* 3 (2): 11.

———. 1981. Fracture Force Changes from Heat Treating and Edge Grinding. *Flintknappers' Exchange* 4 (3): 6–9.

———. 1982. Replication and Classification of Large Size Lithic Debitage. *Lithic Technology* 11 (3): 50–58.

———. 1988. J. B. Sollberger, Archaeologist and Flintknapper. *Bulletin of the Texas Archaeological Society* 59: 19–21.

———. 1990. Characteristics of Bifacial Reduction Flake-Size Distribution. *American Antiquity* 55 (3): 550–558.

Patterson, L. W., and J. B. Sollberger. 1978. Replication and Classification of Small Size Lithic Debitage. *Plains Anthropologist* 23 (40): 103–112.

Perino, Gregory. 1985. *Selected Preforms, Points, and Knives of the North American Indians.* Idabel, Okla.: Points and Barbs Press.

———. 1996. Points and Barbs. *Central States Archaeological Journal* 43 (4): 211.

Peters, Gordon. 1994. What Were They Doing? *Platform* 6 (1): 2–3; 6 (2): 5–6; 6 (3): 2–3.

Phillips, Phillip, and James A. Brown. 1984. *Pre-Columbian Shell Engravings from the Craig Mound at Spiro, Oklahoma.* Cambridge, Mass.: Peabody Museum Press.

Pitblado, Bonnie L. 2003. *Late Paleoindian Occupation of the Southern Rocky Mountains: Early Holocene Projectile Points and Land Use in the High Country.* Boulder: University Press of Colorado.

Pitt-Rivers, Augustus Henry Lane Fox. 1906. *The Evolution of Culture and Other Essays.* Oxford: Clarendon Press.

Pond, Alonzo W. 1930. Primitive Methods of Working Stone: Based on Experiments of Halvor L. Skavlem. *Logan Museum Bulletin* 2 (1): 1–143.

Potter, Mike. 1993. Buying Material. *Chips* 5 (2): 10–11.

Preston, Douglas. 1995. The Mystery of Sandia Cave. *New Yorker* 71 (16): 66–83.

———. 1997. The Lost Man. *New Yorker* 73 (16): 70–81.

———. 1998. Cannibals of the Canyon. *New Yorker* 74 (37): 76–89.

———. 1999. Woody's Dream. *New Yorker* 75 (34): 80–87.

Preston, Douglas, and Lincoln Child. 1999. *Thunderhead.* New York: Warner Books.

Rathje, William, and Cullen Murphy. 2001. *Rubbish! The Archaeology of Garbage.* Tucson: University of Arizona Press.

Ray, Jack H. 1985. An Overview of Chipped Stone Resources in Southern Missouri. In *Lithic Resources Procurement: Proceedings from the Second Conference on Prehistoric Chert Exploitation,* ed. S. Vehik, pp. 225–250. Center for Archaeological Investigations, Occasional Paper 4. Carbondale: Southern Illinois University.

Reeder, A. 1936. Delicate Flint Implements. *Hobbies* 41 (1): 102.

———. 1937a. Fancy Spears May Be Fakes. *Hobbies* 41 (12): 101.

———. 1937b. Oklahoma Notes. *Hobbies* 41 (11): 99.

Reese, Don. 1957. *Flint Chipping, Indian and Modern Style.* Carlsbad, N.Mex.: Beedle Publishing Co.

Regan, Jim. 1991. Greetings. *Flint Knapper's Exchange* 1 (5): 11–12.

Rick, John V. 1978. *Heat Altered Cherts of the Lower Illinois Valley.* Northwestern Archaeological Program, Prehistoric Records Number 2. Evanston, Ill.: Northwestern University.

Rieth, Adolf. 1970. *Archaeological Fakes.* New York: Praeger Publishers.

Roberts, Frank H. H. 1936. *A Folsom Complex: Preliminary Report on Investigations at the Lindenmeier Site in Northern Colorado.* Smithsonian Miscellaneous Collections 94 (4).

———. 1937. *Additional Information on the Folsom Complex: Report on the Second Season's Investigations at the Lindenmeier Site in Northern Colorado.* Smithsonian Miscellaneous Collections 95 (10).

Roberts, Robert B. 1988. *Encyclopedia of Historic Forts: The Military, Pioneer, and Trading Forts of the United States.* New York: Macmillan Publishing Company.

Rolingson, Martha Ann. 1964. Paleo-Indian Culture in Kentucky: A Study Based on Projectile Points. *University of Kentucky Studies in Anthropology* No. 2.

Romano, Anthony. 1993. Lithic "Clues." *Platform* 5 (3): 3–4.

———. 1994. Gunflint Silica. *Platform* 6 (1): 5–7; 6 (2): 3–4; 6 (3): 5–6.

Rubinstein, Ruth P. 1995. *Dress Codes: Meanings and Messages in American Culture.* Boulder, Colo.: Westview Press.

Russell, Virgil Y. 1962. *Indian Artifacts.* Boulder, Colo.: Johnson Publishing Company.

Sahlins, Marshall. 1972. *Stone Age Economics.* New York: Aldine.

Sassaman, Kenneth E. 1992. Lithic Technology and the Hunter-Gatherer Sexual Division of Labor. *North American Archaeologist* 13 (3): 249–262. Reprinted in *Reader in Gender Archaeology,* ed. Kelley Hays-Gilpin and David S. Whitley, pp. 159–171. New York: Routledge, 1998.

Scheiber, Larry B. 1989a. Great Moments in History: An Ode to Dirty-Hairy. *Chips* 1 (3): 12.

———. 1989b. Newsletter, or Psalm to the Lost Knap-in. *Chips* 1 (4): 13.

———. 1989c. Tips on Deep Notching of Projectile Points. *Chips* 1 (2): 6–7.

———. 1992a. Notes from the Ear-o'Corn Ooga Booga Society. *Chips* 4 (1): 2.

———. 1992b. The Other Side of the Story. *Flint Knapper's Exchange* 2 (2): 9–11.

Selbert, Pamela. 1996. Prehistoric Connection. *Lapidary Journal* 50 (6): 57–58, 60, 62, 64.

Shackleford, Steve. 1987. Blades for the Present from Methods of the Past. *Blade Magazine,* September–October, pp. 20–21, 50, 54–55.

Shackley, M. Steven. 2001. The Stone Tool Technology of Ishi and the Yana of North Central California: Inferences for Hunter-Gatherer Cultural Identity in Historic California. *American Anthropologist* 102 (4): 693–712.

Sheward, Chris. 1989. Replicating the Danish Dagger Type I-C. *Chips* 1 (2): 8–9.

Shewey, Charlie, and D. C. Waldorf. 1998. An Interview with Charlie Shewey. *Chips* 10 (3): 12–20.

Sikes, Gini. 1997. *Eight Ball Chicks: A Year in the Violent World of Girl Gangs.* New York: Doubleday.

Skertchly, Sydney B. J. 1879. *On the Manufacture of Gun-flints, the Methods of Excavating for Flint, the Age of Paleolithic Man, and the Connection between Neolithic Art and the Gun-flint Trade.* Memoirs of the Geological Survey of England and Wales. London: Geological Survey.

Skinner, Craig E., and Kim J. Tremaine. 1993. *Obsidian: An Interdisciplinary Bibliography.* International Association for Obsidian Studies Occasional Paper 1.

Sollberger, J. B. 1968. A Partial Report on Research Work Concerning Lithic Typology and Technology. *Bulletin of the Texas Archaeological Society* 39: 95–109.

———. 1978a. Comment on Point #13 Eden. *Flintknappers' Exchange* 1 (2): 30.

———. 1978b. Lever Flaking as a Credible Alternative to Hand-held Pressure Flaking. *Flintknappers' Exchange* 1 (1): 6–7.

———. 1978c. Percussion with a Flake? *Flintknappers' Exchange* 1 (2): 26–27.

———. 1978d. Save Those Broken Bifaces. *Flintknappers' Exchange* 1 (2): 6–7.

———. 1979a. Solly's Tip Sheet: Hand Anvils. *Flintknappers' Exchange* 2 (1): 9–10.

———. 1979b. Untitled letter. *Flintknappers' Exchange* 2 (2): 5.

———. 1985. A Technique for Folsom Fluting. *Lithic Technology* 14 (1): 41–50.

———. 1986. Lithic Fracture Analysis: A Better Way. *Lithic Technology* 15 (3): 101–105.

Sollberger, J. B., and Errett Callahan. 1978. Craftsman: J. B. Sollberger. *Flintknappers' Exchange* 1 (1): 12–17.

Sollberger, J. B., and L. W. Patterson. 1976. Prismatic Blade Replication. *American Antiquity* 41 (4): 518–531.

Spear, Chas. 1994. Planning and Setting Up a Knap-in. *Chips* 5 (4): 3.

Spradley, James P. 1970. *You Owe Yourself a Drunk: An Ethnography of Urban Nomads*. Boston: Little, Brown. Reprinted, Prospect Heights, Ill.: Waveland Press, 2000.

Stafford, Michael. 1998. In Search of Hindsgavl: Experiments in the Production of Neolithic Danish Flint Daggers. *Antiquity* 72 (276): 338–349.

Stanford, Dennis. 1978. "Comment" on Point #13, Eden. *Flintknappers' Exchange* 1 (1): 20–22.

Stewart, Charles D. 1923. The Arrow-Maker. *Atlantic Monthly* 131 (June): 799–810.

Stuart, George E. 1989. Copan: City of Kings and Commoners. *National Geographic* 176 (4): 488–505.

Tankersley, Kenneth B. 1989. A Close Look at the Big Picture: Eastern Paleoindian Lithic Resource Procurement in the Midwestern United States. In *Eastern Paleoindian Lithic Resource Use*, ed. C. J. Ellis and J. C. Lothrop, pp. 259–292. Boulder, Colo.: Westview Press.

———. 2002. *In Search of Ice Age Americans*. Salt Lake City: Gibbs Smith, Publisher.

Taylor, Jeb. 2000a. Letter Addressed to the *New Yorker*, Attention David Carey. *Indian Artifact Magazine* 19 (1): 4, 80–81.

———. 2000b. More on the Blackwell Affair. *Indian Artifact Magazine* 19 (2): 61–62.

Thomas, David Hurst. 1986. Contemporary Hunter-Gatherer Archaeology in America. In *American Archaeology, Past and Future: A Celebration of the Society for American Archaeology, 1935–1985*, ed. D. J. Meltzer, D. D. Fowler, and J. A. Sabloff, pp. 237–276. Washington, D.C.: Smithsonian Institution Press.

Thoreau, Henry David. 1906. *The Writings of Henry David Thoreau*, ed. Bradford Torrey. Vol. 12, *Journals March 2, 1859–November 30,*

1859. Boston and New York: Houghton Mifflin Company.

Titmus, Gene L. 1980. Large Obsidian Boulder Reduction. *Flintknappers' Exchange* 3 (3): 21–22.

———. 1985. Some Aspects of Stone Tool Notching. In *Stone Tool Analysis: Essays in Honor of Don E. Crabtree*, ed. M. Plew, J. Woods, and M. Pavesic, pp. 243–264. Albuquerque: University of New Mexico Press.

Titmus, Gene, and Errett Callahan. 1980. Craftsman: Gene Titmus. *Flintknappers' Exchange* 3 (1): 19–25.

Titmus, Gene L., and James C. Woods. 1986. An Experimental Study of Projectile Point Fracture Patterns. *Journal of California and Great Basin Anthropology* 8 (1): 37–49.

Tolstoy, Leo. 1953. *What Is Art? and Essay on Art.* Translated by Aylmer Maude. London: Oxford University Press.

Trotta, Paul. 1996. Some Thoughts on Conservation. *Chips* 8 (4): 8–9.

Trout, Matt. 1997. The Rhinehart-McGee Flaking Jig. *Chips* 9 (2): 3–5.

Tubb, Kathryn W., ed. 1995. *Antiquities Trade or Betrayed: Legal, Ethical, and Conservation Issues.* London: Archetype Publications Ltd.

Tunnell, Curtis. 1979. Don't Be a Knapping Vandal. *Lithic Technology* 8 (1). Also reprinted as untitled letter, *Flintknappers' Exchange* 2 (2): 2 (1979), and in *Bulletin of Primitive Technology* 5: 71 (1993).

Turner, Victor. 1969. *The Ritual Process: Structure and Anti-Structure.* Chicago: Aldine Publishing Co.

United States Census Bureau. 1995. *Statistical Abstract of the United States.* Washington, D.C.: United States Census Bureau.

Van Arsdale, Scott. 1995. Letter. *Chips* 7 (2): 1.

———. 2000. 10th Annual Stone Tool Craftsman's Show. *Chips* 12 (1): 12–15.

Van Gennep, Arnold. 1960. *The Rites of Passage.* Translated by Monika B. Vizedom and Gabrielle L. Caffee. London: Routledge and Kegan Paul.

Waldorf, D. C. 1980. Untitled Letter. *Flintknappers' Exchange* 3 (2): 1–2.

———. 1989a. Dr. Flint: Comments on Notching. *Chips* 1 (3): 8–10.

———. 1989b. Editorial. *Chips* 1 (1): 1.

———. 1989c. An Interview with Jim Spears. *Chips* 1 (1): 3–5.

———. 1989d. Marking Your Points. *Chips* 1 (2): 3.

---. 1990. From the President. *Chips* 2 (1): 2–6.
---. 1991. Finding the Pony. *Chips* 3 (1): 2–4.
---. 1993. *The Art of Flint Knapping.* 4th ed. Branson, Mo.: Mound Builder Books.
---. 1994a. Destination Denmark. *Chips* 6 (1): 3–5.
---. 1994b. Some Notes on Danish Flint. *Chips* 6 (1): 10.
---. 1994c. Whatever Happened to Flint Knappers Guild International? *Chips* 6 (2): 1–2.
---. 1995a. Machine Pressure Flaking (or How to Win a Tasmanian Virgin). *Chips* 7 (1): 6–7.
---. 1995b. Who's Da Judge?: Editorial. *Chips* 7 (1): 4–6.
---. 1996. Of Ballast and Washing Machines. *Chips* 8 (1): 2–18.
---. 1997. Grey Ghosts and Old Timers. *Chips* 9 (1): 9–11.
---. 1998. *Roasting Rocks: The Art and Science of Heat Treating—The Recipe Book.* Branson, Mo.: Mound Builder Books.
---. 2000. Clovis Points Then and Now. *Chips* 12 (4): 11–19.
Waldorf, Val. 1989a. The Flint Knapper's Back Seat. *Chips* 1 (1): 13.
---. 1989b. Knap-in News. *Chips* 1 (4): 10.
---. 1989c. Rocky Hollow Knap-in, 1989. *Chips* 1 (2): 10.
---. 1993. Other Knap-in News. *Chips* 5 (4): 3.
---. 1999. Flint Costs What?!! *Chips* 11 (4): 23–25.
Waldorf, Val, and D. C. Waldorf. 1987. *Story in Stone: Flint Types of the Central and Southern U.S.* Branson, Mo.: Mound Builder Books.

Warner, Ken. 1986. A Return to a Sharper Time. In *Knives '86*, ed. K. Warner, pp. 32–35. Northbrook, Ill.: DBI Books Inc.
Warren, Richard. 1978. Untitled letter. *Flintknappers' Exchange* 1 (3): 4.
Watts, Steve. 1991. The Society of Primitive Technology Organized. *Bulletin of Primitive Technology* 1: 7.
Wenger, Etienne. 1998. *Communities of Practice: Learning, Meaning, and Identity.* Cambridge: Cambridge University Press.
Whittaker, John C. 1992. The Curse of the Runestone: Deathless Hoaxes. *Skeptical Inquirer* 17 (1) 57–63.
---. 1994. *Flintknapping: Making and Understanding Stone Tools.* Austin: University of Texas Press.
---. 1995. Silica on Celluloid: Some Current Flintknapping Videos. *Lithic Technology* 20 (2): 149–152.

———. 1996a. Primitive Technology Experiments: Further Comments. *Primitive Technology Newsletter* 2: 5–6.

———. 1996b. Reproducing a Bronze Age Dagger from the Thames: Statements and Questions. *London Archaeologist* 8 (2): 51–54.

———. 2001a. Knapping Building Flints in Norfolk. *Lithic Technology* 26 (1): 71–80.

———. 2001b. "The Oldest British Industry": Continuity and Obsolescence in a Flintknapper's Sample Set. *Antiquity* 75 (288): 382–390.

Whittaker, John C., and Matt Hedman. 1996. Fort Osage Knappers: Survey Results. *Chips* 8 (2): 5.

———. 1997. How Knappers Learn: Survey Results. *Chips* 9 (3): 10.

Whittaker, John C., and Anthony D. Romano. 1996. Some Prehistoric Copper Flaking Tools in Minnesota. *Wisconsin Archaeologist* 77 (1): 3–10.

Whittaker, John C., and Michael Stafford. 1999. Replicas, Fakes, and Art: The Twentieth Century Stone Age and Its Effects on Archaeology. *American Antiquity* 64 (2): 203–214. Reprinted 2000 in *Arkansas Archaeologist* 39: 19–30 (1998 issue).

Willey, Gordon R. 1972. *The Artifacts of Altar de Sacrificios.* Papers of the Peabody Museum of American Anthropology and Ethnology 64 (1). Cambridge, Mass.: Harvard University Press.

Willey, Gordon R., William R. Bullard, John B. Glass, and James C. Gifford. 1965. *Prehistoric Maya Settlements in the Belize Valley.* Papers of the Peabody Museum of American Anthropology and Ethnology 54. Cambridge, Mass.: Peabody Museum.

Wilmsen, Edwin, and Frank H. H. Roberts. 1978. *Lindenmeier, 1934–1974: Concluding Report on Investigations.* Smithsonian Contributions to Anthropology 24. Washington, D.C.: Smithsonian Institution Press.

Wilson, Thomas. 1888. Fraudulent Spear or Arrowheads of Curious Forms. *American Naturalist* 22: 554–555.

Winters, Howard D. 1984. The Significance of Chert Procurement and Exchange in the Middle Woodland Traditions of the Illinois Area. In *Prehistoric Chert Exploitation: Studies from the Midcontinent,* ed. B. M. Butler and E. E. May, pp. 3–22. Center for Archaeological Investigations, Occasional Paper 2. Carbondale: Southern Illinois University.

Witcher, Gerald. 1997. *Counterfeiting Antique Cutlery.* Brentwood, Tenn.: National Brokerage and Sales, Inc.

Woods, James C., and Gene L. Titmus. 1996. Stone on Stone: Perspectives on Maya Civilization from Lithic Studies. In *Eighth Palenque Round Table 1993,* ed. M. G. Robertson, pp. 479–489. San Francisco: Pre-columbian Art Research Institute.

Wormington, H. Marie. 1949. *Ancient Man in North America.* 3d ed. Denver: Denver Museum of Natural History.

Notes

3. From Fakes and Experiments to Knap-ins

1. Various spellings are used in the knapper literature, Brian, Bryan, and Bryon, and Rhinehart, Reinhardt, and Rinehart. Errett Callahan (2001b) says he has correspondence signed Bryon Rinehart.

2. Listed for Wyoming: Don Crabtree, Gene Titmus, Jeff Flenniken, Rod Reiner, Bob Patten, Errett Callahan, Larry Belitz; and for Texas: J. B. Sollberger, W. B. Carroll, L. W. Patterson, Cary Weber, Bob Vernon, Harry Shafer, Glen Goode, Phil Bandy.

4. The Knap-in: People and Organization

1. At the Spring 2003 knap-in, as this book was being edited, we learned that the knap-in would have to move. The park planned to build a new museum on the site, and some neighbors were eager to remove the evening noise of four knap-in nights a year. Bob Hunt was confident that a new location would be found.

2. Also, my mailing lists came from Bob Hunt in Missouri, and from Steve Behrnes, who had started his list with one from Ray Harwood, who was based in California.

7. Art, Craft, or Reproduction

1. *The Texas Cache,* later calling itself the newsletter of the Texas Amateur Archaeological Society, is unfortunately an example of the kind of collector literature that disgusts archaeologists. While claiming to promote amateur archaeology and document the past, it organizes and advertises "digs" where members pay a fee to pick and shovel through prehistoric sites and find arrowheads. Any useful information is

destroyed, and "documentation" consists of photographing the goodies. This is looting, not archaeology.

10. *Knappers, Collectors, Archaeologists*

1. An exception was Errett Callahan, who now thinks our estimate is "a fallacy" and "wishful thinking." (2001a). My feeling is rather that he finds the truth distasteful.

11. *Silicon and Society*

1. Silicon is the element, and is used in modern computer circuitry, famously lending its name to Silicon Valley. Silica, SiO_2, silicon dioxide, is the mineral forming quartz, flint, glass, and other knappable materials.

Index

Africa, 18
Alexander, Larry, 238
Altiere, Gene, 97–98, 143, 304
Anthropology, 9–10
Antiquities, 6, 8
Archaeological evidence, 31
Archaeologists: and fakes, 38, 57, 248, 255, 258, 271; point of view of, 12, 71, 140, 169–171; relations of, with collectors, 37, 44, 67–69, 262, 279–282; relations of, with knappers, 2, 58, 61, 67, 98, 260, 262, 280–281, 283, 299
Archaeology: experimental, 2, 27, 37, 59–61; and female knappers, 126; and knapping, 7–8
Archery, 85, 145, 149
Arles, Brad, 101
Art, knapping as, 6–8, 55–56, 76, 102, 137, 145, 169–180, 190, 200, 233, 237–241, 244, 247–248, 250, 257, 258, 268, 273, 285
Ash, Mike, 143, 169, 178, 180
Atkinson, Percy, 81–83

Atlatls, 96, 104, 105, 110, 149, 232, 295
Authenticators, 258, 275–279, 286
Authenticity, 270, 272
Axes, 82

Barbieri, Joseph, 58
Behrnes, Steve, 101, 184, 189, 206
Berg, Bob, 104, 105, 110, 191
Bibby, Art, 180
Biface, 18, 22, 28, 30, 117, 126, 158, 221
Blackwell, Woody, 31, 119, 123, 131, 177, 254–260, 273, 284–287
Blades, 24, 26
Boley, Jamie, 289, 290
Bollinger, Fred, 73
Bonnichsen, Rob, 63, 64
Bordes, François, 59, 60
Bostrom, Pete, 45, 211, 228
Boucher de Perthes, Jacques, 38–39
Bracken, Mark, 93, 195
Bradley, Bruce, 118, 170
Brownlow, Russ, 295
Bulb of Percussion, 19–20

Callahan, Errett, 30, 31, 51, 61, 62, 64, 65, 121, 123, 124, 150–151, 152, 177–178, 182, 240, 244, 245–246, 248, 264, 266
Calvert, Jerry, 30, 232, 232–234
Cannon, Dale, 32, 119, 156, 241–247
Cantrell, Alan, 26
Chert. *See* Stone
Chips, 14, 84
Cianfarani, John, 286
Collectors: of art knapping, 238, 259; ethos of, 269–272; and fakes, 57, 252–253, 255, 261, 277, 279–281; of knives, 240; relations of, with archaeologists, 37, 44, 67–69, 262, 279–282; relations of, with knappers, 36, 259, 263, 284–285
Communities, 5, 153, 298–299; of practice, 113–114, 123, 140, 145, 283
Competition, 6, 7, 106, 110, 124, 147, 149, 156, 168, 186–193
Computers. *See* Internet
Conchoidal fracture, 19
Contest, 186–193
Cook, Mike, 182
Core, 19, 20, 22
Crabtree, Don, 59–61, 63, 65, 118, 121, 262
Culture, 6, 113–114
Cushing, Frank H., 37

Daggers, Danish, 161, 245, 248, 266
Daniel, H. T., 46, 48
Debitage, 282, 283
Dempsey, Ken, 166
Devil's Hole. *See* Mid-West Flintknappers' Convention
Dillard, Tim, 195
Dixon, Jim, 73
Dothager, Mike, 70

Dowell, Carl, 73, 209
Dreisoerner, Don, 73, 164–165

Eccentrics, 40, 42–43, 45, 55, 178, 192, 239–240
Eklund, George, 28, 73, 76–77, 117, 165–166, 182, 225, 240, 249
Ellis, H. Holmes, 43, 59
Elsing, Willard, 45
Ericson, Lewis, 39
Esthetics, 6–7, 30, 140, 164, 170–173, 180–194, 200–202, 208, 245, 250
Ethics, 123, 152, 251, 273, 299
Ethnicity, 125
Ethos, 4, 6, 25, 123–125, 147, 151, 159, 163, 188, 298
Evergreen Lake Knap-in, 8, 99–101
Experiments, 2, 27, 30, 37, 59–61, 66

Fagan, Carl, 64
Fairview Heights Knap-in. *See* Mid-West Flintknappers' Convention
Fakes, 2, 8, 22, 38, 39, 43, 57, 69, 76, 136, 152, 233, 236, 248, 250–255, 257, 260–263, 271–282, 284–285
Fenn, Forrest, 254–255, 260, 269
Fenn cache, 254, 257
Ferrell, Craig, 108
Flake, 19, 45, 238, 249–255, 257–263, 267–269, 271–282, 283–287
Flake-over-grinding. *See* Lap knapping
Flenniken, Jeff, 61, 63
Flint. *See* Stone
"Flint Jack" (Edward Simpson), 39
Flintknapping, 1
Flint Ridge Knap-in, 8, 93, 107–111
Fluting, 24, 80, 97, 115, 134, 158, 162, 201
F.o.g. knapping. *See* Lap knapping
Fogelman, Gary, 189

Folsom, 47, 49
Fort Osage Knap-in, 3, 8, 13, 14, 15, 16, 29, 66, 84, 93, 113, 140, 149–150, 153, 180, 215, 226, 246, 249, 263, 289; food at, 75; people at, 72–86, 86–92, 92–94, 121, 125, 127, 128, 228–230, 236, 238, 241–247, 275–276
Frank, Ted, 24, 30, 195
Fry, Carl, 107
Fuller, Ron, 23, 93, 232, 234

Genesee Knap-in, 8, 101–107, 150, 154, 187, 189–191
Ghost Dance, 145
Goth, Gerry, 107
Gower, Jeff, 176, 195, 235–237
Graesch, Matt, 112, 115, 198
Grey Ghosts, 50–55, 250
Grybush, Dick, 184, 195, 208, 213
Grybush, Jim, 135, 208, 213
Gunflints, 19, 27, 38, 178

Hardy, Gary, 110
Harper, Hershel, 238
Harrison, J., 152
Harvey, Tom, 204
Harwood, Ray, 69, 150
Hayes, Virgil, 149
Heat treatment, 54, 204, 222, 232, 294
He Crow, Mike, 127, 204
Heritage, 6
Hewitt, Joe, 104, 156
Hierarchy, 6, 7, 124
Hobby, 2, 8, 143
Holmes, William H., 37
Hopkins, Angela, 127
Hopper, Jim, 53, 116–117, 160, 183, 211, 233, 242
Howard, Calvin, 286

Howe, Lear, 46
Humor, 70, 101, 104, 128–133, 155, 156, 212–215
Hunt, Bob, 15, 35, 72–75, 83, 115, 117, 123, 148, 156, 158, 164, 167, 187, 195, 205, 206, 209
Hurst, Cole, 179

Identity, 5, 11, 12, 114, 115, 117, 128–132, 136, 141, 302, 303
Imitation, 193–194
Individualism, 145, 301–302
Injuries, 207, 237
Internet, 9, 13, 119, 148, 265, 289–297; EBay, 268, 284–285; FlintFORUM, 291–292; Knappers Anonymous, 297; Knapper's Corner, 297; listservers, 290–291, 296; The Pack, 284–285; The Tarp, 13, 229, 285–286, 292–293, 299, 304; Web pages, 70, 289, 292, 296
Interviews, 9, 12
Ishi, 24, 35, 40, 41
Ishi stick, 24, 25, 29

Jay, Don, 204
Jenks, Albert, 39
Jines, Leroy, 92–94
Johnson, Carolyn, 238
Jones, Ingrid & Earnie, 84–85

Karrow, Terry, 30
Keiper, Bob, 242, 247
Kinsella, Larry, 73, 85, 94, 96, 131, 164
Klein, Dana, 102, 155, 191, 215
Klostermeier, Dave, 73, 94, 96
Knap-ins, 3, 8, 61, 64–65, 67, 70–71, 120; demography of, 86–92, 125, 127, 141; organization of, 75, 86, 96, 99–101, 104–106, 109–111,

Index

147–150, 157. *See also* Flint Ridge Knap-in; Fort Osage Knap-in; Genesee Knap-in; Mid-West Knap-in; Pine City Knap-in

Knappers: ages of, 88–89; backgrounds of, 90; commercial, 90, 98, 139, 152, 166, 176, 227–228, 235–237, 251–252, 265, 267, 278, 299; female, 88, 125–127: hobby, 90, 130, 139, 227, 251, 265; location of, 86–88; skill levels of, 89–90, 116–117

Knapping techniques, 17–33
Knives, Egyptian, 173, 174, 243
Knives, stone, 177, 178, 179, 240–247
Knudson, Ruthann, 62, 64
Kylberg, Don, 85, 123, 162, 189

Langford, Larry, 240
Lap knapping, 31, 32, 53, 160–161, 183, 184, 189
Learning, 7, 113, 118–125
Leesman, Glenn, 99, 132, 195
License plates, 132
Lindenbaum, Tim, 99
Long, Dan, 104
Looters, 262, 268, 272
Lowry, Ron, 246
Lubbock, Sir John, 39

Magic, 134–135, 270
Magruder, Art, 304
Manna, 167, 211, 270, 272, 279
Markets, 69; for points, 92, 227–248, 251, 267–269, 271–272; for stone, 79–80, 92, 215–222, 228–230, 234, 235, 246, 282
Martin, Dane, 84, 155
Martin, Mary, 84
Martis, Ron, 247

McCardie, Don, 73
McCormick, Marvin, 37, 47–49
McLean, Derek, 228, 286, 304
Megafauna, 294–295
Meister, Al, 73
Membership, 5
Metcalfe, Bill, 118
Mid-West Flintknappers' Convention (Fairview Heights Knap-in), 8, 94–97, 161
Miller, Jim, 240
Miller, Joe, 255, 256
Miller, Roy, 107
Minard, Dan, 107
Minnesota, 8
Mondino, John, 81, 180
Mondino, Sharon, 211
Moore, Mark, 194
Morton, Bill, 73
Motley, Roy, 73, 166, 167, 240, 263, 275–276, 278

Nelson, Larry, 50, 53–56
Newbert, David DeTar, 252
Newsletters, 13, 61–64, 120, 151, 229; *Bulletin of Primitive Technology*, 151, 152, 264; *Chips*, 66, 69–70, 83, 94, 148, 150, 155, 217–220, 264, 297; *Flintknappers Digest*, 70; *Flintknappers' Exchange*, 62–64, 66, 69, 70, 264; *The Flint Knapper's Exchange*, 70, 264; *Flintknapping Digest*, 69; *Indian Artifact Magazine*, 189; *Lithic Technology*, 61–62, 264; *The Platform*, 70, 97–98; *Texas Cache*, 192
New York Knap-in. *See* Genesee Knap-in
Nicholas, Jacqueline, 62, 65
Norgard, Stan, 233

Obsidian, 19, 207–208, 234, 294
Odell, George, 62, 264
Ollinger, Jamie, 156
Ooga-Booga, 153–156, 157, 229, 244
Orcutt, Ted, 40
Organizations, 7
Owens, Steve, 204, 260
Oyler, Jim, 294

Parker, Dick, 104
Participant, 10, 11
Patten, Bob, 61, 65, 93, 182, 247, 264
Patterson, L. W., 61
Paynes Prairie Knap-in, 93
Pedlow, Tom, 104
Pelfrey, George, 101, 211, 284
Percussion, hard hammer, 21, 22
Percussion, indirect, 21, 22, 24
Percussion, soft hammer, 21, 22
Performance, 17, 114–117, 128–129, 142, 158–163
Perino, Gregory, 124, 276, 286
Pfaltzgraff, Jim, 294
Pigg Farm Knap-in, 93
Pine City Knap-in, 8, 97–99, 241, 304–306
Plankers, Dave, 78, 304–305
Platforms, 19
Points: Adena, 196; Archaic, 142, 180, 192, 195, 196, 268, 280; Cahokia, 182; Calf Creek, 196; Clovis, 25, 131, 170, 195, 197, 198, 200, 201, 209, 253, 255, 259–260, 268, 269, 272, 282, 287, 294; Dalton, 126, 176, 196, 197, 209; Dovetails, 196; Eden, 196, 199; Elko, 194; Etley, 196; Fluted, 47–48, 57, 176, 189, 192, 195; Folsom, 25, 162, 195, 201; Hardin, 181, 196; Mexican, 171, 172, 185, 231; Scottsbluff, 196,
197–199; Snyder, 196; Thebes, 126, 190, 196; Turkey Tail, 180, 181, 190, 196; Woodland, 142
Politics, 125, 128, 143
Pond, Alonzo, 58
Pressure flaking, 23, 24, 26, 29, 32
Projectile point, 18, 126
Provenance, 280
Punches, 22

Quartzite, Arizona, 94, 230–235
Questionnaire. *See* Survey

Rast, Tim, 289, 297
Ratzat, Craig, 104, 109, 119, 211, 216, 220, 233, 247
Redfearn, Jim, 118, 201
Regan, Jim, 30, 77–78, 97–98, 115, 129, 143, 215, 304–305
Regan, Pat, 78, 86
Replicas, 2, 169, 180, 181, 184, 193–194, 200–201, 236, 238, 250–251, 253, 262, 269, 303
Reuter, Marty, 235–237
Reynolds, John, 166
Richter, Tom, 30, 220
Rinehart, Bryon, 50–53
Rite of passage, 153
Ritual, 134, 153–154, 163–168
Robinson, Robbie, 155, 190
Rock. *See* Stone
Romano, Tony, 31, 97–98, 129, 143, 158, 304

Sanchez, Richard, 289, 290–293, 296, 302, 304
Sandia Cave, 281
Scheiber, Larry, 154, 155, 156
Schilkofski, Paul, 99, 212
Schismogenesis, 299

Schorn, Dave, 195, 240, 248
Sculpture, 56, 177, 178, 209
Shelden, Billy Joe, 247
Shewey, Charlie, 28, 34–37, 40, 45, 47, 54, 68, 73, 76, 81, 83, 197–198, 211, 238, 251–252, 256, 258, 271, 272
Shows, 17
Silsby, Scott, 161, 179
Simpson, Edward ("Flint Jack"), 39
Size of points, 181–182, 193, 194, 198
Skavlem, Halvor, 58–59
Sociogenesis, 298
Sollberger, J. B., 27, 51, 61, 63, 64, 121, 123, 131, 255
Spears, Jim, 30, 81, 159, 162–163, 182, 183, 198, 235–236, 266
Spiro, 44–46, 68
Stafford, Mike, 24, 123, 161, 163, 166, 191, 216, 242, 244, 247, 248, 253
Stapleton, Gene, 30, 79–81, 123, 197–199, 227
Status, 7, 147, 156–157, 225
Stevens, Frank, 163, 228–230, 297
Stone, 203–226; hunting, 211–214; prices, 220, 221–222, 223, 232; qualities, 19, 210–211; selling, 79–80, 92, 215–222, 228–230, 234, 235, 246, 282; slabs, 222, 223; sources, 107–109, 203–204, 222–223, 283; waste, 223–225, 282–283
—types: Brandon flint, 220; Burlington chert, 93, 203–205, 212, 221, 223, 226; chert, 19, 93, 206; Citronel chert, 93; Coastal Plains chert, 93; Crescent chert, 205; dacite, 93; Edwards chert, 93; Edwards flint, 93; Edwards Plateau chert, 206; fiber optic glass, 186, 211; flint, 19, 206, 209; Flint Ridge chert, 107; Florida chert, 93; Georgetown flint, 93, 206, 221; Hixton quartzite, 208, 213; Kay County chert, 93; Knife River flint, 221; mozarkite, 164, 205; novaculite, 45, 80, 93; obsidian, 93, 207–208, 209, 216; Onondaga chert, 106; opal, 211, 221; Pedernales chert, 93, 206; Texas chert, 205–206, 213, 234; White River flint, 206
Strategy, 19
Strischek, Ray, 110
Subculture, 4, 5, 145
Survey, 12, 86–92, 119–121, 137–139, 265–266, 273, 274–275

Teaching, 6, 7, 118–122, 129, 152, 159, 167, 303
Teleolithics, 55
Thinness, 156, 181, 182, 184, 186, 193
Thomas, Bob, 240
Tie-signs, 130, 132
Titmus, Gene, 61, 63, 122, 239–240
Tonn, Virgil, 233
Tools, 1–2, 135, 158; antler tools, 27, 28, 29, 30, 162, 228, 236; copper tools, 27, 28, 29, 30, 31, 33, 76, 77–78, 80, 85, 152, 228, 236, 277, 294; levers, 24, 25, 50, 52, 158, 255; wooden tools, 28
Tradition, 6, 31, 33
Trout, Matt, 52
T-shirts, 131–132, 228, 304
Tussinger, Mack, 40–46, 179

Van Arsdale, Scott, 188
Videos, 14, 118–119, 245

Waldorf, D. C., 14, 25, 52, 65–67, 83–84, 118, 119, 123, 136, 150, 161, 166, 168, 176, 187, 189–190, 214, 248, 264, 266
Waldorf, Val, 14, 65–67, 70, 83–84, 126, 150, 228, 264
Wall, Steve, 233
Wallace, Kenny, 102
Warmuskerken, Roger, 118
Warren, Richard, 50, 53–57, 160, 178
Washing machines, 261
Water Creek Knap-in, 93
Wells, Quentin, 25
Wilson, Thomas, 39
Woodring, Jim, 155
Woods, James, 240

www.ingramcontent.com/pod-product-compliance
Lightning Source LLC
Jackson TN
JSHW021124160426
100741JS00013B/12